Valency

Trends in Linguistics
Studies and Monographs 187

Editors

Walter Bisang
(main editor for this volume)
Hans Henrich Hock
Werner Winter

Mouton de Gruyter
Berlin · New York

Valency

Theoretical, Descriptive and Cognitive Issues

edited by

Thomas Herbst
Katrin Götz-Votteler

Mouton de Gruyter
Berlin · New York

Mouton de Gruyter (formerly Mouton, The Hague)
is a Division of Walter de Gruyter GmbH & Co. KG, Berlin.

♾ Printed on acid-free paper which falls within the guidelines
of the ANSI to ensure permanence and durability.

Library of Congress Cataloging-in-Publication Data

Valency : theoretical, descriptive, and cognitive issues / edited by Thomas Herbst, Katrin Götz-Votteler.
p. cm. – (Trends in linguistics. Studies and monographs ; 187)
Includes bibliographical references and index.
ISBN 978-3-11-019573-6 (hardcover : alk. paper)
1. Dependency grammar. 2. Cognitive grammar. 3. Contrastive linguistics. 4. Computational linguistics. 5. Semantics. I. Herbst, Thomas. II. Götz-Votteler, Katrin, 1975–
P162.V345 2007
415–dc22
2007031827

ISBN 978-3-11-019573-6
ISSN 1861-4302

Bibliographic information published by the Deutsche Nationalbibliothek

The Deutsche Nationalbibliothek lists this publication in the Deutsche Nationalbibliografie; detailed bibliographic data are available in the Internet at <http://dnb.d-nb.de>.

Cover design: Christopher Schneider, Berlin.
Printed in Germany.

Preface: Valency – theoretical, descriptive and cognitive issues

Thomas Herbst and Katrin Götz-Votteler

As with most other concepts in linguistics, in the discussion of valency one must distinguish between the linguistic phenomenon of valency on the one hand and the use of the term *valency* and the development of theoretical frameworks associated with it on the other. As far as the former is concerned, it is obvious that valency phenomena have been treated in linguistics under a variety of different labels ranging from *government* or *Rektion* in traditional grammar to *subcategorization* in generative frameworks or comparatively neutral labels such as *complementation* in descriptive grammars such as the *Comprehensive Grammar of the English Language*. Obviously, up to a point the use of different terms suggests different ways of viewing the phenomenon in question.

The notion of valency as such is generally linked with Tesnière's dependency grammar, although similar concepts had been put forward for example by Bühler (1934) and de Groot (1949).[1] It is probably fair to say that very significant contributions to the development of a theory of valency have been made by German linguistics since the 1960s. It is particularly the work of Gerhard Helbig and the emergence of a number of German valency dictionaries (Helbig and Schenkel 1969; Engel and Schumacher 1976; VALBU 2004) that are of importance here. Both lexicographically oriented and theoretical work on valency have resulted in an extensive discussion of criteria for the distinction between complements and adjuncts and a distinction between different types of complements with respect to their various degrees of obligatoriness. In recent years, the term valency has increasingly been used for the description of English, sometimes with explicit reference to the European tradition of valency theory and the concepts and criteria developed there,[2] sometimes just as a new term for complementation phenomena.

This volume comprises articles which deal with both the theoretical notion of valency and the analysis of valency phenomena. The articles in the first section, theoretical and descriptive aspects of valency, discuss the valency concept in its theoretical context (Peter Matthews) and the question of how valency phenomena can be described most appropriately with reference to certain distinctions such as complement inventories or valency patterns or semantic or syntactic valency (Thomas Herbst, Katrin Götz-Votteler). Other papers focus on different concepts of grammaticalization (Lene Schøsler, Dirk Noël) and particular problems of valency in synchronic and diachronic descriptions (Mechthild Habermann, Michael Klotz, Ilka Mindt). Finally, this section contains an outline of the treatment of valency phenomena and the underlying theoretical concept in the Berkeley FrameNet project (Charles Fillmore).

Section II focuses on the important issue of the role of valency phenomena in cognitive linguistics (Gert Rickheit and Lorenz Sichelschmidt, Rudolf Emons), where the acquisition of valency structures is of course a particularly important aspect (Heike Behrens).

Section III contains a number of papers with a contrastive orientation, which ranges from descriptive issues comparing different aspects of valency in English and German (Klaus Fischer, Irene Ickler, Brigitta Mittmann) and English, German and Norwegian (Stig Johansson) to a more pedagogically oriented account of valency errors in the performance of German and English learners (Ian Roe).

Finally, Section IV is concerned with computational aspects of valency analysis, where possible ways of using existing valency descriptions such as the *Valency Dictionary of English* (2004) as the basis for programs of word recognition are demonstrated (Dieter Götz, Ulrich Heid) and other approaches towards the automatic analysis of valency structures in computational linguistics are outlined (Roland Hausser, Besim Kabashi, Günther Görz and Bernd Ludwig).

The volume comprises papers given at a conference entitled *Valency: Valenz – Theoretical, Descriptive and Cognitive Issues* held at the Friedrich-Alexander-Universität Erlangen-Nürnberg in April 2005, which was supported by the Deutsche Forschungsgemeinschaft and the Dr.-Alfred-Vinzl-Stiftung. The editors would like to thank these institutions for the generous support they gave to the conference, Dr. Anke Beck for attending the conference and her support of the present volume, David Heath for his help and advice in all matters linguistic and Susen Schüller for her work on the index. Above all, our thanks go to all participants of the conference.

Notes

1. Cf. de Groot (1949/1964: 114-115) and Matthews (1981: 117). For the history of the concept of valency see Ágel (2000); for valency models in German linguistics see Herbst, Heath, and Dederding (1980) and Helbig (1992).

2. See, e.g., Emons (1974), Allerton (1982) and VDE (Herbst et al. 2004).

References

Ágel, Vilmos
2000 *Valenztheorie*. Tübingen: Gunter Narr Verlag.

Allerton, David J.
1982 *Valency and the English Verb*. London/New York: Academic Press.

Bühler, Karl
1934 *Sprachtheorie. Die Darstellungsfunktion der Sprache*. Jena: Fischer Verlag.

Engel, Ulrich, and Helmut Schumacher
1976 *Kleines Valenzlexikon deutscher Verben*. Tübingen: Gunter Narr Verlag.

Emons, Rudolf
1974 *Valenzen englischer Prädikatsverben*. Tübingen: Max Niemeyer Verlag.

de Groot, Albert W.
1964 Reprint. *Structurele Syntaxis*. The Hague: Servire. Original edition, The Hague: Servire, 1949.

Helbig, Gerhard
1992 *Probleme der Valenz- und Kasustheorie*. Tübingen: Max Niemeyer Verlag.

Helbig, Gerhard, and Wolfgang Schenkel
1969 *Wörterbuch zur Valenz und Distribution deutscher Verben*. Leipzig: VEB Verlag Enzyklopädie.

Herbst, Thomas, David Heath, and Hans-Martin Dederding
1980 *Grimm's Grandchildren. Current Topics in German Linguistics*. London/New York: Longman.

Herbst, Thomas, David Heath, Ian Roe, and Dieter Götz (eds.)
2004 *A Valency Dictionary of English. A Corpus-Based Analysis of the Complementation Patterns of English Verbs, Nouns and Adjectives*. Berlin/New York: Mouton de Gruyter. [VDE]

Matthews, Peter
1981 *Syntax*. Cambridge: Cambridge University Press.

Quirk, Randolph, Sydney Greenbaum, Geoffrey Leech, and Jan Svartvik
1985 *A Comprehensive Grammar of the English Language*. London: Longman.

Schumacher, Helmut, Jacqueline Kubczak, Renate Schmidt, and Vera de Ruiter (eds.)
2004 *VALBU – Valenzwörterbuch deutscher Verben*. Tübingen: Gunter Narr Verlag [VALBU].

Tesnière, Lucien
1959 *Éléments de Syntaxe Structurale*. Paris: Klincksieck.

Contents

Section 2: Cognitive issues and valency phenomena

Section 3: Contrastive aspects of valency

Section 4: Computational aspects of valency analysis

Section 1
Theoretical and descriptive aspects of valency

The scope of valency in grammar

Peter Matthews

1.

Valency or *valence* is a term originally restricted to the syntax of verbs: "nombre d'*actants*", as Tesnière defined it in the glossary to his *Éléments*, "qu'un verbe est susceptible de *régir*" (1959: 670). It was also linked, by the same definition, to dependency. Thus, in *Alfred parle* ['Alfred speaks'], the verb as a governor (*régissant*) "commanded" the *actant*, *Alfred*, as a subordinate term depending on it (Tesnière 1959: ch. 2.1–3). The early development of valency theory (*Valenztheorie*) was therefore closely linked with that of a dependency grammar (*Dependenzgrammatik*), in Germany especially, in the 1970's.

This line of thinking was neatly summarised in English, at the end of that decade, by Thomas Herbst and his colleagues (1980: ch. 4). It was obvious, however, that words of other categories could have "semantic properties", as I initially put it somewhat nervously, "akin to valency" (Matthews 1981: 115). Later definitions therefore, following later usage, have in that respect become more general. In, for example, my own dictionary of linguistics, valency is of "a verb or other lexical unit" (Matthews 1997: 394). For the late Lawrence Trask, whose dictionary of grammar was familiar to me when I chose this form of wording, the term had both a narrower and a broader definition: "1. The number of arguments for which a particular verb subcategorizes, ... 2. More generally, the subcategorization requirements of any lexical item" (Trask 1993: 296; *argument* defined 20, *lexical item* 158). One problem, therefore, is how far the scope of valency should be extended. This can, if we like, be cast in terms of such a definition. The questions, that is, are what is a *lexical item* or a *lexical unit*, and what exactly is meant by *subcategorisation*.

Note too, however, that while Trask's first definition is in the main close to Tesnière's, it says nothing about verbs as governors or their arguments as depending on them. Neither does the definition I gave, which refers simply to a "range of syntactic elements", with no further stipulation of the relations, whether implicitly of dependence or otherwise, in which they stand. This may perhaps not quite reflect the way all linguists see things, outside what one might be tempted to call, however spuriously, an "Anglo-Saxon" tradition. But dependency and valency are potentially separate. To say, for example, that a verb is transitive is one thing; and, if the facts are agreed, the finding will not be controversial. To say that verbs take objects as dependents is another, and in some accounts at least no such relation has been posited. A second problem, therefore, is how far a link between dependency and valency is justified, especially for categories other than verbs. If *X* is a lexical item, and its subcategorisation either allows it or requires it to take other units, is it always the governor, in Tesnière's sense, in its relation to them?

2.

The valency of atoms, as defined in chemistry, refers to their capacity to combine with other atoms, or with groups of atoms, in the formation of compounds. A verb then, as Tesnière perceived it, could be compared to "une sorte d'atome crochu" (1959: ch. 97.3), which determined the number of *actants* that it too can combine with. To "number" we may add "types"; and, if units other than verbs can be similar "atoms", there will be none which do not in some sense allow some combinations while excluding others. Not all definitions in linguistics stress the parallel with chemistry. But for Crystal, who does, valency refers in general to "the number and type of bonds which syntactic elements may form with each other" (2003: s.v., "syntactic elements" in capitals). If two elements, therefore, of whatever category can combine in any specific construction, it will be because one or the other, or perhaps both, has a valency that allows it.

By "syntactic elements" Crystal means, or seems to mean, all units that form a constituent in a hierarchy (s.v. *element*). Valency in that sense, which again is similar to valency in chemistry, would be the foundation not just of the syntax of verbs, or of verbs and other lexical units, but of syntax generally. In most accounts, however, its sense is narrower in two ways. First it is a property of, more precisely, *lexemes*: of words, that is, as entered in a lexicon or dictionary. Secondly, it has to do, again as Trask defines it, with subcategorisation. Thus, in this view, it is not part of the valency of *clear* that it can combine with an intensifying adverb: *very clear*, *quite clear* and so on. This is instead a property of adjectives in general, or of adjectives in general with specific exceptions. But adjectives in general cannot be construed with, for example, nominal clauses: thus predicatively in *It was clear that they were coming*. This is a property of a particular subcategory of adjectives, of which *clear* is a member. Therefore it is part of the valency of *clear*, and of every other adjective that in this respect is like it.

This plainly raises problems. There are potential grounds for disagreement as to how we should distinguish lexemes; as to what are categories and what are subcategories; as to what is a subcategory and what are no more than "exceptions". It is now, however, still more obvious that where the scope of valency might be disputed, issues of dependency in syntax have no bearing on the argument one way or the other. Most linguists will agree that in, for example, *This is quite clear* the intensifier depends on the adjective. They may use other terminology: *quite*, for example, is *subordinate* to *clear*, or *clear* is the *head* of *quite clear*, or the adjective is again a *governor*. Many at least will also see the nominal or *that*-clause as dependent, or subordinate, in *It was clear that they were coming*. But suppose that it were not a dependent, or that *clear* is not a head or governor in relation to it. If so, it would still belong to the same major category as all other adjectives. Therefore, once more, that it takes such clauses would be a matter of subcategorisation. If someone were, despite tradition, to assign it to another category, it would again not be for such a reason.

Dependency, for its part, was a term that Tesnière did not define in his glossary. It is simply, in the passage referred to earlier, the equivalent of being *governed*. In another account, which is that of, in particular, the recent *Cambridge Grammar of the English Language*, it is similarly the converse of *headship*. In *This is quite clear*, a phrase, *quite clear*, would be headed by *clear*; and, in the same breath, *quite* would be a dependent combining with the adjective (compare Huddleston and Pullum 2002: 24). "The term dependent", as it is then explained, "reflects the fact that in any given construction what kinds of dependent are permitted depends on the head". Thus, for example, *quite* or *very* are permitted dependents of head adjectives, but not of nouns. A clause like *that they were coming* is again a permitted dependent of an adjective like *clear*, but not of, for example, *pink* or *pretty*.

Valency is thus implicitly, as it could have been for Tesnière, a sufficient criterion for dependency. In, for example, *Alfred liked me* both the subject and the object are within the valency of *to like*. There are some verbs, that is, which exclude or only optionally take an object; and there are others, in Tesnière's term *avalent*, which in a more sophisticated sense exclude a subject. Therefore *Alfred* and *me*, as "permitted" units, depend on, in this formulation, a head *liked*. But the way this evidence is interpreted could in principle be quite the opposite. Under what conditions, we may begin by asking, can a strictly transitive verb, such as *to like*, enter into a construction? Part of the answer is, of course, that there must be a subject and an object with which it can combine. The presence, therefore, of forms such as *liked* depends, still in a perfectly natural sense of this term, on the presence of units such as *Alfred* and *me*, by which these conditions can be satisfied. More generally, therefore, if *X* has a valency, the units it takes do not depend on it. In this view, it instead depends on each of them.

For this concept of dependence compare, for example, the later work of Zellig Harris (briefly in Harris 1988: 12f. and elsewhere). It is also matched, for such a sentence, by the much earlier analysis of the Modistae (survey in, for example, Rosier 1983). Even, however, if this view can be discounted, the criterion proposed is soon found to conflict with others. Dependence, in this formulation, is again on heads of phrases: that of an object, for example, on a verb as head of a verb phrase. But headship is notoriously problematic, and evidence that a proposed head has a valency can conflict with other arguments that potentially bear on it.

3.

The problem can be seen most clearly in the case of prepositions. In English especially, different prepositions do take different constructions. In that way they have properties at least "akin", once more, to valencies. But it is far less certain that they are heads, if current definitions of a head are taken seriously.

For Huddleston and Pullum prepositions include, for example, *after* in *after I left* and, in its wake, most other subordinating conjunctions (2002: 599f.). Some prepositions take accordingly both clauses and noun phrases; others, such as *at*, take only phrases; others, like *when*, only clauses. In most other accounts the category remains much smaller. But even then, a preposition such as *on* has one construction in *on the floor* and another in *on leaving the building*, while, for example, *at* has only the first. *Until*, for example, can combine with adverbs such as *recently* (Huddleston and Pullum 2002: 599), but *during* cannot, and so on. In another view, which Huddleston and Pullum also follow, words such as *since*, in *I've seen her since Saturday*, are still prepositions, not reclassed as adverbs, in *I've seen her since*. With some members, therefore, of this category a complement can be optional while with others it is obligatory. If we talk in this light of the valency of prepositions, there will obviously be many problems in distinguishing in detail the constructions they can take. But in one analysis or another, different prepositions would have partly different entries in a lexicon.

The complement of a preposition might thus be "similar", as I put it in the early 1980's, "to the direct object of a verb, with valencies determining when it is obligatory, optional and excluded" (1981: 151). "Therefore", I continued, it was a dependent. But this "therefore", even at that date, was rather careless. It is even more so if dependency is defined as the converse of headship.

In an "informal characterization", the head of a phrase was "one of its constituents which in some sense dominates and represents the whole phrase" (Corbett, Fraser, and McGlashan 1993: 1). In what sense is, of course, the problem; and, as Zwicky made clear over twenty years ago (1985), there are several possible candidates. But the formula which many linguists have since favoured talks of heads as units that "determine" the external syntax of a whole of which they are part. It is hard to find an illustration that does not raise difficulties. But in, for example, *very angry people* it is easy to establish a relation between *very* and *angry*: there is a class of adverbs, as they are called, by which adjectives can be modified. There is also a relation between *angry* and *people*: one role of adjectives, that is, is as modifiers of nouns. But it is hard at least to establish any independent relation between *very* and *people*. Substitute for *very* any other adverb that forms a similar combination, and it is still the adjective alone that determines the "distribution", as a definition on these lines is often formulated, of the intensifier and the adjective together.

For Huddleston and Pullum the head, "normally obligatory, plays the primary role in determining the distribution of the phrase, i.e. whereabouts in sentence structure it can occur" (2002: 24, "distribution" in bold face). Note, in passing, that the "distribution" of a phrase is relative to "sentence structure"; also that, though "normally obligatory", a head can be elliptical. The main difficulty, however, now lies in the qualification "primary". The syntax of a whole can by implication be determined by both a head and a dependent. But the role of the dependent would be seen as secondary.

It is obvious why thc qualification is needed. The distribution of, for example, *angry with me* is in general, one might claim, determined by the adjective; but its position as a post-modifier, in *the people angry with me*, reflects in part the presence of *with me* as its complement. Is it always clear, though, what is primary and what is secondary? Take, for example, a phrase such as *on leaving the building*. Its distribution is not simply that of *on X*; of the preposition as such plus whatever can then follow it. Compare, for example, *Put it on the floor*, *Put it on leaving the building*. But does the preposition even "primarily" determine the constructions in which these different units can stand? In *Put it on the floor*, the role of *on the floor* is as a locative. In that respect it goes with, for example, *here* in *Put it here*, or *where you like* in *Put it where you like*, in neither of which a preposition is included. In *Turn right on leaving the building*, the unit introduced by *on* belongs instead with clauses such as *when you leave the building*; and, like these, it includes a verbal unit. In another view it is these categories that are primary, and it is the presence of a preposition, in one kind of locative or in certain kinds of reduced clause, that would then be secondary.

The headship of prepositions could, of course, be saved by technical devices. In *Put it on the floor*, what is locative might in one solution be a preposition, *on*$_{\text{loc}}$, which is different from other *on*s, which merely happen to be homonyms, in *on leaving the building* or, for example, *on Saturday*. The distribution of a phrase like *on*$_{\text{loc}}$ *the floor* could accordingly be said to be determined, absolutely and not merely primarily, by the specific presence of *on*$_{\text{loc}}$; that of *on leaving the building* by a different preposition, *on*$_{\text{ing}}$ that we might establish there, and so on. But this is a solution of a kind not needed in the same way for verbs, nouns and adjectives. The headship of, for example, *left* in *left the building*, of *people* in *people angry with me*, or again of *angry* in *angry with me*, all fit Huddleston and Pullum's definition much more easily.

4.

The dependency of complements on prepositions is, in this light, at least problematic. But let us suppose, for the sake of argument, that prepositions are not heads. *On*, for example, will still take a range of possible constructions, distinct from those of other prepositions such as *at*, or *under*, or *during*. This could still be valency, if that term applies appropriately to it.

The widest application would again be as implied by Crystal's dictionary. Not only, then, does *on* as one syntactic element form a "bond" with *the floor* or with *leaving the building*; but, for example, *building* would form a bond with *the*, *on leaving the building*, in *Turn right on leaving the building*, would form a bond with *turn right*, and so on. These are bonds of different types, and in Crystal's definition, which in itself is perfectly coherent, they reflect not only the valencies of words like *at* and *building* but also, since a phrase is a syntactic element, of the constituents of which they form part at all levels. In other accounts, however, valency is again restricted to lexical units. The syntactic elements that they take, moreover, are traditionally *constructions*: not constituents individually, but the general patterns in which any similar constituent will stand.

Take for comparison a straightforward relation of agreement. The construction of, say, *die Frau* ['the woman'] is the same, at least as linguists usually describe it, as that of *der Mann* ['the man']: of, in general, a noun with an article. It is then a property of certain lexemes, such as *Frau*, that they form bonds with articles, such as *die*, in the feminine. But in this light it is not a property of valency. One justification is that rules for gender are bound up with those affecting number or case, which are not inherently of lexical units. Another, however, might be that relations like this are less obviously asymmetrical. A construction is one thing, and a lexical unit, which in the traditional term "takes" or "requires" it, is another. But *Frau* is a word and *die* too is a word, and, while grammars have traditionally talked of articles "agreeing with" nouns, or of nouns as determining the form that they will take, it would technically be possible to say precisely the opposite. In *die Frau*, that is, *die* is inherently feminine; therefore, in an alternative formulation, it requires nouns, such as *Frau*, whose properties will match it. For many linguists, this account fits beautifully with the hypothesis, as they present it, that the construction is of a *determiner phrase*, with *die* as its head determiner.

What do we mean then, more exactly, by constructions? Since the 1980's this term has taken on a new life, in the work of Fillmore and others (Fillmore, Kay, and O'Connor 1988; Goldberg 1995). One point, however, that we need to emphasise is thoroughly traditional: that constructions are wholes that may not always reduce to a simple hierarchy of parts.

At school, for example, I was taught that certain verbs in Latin, such as *doceo* ['I teach'], took a "double accusative", or the "double accusative construction". The purpose, no doubt, was in practice to discourage me from putting nouns that should be accusative into the dative, on the model of, in English, sentences such as *I taught it to the children*. But this view of their construction does reflect a fundamental truth, which is brought out beautifully, from a lexicographer's viewpoint, by Thomas Herbst in this volume. A verb, in particular, does not bond independently with individual syntactic elements, subject only to restrictions that affect each combination separately. Its valency is a whole of which such elements are parts, and its relation to each element, as to each of the accusatives in a double accusative construction, may be bound up with the ones it bears to others, or that these elements bear among themselves.

Divisions among elements will then be secondary; and in many cases, as with the constructions of *doceo* in Latin or *to teach* in English, they are not a problem. But take, for a notorious example, the constructions of what Quirk and his colleagues have called *complex transitives*. In *They made her their leader*, the verb is followed, as they and many other linguists see it, by two separate elements: first an object, *her*, and then an *object complement, their leader*. In this sense, therefore, *made* will form bonds with *they*, as subject, and with each of these. Other complements of an object, similar in that way to noun phrases like *their leader*, include adjective phrases, as in, for example, *That drove* [*him*] [*crazy*]; infinitives, as in *I felt* [*it*] [*to be falling apart*], and so on (Quirk et al. 1985: 1195ff.). But this is, of course, just one analysis. In another common view, such verbs will take two elements only: *they* as subject and a clause of which the so-called "object" is instead the subject. In two of the examples given, this is of the kind that followers of Chomsky class as "small": thus, with brackets again, *They made* [*her their leader*], *They drove* [*him crazy*] (compare Fromkin 2000: 133f.). In the third example, it is a clause like others generally, except that it is not tensed: *I felt* [*it to be falling apart*].

Which treatment should we follow? One well-known compromise would hold that both are right; but at two different levels. In an underlying structure *her* remains a subject, in the same role as the subjective pronoun in *He was their leader*. But it is superficially "raised"; and, after raising, it becomes an object. This was an analysis defended at length, thirty years ago, by Postal (1974). Alternatively, the syntax is of an object and its complement; but the relation between these is semantically like that of predication. With infinitives in particular, this relation then distinguishes a *raising verb*, as many linguists call it, from *control verbs*, as again a follower of Chomsky calls them, such as *to persuade* or *to ask*. In syntax, that is, both will take the same constructions. But with verbs of the control kind, as described by Huddleston and Pullum, "the syntactic structure matches the semantics quite straightforwardly" (2002: 1201): compare, for example, *They asked* [*me*] [*to leave*]. With "raised object verbs", there is instead a mismatch. In, for example, *They intended* [*me*] [*to leave*], the syntactic object is not an argument, at the level of propositional meaning, of *to intend*; but simply of the subordinate verb *to leave* (Hudddleston and Pullum 2002: 1201; "propositional meaning" 226). Whatever the solution, however, there will now be further difficulties. Is there also a "small clause", if that is the way we want to describe it, in, for example, *They found him ill* or *They found him in distress*? Or are *ill* and *in distress* no more than separate adjuncts? Which kind of verb is, for example, *to expect* in *I expect you to leave*? Is *you*, "syntactically" if we so perceive it, no more than the subject of *to leave*? What is expected, that is, is an event which involves the addressee's departure. Or does the speaker expect it of the addressee, as an individual or set of individuals, that he, she or they will go away? That might suggest that *you* is an object, and the subject of the infinitive, again in one analysis, a zero "controlled" by it. Or is the sentence structurally ambiguous, in its syntax or again in no more than its semantics, as we prefer?

Such issues are familiar and it is hard to see how indeterminacy can be avoided. It seems clear, however, that at least some verbs take networks of relations. In *That drove him crazy*, there is a link of some kind between *him* and *crazy*. The dispute is simply as to whether it is syntactic or semantic. Either *him*, in one account, or *him crazy*, in another, are in turn related to *drove*. But so too, on its own, is *crazy*. *To drive* can take a small clause, if that is how we want to see it, where the predicate is an adjective; or, for example, an infinitive (*That drove him to commit suicide*). But, unlike *to make*, it does not generally take a noun or noun phrase (compare, for example, **That drove him a suicide*). There are also limits to the adjectives it normally goes with (compare, for example *That drove him angry* or ?*That drove him happy*), as with other verbs of this class. Compare, for example, *They painted it green* with ?*They painted it pretty*; or *They cut it short* with ?*They cut it brief*. The construction is a whole in that sense, in that all its elements are interrelated. But within the class of verbs that take it, whose valency is at a general level complex transitive, there are again some where, at a subsidiary level, one relation or the other will be weaker. The link of verbs to object complements is strongest with what may be called "group verbs" (Denison 1998: 221ff.) or idioms, such as, we might say, *to cut short*. But it is certainly weaker in, for example, *The crash left her penniless* or *They found him ill*. The link of verbs to objects is weaker with so-called "raising verbs", as in *I felt it to be falling apart*; and so on. But the problems this can lead to, in saying what exactly, for example, is the valency of *to expect* or *to want*, are precisely no more than subsidiary.

The network does not, in this case, so obviously include the subject. But there is also the construction first described by me, I think, as "complex intransitive" (Matthews 1980). In, for example, *She turned green* this is again a whole in which the relation between no two syntactic elements (subject, verb and subject complement) can be detached from the others.

5.

Valency, to sum up, is in principle independent of dependency, headship or governorship; it is a property of lexical units in relation to constructions; and it is specifically of units assigned to subcategories. The remaining question is, which lexical units? Or, if the answer is all, what is a lexical unit?

One definition might appeal to a distinction between closed and open categories. The distinction itself is central for, among others, Quirk and his colleagues (1985: 67, 71ff.); and in this sense prepositions, in particular, are not lexical but grammatical. Therefore the bonds they form in varying constructions, though "akin" to valency, could belong with those of other members of closed categories, such as conjunctions, modal verbs, or articles. In another view, however, they too form a lexical category. The reasons vary; but one argument might be precisely that each preposition has a valency. Like verbs, that is, each takes or in more fashionable jargon "licenses" a specific range of structures.

The truth, however, is that no single category is quite like the others. The properties of verbs, in this respect, are clearly lexical. Not only does each member of the category have a valency; but exactly what it is can vary between speakers and can change quite easily. Judgments, therefore, are notoriously difficult. Can *to start*, for example, be used as a complex transitive: thus *The rain is starting the tunnel to collapse*? Can *to demand* take the construction of *They demanded someone to come*, or *to accord* that of *They accorded it with this title*? These are modelled, naturally, on examples I have collected. "Chaque mot", one might say, "a sa valence"; and although the instinct of many linguists has been to establish ordered series of subcategories, distinguished by fixed ranges of constructions and semantic or "cognitive" properties corresponding to them, they are liable to be defeated, in the end if not from the outset, by the operations of analogy on the use of lexemes individually. To say of an intransitive verb that it simply cannot be used transitively is already imprudent.

If prepositions are grammatical it is, in this light, not just because they are closed. That statement may in any case need to be qualified. It is because their meanings and their syntax are fragmented. *On*, for example, enters into different contrasts with different sets of opposed units: as a locative in *Put it on the floor*; in expressions of time such as *on Saturday*: in combination with an *ing*-form in *on leaving the building*; in individual group verbs such as *to look on* or *to run on*; and so on. Each use is therefore subject to its own rules. *By*, for example, is another preposition that can take an *ing*-form: thus *by leaving the building*. It also enters into locative constructions, as in *I was walking by the river*; and, in that use, it can have a meaning partly similar to that of *along*, in *I was walking along the river*. But there is no basis here for analogical extensions like those that we find with verbs: *by leaving the building*, that is; therefore *along leaving the building*.

In this respect most adjectives and nouns are also lexical. But nouns especially raise other problems, which in turn are well-known. Not all, of course, take even optional complements: *the news of their success*, not *the cat of their success*; *her letter to the council*, not *her cat to the council*; and so on. Is *cat* to be described in this light as a noun which has a zero valency, on the lines of verbs such as *to rain*? Or do such nouns simply have no valency at all? With nouns like *news* or *letter*, complements are then rarely obligatory. Many such nouns are derived, moreover, from verbs: *announcement* from *to announce*; *speech*, although irregularly, from *to speak*, and so on. Their valencies, if that is how we should again describe them, are in many cases also temptingly derivative: *He announced his resignation* or *She spoke to parliament*; hence, as many will argue, *the announcement of his resignation* or *her speech to parliament*. Now the meaning of *speech* in this example is narrower than that of *spoke*. But how far, despite that, are their valencies that of a common stem and not of nominal and verbal lexemes separately?

The way we answer questions like these may, however, not be that important. That valencies are above all properties of verbs has been acknowledged from the outset, and most linguists, whether or not they use the term themselves, see individual *argument structures*, or what Quirk and his colleagues call their *complementation*, as fundamental to their meanings. The same is arguably true of adjectives such as *clear* in *It was clear that they were coming*, or *sure* in *I was sure that they were coming*, where, in predicative position, they may take complements optional only under ellipsis. Here too, moreover, usage can be fluid. But many other adjectives, like many nouns, take modifiers only or have valencies that are temptingly, again, derivative. If prepositions did have meanings like verbs, their status as *atomes crochus* could again be seen as similar: both primitive and fundamental to the whole class. If Tesnière did not describe them in that way it was because, in his analysis, they were grammatical *markers* and not *governors*. But even if governorship is irrelevant, or the definition of a head can somehow be made to cover them, there would still be problems that might lead us to explain their syntax differently.

References

Corbett, Greville G., Norman M. Fraser, and Scott McGlashan (eds.)
1993 *Heads in Grammatical Theory*. Cambridge: Cambridge University Press.

Crystal, David
2003 *A Dictionary of Phonetics and Linguistics*. 5th ed. Oxford: Blackwell.

Denison, David
1998 Syntax. In *The Cambridge History of the English Language 1776-1997*, Vol. 4. Richard Hogg, and Suzanne Romaine (eds.), 92–329. Cambridge: Cambridge University Press.

Fillmore, Charles, Paul Kay, and Mary Catherine O'Connor
1988 Regularity and idiomaticity in grammatical constructions: The case of *let alone*. *Language*, 501–538.
Fromkin, Victoria (ed.)
2000 *Linguistics: An Introduction to Linguistic Theory*. Oxford: Blackwell.
Goldberg, Adele E.
1995 *Constructions: A Construction Grammar Approach to Argument Structure*. Chicago: University of Chicago Press.
Harris, Zellig S.
1988 *Language and Information*. New York: Columbia University Press.
Herbst, Thomas, David Heath, and Hans-Martin Dederding
1980 *Grimm's Grandchildren: Current Topics in German Linguistics*. London: Longman.
Herbst, Thomas
2007 Valency complements or valency patterns? This volume.
Matthews, Peter H.
1980 Complex intransitive constructions. In *Studies in English Linguistics for Randolph Quirk,* Sidney Greenbaum, Geoffrey Leech, and Jan Svartvik (eds.), 41–60. London: Longman.
1981 *Syntax*. Cambridge: Cambridge University Press.
1997 *The Concise Oxford Dictionary of Linguistics*. Oxford: Oxford University Press.
Postal, Paul M.
1974 *On Raising*. Cambridge, Mass.: MIT Press.
Quirk, Randolph, Sidney Greenbaum, Geoffrey Leech, and Jan Svartvik
1985 *A Comprehensive Grammar of the English Language*. London: Longman.
Rosier, Irène
1983 *La Grammaire Spéculative des Modistes*. Lille: Presses Universitaires de Lille.
Tesnière, Lucien
1959 *Éléments de Syntaxe Structurale*. Paris: Klincksieck.
Trask, R. Lawrence
1993 *A Dictionary of Grammatical Terms in Linguistics*. London: Routledge.
Zwicky, Arnold
1985 Heads. *Journal of Linguistics* 21: 1–29.

Valency complements or valency patterns?

Thomas Herbst

1. Valency and the idiom principle

1.1. Valency as a property specific to lexical units

The valency approach as it was developed in German *Germanistik* can probably claim to be one of the most systematic attempts to describe complementation structures of verbs, adjectives and nouns. One of its most important assets is that it has always devoted considerable attention to the distinction between such elements whose occurrence is dependent on the presence of a particular valency carrier, i.e. the complements (*Ergänzungen*), and such elements whose occurrence in a clause is structurally independent of the presence of particular other words, i.e. the adjuncts or peripheral elements (*Angaben*). Although the distinction between complements (or, in more refined versions of the approach, different types of complement) and adjuncts takes the form of a gradient rather than that of two clearly distinct categories, it can be said that within valency frameworks what is to be considered a complement of a valency carrier is not left to intuition but based on a number of test criteria.

The phenomenon of valency is one part of the unpredictable, unsystematic aspects of language. It is thus probably more than a historical coincidence that pioneering work within the valency framework has been done within a general context of foreign language learning and foreign language teaching, which is equally true, for example, of Gerhard Helbig's contributions to the development of valency theory in the GDR and of early valency work in West Germany (e.g. Engel and Schumacher 1976).[1] Equally, it can hardly be considered a coincidence that valency research should have resulted in valency dictionaries since valency structures represent idiosyncratic, word-specific types of information (e.g. Helbig and Schenkel [2]1973; Engel and Schumacher 1976; VALBU 2004 for German or VDE 2004 for English). Although valency is also an important concept within many syntactic theories, especially those with a dependency component (Matthews 1981; Heringer 1970 or 1996; Herbst and Schüller forthcoming), it is primarily to be seen as a property of lexical items or, to be more precise, as a property of lexical units. This is, of course, no contradiction since, in fact, the determining influence of individual lexical units on the structure of sentences has received increasing attention in many theoretical frameworks.[2]

1.2. Tidy and messy aspects of language

Unpredictability in language is not restricted to valency, however. A further case in point is presented by combinations such as *guilty conscience* or *lay the table*, which can be called institutionalized collocations and which can be characterized as "typical, specific and characteristic relations between two words" (Hausmann 1985: 118). Again, the idiosyncratic nature of such combinations is revealed by the comparison with other languages. Neither **schuldiges Gewissen* nor **den Tisch legen* would be acceptable translations in German, for instance. In general, one could argue that the fact that the well-formedness of sentences or texts cannot easily be described as the result of applying syntactic rules of some kind is probably particularly apparent in the context of a type of linguistics that takes into account aspects of foreign language teaching and of translation theory. At a very basic level, this kind of insight takes the form of the common experience that learners' utterances produced in essays or translations which do not violate any grammatical rules of the target language are nevertheless often judged not to "sound right" by native speakers although it is difficult to formulate this in more concrete terms. It is important to realize that although the unsystematicity of language, for which such observations provide evidence, may be particularly noticeable in foreign language contexts, it is a central feature of the phenomenon of language as such and thus has to play an appropriate role in any comprehensive theory of language.

On the other hand, it cannot be denied that other aspects of language can indeed be accounted for in terms of general rules or principles. Just as it is obvious that institutionalized collocations such as *guilty conscience, white coffee* or *strong tea* cannot be explained in terms of rules, one would definitely assume that at the other end of the extreme the interpretation of utterances is determined by general pragmatic principles.[3] Thus an announcement of the type as is made on trains running from Westerland (Sylt) to Hamburg

(1) *In Kürze erreichen wir Husum. In Husum steigen Sie bitte in Fahrtrichtung rechts aus.*
'We'll shortly be arriving at Husum. At Husum please alight using the doors on the right-hand side of the train.'

is not interpreted by any passenger to mean that one is obliged to get off at Husum although this would be a literal interpretation of what is being said.

Up to a point, distinctions such as de Saussure's (1916) between *langue* and *parole*, Coseriu's (1973) between *System* and *Norm*,[4] Sinclair's (1991) between the open choice principle and the idiom principle[5] or Chomsky's (1986) between *core* and *periphery* recognize the fact that some aspects of language can be explained rather well in terms of general rules whereas others apparently cannot. The question is, however, how much importance is attributed to these two aspects. Chomsky (1986: 221), already in his choice of terms but also in the description of the concepts, clearly takes core grammar to be the central aspect of language:

> The core, then, consists of the set of values selected for parameters of the core system of S_0; this is the essential part of what is "learned", if that is the correct term for this process of fixing knowledge of a particular language. The grammar of the language L is the linguist's theory of L, consisting of a core grammar and an account of the periphery.

Whether core grammar in the sense described by Chomsky is the "essential part of what is being 'learned'" or not depends very much on the number of linguistic facts that – like valency and collocation – fall under the heading of the unpredictable, idiosyncratic or idiomatic. Opposing Chomsky, Sinclair (1991: 110) argues that the principle of idiom, "has been relegated to an inferior position in most current linguistics, because it does not fit the open-choice model."

It is interesting to see that a lot of the empirical research carried out in corpus linguistics also underlines the importance of idiosyncratic features as far as the co-occurrence of words in texts is concerned. It is in this light that Sinclair's (1991: 110) concept of the idiom principle – "that a language user has available to him or her a large number of semi-preconstructed phrases that constitute single choices, even though they might appear to be analysable into segments" – appears so remarkable. It seems that a considerable amount of the evidence provided by corpus research and the experience gained in contexts such as that of foreign language teaching must lead to the conclusion that the idiosyncratic or idiomatic aspect of language may well be much more important than is often assumed even if this means that language as a whole appears less tidy and perhaps slightly messy.[6]

It is obvious that the relationship between the rule-driven, tidy and the messy, idiomatic components of language is of particular relevance to cognitive or psycholinguistic issues. Idiomatic or idiosyncratic aspects require storage; open choice aspects can be accounted for in terms of rules – irrespective of whether such rules are learned or acquired as rules or emerge from data that are acquired in some form or another. While the investigation of various valency phenomena provides a considerable amount of evidence to assume that the idiosyncratic component is rather important (Götz-Votteler, this volume; Klotz, this volume; Herbst, forthcoming), this article will address the problem from a slightly different angle – namely by looking at the question of how valency relations are best described.

2. Valency patterns or valency complements?

2.1. Complement inventories

Valency is most often seen as the property of a word – or, more precisely, of a lexical unit as "the union of a single sense with a lexical form" (Cruse 1986: 80) – to determine the occurrence of other elements in a clause. Thus Helbig and Schenkel (^{2}1973: 49) define syntactic valency in the following way:[7]

> ... die Fähigkeit des Verbs, bestimmte Leerstellen um sich herum zu eröffnen, die durch obligatorische oder fakultative Mitspieler zu besetzen sind.
> [... the ability of the verb to open up certain positions in its syntactic environment, which can be filled by obligatory or optional complements.]

This view of valency is expressed in a very similar way in Emons's (1978: 4) definition of valency:

> Die Eigenschaft eines Prädikats, eine bestimmte Anzahl von Ergänzungen zu fordern, nennen wir seine V a l e n z.
> [The property of a predicate to demand a certain number of complements is referred to as its valency.]

Very similar descriptions can be found in other frameworks, for instance, when Haegeman (1991: 41) says the "verb **theta-marks** its arguments" or in Chomsky's (2004: 111) description of the character of lexical entries of verbs:

... every lexical item carries along with it a certain set of thematic roles, theta-roles, which have to be filled. That is its lexical entry ...

What all these conceptions have in common is that a verb can be associated with a kind of inventory of syntactic elements, which, depending on the theoretical framework and terminology, can be described in terms of semantic cases, theta-roles or as arguments or complements. This view of valency is represented in the *Valency Dictionary of English* (VDE) in the form of complement inventories, in which the complements of a particular lexical unit (e.g. *convince*) are listed.

	Active: 2 / 3	Passive: 1 / 3	General: 0
I	**$[N]_A$ / [by N]**		
	$[V\text{-}ing]_A$	D	T1–3
	$[that\text{-}CL]_A$	D	T1–3
	$[N\ V\text{-}ing]_A$	D	T1–3
II obl	**$[N]_P$**	D	T1–3
III	**[to-INF]**		T1
IV	**[that-CL]**		T2
	[of N]		T3

The alternative to such a view of valency as an inventory of complements is to regard valency specifications as information about particular patterns in which a lexical unit can occur. In the VDE such patterns are indicated (however usually without any specifications regarding subjects) in the patterns and examples section following the complement inventory. Thus, in the case of *convince*, one divalent active pattern and three trivalent active patterns are identified:

D **+ N_P** No I'm stuck you know I'm going to be stuck with my opinion and that is that and you're not going to *convince* me. (only if clear from context) ◦ I think we would have *convinced* anyone, although, come to think of it, we could not have had a more difficult audience than Florence. (only if clear from context)

T1 **+ N_P + to-INF** Sometimes the young person involved and their parents will have to attend a meeting of the school governors to try to *convince* them not to go ahead with the expulsion.

T2 **+ N_P + (that)-CL** The few shining examples of new working-class accommodation which he saw on his tours around the country *convinced* him that far more could be done. ◦ They were unable to *convince* him that his tape recorder played both sides without first having to rewind the cassette. ◦ It took her a moment, after waking, to *convince* herself that she had not heard the voice at all. ◦ In extreme fevers – and there are records of many such in history – nothing will *convince* you you are unwell.

T3 **+ N_P + of N** The mere suspicion was enough to *convince* him of Andy's guilt.

Such a pattern-related view of valency is also reflected in the concept of *Satzbaupläne* as outlined by Engelen (1975) or Engel (1977).[8] Similarly, one could argue that Fillmore's (1968: 27) statement that the "insertion of verbs ... depends on the particular array of cases, the 'case frame' provided by the sentence" can be taken to refer to a pattern oriented view of such phenomena.

In many respects, both views of valency – in terms of an inventory of complements or in terms of valency patterns – are compatible with one another. The question to be discussed here is, however, whether there are linguistic facts which can be described more appropriately in terms of the one framework rather than the other.

This will be discussed with respect to the following four levels of description which a comprehensive valency description as attempted in VDE should comprise, namely statements about:

(i) the minimum and maximum valency of the lexical unit in question,
(ii) the degree of optionality of the complements as obligatory, contextually-optional or optional,[9]
(iii) the formal and functional properties of the complements,[10]
(iv) the lexical, semantic and collocational description of the complements.[11]

2.2. Quantitative valency

The complement inventory account and the pattern-oriented view of verb valency may already be in conflict when it comes to the relatively simple question of quantitative valency, which is usually seen as being determined by the number of obligatory and optional complements a verb requires. Thus it would be common practice to classify a verb such as *meet* as divalent on the basis of a sentence such as

(2) *This time, <u>she</u>* met *<u>Jamie</u> at Rital's wine bar at lunchtime.*$_{\text{BNC}}$[12]

since neither the $[\text{N}]_{\text{A}}$-complement *she* nor the $[\text{N}]_{\text{P}}$-complement *Jamie* can be deleted without making the sentence ungrammatical. However, monovalent uses of *meet* can be found in sentences such as

(3) *These days <u>they</u>* meet *at conferences ...*$_{\text{BNC}}$
(4) *<u>A Cabinet committee</u>* meets *tomorrow to agree to slash public spending by billions.*$_{\text{BNC}}$

The problem with verbs such as *meet* or *kiss* is that there is a difference between syntactic and semantic valency. One could argue that at the semantic level such verbs have an obligatory valency of 2 in that they require two arguments whose semantic roles could be described as that of a 'MEETER' (i.e. a person who meets someone) and that of a 'MEETEE' (i.e. a person who is met by someone). At the syntactic level, however, both these arguments can be expressed by one complement, which can consist of a coordinated noun phrase or a plural noun phrase as in (3) or of a noun phrase containing a singular group noun. In VDE this is represented in a form which combines the two arguments I + II and provides a list of possible complements:

I + II	**[N]$_A$ / [by N] + [N]$_P$**		D1	T1–2
	[N$_{pl/group}$]$_A$	M		T2
	[N and N]$_A$	M		T2
	[N]$_A$ + [with N]		D4	T2

Although such an account describes the syntactic possibilities accurately, it is not entirely unproblematical from a theoretical point of view. First of all, the monovalent uses of such verbs raise the question of whether the [N]$_A$-complement (the subject) actually represents the two semantic roles of 'MEETER' and 'MEETEE' or whether such role assignment is misguided in such cases. One could indeed argue that since activities such as 'meeting' involve more than one person, the unacceptability of a sentence such as

(2) a. **This time, she* met *at Rital's wine bar at lunchtime.*

is due to a general semantic or even pragmatic rule. More importantly in the present context, however, the complement inventory presented in VDE already contains aspects of a pattern-oriented view of valency since it demonstrates the interrelationship between different kinds of possible realizations of the arguments identified. In any case, one can conclude that statements about the minimum or maximum valency of verbs are difficult to make without taking into account the precise form a complement such as [N]$_A$ takes in a particular realization.[13]

2.3. Optionality

It is common in valency theory to make a distinction between different kinds of complement with regard to their degree of optionality. Thus it would be generally accepted to classify [from N] in

(5) *We'd love to* hear *from you about it*.$_{VDE}$

as an optional complement since the verb *hear* can be used in the same meaning without that complement, as in

(6) *I want to* hear *about it*.$_{BNC}$

At the same time there are uses such as

(7) *We'll* hear *from an economics writer on why the economy is expanding faster than unemployment is decreasing.*$_{VDE}$

where the [from N] complement cannot be deleted:

(7) a. **We'll* hear *on why the economy is expanding faster than unemployment is decreasing.*

This situation is difficult to describe in terms of a complement inventory since [from N] is optional in patterns with [about N] but obligatory in patterns with [on N].[14] An accurate description of the optionality of complements is complicated further by the fact that with some verbs it may be affected by special types of text and the grammatical construction in which the verb is used. A typical example of this is presented by instructions typical of cookery books:

(8) Fix *and* wash *carefully.*$_{VDE}$
(9) *Boil the lime flowers and nettles together in the water,* cover *and* leave *to simmer for ten minutes*.$_{VDE}$

2.4. Alternative realizations

A further problem for an inventory-oriented approach towards the description of valency is presented by alternative patterns which can be considered to be more or less synonymous. Thus in cases such as

(10) *I hurried to* pack *my things*^{II}.$_{BNC}$
(11) *I rushed to* pack *my suitcase*^{III}.$_{BNC}$
(12) *I*^{I} pack *them*^{II} *into big bags*^{III}.$_{VDE}$
(13) *The old fellow has no idea how to* pack *a shopping basket*^{III} *with goods*^{II}.$_{VDE}$

it makes sense to consider the underlined elements as representing one type of complement and the elements marked by dotted underlining as representing another type of complement. The first one could be seen as representing an argument that could be described as 'CONTAINER', the second one as an argument labelled 'ÆFFECTED' in VDE. The VDE complement inventory of *pack* contains the following information:

A	... suitcase		
	Active: 1/3 Passive: 1/3		General: 0
I	**[N]$_A$ / [by N]**		
II	**[N]$_{P-2}$** *ÆFFECTED*	D1	T1–2
	[with N]		T3
III	**[N]$_{P-2}$** *CONTAINER*	D1	T1.3
	[into N]		T2
IV	**[N]$_{P-1}$** *BEN/REC*		T1

What is remarkable about this is that a mere list of complements without any reference to the patterns in which they can occur would not be sufficiently specific because it would not rule out unacceptable sentences of the type

(14) a. **I rushed to* pack *into my suitcase*^{III} *with my things*^{II}.
b. **I rushed to* pack *with my things*^{II} *into my suitcase*^{III}.

Only the fact that [with N] is specified as occurring only in pattern T3 (of which [13] is an example) and [into N] as occurring only in pattern T2 (as in [12]) rules out (14a) and (14b). Combinations of two noun phrases of the type

(14) c. **I rushed to* pack *my things*^{II} *my suitcase*^{III}.
d. **I rushed to* pack *my suitcase*^{III} *my things*^{II}.

are also excluded by the description of the complements as [N]$_{P-2}$, which means that they can occur only as the second noun phrase in a pattern T1 as in

(15) *Shelagh*^{I} packed *them*^{IV} *a lunch box*^{II}. $_{VDE}$

One could argue, of course, that specifying a complement with respect to its place in a pattern (as indicated by the indices 1 and 2) already provides information about patterns in the description of the complements. Although these examples show that referring to the valency patterns of a verb is an essential component of the description of its valency, this does not mean, however, that identifying complements as such and establishing a complement inventory is a pointless or redundant exercise. One should not forget that it is this kind of complement inventory that provides information about the semantic roles of the complements in various patterns.

2.5. Semantic and lexical properties

A similar kind of problem is presented by rivalling patterns if one takes the lexical level into account. Klotz (2000) points out that the two trivalent patterns of the verb *cause* do not allow the same lexical elements. Thus although the complements marked by single and double underlining in

(16) ... *there are people whose drinking* causes *them medical or social harm*.BNC

and

(17) *It can now be stated that passive smoking* causes *lung cancer in non-smokers and serious respiratory illness in babies*.BNC

express the same or very similar semantic roles, a sentence such as

(17) a. **passive smoking* causes *babies serious respiratory illness*.

is not acceptable. A similar example is presented by the fact that in the case of so-called ergative verbs such as

(18) *They*[I] closed *the door*[II] *behind them*.VDE
(19) *The heavy wooden door*[II] closed *with a thump*.VDE

ergativity (in the sense that the $[N]_P$-complement can also occur as an $[N]_A$) is restricted to certain lexical items:

(20) *He* closed *his book and gazed into the flames*.VDE
(21) **His book* closed.
(22) ... *this book* closes *with the end of the 1988 season*.BNC

where (22) obviously does not correspond semantically to (20). A similar example is presented by *open*, where one finds

(23) *Suddenly the kitchen door* opened ...VDE
(24) *He* opened *the kitchen door and came in and shut it before he turned to face them*.BNC
(25) *He* opened *a bottle of champagne*.BNC

but not:

(25) a. *<u>*A bottle of champagne*</u> opened.

Observations like these stress the argument that speakers seem to have available to them information about possible realizations of particular complements in particular patterns and not just information about the complements of a particular verb.

3. Semantic and lexical information about complements

If valency information comprises not only information about possible complements of a verb (or other valency carriers) but specific knowledge about the possible combinations in certain valency patterns including lexical information of the kind which lexical items or sets of lexical items can realize a complement in a particular pattern, then this certainly increases the amount of idiosyncratic or idiomatic knowledge that has to be acquired and stored by the speakers of a language.

This applies particularly to the question of whether it is possible to provide a description of the semantics of complements that would actually account for all the lexical items that can realize this complement and exclude others. Empirical work in this field has shown that a finite set of semantic cases as originally proposed by Fillmore (1968) poses a great number of descriptive problems and is probably not refined enough to provide a comprehensive description. Helbig and Schenkel (^{2}1973) make use of semantic components to characterize semantic properties of complements; Helbig (1992: 154–155) suggests integrating both semantic components (*Stufe II*) and case roles (*Stufe III*). Although VDE adopts a very flexible policy and includes semantic descriptions that correspond to stages II and III of Helbig's model, it is interesting to see that VDE, VALBU and FrameNet independently of each other generally provide descriptions of the semantics of complements which are rather specific to the particular verb. Thus VALBU characterizes the nominative complement (NomE) and accusative complement (AkkE) of a lexical unit such as *gründen* (sense 1) as follows:

> NomE: derjenige, der etwas ins Leben ruft: Person/Institution
> AkkE: dasjenige, das ins Leben gerufen wird: Institution/Gremium [Kommission, Bürgerinitiative, Selbsthilfegruppe o.Ä.]

This is rather similar to the descriptions provided in VDE for a verb such as *deny*:

> **A person or something written or said by a person[I] can deny**
> (i) **something they are accused of or that has been said about them[II]**
> (ii) **that something is the case or exists[II].**

Similarly, FrameNet, which establishes categories that cover more than a single lexical unit, uses categories that are much more specific than those of traditional case grammar. Thus the *closure* frame, to which the verb *open* belongs, operates with categories such as 'Agent', 'Fastener', 'Containing object', 'Enclosed region', 'Container portal' or 'Manipulator'. Again, a parallel can be found to the description provided in VDE:

> A *Open* can mean 'become open'.
> (i) **A door, window, etc.[II] can open or be opened by someone[I] or something[V] or open easily.**
> (ii) **A container such as a tin[II] can be opened by someone[I] or something[V] or open easily.**
> → M D1 D8 T2 T3
> B **A public place, a shop, a business, an exhibition, an event, a discussion, etc.[II] can open or be opened,** i.e. start to be open to the public or do business.

The description of sense B in VDE finds an interesting parallel in VALBU's definition 6 of *öffnen*:

> jemand [Person [als Funktionsträger]/Institution] veranlasst, dass etwas [Institution: Geschäft, Praxis, Behörde o.Ä./[indirekt Räumlichkeit]] irgendwann für den Kunden-, Publikumsverkehr zugänglich ist; aufmachen.

What is interesting about the lexicographical treatment of the non-formal side of the characterization of complements in VDE or VALBU is that both dictionaries make use of general categories such as *someone* or *derjenige* (which can be seen as equivalent to Helbig's semantic feature + HUM) but nevertheless find it necessary to give relatively specific lists of lexical items such as *door, window, etc.* or *Kommission, Bürgerinitiative*. Very often this is because no suitable label can be found as in the case of the note for the verb *set* in VDE

> **A person[I] can set someone[III] something such as a deadline, a target, a task, a test, an examination, etc[II] .**

where it seemed impossible to subsume all possible realizations of complement II under a general heading.

All this provides strong evidence for the messy side of the scale.

4. Conclusions and questions

4.1. Conclusions

With regard to the question of whether valency phenomena are to be described more appropriately in terms of a complement inventory or in terms of valency patterns, it seems that both views will have to be considered. Valency patterns can be seen as the basis for generalizations in terms of a complement inventory or also in terms of argument structure constructions of the kind discussed, for instance, by Goldberg (2006). The identification of separate complements in a complement inventory allows certain generalizations to be made, especially with regard to the semantic contribution of the complement (in terms of semantic roles or whatever) that must be part of a valency description. However, the above discussion has revealed that very important facts about the valency structures of a lexical unit cannot be covered by a complement inventory: these range from the possible combinations of complements and their position to the question of the possible lexical realizations of the complements in different valency patterns.[15] That valency dictionaries should provide *Satzbaupläne* as in VALBU or valency patterns as in VDE thus is not merely due to considerations of lexicographical or didactic presentation but reflects the nature of valency phenomena as such. This insight is also of psycholinguistic relevance in that it shows the need to specify valency patterns in the design of a mental lexicon.

The discussion has also shown that valency is definitely one of the more messy aspects of language. Although nobody will deny that certain general tendencies are also at work – for instance generalizations of the type that subjects of English active declarative clauses tend to be the most agent-like entity in the clause –, the discussion has provided ample evidence to illustrate that the amount of idiosyncratic word specific knowledge that is involved is considerable.

4.2. Questions

If one considers valency phenomena not only from the point of view of descriptive linguistics or lexicography but with respect to psycholinguistic or cognitive questions, then the conclusions outlined above raise a number of questions. What is obvious is that the messy character of valency phenomena as such and the role attributed to valency patterns – which are neither general patterns like the patterns of early American structuralism nor identical with the constructions of construction grammar[16] – increases the amount of information that has to be stored in the mental lexicon.

However, if storage is such an important factor in this area, one might take the issue further and question the idea of valency as a property of lexical units altogether. Does it make sense to assume that we store different senses of a lexeme, which then have certain properties such as a particular valency structure? To what extent are we justified in assuming that

(26) *Her excitement shone in her eyes as she* showed *him her sketches.*$_{\text{VDE}}$

represents a different meaning of *show* from that exemplified by

(27) *Nicholson seized every opportunity to* show *his work in the mixed exhibitions now being arranged.*$_{\text{AC}}$
(28) *Patrick Heron's work was* shown *by the Waddington Galleries.*$_{\text{AC}}$

simply because (27) and (28) represent divalent uses and semantically are instances of public showing? Does

(29) *Children in this phase* show *no special anxiety at being separated from their parent; and no fear of strangers.*$_{\text{VDE}}$

have to be treated as a separate sense of *show* because the showing is non-intentional? It is obvious that these are questions any descriptive semanticist or lexicographer is faced with every day, and it is equally obvious that polysemy is not necessarily a property lexical items possess but a property that is imposed on them by analysts, but nevertheless the question remains about how such facts are dealt with in language acquisition and how they are processed and stored in the brain and what role general rules play.

Perhaps it is useful to draw an analogy with regular and irregular phenomena in morphology. Contrary to general opinion, Bybee (1995: 428) argues that it is not only so-called irregular past tense forms such as *stuck* or *struck* that are stored in the brain but also the regular forms of high frequency verbs such as *covered* and that past tense forms of a low frequency words such as *hovered* can be produced on the basis of the stored information:

> The basic proposal is that morphological properties of words, paradigms and morphological patterns once described as rules emerge from associations made among related words in lexical representation.

The question to be asked in the valency context is whether storage of unanalysed information could not equally serve as an explanation for (a) the apparently idiosyncratic character of many valency phenomena and (b) those generalizations about the use of certain complements or valency patterns that are actually possible.

Take a simple example such as the verb *meet*. Presumably one can safely assume that in the language acquisition process a child will first encounter sentences of the type

(2) *This time, she* met *Jamie at Rital's wine bar at lunchtime.* BNC
(30) *This morning he'll* meet *President Vaclav Havel* ... BNC
(3) *These days they* meet *at conferences* ... BNC
(4) *A Cabinet committee* meets *tomorrow to agree to slash public spending by billions.* BNC
(31) *Heron had* met *Delia almost immediately on arrival in Welwyn in 1929, when they attended the same school.* AC
(32) *We had never* met *before.* AC

All of these sentences represent the concept of a coming together of two or possibly more people, which can be seen as a very simple representation of the meaning of the verb and a very basic concept of what one might call its argument structure. If children "are indeed learning utterance-level constructions as linguistic gestalts", as Tomasello (2003: 169) supposes, then these sentences can serve as the basis for abstractions concerning the semantic features ('+ human' or 'PERSON') and semantic roles of the complements. However, that the character of the "meeting" described in these utterances differs can be concluded from one's world knowledge rather than from the semantics of the verb. The fact that dictionaries distinguish between different senses on the grounds of such features as 'by arrangement', 'by chance' or 'for the first time' is an attempt to describe the scope of situations in which the verb *meet* can be used rather than a semantic description; this is made clear by the ambiguity of some of the sentences above (Herbst and Klotz 2003: 40–41). What one has to bear in mind, however, is that while for lexicographical purposes it may be necessary to distinguish between different senses of a verb such as *meet*, psychologically this need not be so – at least not for perception purposes. In order to understand sentences such as the ones above, a very general understanding of what *meet* 'means' together with knowledge of certain facts of the world or what one could call pragmatic rules is sufficient.

On that basis, it is also possible to understand sentences such as

(33) *Each service is* met *by a bus at Dunwich.*BNC
(34) *Where the land* meets *the sea, there are hundreds of beaches and coves …*BNC

in which the arguments are not '+ human' any more. Equally, a sentence such as

(35) *We are moving slowly and carefully to find the best ways to* meet *the individual needs of those gifted in math or gifted in any area …*BNC

can be interpreted without any difficulty. The basic suggestion is that on the basis of storage of highly frequent and thus prototypical uses of a verb such as *meet* speakers gain knowledge about the kinds of situations to which this verb can be applied together with some notion of its meaning. Encountering less frequent uses does not present any problems of comprehension and results in further storage of possible uses of that word. Certainly one would assume that no foreign learner of English who is familiar with the prototypical uses of *meet* referring to the encounter of two or more people will find it impossible to understand what sentences such as (33–35) mean. On the other hand it is unlikely that any foreign learner would use such sentences before having heard or read a verb being used in such a context. In fact, one might argue that this is precisely the reason why many users of monolingual dictionaries find examples more useful than definitions. What kind of sentence would a learner be able to produce on the basis of the definition "to experience a problem, attitude, or situation" without the example *Wherever she went she met hostility and prejudice* (LDOCE4)?

Such an account of verb valency emphasizes storage in combination with the application of general pragmatic rules. It leaves open the question of the precise form or amount of the information that is being stored and the status of generalizations in terms of rules or general principles that certainly also have to be accommodated, although some of the ideas that have been proposed under the heading of emergentism seem to promise new explanatory potential in this respect.[17] There seems to be very convincing evidence that repetition and storage play a major role in language acquisition. Tomasello (2003: 112), for instance, points out "that many, indeed the majority of the utterances children hear are grounded in highly-repetitive item-based frames that they experience dozens, in some cases hundreds, of times every day".

What would make such a model attractive to descriptive linguistics is that it would account for the impossibility of making a clear distinction between various senses of a word and it would account for the fact why much valency information seems messy rather than systematic.

The fact that the descriptive analysis of valency phenomena sometimes results in rather clear and straightforward generalizations but sometimes only leads to seemingly unsatisfactory or messy accounts of a phraseological or quasi-collocational nature seems highly compatible with Goldberg's (2006: 62) view that "both item-specific knowledge and generalizations coexist" and with the following conclusion reached by Tomasello (2003: 98):

> The level of abstraction at which the speaker is working in particular cases may or may not correspond to the most abstract level the linguist can find; it is in all cases an empirical question that most often needs psychological experimentation.

What is interesting in the case of valency is that linguists or lexicographers do not always seem to be able to find abstract representations – in any case, empirical psychological evidence would be extremely helpful also for the design, and the assessment of the plausibility, of various models of valency phenomena within descriptive linguistics.

Notes

1. For an account of early German valency see Herbst, Heath, and Dederding (1980).
2. See Sinclair (2004b: 164-165) and Herbst (forthcoming).
3. For the difference between rules and principles see Leech (1983).
4. For a discussion of valency phenomena in terms of *Norm* see Herbst (1983).
5. See also Sinclair (2004a).
6. Compare also Fillmore, Kay, and O'Connor (1988) for the importance of idiomaticity.
7. Compare also Helbig (1992: 3–18) and Ágel (2000).
8. Engel (1977: 180) defines *Satzmuster* as follows: "Die Struktur des Satzes wird zwar entscheidend durch die Struktur des Verbs bestimmt; dabei spielt aber die Art der jeweiligen Ergänzung eine wenigstens ebenso große Rolle wie ihre Anzahl. Ein Überblick über die Kombinationsmöglichkeiten von Ergänzungen hat also deren Zahl und Art zu berücksichtigen. Solchermaßen festgelegte Kombinationsmöglichkeiten werden Satzmuster genannt." Engel (1977: 181) distinguishes *Satzmuster* from *Satzbaupläne*: "In den Satzmustern werden zwar die kombinierbaren E. zusammengestellt, es wird aber zwischen

obligatorischen und fakultativen E. nicht unterschieden. Dieser wichtige Unterschied gehört ebenfalls zur Valenz, ist also wie die Zahl und Art der E. vom Verb gesteuert. Man berücksichtigt ihn in der Kodierung am besten, indem man alle fakultativen E. einklammert. Auf diese Art entstehen aus Satzmustern Satzbaupläne." Such valency descriptions in terms of *Satzbaupläne* take the form of *essen*$_{<0(1)>}$ or *sagen*$_{<01(3)>}$ (Engel 1977: 182).

9. For the treatment of these cases in FrameNet see Fillmore (this volume).
10. In VDE complements are characterised in terms of their morphological form – [N] for noun phrase or [V-ing] for an *ing*-clause – and in terms of possible functions in a clause – the index $_{A}$ indicating the ability of a complement to occur as the subject in an active clause; $_{P}$ indicating the ability to function as a subject in a passive clause.
11. The first three levels are covered by the information given in the complement inventory and taken up by the patterns, which are given in the main part of the entry together with the examples. The fourth level of the description is indicated by separate notes at the end of a dictionary entry.
12. Examples marked BNC are taken from the British National Corpus, those marked VDE are taken from the *Valency Dictionary of English*, which is based on the Bank of English. AC refers to general authentic language material.
13. For a more detailed discussion of such problems see Herbst and Klotz (2002).
14. Within the VDE framework, a complement of a verb is classified as obligatory if it has to be realized when the verb is used. This is different from approaches in which the distinction between obligatory and optional complements is based on the use of a verb in active declarative clauses. Cf. Herbst et al. (2004: xxx–xxxiii).
15. Valency patterns are to be seen as verb specific patterns not as general patterns in the sense that the concept of patterns was used in early structuralism. In this respect, the concept of valency patterns also differs from similar ideas in construction grammar. In particular, no claims will be made as to the meaning of certain valency patterns, which is a position also taken by Engel (1977: 182): "Insbesondere scheint es mir nicht möglich, jedem Satzbauplan, wie Weisgerber offenbar wollte, eine spezifische Bedeutung zuzuschreiben." Valency patterns can be modified in their syntactic realization by other syntactic factors such as theme/rheme considerations, types of clauses etc. For possible variations on *Satzbaupläne* see Engel (1977: 183).
16. See, for instance, Croft and Cruse (2004).
17. Compare also MacWhinney (1998 or 2001) for accounts of emergentist approaches.

References

Ágel, Vilmos
 2000 *Valenztheorie*. Tübingen: Gunter Narr Verlag.

Bybee, Joan
 1995 Regular morphology and the lexicon. *Language and cognitive processes* 10 (5): 425–455.

Chomsky, Noam
 1986 *Knowledge of Language: Its Nature, Origin and Use*. New York/Westport, Connecticut/London: Praeger Publishers.
 2004 *The Generative Enterprise Revisited.* Berlin/New York: Mouton de Gruyter.

Coseriu, Eugenio
 1973 *Probleme der strukturellen Semantik.* Tübingen: Gunter Narr Verlag.

Croft, William and D. Alan Cruse
 2004 *Cognitive Linguistics*. Cambridge: Cambridge University Press.

Cruse, David A.
 1986 *Lexical Semantics*. Cambridge: Cambridge University Press.

de Saussure, Ferdinand
 1916 *Cours de Linguistique Générale* (ed. by Charles Bally and Albert Séchehaye). Berlin: Mouton de Gruyter.

Emons, Rudolf
 1974 *Valenzen englischer Prädikatsverben.* Tübingen: Max Niemeyer Verlag.
 1978 *Valenzgrammatik für das Englische.* Tübingen: Max Niemeyer Verlag.

Engel, Ulrich
 1977 *Syntax der deutschen Gegenwartssprache.* Berlin: Erich Schmidt Verlag.

Engel, Ulrich, and Helmut Schumacher
 1976 *Kleines Valenzlexikon deutscher Verben.* Tübingen: Gunter Narr Verlag.

Engelen, Bernhard
 1975 *Untersuchungen zu Satzbauplan und Wortfeld in der geschriebenen deutschen Sprache der Gegenwart*. München: Max Hueber Verlag.

Fillmore, Charles
 1968 The case for case. In *Universals in Linguistic Theory*, Emmon Bach, and Robert T. Harms (eds.), 1–88. New York: Holt, Rinehart and Winston.
 2007 Valency issues in FrameNet. This volume.

Fillmore, Charles, Paul Kay, and Mary Catherine O'Connor
 1988 Regularity and idiomaticity in grammatical constructions: The case of *let alone*. *Language*, 501–538.

Götz-Votteler, Katrin
 2007 Describing semantic valency. This volume.

Goldberg, Adele
2006 *Constructions at Work. The Nature of Generalizations in Language.* Oxford/New York: Oxford University Press.

Haegeman, Liliane
1991 *Introduction to Government & Binding Theory*. Oxford/Cambridge: Blackwell.

Hausmann, Franz Josef
1985 Kollokationen im deutschen Wörterbuch. Ein Beitrag zur Theorie des lexikographischen Beispiels. *Lexikographie und Grammatik*, Henning Bergenholtz, and Joachim Mugdan (eds.), 118–129. Tübingen: Niemeyer.

Helbig, Gerhard
1992 *Probleme der Valenz- und Kasustheorie.* Tübingen: Max Niemeyer Verlag.

Helbig, Gerhard, and Wolfgang Schenkel
1973 *Wörterbuch zur Valenz und Distribution deutscher Verben.* 2d ed. Leipzig: VEB Verlag Enzyklopädie.

Herbst, Thomas
1983 *Untersuchungen zur Valenz englischer Adjektive und ihrer Nominalisierungen.* Tübingen: Gunter Narr Verlag.
forthc. "Valency – item-specificity and idiom principle." *Exploring the Grammar-Lexis Interface.* Ute Römer, and Rainer Schulze (eds.). Amsterdam/Philadelphia: John Benjamins.

Herbst, Thomas, and Michael Klotz
2002 *Meeting* and *Kissing* as valency problems – some remarks on the treatment of reciprocity and reflexivity in a valency description of English. In *Reflexives and Intensifiers: The Use of* self-*Forms in English*, Ekkehard König, and Volker Gast (eds.), 239–249. (*Zeitschrift für Anglistik und Amerikanistik* 2002.3.) Tübingen: Stauffenburg Verlag.
2003 *Lexikografie*. Paderborn: Schöninghh (UTB).

Herbst, Thomas, David Heath, and Hans-Martin Dederding
1980 *Grimm's Grandchildren. Current Topics in German Linguistics.* London/New York: London.

Herbst, Thomas, David Heath, Ian Roe, and Dieter Götz
2004 *A Valency Dictionary of English. A Corpus-Based Analysis of the Complementation Patterns of English Verbs, Nouns and Adjectives.* Berlin/New York: Mouton de Gruyter. [VDE]

Herbst, Thomas, and Susen Schüller
forthc. *Introduction to Syntactic Analysis. A Valency Approach.* Tübingen: Narr.

Heringer, Hans Jürgen
1970 *Theorie der deutschen Syntax*. München: Max Hueber Verlag.
1996 *Deutsche Syntax Dependentiell.* Tübingen: Stauffenburg.

Klotz, Michael
2000 *Grammatik und Lexik: Studien zur Syntagmatik englischer Verben.* Tübingen: Stauffenburg.
2007 Valency rules? The case of verbs with propositional complements. This volume.
Leech, Geoffrey
1983 *Principles of Pragmatics.* London/New York: Longman.
Matthews, Peter
1981 *Syntax.* Cambridge: Cambridge University Press.
MacWhinney, Brian
1998 Models of the emergence of language. *Annual Review of Psychology* 49: 199–227.
2001 Emergentist approaches to language. In *Frequency and the Emergence of Linguistic Structrure,* Joan Bybee, and Paul Hopper (eds.), 449–470. Amsterdam/Philadelphia: Benjamins.
Schumacher, Helmut, Jacqueline Kubczak, Renate Schmidt, and Vera de Ruiter
2004 *VALBU – Valenzwörterbuch deutscher Verben.* Tübingen: Gunter Narr Verlag [VALBU].
Sinclair, John
1991 *Corpus, Concordance, Collocation.* Oxford: Oxford University Press.
2004a The search for units of meaning. In *Trust the Text. Language, corpus and discourse*, John Sinclair (ed., with Ronald Carter), 24–48. London/New York: Routledge.
2004b Lexical grammar. In *Trust the Text. Language, corpus and discourse,* John Sinclair (ed., with Ronald Carter), 164–193. London/New York: Routledge.
Tomasello, Michael
2003 *Constructing a Language. A Usage-Based Theory of Language Acquisition.* Cambridge, Mass./London: Harvard University Press.

Framenet: http://framenet.icsi.berkeley.edu/

Describing semantic valency

Katrin Götz-Votteler

1. Semantic valency

Valency theory as outlined by Tesnière in the 1950s was a primarily syntactic theory. But Tesnière already briefly characterized the *actants* of a verb according to their semantic function or, to use his metaphor, according to their roles as actors in a *petit drame* (Tesnière 1965: 102). The *prime actant* is said to carry out the action ("fait l'action"), the *second actant* in an active sentence to support the action ("supporte l'action"), and the *tiers actant* to be the one that profits or suffers from the action ("l'action se fait à son profit ou à son détriment"; Tesnière 1965: 111).

Since then, valency has not only been specified as a theory, but also been applied as an approach for linguistic description, as in the syntactical description of such languages as German, English or Danish, for the cognitive exploration of grammar or in computational linguistics.[1] As a consequence, the theory has increasingly opened up to semantic, communicative or cognitive aspects.

In more recent models of valency this has led to a distinction between different levels of valency: Allerton, for example, establishes three levels of analysis in valency patterns: the first is concerned with *semantic roles and processes*, the second deals with *valency structures*, i.e. with the complements required by a verb, and the third examines *surface structures* like dummy subjects or transformations of active into passive clauses (Allerton 1982: 40–48).

Helbig also assumes three levels of valency, which differ however from those established by Allerton: on his first level, *logical valency*, mental relations between logical predicates and related elements are analysed. The logical structure of *swim*, for instance, comprises one element, called *argument* ("Argument"), as swimming is usually done by only one person, the logical structure of *visit*, on the other hand, consists of two elements, as visiting requires a visitor as well as a visitee (Helbig 1992: 7).

At the second level, *semantic valency*, the semantic properties of the arguments are specified by using semantic properties as well as semantic cases (Helbig 1992: 8). The third level, *syntactic valency*, then deals with the syntactic properties of arguments, which are at this level called *actants* or *complements* ("Aktanten" / "Ergänzungen") i.e. it concerns their syntactic realisation or their status in relation to optionality or obligatoriness (Helbig 1992: 9).

What these two models have in common is that they establish a syntactic side of valency on the one hand, a semantic side on the other and some kind of relationship between the two. The nature of this relationship, however, is contested: syntactic valency can be seen as an indirect reflection of semantic relations, it can be regarded as being directly determined by the verb meaning, or valency can be considered an exclusively semantic phenomenon, i.e. as part of the meaning itself (Helbig 1992: 16).[2]

While no agreement concerning the exact nature of the relationship between syntactic and semantic valency has yet been reached, common ground is shared in the acceptance of the utility of some kind of semantic description in a valency model. As summarised by the *Valency Dictionary of English* (VDE 2004: xxix): "The semantic analysis of valency complements addresses two questions: firstly, the meanings of the complements, especially the difference or parallels in meaning between various complements of the same word; secondly, which lexical items can (or cannot) occur as a particular complement."

2. Possible ways of describing semantic valency

It is not only the relationship between syntactic and semantic valency that has not yet been agreed upon, but also which method to use in order to describe the meaning of complements. Basically, four approaches can be distinguished here: semantic roles, semantic components, semantic categories and a verb-specific description.

The concept of a more or less fixed set of *semantic roles* (also called "deep cases", "thematic roles" or "theta-roles") goes back to Charles Fillmore (1968) and is mainly used in theoretical approaches to valency.[3] The following chart taken from Allerton (1982: 52) shows a semantic description of several zero-, mono-, di- or trivalent verbs applying a semantic role model:

rain:	(0)
sneeze:	(1) subject "patient"
blow:	(1) subject "agent/force", (2) (object "patient/result")
see:	(1) subject "experiencer", (2) object "mental focus"

read: (1) subject "agent",
(2) (object "mental focus")

tear: (1) subject "agent",
(2) object "patient"

give: (1) subject "agent",
(2) object "patient",
(3) indirect object "recipient"

More applied approaches, such as VerbNet, also use semantic roles as part of – in this case – the lexicographical description of a verb, as the following extract from the entry *blow* (in the meaning "free of obstruction by blowing air through: 'blow one's nose'") shows:

Agent[+animate]
Cause[]
Patient[+body_part]
Recipient[+animate]
Theme[+communication]
(http://www.cis.upenn.edu/group/verbnet/)

As can be seen from this entry, VerbNet complements the semantic description by additionally listing *semantic components*. Such components as e.g. +/-animate, +/-human or +/-abstract serve to identify semantic properties of the noun usually used as complement with a certain verb, as the following entry from Helbig and Schenkel's *Wörterbuch zur Valenz und Distribution deutscher Verben* ([5]1980: 176) shows:

zwingen

I. $zwingen_3$
II. zwingen → Sn, Sa, pS/$NS_{daß}$/Inf

III. Sn →	1. +Anim (*Der Junge, der Hund* zwang das Kind zur Umkehr.)
	2. –Anim (*Die Schlacht* zwang sie zu einem Umweg.)
	3. Abstr (*Die Kritik* zwang ihn zur Darlegung seiner Gründe.)
	4. Act (*Das Lärmen* zwingt uns zu einer Pause.)
Sa →	1. Hum (Die Situation zwingt *den Jungen* zum Nachdenken.)
	2. Abstr (als Hum) (Die Demonstration zwingt *die Regierung* zur Überprüfung ihrer Politik.)
	3. Sa = Sn (Refl) (Er zwingt *sich* zur Arbeit.)
p = zu,	
pSd →	1. Abstr (Er zwingt ihn *zu dieser Maßnahme*.)
	2. Act (Er zwingt den Jungen *zum Schwimmen*.)
NS →	Act (Er zwingt ihn dazu, *daß er spricht*.)
Inf →	Act (Er zwingt ihn dazu, *zu sprechen*.)

In contrast to semantic roles, semantic components do not depend on the meaning of the verb, but can be regarded as properties of the noun, i.e. they are noun-inherent.

Related to the description of semantic valency with semantic components is a third option, namely the classification of syntactical complements into *semantic categories*. This is done for example in the *Valenzwörterbuch deutscher Verben VALBU*, which identifies for each complement possible categories the expression can refer to, like person, animal, object or force (VALBU 2004: 89).[4] In contrast to semantic components, semantic categories as defined in VALBU do not refer to inherent properties of a noun, but to the usage of a noun within the semantic range of a certain category:

> Diese Bestimmungen sind nicht so zu verstehen, dass den Wörtern, die an diesen Stellen eingesetzt werden können, diese Kategorien als inhärente Merkmale zukommen. Es wird damit behauptet, dass ein Sprecher, der diese Verbvariante korrekt verwendet, die Belegung der NomE als einen Ausdruck interpretiert wissen will, der auf eine Person oder ein Gremium oder eine Institution referiert. (VALBU 2002: 62)
> [These descriptions cannot be regarded as inherent properties of the words used as complements. They signify that a speaker using this verb correctly in this meaning wants the expression to be interpreted as a person or a group or an institution.]

VALBU employs semantic categories in combination with a further option of describing semantic valency, the *verb-specific description of participants*. Therefore, the nominative complement of *sich verletzen 1*, for example, is characterized as follows: "dasjenige, das eine Verletzung durch etwas erleidet: Person/Tier" (VALBU 2004: 790).

The advantages of a verb-specific description lie in its accuracy and completion of the verb meaning. This is why this method is mostly used in lexicographical frameworks, as in VALBU or VDE (2004):

A (i) **A person or a group of people such as an army^{I} can attack another person, a group or a country^{II} with a particular weapon^{III}**, i.e. use force against them.
(ii) **A person or something written by a person such as an article^{I} can attack a person, a particular approach or point of view, etc.^{II}**, i.e. criticize them.
→ M D1 D2 T1 T3 T5

B **A person^{I} or an institution can attack a problem or issue^{II}**, i.e. make a serious attempt to tackle it.
→ D1 T2 T4

These four different methods of specifying semantic valency, semantic roles, semantic components, semantic categories and verb-specific description, draw on different starting points of description, as already suggested above: the semantics of complements can be seen as a result of the verb meaning; this is the case with semantic role models and verb-specific description. Characterization of complements via semantic components uses however noun-inherent properties, so that the head of the noun phrase becomes the determining factor of description. Finally, semantic categories are understood as usage-based categories and therefore as a reflection of verb pragmatics.

As verbs can be regarded as the core of valency theory, the two methods that take the verb as starting point appear particularly attractive within a valency framework. The following section therefore concentrates on these two methods, semantic roles and verb-specific description, evaluating their application in descriptions of semantic valency.

3. Semantic roles and verb-specific description

The usefulness of descriptive methods is best assessed by their application. The following examples show usages of the verb *fly*; in examples (1–12) *fly* takes two noun phrase complements and possibly one or more adverbial complements, examples (13–16) illustrate a divalent use of *fly* with one noun phrase complement and one adverbial complement. The labels after the examples refer to verb-specific classes of participants that occur as complements with *fly*.[5]

(1) *Stan* ***flew*** *helicopters in Vietnam.*$_{\text{LDOCE}}$
→ PILOT / MACHINE

(2) *He* ***had flown*** *a distance of 169 miles in 3 hours 40 minutes and established a record.*$_{\text{VDE}}$
→ PILOT / DISTANCE

(3) *Under the Brabazon recommendations, the aircraft would have six to eight piston or reciprocating engines, possibly replaced by gas turbine engines if available, and a pressurized cabin, and be capable of* ***flying*** *5,000 miles non-stop at 275 miles per hour.*$_{\text{BNC}}$
→ MACHINE / DISTANCE

(4) *I find it a little horrifying to think that some Commercial pilots* ***flying*** *large numbers of passengers may have had very little exposure to reduced 'g'.*$_{\text{BNC}}$
→ PILOT / PASSENGER

(5) *British Airways* ***flies*** *passengers to over 150 destinations around the world and has a cashhandling requirement at each of its airports.*$_{\mathrm{NET}}$
→ AIRLINE / PASSENGER / DESTINATION

(6) *The couple* ***flew*** *British Airways.*$_{\mathrm{VDE}}$
→ PASSENGER / AIRLINE

(7) *The camps were spotted by pilots* ***flying*** *supplies to Nagorny Karabakh, which has been sealed off from the rest of Azerbaijan for several months.*$_{\mathrm{BNC}}$
→ PILOT / GOODS / DESTINATION

(8) *From the hub of the operation, the Ilopango Air Base in El Salvador, creaking aircraft* ***flew*** *supplies to the contras' northern front billetted in Honduras.*$_{\mathrm{BNC}}$
→ MACHINE / GOODS / DESTINATION

(9) *His company* ***flew*** *him to Rio to attend the conference.*$_{\mathrm{LDOCE}}$
→ INSTITUTION / PASSENGER / DESTINATION

(10) *The fully refurbished, vintage plane then* ***flies*** *passengers to Bullo River Station for three nights at the half-million acre, traditional Outback cattle ranch before continuing to Kakadu National Park to accent Aboriginal culture.*$_{\mathrm{NET}}$
→ MACHINE / PASSENGER / DESTINATION

(11) *The airline* ***flew*** *89 flights to Sweden in 1941.*$_{\mathrm{VDE}}$
→ AIRLINE / OPERATION / DESTINATION

(12) *And one of Arrow's pilots, Jacobo Bolivar, was one of the three principals of Sur International, the company which* ***flew*** *weapons from the US to Iran for Lieutenant-Colonel Oliver North in 1985.*$_{\mathrm{BNC}}$
→ INSTITUTION / GOODS / SOURCE / DESTINATION

(13) *Britain cancelled a 1960 no-visa agreement in June and imposed entry visas for all Turks after more than 1,500 Turks* ***flew*** *to Britain and applied for political asylum.*$_{\mathrm{BNC}}$
→ PASSENGER / DESTINATION

(14) *The symptoms are generally worse the further you* ***fly*** *and they are more marked after eastward flights than those to the west.*$_{\mathrm{BNC}}$
→ PASSENGER / DISTANCE

(15) *The plane* ***flew*** *up the fjord, which seemed so narrow that the mountains were on both wing tips at the same time.*$_{BNC}$
→ MACHINE / ROUTE

(16) *While supplies* ***are flying*** *in from all over the world, making sure that everybody over such a large area receives them is another matter.*$_{NET}$
→ GOODS / DESTINATION / SOURCE

Eleven different classes of participants can be identified here: PILOT, MACHINE, AIRLINE, PASSENGER, GOODS, INSTITUTION, OPERATION, DESTINATION, SOURCE, DISTANCE and ROUTE. The categories PILOT, PASSENGER, AIRLINE, MACHINE, INSTITUTION and GOODS can be found in subject position.

So far, the complement description with the above categories has been entirely verb-specific. In order to transfer it to a semantic role model with a fixed set of roles, it would be necessary to assign these labels to specific roles, e.g. PILOT – AGENT, PASSENGER – PATIENT. However, the syntactic arrangement of a clause seems to affect the role of a specific participant, or in other words, seems to reflect the role of the participant in a specific situation. Consider the examples in which the same type of participant is realised in different syntactic positions:

(5) *British Airways* ***flies*** *passengers to over 150 destinations around the world and has a cashhandling requirement at each of its airports.*$_{NET}$
→ AIRLINE / PASSENGER / DESTINATION

(6) *The couple* ***flew*** *British Airways.*$_{VDE}$
→ PASSENGER / AIRLINE

The two participants PASSENGER and AIRLINE both occur once in subject and once in object position, and it seems as if the participant in subject position is interpreted as the more agentive, more performing character: in example (5) *British Airways* can be regarded as the entity doing something, whereas in example (6) *the couple* seems to play a more agentive role than the airline. This result goes hand in hand with findings that agentive entities are usually encoded in a more fronted position than less agentive entities:

> Nominals denoting figures of state and sources of actions consistently precede those denoting grounds and recipients, except in presentative contexts. They are also chosen as perspectives. (Sridhar 1988: 82)

These considerations can lead to the hypothesis that elements in subject position are generally interpreted as the performing character within a specific situation. This hypothesis also includes inanimate entities:

(3) *Under the Brabazon recommendations, the aircraft would have six to eight piston or reciprocating engines, possibly replaced by gas turbine engines if available, and a pressurized cabin, and be capable of **flying** 5,000 miles non-stop at 275 miles per hour*.$_{\text{BNC}}$
→ MACHINE / DISTANCE

(15) *The plane **flew** up the fiord, which seemed so narrow that the mountains were on both wing tips at the same time*.$_{\text{BNC}}$
→ MACHINE / ROUTE

These sentences seem to reflect a perspective within which the MACHINE is perceived as the only entity that fits the description *fly* or as the only relevant entity in that process. Other entities to which the role AGENT could be attributed might either not be perceived, be unknown or just irrelevant. It can therefore be said that the MACHINE is presented as the participant performing the action of flying.

If the subject is generally perceived as the agentive entity, the conclusion must be drawn that semantic roles cannot be separated from syntactic structure. Such separation would only be possible if different lexical units for *fly* in sentences like (5) and (6) were assumed. Then, *fly* in example (5) could be paraphrased as 'operating flights as an airline' and *British Airways* could be identified as acting entity. On the other hand, a sense like 'travel somewhere by plane as a passenger' would assign the agentive role to *the couple*. But even then, the participant in subject position would still be regarded as performing participant, so that the correlation between subjectivity and agentivity would still hold. Furthermore, assuming different lexical units for each type of possible subject would come very close to using a verb-specific description, so that the general applicability of semantic roles would be weakened. It can therefore be concluded that it is not possible to assign general semantic roles to a specific type of participant in a one-to-one relationship.

The hypothesis above can also be extended to ergative verbs. The *Collins Cobuild English Grammar* describes ergative verbs as follows: "Some verbs allow you to describe an action from the point of view of the performer of the action or from the point of view of something which is affected by the action." (1990: 155). In other words: the semantic role of the participant in subject position is that of the PATIENT.

Following the hypothesis outlined above leads, however, to the conclusion that the subject of an ergative verb is not presented in the role of the PATIENT but from a perspective within which it seems as if the entity in subject position were the performer of the action. Consider the following examples:

(17) *He* ***opened*** *the door wide, and gestured for me to come in.*$_{\text{LDOCE}}$
→ OPENER / DOOR

(18) *The new key* ***opened*** *the door but did not work in the ignition.*$_{\text{NET}}$
→ KEY / DOOR

(19) *The bedroom door* ***opened*** *and she rushed in.*$_{\text{BNC}}$
→ DOOR

(20) *After a short discussion with the customs officers, the gates* ***opened*** *and the truck moved off.*$_{\text{LDOCE}}$
→ DOOR

(21) *That window* ***doesn't open***.$_{\text{LDOCE}}$
→ WINDOW

The entities in subject position differ semantically: in example (17) *he* is a human performer; here, the semantic role AGENT can be assigned without much hesitation. In example (18), it seems as if it was not in the power of a human entity to open the door but in the "power" of a key. The key can therefore be regarded to be the entity responsible for the opening action.

The second clause in example (19) makes it clear that the event is described from inside the room. From this point of view, what is seen first is the moving of the door, i.e. the door is the only participant perceived to be performing an action. Consequently, it is presented in the position of the performing participant.

Example (20) is very similar: possibly, the gates open automatically, so that the element causing the movement, be it the mechanism or an officer pressing a button, is not perceived. (By the way, would the mechanism or the officer be regarded as AGENT?) In this specific situation it is again only the gates which can be seen to be moving. Finally, in the last example it is impossible for any human actor or for any tool to open the window. Thus, the "action of non-opening" must be assigned to the window.

Therefore we can sum up our conclusions by saying that in ergative constructions the entity in subject position does not fulfil the semantic role PATIENT. Such constructions reflect a certain perspective on a situation in which the entity in subject position is perceived as the only entity doing something. The real causer is either not perceived, not known or considered irrelevant. As put by William Croft (1994: 95):

> The subject is the "ultimate cause" in that by making a participant a subject, the speaker has chosen – to the extent allowed by the grammar of his or her language – to represent the participant as not significantly acting under control of someone or something else. In the case of human agency, this normally implies that the subject is controlling the action himself/herself; however, lesser degrees of control are not incompatible with being assigned to subject position ....

This does, however, not apply to passive constructions. The form of the verb in a passive clause assigns a passive role to the entity in subject position and leads to the inference that a more agentive entity is present in the situation.[6] I do therefore not agree with the *Collins Cobuild English Grammar*, which states: "Note that ergative verbs perform a similar function to the passive because they allow you to avoid mentioning who or what does the action" (1990: 157). Whereas in the passive construction the verb form indicates the presence of a further, more agentive participant, in the ergative construction the entity in subject position is presented as the perceived performer of the verb action.

4. Conclusion

The analysis above can be summed up as follows:

1. The perception of a certain event that is to be encoded linguistically is selective.
2. The manner in which a specific situation is perceived is reflected in the syntactic realisation of a clause.
3. The subject position is assumed by that entity that seems to be performing the action expressed by the verb. If the "real" causer cannot be perceived or does not play a role in the specific situation, the participant next likely to perform the action or process is realised as subject.
4. It follows therefore that a model that assumes a fixed relationship between a verb-specific participant (e.g. PASSENGER) and a semantic role label (e.g. PATIENT) is not suitable to describe semantic valency.

Thus, it can be concluded that a verb-specific description of participants can be regarded as the linguistically as well as a psychologically more accurate way to describe semantic valency.

The statements above can also explain hierarchies of semantic features that are used to express the likelihood of an entity occurring in subject position. The following chart taken from Givón (1984: 107) sums up the most important of these features:

a. *Humanity*: human > animate > inanimate > abstract
b. *Causation*: direct cause > indirect cause > non-cause
c. *Volition*: strong intent > weak intent > non-voluntary
d. *Control*: clear control > weak control > no control
e. *Saliency*: very obvious / salient > less obvious / salient > unobvious / nonsalient

If the subject refers to the participant perceived as the most agentive one in a situation, then it is just a matter of likelihood that this entity can be described as salient, human and intentionally acting. If such a participant is not present, then the next likely entity to be encoded as the performing character will possibly be a salient, animate and more or less intentionally acting one, and the next one perhaps a less salient, animate, less intentionally acting one and so on:

> To wit, a human is closer to the ego, thus more familiar and obvious. Direct causes tend to be perceptually more obvious, occupying a clear *boundary position* within the chain (as also does the *effect*, which is categorically coded as *patient*). Intermediate points in the chain are less salient. Strong intent creates a higher probability of success, i.e. visible effect. Ditto for strong control. (Givón 1984: 107)

All that has been said so far applies to sentences that linguistically encode a non-linguistic event. It must not be forgotten, however, that apart from semantic suitability, the subject fulfils a second important function in the English language, namely that of the topic in an information unit. Very often, these two aspects, the semantic and informational value of the subject, coincide. But, as quantitative analyses of fictional texts have shown (Götz-Votteler forthcoming), up to four percent of the subjects can be said to function primarily as text-organisational devices. It must therefore be borne in mind that a description of the semantic valency of a verb applies to the majority of usages, but cannot embrace all cases of syntactic realisation.

Notes

1. Recent projects that have made use of valency theory as a syntactic model include the *Valenzwörterbuch deutscher Verben* (VALBU), the *Valency Dictionary of English* (VDE), the *Odense Valency Dictionary of Danish* (OVD), *FrameNet*, *Contragram* and the *Prague Dependency Treebank*, to name only a few.
2. For the relationship between syntactic complements and meaning see also Klotz and Schøsler (both this volume).
3. The model of case roles is not only used in valency frameworks; it is, for example, also part of syntactic description within Government and Binding Theory. Haegeman, for instance, lists as possible theta-roles for argument specification AGENT, THEME, EXPERIENCER, BENEFACTIVE/BENEFICIARY, GOAL, SOURCE and LOCATION (1991: 41–42).
5. For a list of the most important categories see VALBU (2004: 89–90).
6. The abbreviations at the beginning of the example denote the source of the sentence: *Longman Dictionary of Contemporary English* (LDOCE), *Valency Dictionary of English* (VDE), *British National Corpus* (BNC), and the internet (NET).
9. See Rickheit/Sichelschmidt (this volume).

References

Allerton, David J.
1982 *Valency and the English Verb*. London/New York: Academic Press.

Croft, William
1994 Voice: Beyond control and affectedness. In *Voice – Form and Function*, Barbara Fox, and Paul J. Hopper (eds.), 89–117. Amsterdam/Philadelphia: John Benjamins Publishing Company.

Fillmore, Charles
1968 The case for case. In *Universals in Linguistic Theory,* Emmon Bach, and Robert T. Harms (eds.), 1–88. New York: Holt, Rinehart and Winston.

Givón, Gerhard
1984 *Syntax – A Functional-typological Introduction* Vol. 1. Amsterdam/Philadelphia: John Benjamins Publishing Company.

Götz-Votteler, Katrin
forthc. Aspekte der Informationsentwicklung im Erzähltext.

Haegeman, Liliane
2003 Reprint. *Introduction to Government & Binding Theory*. Oxford/Cambridge, Mass.: Blackwell.

Helbig, Gerhard
1992 *Probleme der Valenz- und Kasustheorie*. Tübingen: Max Niemeyer Verlag.

Helbig, Gerhard, and Wolfgang Schenkel
1980 *Wörterbuch zur Valenz und Distribution deutscher Verben*. 5th edition. Leipzig: Bibliographisches Institut.
Herbst, Thomas, David Heath, Ian Roe, and Dieter Götz (eds.)
2004 *A Valency Dictionary of English*. Berlin/New York: Mouton de Gruyter.
Klotz, Michael
2007 Valency rules? The case of verbs with propositional complements. This volume.
Rickheit, Gert, and Lorenz Sichelschmidt
2007 Valency and cognition – a notion in transition. This volume.
Sridhar, Shikaripur N.
1988 *Cognition and Sentence Production – A Cross-linguistic Study*. New York/Berlin/Heidelberg/London/Paris/Tokyo: Springer-Verlag.
Schøsler, Lene
2007 The status of valency patterns. This volume.
Schumacher, Helmut, Jacqueline Kubczak, Renate Schmidt, and Vera de Ruiter (eds.)
2004 *VALBU – Valenzwörterbuch deutscher Verben*, Tübingen: Gunter Narr Verlag.
Sinclair, John
1990 *Collins Cobuild English Grammar*. London/Glasgow: Collins.
Summers, Della
2005 *Longman Dictionary of Contemporary English*. 4th edition. Harlow: Longman.
Tesnière, Lucien
1965 *Éléments de Syntaxe Structurale*. 2d edition. Paris: Librairie C. Klincksieck.

VerbNet: http://www.cis.upenn.edu/group/verbnet/

The status of valency patterns[1]

Lene Schøsler

Twas brillig, and the slithy toves
Did gyre and gimble in the wabe;
All mimsy were the borogoves,
And the mome raths outgrabe.
Lewis Carroll: *Through the Looking Glass,* Jabberwocky

The aim of my paper is to discuss the following questions: is valency a formal category or a content category in languages like French, English, and Danish? And if so – or if this is so in part – does such a thing as *grammaticalisation of valency patterns* exist?[2]

Concerning the first question, the status of valency, this question can be rephrased in the following two hypotheses:

a. The valency pattern expresses a cognitive structure; there is a link or an iconic relation between a valency pattern and the semantic content of the same pattern;
b. The valency pattern does not express a cognitive structure; there is a purely grammatical structuration without any link or iconic relation between expression and content.

When Hopper and Thompson (1980), for example, talk about prototypical relations of transitivity, they mean a human agent carrying out an action having an impact on a non-human object. This way of seeing things implies a valency structuration of the world with, at its centre, an active human being. So this view suggests an interpretation of valency patterns following hypothesis (a). On the other hand, hypothesis (a) has to be rejected if we consider e.g. verbs of perception and verbs of emotion, as already pointed out, e.g. by Krefeld (1998), because these verbs do not have a prototypical agent as subject. Others, e.g. François and Broschart (1994: 40–41) insist that valency patterns are not very informative on the meaning conveyed by the constructions. Hypothesis (a) is easily adapted to a functional approach and hypothesis (b) to a formal approach. The goal of my paper is to show that hypothesis (a) is confirmed at least in some cases and that these cases can be considered to be cases of *specialisation* or *grammaticalisation* of the valency pattern. My discussion of the status of valency is based on synchronic arguments from Danish, French and English and on diachronic arguments from French and Danish.

When we consider quantitative valency patterns, it appears that some patterns seem to be very common and others fairly rare. Thus, in e.g. the *Odense Valency Dictionary of Danish* (OVD)[3], there are eight valency transitive patterns,[4] of which two are extremely common (see table 1) and do not contain verbs having the same or similar content (see examples 1a and 1b), whereas five other patterns, less frequent ones, contain verbs with related content (see examples 1c-h). This suggests that at least some patterns specialise to provide a particular content, whereas others do not. Thus, in many languages meteorological verbs are avalent,[5] and with respect to valency, they constitute a formal class with a specific content. They are even productive in the sense that other verbs when used with this specific pattern will provide a meteorological sense. This is the case in (2a), where the Danish verb *pøse* ('pour'), especially with the particle *ned* ('down'), is used to indicate heavy rain, which is not the sense of the verb when used with a referential subject (2b). A non-referential subject is impossible with the divalent valency pattern of the verb *pøse* (2c).

Table 1. Valency patterns of the OVD.[6] Patterns provided with the symbol # contain verbs with related content.

Valency patterns with direct object		number of verbs in the OVD
subject – object	(1a)	907
subject - object - indirect object # verbs of donation and transfer	(1b)	33
subject - object - prepositional object	(1c)	335
subject - object - prepositional object_1 – prepositional object_2 # verbs indicating change of state or change of concrete or abstract location	(1d)	12
subject - object - locative object	(1e)	37
subject - object - directional object # causative verbs of movement	(1f)	40
subject - object - object of quantity # verbs of weighing and paying	(1g)	4
subject - object - object of manner # verbs of personal evaluation or of utilisation	(1h)	54
		1422

(1) a. *Hun afskedigede ham*
'she dismissed him'
b. *Hun gav ham bogen*
'she gave him the book'
c. *Hun minder mig om hendes mor*
'she reminds me of her mother'
d. *Hun oversætter bogen fra dansk til fransk*
'she translates the book from Danish into French'
e. *Hun lægger bogen på bordet*
'she puts the book on the table'
f. *Han sænker dykkerklokken ned mod havets bund*
'he lowers the diving bell towards the bottom of the sea'
g. *Hun betaler ham en million euro*
'she pays him a million euros'
h. *Han betragter ham som sin ven*
'he considers him his friend'

(2) a. *Det pøsede ned i haven*
lit. 'it poured down in the garden, it rained heavily in the garden'
b. *Han pøser suppe ned i skålen*
'he pours soup into the bowl'
c. **Det pøser suppe ned i skålen*
lit. 'it pours soup into the bowl'

The conclusions to be drawn from the above are: 1, that some valency patterns clearly provide information on the content of verbs having this pattern (1b, 1d, 1f-h) and 2, that change of pattern, e.g. from avalent to valent constructions (2a-b), implies change of content. These points are arguments in favour of a "light" version of hypothesis (a), implying that at least in some cases valency is a content category.

Now, let us consider more examples in order to see how widespread changes of patterns implying change of content are. Cases like these could indeed be arguments in favour of considering valency patterns a sort of expression-content-paradigm for verbs, which is a condition for interpreting these patterns as part of the grammar and not exclusively as part of the lexicon.

Beth Levin has studied verbal alternations as e.g. in (3a-5b) for English; see table 2. These cases of alternation imply: 1, a change of verbal aspect (the a-examples being telic, the b-cases imperfective, as illustrated by the adverbs); 2, a change of entailment (the a-cases implying that the action has been completed); and 3, a change of focus (the focus being on the direct objects). Changes like these are known in several languages; (6) is a translation of (4) into French, and (7) into Danish, with corresponding differences of verbal aspect, entailment and focus, meaning that in the a-examples the wall is painted, the car is full of boxes and John has learnt linguistics, whereas in the b-examples the activity has not come to a (successful) completion. In Danish, this alternation is very productive and has recently spread to contexts where it did not exist previously. The pattern shown in (8-9), with the preposition *på* ['on'], is especially frequent. The construction without the preposition *på* is telic, it implies that the activity expressed by the verb has been completed. The construction with the preposition *på* is imperfective; it implies that the activity is ongoing and that it is not (yet) completed. In other words, the direct construction indicates that the president is dead and the book is finished, whereas the indirect construction indicates that the president is still alive and the book was not – perhaps never – finished (see Durst-Andersen and Herslund 1996). The productivity of these patterns confirms, I think, my interpretation of them as valency-paradigms with specific content.

Table 2. Alternations of valency patterns

telic action		imperfective activity	
(3a)	*John sprayed the wall with paint (in an hour)*	(3b)	*John sprayed paint on the wall (for an hour)*
(4a)	*Julie loaded the car with boxes (in an hour)*	(4b)	*Julie loaded boxes into the car (for an hour)*
(5a)	*Mary taught John linguistics (in an hour)*	(5b)	*Mary taught linguistics to John (for an hour)*
(6a)	*Julie a chargé la voiture de caisses (en une heure)*	(6b)	*Julie a chargé des caisses sur la voiture (pendant une heure)*
(7a)	*Julie har læsset vognen med kasser (på en time)*	(7b)	*Julie har læsset kasser på vognen (i en time)*
(8a)	*skyde præsidenten* ['shoot the president']	(8b)	*skyde på præsidenten* [lit. 'shoot on the president']
(9a)	*skrive en bog* ['write a book']	(9b)	*skrive på en bog* [lit. 'write on a book']

Alternating constructions of the type *Marie lui casse le bras, Marie casse son bras* [lit. 'Marie him breaks the arm' – 'Mary breaks his arm'], with alternating patterns combined with inalienable possession, provide other well-known pairs that I will consider as valency-paradigms with specific content. The case is especially clear in Danish, where we find two different alternation patterns depending on the nature of the verb, a pleasant or an unpleasant action; see examples (10-11).[7]

(10)	a.	*jeg kysser ham på kinden* lit. 'I kiss him on the cheek'	b.	*jeg kysser hans kind* 'I kiss his cheek'
(11)	a.	*jeg bider ham i kinden* lit. 'I bite him in the cheek'	b.	*jeg bider i hans kind* lit. 'I bite in his cheek'

In both cases, there is an agent (*I*) a possessor (*he*) and a possessum (*the cheek*). In all four examples, *I* am doing something to *him*. In the a-constructions, *I* am kissing or biting an inalienable part of *him*, i.e. his cheek. In the b-constructions, the cheek is presented as not forming an inalienable part of *him*, indeed, the cheek may not be a part of *him* at all – *he* could be a student of medicine, having a cheek-sample for experimentation. The difference in the constructions (10) and (11) lies in the way the same constituents are expressed in the parallel constructions. In the a-constructions, the possessor is expressed as a direct object and the possessum is expressed as a locative; in (10b), they are merged together as the direct object in the alternating construction; in (11b), they are merged together as a locative in the alternating construction. Pleasant action-verbs behave like (10), unpleasant like (11).

Having found valency patterns with specific content and even the possibility of alternation patterns with alternating content, I find it legitimate to conclude that valency patterns are not purely formal categories, they are – at least sometimes – content categories. Now, the question is whether we can find cases where these patterns become "more grammatical", in the sense that patterns that used to be open to different verb senses specialise in order to contain only verbs of the same or related sense. If such a case exists, I would propose that we have here a case of grammaticalisation of a valency pattern.

The verbs listed in table 4 of Maurice Gross' verb lexicon (Gross 1975) with the divalent pattern subject-indirect object are, I believe, such a case.[8] In spite of some differences between the verbs that I cannot comment on here,[9] the verbs of Gross' table 4 share the particular feature that they all express – more or less clearly – a psychological relation between on the one hand a human being who is the experiencer that I will label E and who has pleasant or unpleasant feelings, and on the other hand another human being or an object being the cause of these feelings that I will label O. The verbs of Gross' table 4 have in common the fact that E is expressed as the indirect object and O as the subject. Interestingly, the valency patterns of these verbs have changed over time. Let us just consider three verbs belonging to our list, *obéir, ressembler* and *mentir* in a diachronic perspective.[10] None of these verbs exhibit identical patterns in Latin: the etymon of *obéir* ('obey') was followed by the dative, the etymon of *mentir* ('lie') was followed by the accusative, and the etymon of *ressembler* ('ressemble') had both constructions. In Old French the three verbs had both patterns, and it is not before Modern French that we find one and the same pattern SVIO for all three verbs; see table 3, where I present the case-indications throughout the periods: "accusative" for the direct object and "dative" for the indirect object.

Table 3. The evolution of the case-marking for the etymons of the French verbs *obéir, ressembler* and *mentir*

	Latin	Old French	Middle French	16th century	17th century	Modern French
obéir	---	accus	accus	accus	---	---
	dative	dative	dative	---	dative	dative
ressembler	accus	accus	accus	accus	accus	---
	dative	dative	dative	dative	dative	dative
mentir	accus	accus	accus	accus	---	---
	---	dative	---	---	dative	dative

Now, let us consider a few cases more closely. Following Koch (2001), I will consider that the verbs of the list, such as *plaire, déplaire, répugner* express what can be called "the perspective of O", implying that O is coded as subject. Other verbs, that do not belong to the list, such as *adorer, aimer, apprécier, détester*, express what can be called "the perspective of E", implying that E – the experiencer – is coded as subject. Table 4 illustrates how the verbs are opposed with respect to this perspective.

Table 4. Expression of the perspective of O vs. E with different verbs

O = subject; SVIO	E = subject; SVO
plaire ['please']	*adorer, aimer, apprécier* ['like']
déplaire, répugner etc. ['displease']	*détester, ne pas aimer* ['dislike']
il me semble que cela est bon [lit. 'it seems to me that this is good']	*je trouve que cela est bon* [lit. 'I find that this is fine']

On the other hand we sometimes find a quite different case, as in table 5, where the same verbs choose the pattern SVIO when the O-perspective is chosen, and SVPP when the E-perspective is chosen.

Table 5. Expression of the perspective of O vs. E with the same verbs, but different patterns

O = subject; SVIO	E = subject; SVPP
bénéficier à ['be useful']	*bénéficier de* ['profit from']
manquer à ['miss']	*manquer de* ['lack']
profiter à ['be useful']	*profiter de* ['profit from']
réussir à (=lui) ['succeed in']	*réussir à* (=y) ['be successful']

These cases show, I believe, that the pattern SVIO has specialised as expression of a relation between E and O in such a way that O is the subject of the sentence. As none of these verbs passivise, the E-perspective cannot be expressed by means of a passive; the E-perspective is expressed either by a different verb as seen in table 4, or by a different pattern of the same verb, as seen in table 5.

So, in certain cases, like the SVIO-pattern, the evolution of language has as a result a specialisation of the valency pattern which expresses a specific cognitive relation. We saw above, in table 3, that verbs belonging to Gross' table 4 have adopted this pattern recently, after some hesitation. Other verbs that did not match the content of this pattern have indeed been ejected from it. Let us consider the case of verbs meaning 'help'. In Old French these verbs had very different ways of marking the person to whom help is given: *conforter* and *rescorre* were divalent (SVO), *secourir* was divalent, but hesitated between the two patterns SVO and SVIO. Later, they all adopted the pattern SVO. In Modern French the trivalent *aider* has a direct object instead of an IO indicating the person to whom help is given. In Old French, *assister* and *servir* also had an IO. Later, all the verbs meaning 'help' still in use express the person helped by means of a direct object.[11] I will claim that these verbs changed their pattern because they did not conform to what had specialised as the content of the SVIO-pattern and I will consider this evolution a case of grammaticalisation of the valency pattern.

Danish provides another case of what I will consider grammaticalisation, where alternations of valency pattern replace previous lexical alternations. So this is a change implying transfer from lexicon to grammar in the way of marking a difference of content. Danish had and still has a series of verb pairs offering the choice between a verb indicating a situation (12a-

14a) and a related causative verb (12b-14b), like the English pair *to lie – to lay*. In Danish, the two verbs have fused in some cases, and instead of a previous lexical alternation visible at least in the past tense, see (15a-b), we find an alternation between two valency patterns of what appears to be one and the same verb (16a-b). According to Skafte Jensen (2002) Swedish still distinguishes lexical alternations (17) in cases where Danish has alternating valency patterns (18). Valency patterns alternating between an intransitive and a causative (transitive) pattern are well known in other languages as well, see (19) and (20). I believe that the change from lexical alternation to valency alternation in Danish confirms my claim that valency patterns combine expression and content in a paradigmatic way.

		intransitive situation		causative action
(12)	a.	*stå* ['be situated']	b.	*stille noget et sted* ['put something somewhere']
(13)	a.	*sidde* ['sit']	b.	*sætte noget et sted* ['put something somewhere']
(14)	a.	*ligge* ['lie']	b.	*lægge noget et sted* ['lay something somewhere']
(15)	a.	*hænge / hang* ['hang / hung']	b.	*hænge noget et sted / hængte* ['hang something somewhere / hanged']
(16)	a.	*hænge / hængte*	b.	*hænge noget et sted / hængte*
(17)	a.	*brinna / brann / brunnet* ['burn / burned, burnt']	b.	*bränna noget / brände / bränt* ['burn something / burned, burnt']
(18)	a.	*brænde / brændte / brændt* ['burn / burned, burnt']	b.	*brænde noget / brændte / brændt* ['burn, burned, burnt']
(19)	a.	*the branch broke*	b.	*Peter broke the branch*
(20)	a.	*la branche a cassé*	b.	*Pierre a cassé la branche*

If my claim about the grammaticalisation of valency patterns is correct, it should be possible to test it on new verbs being brought into use. Danish, like other modern languages, has introduced new verbs borrowed from English, such as those meaning e.g. 'e-mail' and 'fax'. These have adopted the models for Danish verbs with related meanings. Thus, the Modern Danish verbs *maile, faxe* are trivalent, adopting the Danish model of *to write* or *to send*. But the new Danish verb *brainstorme*, meaning to meet in order to solve a problem (in American English: *to have a brainstorm*),[12] does not have such a clear Danish model, and speakers are clearly testing different valency patterns for the verb, mostly by means of different prepositions, especially the preposition *på* ['on'] (21a-c). Even a transitive construction is found (21d), as appears from the following examples taken from Google:

(21) Innovative Danish
- a. *vi **brainstormer** på egne og andres ideer*
  [lit. 'we b. on our own and others' ideas']
- b. *vi forsøgte at **brainstorme** over emnet*
  [lit. 'we tried to b. upon the topic']
- c. *det er muligt at **brainstorme** frem til en kommerciel idé*
  [lit. 'it is possible to b. on to a commercial idea']
- d. *Lederen beder deltagerne om at "**brainstorme**" et emne*
  [lit. 'the leader asks the participants to b. a topic']

We have a comparable situation when a verb cannot be understood, either because we have not heard the verb before or because the verb is a nonsense verb. In both cases, the person trying to interpret the unknown verb will apply different strategies, i.e. deriving the sense of the verb from the context. This strategy makes us understand e.g. that the verbs *to whiffle*, *to burble* and *to galumph* indicate sounds and manners of movement in the following passage:

(22) *And as in uffish thought he stood,*
The Jabberwock, with eyes of flame,
*Came **whiffling** through the tulgey wood,*
*And **burbled** as it came!*
One, two! One, two!
And through and through
The vorpal blade went snicker-snack!
He left it dead, and with its head
*He went **galumphing** back.*
(Lewis Carroll: *Through the Looking Glass,* Jabberwocky)

The two verbs found at the start of the poem (*the slithy toves did **gyre** and **gimble** in the wabe)* are clearly verbs of movement: *to gyre* is to go round like a gyroscope, and *to gimble* is to make holes like a gimlet.[13] But the context does not help us to understand *outgrabe* quoted at the beginning of this paper: *and the mome raths **outgrabe**.* According to Humpty Dumpty, *outgrabe* is the past tense of the intransitive verb *outgribe*, indicating a special sound. I will claim that if the pattern of this nonsense verb had been different and more specific, e.g. *he outgrabe her on the back*, or *he outgrabe it from Latin into English*, we would clearly interpret this as a verb of action like *to scratch* or a verb of transfer like *to translate*, as these valency patterns clearly combine expression and content, as shown for Danish in table 1. I will come back to the implications of this way of reasoning in the following, as the contribution to this volume by Dirk Noël[14] motivates me to further clarify some key notions of my paper, especially *valency patterns* vs. "constructions" and *grammaticalisation*. I will also need to define what is included in grammar according to my analysis which is conform to that of the Danish Functional School (most clearly defined in Engberg-Pedersen et al. 1996), as this view is clearly not shared by Dirk Noël.

The notion of valency patterns used here should not be confused with "constructions" in the sense of Goldberg (1995) or Croft (2001). It is, however, not easy to define exactly what constitutes a *construction*: is it an abstraction derived from the lexical semantics of verbs having a special valency pattern? Or does a *construction* correspond to the pattern and its arguments having a specific, but necessarily abstract, meaning? It appears from the literature that *constructions* should probably best be understood in an onomasiological way, related to the meaning of *frames,* rather than a semasiological one, derived from verbs. But still, in the literature, *constructions* are always defined in terms of prototypical and derived cases. My approach is different, as my starting point is the valency patterns and the possibility of interpreting them as expressions of a specific content, as we have seen above. In order to investigate this possibility, I have applied Hjelmslev's commutation principle (Harder 1996: 439) on changes of patterns linked to change of content (examples 2a-b) and on alternations of patterns with corresponding alternations of content (examples 3-11). Thus, my answer to the question asked by Dirk Noël in his paper is in the affirmative: these are indeed cases of patterns having a grammatical meaning. My goal has been to defend the point of view that we should consider the existence of paradigms not only in morphology, but also in syntax, and that the valency patterns illustrated here are comparable to morphological paradigms, thus belonging to grammar and not to lexicon. A similar argumentation concerning a paradigmatic conception of another domain of syntax, i.e. word order, is put forward by Heltoft (1996: 478ff.). A more general discussion of "sets of options" constituting a "paradigm" is presented by Harder (1996: 440), and by Andersen (forthcoming b) who uses the term *paradigm* "not in the narrow sense of 'inflectional paradigm', but in the general sense of 'selectional set', a usage that has been traditional since Saussure."

Now, having defined the valency patterns under discussion as paradigmatic expressions of specific content, it is legitimate to consider the possibility of a grammaticalisation of these patterns. Dirk Noël rejects this possibility, firstly, because he has a narrower definition of grammaticalisation than I have, and secondly, because he considers it a case of increase of meaning, which goes against one of the principles of grammaticalisation. Let us consider some of the principles of grammaticalisation.

The traditional grammaticalisation cline confuses different levels of analyses, see Andersen (forthcoming b): "Somehow many historical linguists who accepted this 'cline' did not notice that it confuses content, morphosyntax, and expression: lexical > grammatical is a change in content, word > clitic > affix is a development in morphosyntax, and item > Ø refers to phonological attrition." Moreover, the "cline" is dependent on the type of language: in analytical languages we will not expect grammaticalisation to result in affixes, so we should not cling too heavily to the "cline", but instead, as proposed by Andersen (forthcoming b) accept that lexical and grammatical categories form paradigms, and that content changes should be divided into "(i) changes into, (ii) changes within or among, and (iii) changes out of lexical or grammatical paradigms". I consider the grammaticalisation of valency patterns as cases of (ii).

The second point raised by Dirk Noël concerning loss or increase of meaning is interesting. As I see it, we have loss of lexical meaning and increase of grammatical meaning. I suggest that the grammaticalisation of valency patterns is the result of a reanalysis where (part of) the meaning of the lexical verb has been inferred to the pattern.

Dirk Noël is right in pointing out that grammaticalisation is normally followed by expansion rather than reduction. However, we find both: in the case of productive patterns, e.g. the pattern of Danish illustrated by example (21a), we find that it is actually rapidly spreading to verbs that did not present this pattern previously. On the other hand, we find patterns that are not productive any more, but remain a closed, consolidated class, like the one presented in table 3.

Other scholars might prefer to interpret the facts that I have put forward here in a different way. They might propose that valency patterns are reflections of our experience of the world, having agents doing something to persons or things in plurivalent patterns or entities moving by themselves in monovalent patterns, etc.; to put it differently, that we have what we could call "natural patterns". This is probably the way Hopper and Thompson (1980) see it. But such a view does not account for the fact that although languages often organise their valency patterns in similar ways, there are important differences, even between closely related languages such as the ones referred to in this paper. Moreover, it cannot account for systematic changes such as those presented above, for innovation with adoption of existing valency patterns for new verbs (the case of the Danish verb *brainstorme*) nor for the speaker's reasonable interpretations of unknown verbs based on existing patterns (see Jabberwocky, *Through the Looking Glass*).

If we include valency patterns as part of the grammar and accept the changes presented here as results of inference from lexicon to grammar and as cases of paradigmatisation of valency patterns, then it is legitimate to refer to these changes as "grammaticalisations",[15] or rather, following Henning Andersen's terminology, as cases of "regramma(ticalisa)tion".[16]

Notes

1. This article is part of the project "Linguistic Theory and Grammatical Change", conducted at the Centre for Advanced Study (CAS) in Oslo in 2004/05. I want to thank Roger Wright for help, especially for his many useful comments on a previous version.
2. Here I use the term *valency pattern* in the most common sense, I think, i.e. in the sense of quantitative *and* qualitative valency, implying the number of valency bound elements, the grammatical and semantic features of the valency bound elements, etc.
3. The OVD was a project supported by the Danish research council in the 1990s with the aim of developing the first valency dictionary for Danish verbs to be used for human inspection as well as in computational applications. It contains approximately 4000 verb senses corresponding to 1,900 Danish verbs. The verbs were selected using the criteria of frequency. The OVD records different types of information about the verb and its combinatory potential and is developed as an application of the so-called Pronominal Approach, see Schøsler and Van Durme (1996) and Schøsler and Kirchmeier-Andersen (1997).
4. I.e. valency patterns with a subject and a direct object.
5. The term *avalent* (from Tesnière) is used for convenience, referring to verbs like Latin *pluit*, whose subject is not referential. Avalent verbs are not included in table 1 as they have no direct object.
6. Schøsler and Kirchmeier-Andersen (1998) contains a presentation of these patterns and a detailed discussion of examples.
7. A thorough description of these, very frequent, alternations in found in Schøsler and Kirchmeier-Andersen (1998).
8. The verbs are: *agréer*, *aller*, *appartenir*, *arriver*, *bénéficier*, *chanter*, *convenir*, *coûter*, *déplaire*, *échapper*, *échoir*, *importer*, *incomber*, *manquer*, *mentir*, *messoir*, *nuire*, *obéir*, *parvenir*, *peser*, *plaire*, *prendre*, *profiter*, *répugner*, *ressembler*, *réussir*, *revenir*, *seoir*, *sourire*, *tarder*.
9. See Schøsler (2003) for a detailed study of these verbs.
10. See Goyens (2001).

11. Thus it is too simple to claim, as does Hans Geisler (1988), that Modern French has a strong tendency towards the SVO-pattern – this claim is in fact inconsistent with the development of the SVIO-pattern.
12. In (21) the verb is abbreviated as b. in my translations.
13. See the explanation of the nonsense words of the poem by Humpty Dumpty in chapter 6 of *Through the Looking Glass.*
14. I want to thank the editors for providing the possibility of commenting on Dirk Noël's paper. Unfortunately, space does not allow me to go into details, but I sincerely hope that this interesting discussion on valency, constructions and grammaticalisation will continue.
15. See Heltoft, Sørensen, and Schøsler (2005).
16. Regrammaticalisation or, more recently, regrammation, is the term proposed by Henning Andersen (forthcoming a) to cover Lehmann's "from grammatical to more grammatical".

References

Andersen, Henning
forthc. a Grammation, regrammation, and degrammation – tense loss in Russian.
forthc. b Grammaticalization in a speaker-oriented theory of change.

Blanche-Benveniste, Claire, José Deulofeu, Karel van der Eynde, and Jean Stefanini
1987 *Pronom et Syntaxe. L'Approche Pronominale et son Application au Français*. 2d ed. Paris: Selaf.

Bybee, Joan L.
1985 *Morphology: A Study of the Relation between Meaning and Form.* Amsterdam: Benjamins.

Carroll, Lewis
1986 *Through the Looking Glass.* In *The Complete Illustrated Works of Lewis Carroll.* London: Octopus Publishing Group Ltd.

Croft, William
2001 *Radical Construction Grammar. Syntactic Theory in Typological Perspective.* Oxford: Oxford University Press.

Durst-Andersen, Per, and Michael Herslund
1996 The syntax of Danish verbs: Lexical and syntactic transitivity. In *Content, Expression and Structure. Studies in Danish Functional Grammar*, Elisabeth Engberg-Pedersen, Michael Fortescue, Peter Harder, Lars Heltoft, and Lisbeth Falster Jakobsen (eds.), 65–102. Amsterdam: Benjamins.

Engberg-Pedersen, Elisabeth, Michael Fortescue, Peter Harder, Lars Heltoft, and Lisbeth Falster Jakobsen (eds.)
1996 *Content, Expression and Structure. Studies in Danish Functional Grammar.* Amsterdam: Benjamins.

François, Jacques, and Günter Broschart
1994 La mise en ordre des relations actancielles: Les conditions d'accès des rôles sémantiques aux fonctions de sujet et d'objet. In *Les Relations Actancielles. Sémantique, Syntaxe, Morphologie*, Jacques François, and Gisa Rauh (eds.), 7–44. (Langages 113.) Paris: Larousse.

Gaatone, David
1998 *Le Passif en Français*. Paris/Bruxelles: Duculot.

Geisler, Hans
1988 Das Verhältnis von semantischer und syntaktischer Transitivität im Französischen. *Romanistisches Jahrbuch* 39: 22–35.

Goldberg, Adele
1995 *A Construction Grammar Approach to Argument Structure*. Chicago: The University of Chicago Press.

Goyens, Michèle
2001 L'origine des verbes français a construction dative. In *La Valence, Perspectives Romanes et Diachroniques*, Lene Schøsler (ed.), 43–58. (ZFSL Beihefte 30.) Stuttgart: Franz Steiner Verlag.

Gross, Gaston
1989 *Les Constructions Converses du Français*. Genève: Droz.

Gross, Maurice
1975 *Méthodes en Syntaxe. Régime des Constructions Complétives*. Paris: Hermann.

Harder, Peter
1996 Linguistic structure in a functional grammar. In *Content, Expression and Structure. Studies in Danish Functional Grammar*, Elisabeth Engberg-Pedersen, Michael Fortescue, Peter Harder, Lars Heltoft, and Lisbeth Falster Jakobsen (eds.), 423–452. Amsterdam: Benjamins.

Heltoft, Lars
1996 Paradigmatic structure, word order and grammaticalisation. In *Content, Expression and Structure. Studies in Danish Functional Grammar*, Elisabeth Engberg-Pedersen, Michael Fortescue, Peter Harder, Lars Heltoft, and Lisbeth Falster Jakobsen (eds.), 469–494. Amsterdam: Benjamins.

Heltoft, Lars, Jens Nørgård Sørensen, and Lene Schøsler (eds.)
2005 *Grammatikalisering og Struktur* [Grammaticalisation and structure]. København: Museum Tusculanum Press.

Herslund, Michael
1997 Syntaktiske alternationer og funktionelle kategorier [Syntactic alternations and functional categories]. In *Ny Forskning i Grammatik* [New research on grammar], Lisbeth Falster Jakobsen, and Gunver Skytte (eds.), 49–70. (Fællespublikation 4.) Odense: Odense Universitetsforlag.

Hopper, Paul J., and Sandra A. Thompson
1980 Transitivity in grammar and discourse. *Language* 56: 251–299.

Koch, Peter
2001 As you like it. Les métataxes actantielles entre expérient et phénomène. In *La Valence, Perspectives Romanes et Diachroniques*, Lene Schøsler (ed.), 59–81. (ZFSL Beihefte 30.) Stuttgart: Franz Steiner Verlag.

Krefeld, Thomas
1998 Transitivität aus rollensemantischer Sicht. Eine Fallstudie am Beispiel französischer und italienischer Wahrnehmungsverben. In *Transitivität und Diathese in romanischen Sprachen*, Hans Geisler, and Daniel Jacob (eds.), 155–173. Tübingen: Max Niemeyer Verlag.

Koch, Peter, and Thomas Krefeld (eds.)
1991 *Connexiones Romanicae. Dependenz und Valenz in romanischen Sprachen*. (Linguistische Arbeiten 268.) Tübingen: Max Niemeyer Verlag.

Lehmann, Christian
1985 Grammaticalization: Synchronic variation and diachronic change. *Lingua e Stile* 20: 303–318.

Levin, Beth
2003 Objecthood and object alternations, http://www-csli.stanford.edu/~beth/pubs.html

Noël, Dirk
2007 Verb valency patterns, constructions and grammaticalization. This volume.

Oesterreicher, Wulf
1991a Verbvalenz und Informationsstruktur. In *Connexiones Romanicae. Dependenz und Valenz in romanischen Sprachen*, Peter Koch, and Thomas Krefeld (eds.), 349–384. (Linguistische Arbeiten 268.) Tübingen: Max Niemeyer Verlag.

1991b Gemeinromanische Tendenzen: Morphosyntax. In *Lexikon der Romanistischen Linguistik Band II*, Gunter Holtus, Michael Metzeltin, and Christian Schmitt (eds.), Tübingen: Max Niemeyer Verlag.

Schøsler, Lene
1999a La valence verbale et l'identification des membres valentiels. In *Autour de Jacques Monfrin. Néologie et Création Verbale*, Giuseppe Di Stefano, and Rose M. Bidler (eds.), 527–554. Montréal: CERES.

1999b Réflexions sur optionalité des compléments d'objet direct, en latin, en ancien français, en moyen français et en français moderne. *Etudes Romanes* 44: 9–28.

2000 Le statut de la forme zéro du complément d'objet direct en français moderne. *Etudes Romanes* 47: 105–129.

2001 La valence verbale dans une perspective diachronique: Quelques problèmes méthodologiques. In *La Valence, Perspectives Romanes et Diachroniques*, Lene Schøsler (ed.), 98–112. (ZFSL 30.) Stuttgart: Franz Steiner Verlag.

2003 Le rôle de la valence pour une classification sémantique des verbes. In *La Cognition dans le Temps. Etudes Cognitives dans le Champ Historique des Langues et des Textes*, Peter Blumenthal, and Jean Tyvaert (eds.), 145–159. Tübingen: Max Niemeyer Verlag.

Schøsler, Lene (ed.)
2001 *La Valence, Perspectives Romanes et Diachroniques,* Stuttgart: Steiner. (ZFSL 30.)

Schøsler, Lene, and Karen Van Durme
1996 *The Odense Valency Dictionary*. (Odense Working Papers in Language and Communication 13.) Odense University.

Schøsler, Lene, and Sabine Kirchmeier-Andersen
1997 *Studies in Valency II: The Pronominal Approach Applied to Danish.* (RASK Supplement 5), Odense: Odense University Press.
1998 The role of the object in a syntactico-semantic classification of Danish verbs. *Leuvense bijdragen: Tijdschrift voor Germaanse Filologie* 86 (4): 391–412.

Selig, Maria
1991 Inhaltskonturen des 'Dativs'. Zur Ablösung des lateinischen Dativs durch *ad* und zur differentiellen Objektmarkierung. In *Connexiones Romanicae. Dependenz und Valenz in romanischen Sprachen*, Peter Koch, and Thomas Krefeld (eds.), 187–211. (Linguistische Arbeiten 268.) Tübingen: Max Niemeyer Verlag.

Skafte Jensen, Eva
2002 Historisk lingvistik [Historical linguistics]. *Nydanske Sprogstudier* [New Danish studies in language] 31: 7–32.

Verb valency patterns, constructions and grammaticalization

Dirk Noël

1. Introduction[1]

Adele Goldberg's seminal work on argument structure constructions (Goldberg 1995) has brought to the fore that verb valency patterns have the potential at least of being symbolic units: valency patterns might not merely be formal patterns, but pairings of form and meaning. The trivalent pattern in which a verb is combined with a subject and two nominal complements, for instance, is argued by Goldberg (1995: 151) "to be associated with a highly specific semantic structure, that of successful transfer between a volitional agent and a willing recipient", with a number of "systematic metaphors" "licens[ing] extensions from the basic sense" (the basic sense of the construction is illustrated by the sentences in (1), selected from chapters 1 and 5 in Goldberg 1995; the sentences in (2), selected from chapter 6, exemplify some of the extensions).

(1) a. *Joe gave the earthquake relief fund $5.*
    b. *I brought Pat a glass of water.*
    c. *She threw him a cannonball.*

(2) a. *She gave me the flu.*
    b. *She gave Jo her thoughts on the subject.*
    c. *She gave him a wink.*

More recently, Goldberg has engaged in corpus and experimental psycholinguistic research to tackle the question of how argument structure schemas like this ditransitive construction come to be part of the language user's linguistic knowledge (Goldberg, Casenhiser, and Sethuraman 2004). The frequency in the language infants are confronted with of verbs whose meaning the meaning of the construction can be reduced to appears to play a crucial role in this process. Native speakers of English, for instance, first, and most frequently, encounter the ditransive pattern together with the verb *give*. A phylogenetic explanation for how such constructions come to be part and parcel of the repertory of the means of expression available in a language may be hypothesized to run along similar lines. The ditransitive construction could ultimately owe its place as a schematic construction in the grammar of English to the early and ongoing omnipresence in English of the verb *give*. The diachronic investigation of argument structure constructions is still largely a virgin territory, however. So far, there have only been a few studies of partially substantive constructions (i.e. constructions whose lexical fillers are partly specified; cf. Croft and Cruse 2004: 248); Israel (1996) and Verhagen (2002), for instance, are enquiries into the history of Goldberg's "*way*-construction" and its Dutch cognate, and Kemmer and Hilpert (2005) investigate the development of the English *make*-causative. The only work I am aware of that could qualify as a tentative exploration of the diachrony of fully schematic argument structure constructions is Schøsler's (2003, this volume, and forthcoming) treatment of valency patterns in French.

If we accept that schematic argument structure constructions form part of the grammar of a language, the question arises of whether their entry into the grammar is a case of grammaticalization in the technical sense of the term, i.e. in the sense in which the term is used in grammaticalization theory, the "research framework for studying the relationships between lexical, constructional, and grammatical material in language, diachronically and synchronically" (Hopper and Traugott 2003: 18) that became established during the last decade of the previous century.[2] Nutshell definitions of the phenomenon like the one offered in Hopper and Traugott's textbook appear at first sight not to disallow that the entrenchment of a construction in a language is characterized in terms of grammaticalization: grammaticalization is "the change whereby lexical items *and constructions* come in certain linguistic contexts to serve grammatical functions and, once grammaticalized, continue to develop new grammatical functions" (Hopper and Traugott 2003: 18, my emphasis). Schøsler (2003, this volume, and forthcoming) is the only researcher to date, however, at least to my knowledge, who has applied the term to a change involving a schematic argument structure construction.[3] The purpose of this contribution is to investigate whether this is warranted. My conclusion will be that it might not be a felicitous option to do so, one reason being that grammaticalization is most often taken to be a change that affects fairly substantive constructions, rather than fully schematic ones. I will start by clarifying this distinction and by exploring the extent to which, and the sense in which, researchers working within the confines of the grammaticalization theoretical framework are considering constructions.

2. Constructions and grammaticalization

Towards the end of the previous century, more or less simultaneously with, but nevertheless independently of, the surge in interest in grammaticalization and grammaticalization theory, a new theoretical approach to language emerged of which the already mentioned Goldberg (1995) is a major exponent: construction grammar.[4] In principle at least, construction grammar is an all-embracing perspective on language, whereas grammaticalization theory "merely" covers a particular kind of language change. Both paradigms can therefore be said to have a different agenda without there being a conflict of interests between them.

At the basis of construction grammar is the hypothesis that all linguistic knowledge is uniformly represented in the speaker's mind as pairings of form and meaning (Croft and Cruse 2004: 255) or form and function (Goldberg 2003), in other words as constructions. Constructions vary along two dimensions: they can either be atomic (morphemes, words) or complex (phrases, or constructions in the pre-theoretical sense, idioms, valency patterns, ...), and more or less abstract. The latter dimension is where the terms substantive and schematic come in. As pointed out by Fillmore, Kay and O'Connor (1988: 505, n. 3) and illustrated in Croft and Cruse (2004: 248), there is a cline from maximally substantive to maximally schematic. Fully substantive constructions are idioms like *It takes one to know one*, in which there are not only no lexically open elements, but all grammatical inflectional categories are specified as well. An example of a slightly more schematic construction is the idiom *kick the bucket*, which is not lexically open (apart from the subject slot) but which has inflectional flexibility (*Jake kicked the bucket / Jake's gonna kick the bucket*). Somewhat more lexically open is the idiom *give NP the lowdown* ('tell NP the news'), which has two open argument slots as well as inflectional flexibility, as in *I / He gave / will give him / Janet the lowdown*. In the *let alone*-construction all content words are lexically open, the only substantive element being the *let alone*-connective, as in *She gave me more candy than I could carry, let alone eat* and *Only a linguist would buy that book, let alone read it*. An example of a maximally schematic construction, in which all elements are lexically open is the resultative construction, illustrated in *He wanted her to kiss him unconscious* and *I had brushed my hair very smooth*.

Since constructionists are intent on making the point that the meaning of utterances cannot be reduced to the meaning of the words they contain, but that structure adds meaning as well, the centre of attention of constructionist research to date has been on fully or partially schematic rather than fully substantive constructions. If partially substantive constructions are described, the focus is not on the meaning of the substantive elements, but on the meaning of the construction as a whole. Fillmore, Kay and O'Connor's (1988) study of the *let alone*-construction, for instance, does not discuss the meaning of the verb *let*, either separately or in combination with *alone*. In other words, the approach is holistic rather than componential, which to a certain extent is also explained by the fact that constructionist descriptive work normally does not venture off the synchronic plane.

Since grammaticalization theory and construction grammar are not mutually exclusive frameworks, there is nothing to stop a student of grammaticalization from subscribing to a construction grammatical view of language. However, though the construction word turns up regularly in work on grammaticalization, more often than not it is used in a non-technical way[5], usually to refer to collocations that turn into fixed units, like *sort of* and *kind of*, discussed (inter alia) in Tabor (1994),[6] and *instead of* (from *in stede of*), *indeed* (from *in dede*), *anyway* (from *any way*), discussed in Traugott (2003). This is also how the word is used in the definition of grammaticalization presented earlier. A notable exception is Croft (2001), a volume that aims to contribute to both constructionist theorizing and grammaticalization theory. Similarly, Joan Bybee, a leading grammaticalization theorist, has written in a multidisciplinary publication that "grammar consists of a large number of rather specific constructions which act as processing units" (Bybee 1998: 272), thereby implicitly subscribing to one of the tenets of constructionist approaches. On the whole, however, grammaticalization theoretical publications refer to a pre-theoretical construction concept, first and foremost in order to include multi-word units as possible sources and outcomes of grammaticalization, but also to drive home the message that neither atomic nor complex items grammaticalize irrespective of the contexts in which they are used. Another example of the first of these two senses in which the term is made use of is the often quoted insight that "[i]t is the entire construction, and not simply the lexical meaning of the stem, which is the precursor, and hence the source, of the grammatical meaning" (Bybee, Perkins, and Pagliuca 1994: 11). The second sense is apparent in Traugott's plea for a "focus on grammaticalization as centrally concerned with the development of lexemes in context-specific constructions (not merely lexemes and constructions)" (Traugott 2003: 627). It is also evident in the following quote from Himmelmann (2004: 31):[7] "Strictly speaking, it is never just the grammaticizing element that undergoes grammaticization. Instead, it is the grammaticizing element in its syntagmatic context which is grammaticized. That is, the unit to which grammaticization properly applies are constructions, not isolated lexical items."

This use of the construction word is what is referred to with "in certain linguistic contexts" in Hopper and Traugott's (2003) definition of grammaticalization, and with "highly constrained morphosyntactic contexts" in Traugott's (2003: 645) personal definition: grammaticalization is "[t]he process whereby lexical material in highly constrained pragmatic and morphosyntactic contexts is assigned grammatical function, and once grammatical, is assigned increasingly grammatical, operator-like function".[8] If "lexical material" in the second definition is taken to include phrases as well as words, both definitions therefore at least imply a double and conceptually different reference to constructions.

Whichever way the construction concept is invoked, however, whether to include non-atomic material as precursors of grammaticalized items or to highlight the contexts in which the grammaticalization takes place, most of the quotes supplied so far reveal that grammaticalization theorists are normally only considering fairly substantive constructions: they are dealing with constructions containing lexical material. Moreover, since the focus of their attention is on the change in meaning of the lexical atoms at the centre of the construction, their approach can be argued to be componential rather than holistic, as opposed to the typical construction grammatical view on things.

Not all grammaticalization theorists would agree with limiting the research subject of grammaticalization theory to non-schematic constructions, though. Haspelmath's (2004: 26) "current definition" of grammaticalization also contains the construction word but there is nothing in the definition to restrict its applicability to at least partially substantive constructions: "[a] grammaticalization is a diachronic change by which the parts of a constructional schema come to have stronger internal dependencies." An attached footnote in fact makes clear that the definition is intended to include fully schematic constructions: "[t]hus, word-order change consisting of a change from freer to more fixed word order falls under grammaticalization as well ..., not just changes involving free words becoming dependent elements ..." (Haspelmath 2004: 38). Yet it is not universally accepted among grammaticalization theorists that the fixation of word order indeed constitutes a case of grammaticalization. For Himmelmann (2004: 33–34), for instance, changes involving fully schematic constructions do not represent examples of the phenomenon:

> ... grammaticization applies only to the context expansion of constructions which include at least one grammaticizing element (the article in art-noun constructions, the preposition in pps, etc.). Context expansion may also occur with other types of constructions, for example a certain word order pat-

> tern, a compounding pattern or a reduplication pattern. These are not considered instances of grammaticization here.

The footnote he adds is relevant as well:

> We may note in passing that there is a tendency in the literature to use grammaticization as a cover term for all kinds of grammatical change, including simple reanalyses, analogical levelings and contact-induced changes. In this way, the concept grammaticization looses [sic] all theoretical significance and becomes simply a synonym for grammatical change. (Himmelmann 2004: 39)

Christian Lehmann, though not himself adverse to including word order fixation in grammaticalization (e.g. see Lehmann 2002), has in a similar vein dissociated himself from definitions of grammaticalization like "grammaticalization is the genesis of grammar/grammatical structure/grammatical items" (Lehmann 2005:155), maintaining that

> it is unwise to elevate grammaticalization to the status of 'creation of grammar' per se. This necessarily renders the concept wide and heterogeneous, with the consequence that it becomes less apt to generate falsifiable empirical generalizations and to be integrated into an articulated theory of language change and language activity. (Lehmann 2005:155)

Hopper and Traugott (2003: 24, 60), for their part, oppose the inclusion of word order. They do discuss Givón's (1979) work on clause combining and clause fusion, which also involves schematic constructions, but at the same time distance themselves from it by saying it can only be included "[i]f grammaticalization is defined broadly so as to encompass the motivations for and development of grammatical structures in general" (Hopper and Traugott 2003: 176).

The recent plea for a construction-based approach to grammaticalization to replace the morphology-based approach (see Wiemer 2004; and Wiemer and Bisang 2004) should therefore not be taken to imply that all grammatical constructions are the result of a narrowly defined grammaticalization, which crucially involves a bundle of changes happening to the substantive element(s) of non-schematic, or at least not fully schematic, constructions.[9] For this reason the term grammaticalization might not apply well to the establishment of verb valency patterns as argument structure constructions. In the next section I will examine whether indeed such an evolution can justifiably be characterized as a case of grammaticalization.

3. Verb valency patterns and grammaticalization

As a spin-off of cognitive linguistics, construction grammatical studies of schematic constructions have so far only considered their ontogenesis (how do they come to be part of the language user's knowledge?), not their phylogenesis (how do they enter the language?). To my knowledge, no paid-up member of the construction grammatical paradigm has so far used the term grammaticalization in connection with schematic constructions (but see Croft 2001 on substantive constructions). The trigger for the present contribution, however, was work by Lene Schøsler, who has consistently applied the term in a series of diachronic studies of valency patterns (Schøsler 2003, this volume, and forthcoming).

Though not a proponent of a fully-fledged constructionist approach herself, Schøsler (forthcoming) also refers to constructions, but restricts the term to "specialized" verb valency patterns, which are patterns that have become "linked to special content". In other words, Schøsler distinguishes between valency patterns she terms "default patterns", which do not express content, and valency patterns she calls "constructions", which do carry content. The latter are claimed to be the result of grammaticalization. One of her illustrations is based on data from Goyens (2001) on the origin of French verbs used in the "dative construction", i.e. verbs used in a divalent pattern taking an indirect object (in addition to a subject). These verbs "share the particular feature that they all express – more or less clearly – a psychological relation between on the one hand a human being who is the experiencer …, and who has pleasant or unpleasant feelings, and on the other hand another human being or an object being the cause of these feelings …", the experiencer being expressed by the indirect object and the cause by the subject (Schøsler this volume: 55). This situation – illustrated in table 1 with reference to the verbs *obéir*, *ressembler*, *mentir* – is a fairly recent development, however, because up until the 17th century the experiencer did not need to be expressed by an indirect object but could also be expressed by a direct object.

Table 1. The evolution of the valency patterning of the etymons of the French verbs *obéir*, *ressembler* and *mentir* (adapted from Goyens 2001: 56)[10]

	Latin	Anc. frç.	Moy. frç.	XVIe s.	XVIIe s.	Frç. mod.
obéir	---	COD	COD	COD	---	---
	datif	COI	COI	---	COI	COI
ressembler	accus.	COD	COD	COD	COD	---
	datif	COI	COI	COI	COI	COI
mentir	accus	COD	COD	COD	---	---
	---	COI	---	---	COI	COI

In other words, there has been a change in the valency patterning of the verbs expressing this "psychological relation", leading to a situation where they need to be used with an indirect object. This valency pattern is therefore said to have become "specialized" – it is exclusively used for the expression of this relation – and such a specialization is interpreted to amount to becoming "more grammatical", i.e. as a case of grammaticalization, more specifically as a case of "secondary grammaticalization" ("the development of an already grammatical form into a yet more grammatical one", Traugott 2004: 143). This means, in effect, that Schøsler (forthcoming) considers the crystallization of a construction (i.e. the establishment of a connection between a morphosyntactic configuration and a meaning) as being subsumed under the heading grammaticalization.

Though one could find fault with Schøsler's (2003, this volume) characterization of this particular construction (is there really an experiencer in the case of *ressembler*? Does the level of abstractness needed to accommodate all verbs that can enter the pattern not preclude its psychological reality?), this is not my intention here. The question I am interested in is the more general one of whether the establishment of a symbolic link between a particular syntactic arrangement and a meaning can indeed be argued to amount to grammaticalization.

A first sub-question that will need to be answered positively to allow this is whether the meaning of argument structure constructions can justifiably be said to be a grammatical meaning. In the words of Hopper and Traugott (2003: 24): "how far we shall be prepared to extend the notion of 'grammaticalization' will be determined by the limits of our understanding of what it means for a construction to be 'grammatical' or have a grammatical function." Given that the meaning of Goldberg's ditransitive construction can be reduced to the meaning of the verb *give*, and given that Schøsler's description of her "experiencer" construction makes reference to feelings incited in somebody by another person or by something, it seems hardly defensible to talk of grammatical notions here, even if we grant that there is no clear boundary between what is lexical and what is grammatical. The notions referred to here are of an unquestionable propositional or ideational nature, whereas grammatical meanings are prototypically non-propositional or interpersonal.[11] Valency patterns are part of grammar to the extent that they assist in organizing the building blocks of a language into meaningful strings, but it does not follow that the content they might convey is of a grammatical nature. For Schøsler, however, the very fact that structure acquires meaning that is typically associated with the lexicon appears reason enough to talk of grammaticalization when she concludes:

> If we include valency patterns as part of the grammar and accept the changes presented here as results of inference from lexicon to grammar and as cases of paradigmatisation of valency patterns, then it is legitimate to refer to these changes as "grammaticalisations", or rather, following Henning Andersen's terminology, as cases of "regramma(ticalisa)tion". (Schøsler this volume: 62)

In Schøsler (forthcoming) the author goes further and claims these constructions to have an ulterior function: they enable speakers and listeners to identify arguments. Latin had no constructions, only default patterns, and arguments "were first and foremost identified by means of the lexicon, i.e. selectional restrictions on predicates and arguments, and by means of the nominal morphology". In modern Romance languages, however, "we find a large variety of grammaticalized devices used to identify the arguments", among which word order, use of prepositions, and specialized valency patterns. Leaving aside that this is a psychological claim in need of psycholinguistic corroboration, and assuming that argument structure constructions actually contribute to argument identification, it still does not follow though that the naissance of such constructions need be the consequence of a grammaticalization change. Were we to conclude this, it would put a whole new teleological interpretation on grammaticalization.

A second question we need to address is the extent to which the coming into being of argument structure constructions is a change that meets the criteria for grammaticalization put forward in the grammaticalization theoretical literature. Here we run into the problem that, since grammaticalization theorists have mainly been interested in non-schematic constructions, these criteria only work well for constructions containing substantive elements (cf. Fischer 2005). Arguments in favour of their applicability to schematic constructions might therefore not yield falsifiable statements. Heine (2003: 579) provides a conveniently concise list of the "mechanisms" involved in grammaticalization (or the "micro-changes" involved in the "macro-change" grammaticalization, in the terminology of Andersen, forthcoming) about which there is a fairly general consensus:

(i) desemanticization (or "bleaching," semantic reduction): loss in meaning content;
(ii) extension (or context generalization): use in new contexts;
(iii) decategorialization: loss in morphosyntactic properties characteristic of the source forms, including the loss of independent word status (cliticization, affixation);
(iv) erosion (or "phonetic reduction"), that is, loss in phonetic substance.

The latter two mechanisms, especially, will not work if there is no substantive grammaticalizing element: only words and phrases can change categories (e.g. from lexical verb to auxiliary, or from main clause verb phrase to adverbial phrase) and lose substance. The first mechanism, on the other hand, has been brought to bear on the fixation of word order to extend the domain of grammaticalization to it ever since the term grammaticalization first entered the linguistic literature (i.e. in Meillet 1912/1958; see Hopper and Traugott 2003: 23). When word order is free it is used to convey pragmatic meaning, which is lost when word order is decided by syntax. Schematic constructions are not immune to meaning loss, therefore. But the converse has happened if, as Schøsler (forthcoming) suggests, argument structure constructions (or "specialized verb valency patterns") succeed "default patterns". Instead of an evolution from more to less meaning, or from "expressive" to grammatical meaning, what we have here is a development from absence of meaning to presence of meaning, or possibly from grammatical meaning to referential meaning. Instead of the loss in referentiality usually associated with grammaticalization we are seeing a gain in referentiality. Rather than a movement away from the ideational plane there is a progression towards it.

The second mechanism, extension, interlocks with the first: the decrease in semantic specificity concurs with context expansion. The dwindling of the expressivity of a particular word order pattern coincides with its generalization, for instance. In the case of the specialization of valency patterns, on the other hand, the schematic construction's expressivity swells rather than dwindles, so that one might expect context reduction instead of expansion. To better examine whether this could indeed be the case, it may be useful to consider the three kinds of context expansion that were teased apart by Himmelmann (2004: 32–33). The first of these is host-class expansion, an expansion of the class of elements a grammaticalizing element is in construction with. Himmelmann's example: "when demonstratives are grammaticized to articles they may start to co-occur regularly with proper names or nouns designating unique entities (such as *sun*, *sky*, *queen*, etc.), i.e. nouns they typically did not co-occur with before" (Himmelmann 2004: 32). Schøsler's example of the French S-V-IO construction seems to illustrate an evolution in the opposite direction, however, when she states that "verbs that did not match the content of this pattern have … been ejected from it" (Schøsler this volume: 57). This amounts to host-class reduction rather than expansion. One of Schøsler's arguments in favour of the grammaticalization of specialized valency patterns therefore in effect detracts from it.

Himmelmann's second kind of context expansion, syntactic context expansion, a change in the larger syntactic context in which the construction is used (e.g. articles occurring in adpositional expressions in addition to the core argument positions they typically occur in first), might not be relevant to argument structure constructions since the context level beyond the one that is defined by these constructions falls outside the scope of syntax. The third kind, semantic-pragmatic context expansion, is illustrated in Himmelmann's "article" example by the fact that adnominal demonstratives occur only in expressions which involve deictic, anaphoric or recognitional reference, whereas articles also have "larger situation uses" (*the queen*, *the pub*) and "associative anaphoric uses" (*a wedding – the bride*, *a house – the front door*; Himmelmann 2004: 33). A semantic widening of some kind could at first glance also appear germane to argument structure constructions when considering Goldberg's extensions of a construction's central sense. Taking up the example of the ditransitive construction again, the following sentences (the examples in [12] in chapter 6 of Goldberg 1995) illustrate an extension of the construction's central sense of a successful transfer between a volitional agent and a willing recipient in that they do not involve a volitional agent.

(3) a. *The medicine brought him relief.*
b. *The rain bought us some time.*
c. *She got me a ticket while distracting me while I was driving.*
d. *She gave me the flu.*
e. *The music lent the party a festive air.*
f. *The missed ball handed him the victory on a silver platter.*

Such metaphorical extensions do not move the construction off the ideational plane, however, and cannot therefore be argued to be constitutive of a grammaticalization change.

The mechanisms that are generally taken to define grammaticalization do not, therefore, seem to be at work in the "specialization" of verb valency patterns, or the creation of argument structure constructions. Some of these mechanisms can only affect substantive constructions, and those that schematic constructions could be subject to do not seem to work in the direction typical of grammaticalization.

4. Conclusion

Schøsler (2003, this volume, and forthcoming) has pointed the way to a whole new area of research, the diachronic study of schematic argument structure constructions, i.e. the study of how and when verb valency patterns crystallize into pairings of form and meaning. If, as Wiemer and Bisang (2004: 4) have advocated, grammaticalization is "extended to all the processes involved in the diachronic change and in the emergence of [grammatical] systems" (systems "of more or less stable, regular and productive form-function mappings"), i.e. if it is taken as "a general perspective from which to analyse changes in the expression formats of grammatical structure or [in] the distribution of certain morphological or syntactic units in the languages of the world", studies in this area will undoubtedly find their place within grammaticalization theory. The nature of their research subject will make them fall outside the bounds of a more narrowly defined grammaticalization, however. Though constructions have, at the least, a double relevance for grammaticalization theory – as grammaticalizing units and as the structural contexts in which grammaticalization takes place – the core business of the field to date has been (at least partially) substantive constructions.[12] It is on their basis that the principles involved in grammaticalization have been defined. Being schematic constructions, argument structure constructions are less susceptible to them. But argument structure constructions also differ from those schematic constructions that have so far been considered by grammaticalization theorists, in that their meaning is propositional rather than grammatical. The semantic change attending their development is a movement towards greater referentiality, rather than the converse. If the diachronic study of argument structure constructions does find a place in grammaticalization theory, such differences will have to be integrated in future taxonomies of the different natured changes subsumed under grammaticalization.

Notes

1. This paper was written during a sponsorship by the Research Fund of the University of Leuven. I am grateful to the Functional Linguistics Leuven research unit, and especially Kristin Davidse, for their hospitality. I must also thank Lene Schøsler for passing on two of her manuscripts (Schøsler this volume and forthcoming). The organizers of the "Valency – Valenz: Theoretical, Descriptive and Cognitive Issues" symposium must be thanked for their kind invitation to contribute a paper, and for prodding me into writing up my contribution. Lieselotte Brems and Timothy Colleman are owed words of gratitude for their comments on an earlier version.
2. Hopper and Traugott (2003) do not themselves refer to *grammaticalization theory* but use the term *grammaticalization* to refer to the phenomena it covers as well as the study of these phenomena, analogous to such linguistic terms as *syntax*, *morphology* and *semantics*. I will employ *grammaticalization theory* for stylistic reasons, not least because it allows reference to grammaticalization *theorists*, in the absence of a coinage like *grammaticalizationists*. *Grammaticists* is already in use but has a much wider reference.
3. In a series of (at the time of writing) unpublished or yet to be published conference papers Suzanne Kemmer has talked about *constructional grammaticalization*, but the term seems so far only to have been applied to constructions containing a substantive element (e.g., see Kemmer and Hilpert 2005).
4. Grammaticalization and constructionism alike are not uniform frameworks. I am using *construction grammar* as a cover term for all constructionist approaches. Croft and Cruse (2004: 257) distinguish between four variants: Construction Grammar (in capital letters; e.g. Kay and Fillmore 1999), construction grammar (without capitals; e.g. Lakoff 1987 and Goldberg 1995), Cognitive Grammar (Langacker 1987, 1991) and Radical Construction Grammar (Croft 2001).
5. Leaving aside certain notational conventions of individual constructionist approaches, very little is "technical" in construction grammar, not least the definition of what constitutes a construction, but I qualify uses of the construction word as "pre-theoretical" or "non-technical" when those who use it do not pledge their adherence to a constructionist stance.
6. Denison (2002) tries out a construction grammatical analysis of these constructions, and thus constitutes an exception to the generalization formulated here.
7. Some grammaticalization theorists prefer the term *grammaticization* to *grammaticalization.*
8. The reference to a *process* rather than a *change* shows that this definition actually predates the one offered in Hopper and Traugott (2003: xv). Elizabeth Traugott has confirmed (personal communication) that the "Constructions in grammaticalization" article was written in 1995 and revised in 1998, to finally come out in 2003.

9. In Fischer's (2005) terminology, these changes require *tokens* as well as *types*, whereas the "grammaticalization" of clause types and the fixation of word order only involve types. (This use of the type/token distinction roughly compares with the way the two concepts are distinguished in "usage-based" cognitive linguistics, tokens being more specific instantiations of more general types (cf. Bybee 1985).) In Andersen's (forthcoming) classification of types of "macro-changes" (which involve a chain of changes) on the basis of "the observer's wider or narrower focus" grammaticalization is categorized as a change that is observed as a result of a "single element view" (as opposed to a "whole-language view" and a "subsystem view") focusing on expressions (rather than content).
10. Goyens' original terminology was replaced by Schøsler's (2003). COD and COI stand for direct object and indirect object, respectively. For another adaptation, see Schøsler (this volume).
11. *Ideational* and *interpersonal* are Hallidayan terms (e.g. see Halliday 1970).
12. A third, paradigmatic, sense in which constructions are relevant for grammaticalization does involve schematic constructions, when these act as triggers for grammaticalization (cf. Bisang 1998a, b; Hoffmann 2004; Fischer 2005; Noël 2005).

References

Andersen, Henning
forthc. Grammaticalization in a speaker-oriented theory of change. In *Grammatical Change and Linguistic Theory: The Rosendal Papers*, Þórhallur Eyþórsson (ed.). Amsterdam: Benjamins.

Bisang, Walter
1998a Grammaticalization and language contact, constructions and positions. In *The Limits of Grammaticalization*, Anna Giacalone Ramat, and Paul J. Hopper (eds.), 13–58. Amsterdam: Benjamins.
1998b Verb serialization and attractor positions: Constructions and their potential impact on language change and language contact. In *Typology of Verbal Categories*, Leonid Kulikov, and Heinz Vater (eds.), 254–271. Tübingen: Niemeyer.

Bisang, Walter, Nikolaus P. Himmelmann, and Björn Wiemer (eds.)
2004 *What Makes Grammaticalization? A Look from its Fringes and its Components*. Berlin: Mouton de Gruyter.

Bybee, Joan
1985 *Morphology: A Study of the Relation between Meaning and Form*. Amsterdam: Benjamins.
1998 A functionalist approach to grammar and its evolution. *Evolution of Communication* 2 (2): 249–278.

Bybee, Joan, Revere Perkins, and William Pagliuca
1994 *The Evolution of Grammar: Tense, Aspect, and Modality in the Languages of the World*. Chicago: The University of Chicago Press.

Croft, William
2001 *Radical Construction Grammar: Syntactic Theory in Typological Perspective*. Oxford: Oxford University Press.

Croft, William, and D. Alan Cruse
2004 *Cognitive Linguistics*. Cambridge: Cambridge University Press.

Denison, David
2002 History of the sort of construction family. Paper presented at the *2nd International Conference on Construction Grammar*, Helsinki.

Eyþórsson, Þórhallur (ed.)
forthc. *Grammatical Change and Linguistic Theory: The Rosendal Papers*. Amsterdam: Benjamins.

Fillmore, Charles John
2006 *Construction Grammar*. Chicago: University of Chicago Press.

Fillmore, Charles John, Paul Kay, and Mary Kay O'Connor
1988 Regularity and idiomaticity in grammatical constructions: The case of *let alone*. *Language* 64: 501–538.

Fischer, Olga
2005 Coming to terms with grammaticalization. Plenary paper read at the international conference *From ideational to interpersonal: Perspectives from grammaticalization*, Leuven, 10-12 February 2005.

Givón, Talmy
1979 *On Understanding Grammar*. New York: Academic Press.

Goldberg, Adele E.
1995 *Constructions: A Construction Grammar Approach to Argument Structure*. Chicago: University of Chicago Press.
2003 Constructions: A new theoretical approach to language. *Trends in Cognitive Sciences* 7 (5): 219–224.

Goldberg, Adele E., Devin M. Casenhiser, and Nitya Sethuraman
2004 Learning argument structure generalizations. *Cognitive Linguistics* 15 (3): 289–316.

Goyens, Michèle
2001 L'origine des verbes français a construction dative. In *La Valence, Perspectives Romanes et Diachroniques*, Lene Schøsler (ed.), 43–58. (= ZFSL Beihefte 30.) Stuttgart: Steiner.

Halliday, Michael Alexander Kirkwood
1970 Language structure and language function. In *New Horizons in Linguistics*, John Lyons (ed.), 140–165. Harmondsworth: Penguin.

Haspelmath, Martin
2004 On directionality in language change with particular reference to grammaticalization. In *Up and Down the Cline: The Nature of Grammaticalization*, Olga Fischer, Muriel Norde, and Harry Perridon (eds.), 17–44. Amsterdam: Benjamins.

Heine, Bernd
2003 Grammaticalization. In *The Handbook of Historical Linguistics*, Brian D. Joseph, and Richard D. Janda (eds.), 575–601. Oxford: Blackwell.

Himmelmann, Nikolaus P.
2004 Lexicalization and grammaticalization: Opposite or orthogonal? In *What makes Grammaticalization? A Look from its Fringes and its Components*, Walter Bisang, Nikolaus P. Himmelmann, and Björn Wiemer (eds.), 21–42. Berlin: Mouton de Gruyter.

Hoffmann, Sebastian
2004 Are low-frequency complex prepositions grammaticalized? On the limits of corpus data – and the importance of intuition. In *Corpus Approaches to Grammaticalization in English*, Hans Lindquist, and Christian Mair (eds.), 171–210. Amsterdam: Benjamins.

Hopper, Paul J., and Elizabeth Closs Traugott
2003 *Grammaticalization.* 2d ed. Cambridge: Cambridge University Press.

Israel, Michael
1996 The way constructions grow. In *Conceptual Structure, Discourse and Language*, Adele Goldberg (ed.), 217–230. Stanford: CSLI.

Kay, Paul, and Charles John Fillmore
1999 Grammatical constructions and linguistic generalizations: The *What's X doing Y?* construction. *Language* 75: 1–33.

Kemmer, Suzanne, and Martin Hilpert
2005 Constructional grammaticalization in the make-causative. Paper presented at the *Workshop on Constructions and Language Change*, held at the XVIIth International Conference on Historical Linguistics, Madison, Wisconsin, 31 July-5 August 2005.

Lakoff, George
1987 *Women, Fire and Dangerous Things: What Categories Reveal about the Mind.* Chicago: University of Chicago Press.

Langacker, Ronald W.
1987 *Foundations of Cognitive Grammar*. Vol. 1: *Theoretical Prerequisites*. Stanford: Stanford University Press.
1991 *Foundations of Cognitive Grammar*. Vol. 2: *Descriptive Application.* Stanford: Stanford University Press.

Lehmann, Christian
2002 *Thoughts on Grammaticalization.* 2d, revised ed. Erfurt: Seminar für Sprachwissenschaft der Universität.
2005 Theory and method in grammaticalization. In *Grammatikalisierung*, Gabriele Diewald (ed.), 152–187. Berlin: de Gruyter [Zeitschrift für Germanistische Linguistik, Themenheft].

Meillet, Antoine
1958 Reprint. L'évolution des formes grammaticales. In *Linguistique historique et linguistique générale*, 130–48. Paris: Champion. Original edition, *Scientia* 12, (26, 6), 1912.

Noël, Dirk
2005 The productivity of a "source of information" construction: Or, where grammaticalization theory and construction grammar meet. Paper read at the international conference *From ideational to interpersonal: Perspectives from grammaticalization*, Leuven, 10-12 February 2005.

Schøsler, Lene
2003 Le role de la valence pour une classification sémantique des verbes. In *La Cognition dans le Temps: Études Cognitives dans le Champ Historique des Langues et des Texts*, Peter Blumenthal, and Jean-Emmanuel Tyvaert (eds.), 145–159. Tübingen: Niemeyer.
2007 The status of valency patterns. This volume.
forthc. Argument marking from Latin to modern Romance languages: An illustration of "combined grammaticalization processes". In *Grammatical Change and Linguistic Theory: The Rosendal Papers*, Þórhallur Eyþórsson (ed.). Amsterdam: Benjamins.

Tabor, Whitney
1994 The gradual development of degree modifier *sort of* and *kind of*: A corpus proximity model. In *Papers from the 29th Regional Meeting of the Chicago Linguistics Society*, Katherine Beals, Gina Cooke, David Kathman, Sotaro Kita, Karl-Erik McCullough, and David Testen (eds.), 451–465. Chicago: Chicago Linguistic Society.

Traugott, Elizabeth Closs
1995 Subjectification in grammaticalisation. In *Subjectivity and Subjectivisation*, Dieter Stein, and Susan Wright (eds.), 31–54. Cambridge: Cambridge University Press.
2003 Constructions in grammaticalization. In *The Handbook of Historical Linguistics*, Brian D. Joseph, and Richard D. Janda (eds.), 624–647. Oxford: Blackwell.
2004 Exaptation and grammaticalization. In *Linguistic Studies Based on Corpora*, Minoji Akimoto (ed.), 133–156. Tokyo: Hituzi Syobo Publishing Co.

Verhagen, Arie
2002 From parts to wholes and back again. *Cognitive Linguistics* 13: 403–439.

Wiemer, Björn
2004 The evolution of passives as grammatical constructions in Northern Slavic and Baltic languages. In *What makes Grammaticalization? A Look from its Fringes and its Components*, Walter Bisang, Nikolaus P. Himmelmann, and Björn Wiemer (eds.), 271–331. Berlin: Mouton de Gruyter.

Wiemer, Björn, and Walter Bisang
2004 What makes grammaticalization? An appraisal of its components and its fringes. In *What makes Grammaticalization? A Look from its Fringes and its Components*, Walter Bisang, Nikolaus P. Himmelmann, and Björn Wiemer (eds.), 3–20. Berlin: Mouton de Gruyter.

Aspects of a diachronic valency syntax of German

Mechthild Habermann

1. Introduction

According to Ágel (2000: 269), research into the historical valency of German has become a neglected area of linguistics due to a condescending attitude towards language dynamics, or rather shifts. Ágel states that what is lacking is a theory of valency dynamics and shifts.

There are only very few studies devoted to the historical valency of German, and those that we have are strictly synchronic. To quote names:

- Albrecht Greule started in 1973 with an article on *Valenz und historische Grammatik* [valency and historical grammar], in the first issue of the *Zeitschrift für Germanistische Linguistik*.
- In 1978, Jarmo Korhonen worked on clause patterns and valency based on texts written by Martin Luther.
- In 1982, Hugh Maxwell wrote a valency grammar for Middle High German verbs based on the Nibelungenlied.
- In his *Habilitationsschrift*, Albrecht Greule (1982) worked on valency in Old High German based on the Gospel by Otfrid von Weißenburg.
- In 1988, Vilmos Ágel wrote a verb valency dictionary based on the Early New German text *Denkwürdigkeiten der Helene Kottannerin (1439–1440)*.

Only rarely are diachronic studies carried out, that is to say, studies which investigate the valency shifts, or the problems of polyvalency in historical language periods, as did, for example, Korhonen (1995).

Today, it is generally agreed that the field of historical valency in the scope of a history of German syntax needs to be investigated in more depth. This is the heritage left by the so-called Neogrammarians of the second half of the 19th century, who directed their attention mainly to phonetics and morphology when dealing with the historical condition and development of language.

Most of the few studies on historical valency are – rightfully – descriptive. They are orientated towards the description of the signifier in terms of the formal means, i.e. the morphological cases, which are then cautiously classified alongside (syntactic-)semantic functions of cases. Analysing and describing the historical texts is the only possible way to improve our knowledge of historical languages and to be able to build up a so-called *Ersatzkompetenz* compensating for the competence of the native speaker.

This is because our sentence structures, our conventional valency schemata and patterns are not of a formal kind, i.e. determined by morphological cases. In addition to this, prototypical case roles are usually assigned to certain formal cases, as, for instance, "agent" for the subject and "patient" for the accusative object. Both, formal structures and the assignment of case roles, are not necessarily the same throughout the different historical language periods.

Werner Abraham (2005: 211–218) sees the difference in the assignment of cases as follows: in his opinion, Old and Middle High German only have an inherent lexical use of cases, whereas New High German developed a structurally, i.e. syntactically governed use.

I would like to extend Werner Abraham's theory: the valency of Old and even Middle High German depends not only on lexical factors but also on text linguistics. The prototypical clause patterns of New High German are different from those of other historical language periods.

My critique of historical syntax valency is centred on a fundamental point: possible solutions to problems arising from the analysis of Modern German are all too often and easily transposed to earlier language periods. As in the present-day language, the main task is to determine complements and adjuncts.[1] Borderline cases, especially adverbial phrases, are categorized quantitatively, i.e. if an adverbial phrase accompanies a verb or meaning of a verb relatively constantly, it is categorized as a complement. Otherwise, it is considered to be an adjunct.[2] However, the question of whether quantitative valency alone can determine whether a phrase is a complement or an adjunct is sometimes left open (in the case of optional complements for instance).

2. Analysing historical valency of German: Difficulties and problems

When examining historical valency, some preconceptions must be revised, or even abandoned since they obstruct the description of historical syntax. These are:

a) Uncertainty as to the limits of a clause. Punctuation is often missing as a clause is punctuated according to pauses in speech, hence there are no criteria for identifying the beginning and the end of sentences. Consequently, a given phrase cannot easily be classified as a complement of a certain verb. The classification is not always unequivocal, on the contrary, it often remains ambiguous or vague.

b) Uncertainty as to the status of the clause. Subordinate clauses are, as such, not unequivocally identified in every case, since the end position of the finite verb first appears as a rule in New High German. In addition, many conjunctions can just as well be read as hypotactic subordinators or coordinating elements. The relative pronouns *der*, *die*, *das* ['who', 'which'] are also demonstrative pronouns. It thus often remains vague whether there is a relationship of dependence or not. To sum up: the difference between parataxis und hypotaxis is nowhere as clear and unequivocal as in Modern German.

c) Uncertainty as to the verbal stem. For a long time, noun compounds and, what is more important for verb valency, verb compounds were not usually written as one word. With regard to the stem and its valency, it is essential to determine whether Middle High German adverbs such as *an*, *auf*, *durch*, or *heran*, *hinauf*, *herum* have the status of phrases or not and whether, as a consequence, they could be complements or adjuncts; or whether we are dealing with verb particles, and thus with verbs which take a particle, as is the case with *ankommen* ['arrive'], *aufsteigen* ['rise, go up'], or *durchfahren* ['pass'].

d) Uncertainty as to the morphological identification of cases. Because of early syncretism of form, especially since Middle High German, certain cases are no longer identifiable. This means that there is a coincidence between the forms of the genitive and the dative singular of feminine nouns.

Thus, *der zît* ['of the time / to the time'] can just as well be genitive singular or dative singular; *der vrouwen* ['of the woman / to the woman, of the women'] can just as well be genitive singular, or dative singular, or even genitive plural feminine.[3]

It is very risqué to transpose conventional valency schemata of New High German to historical language. In Modern German, the use of the dative is more plausible than assuming a genitive complement, whereas for Middle High German, this assumption would be no more than a shallow prejudice.

e) The polyvalency of verbs. In contrast to New High German verbs, Old and even Middle High German verbs do not have a stable, or should I say prototypical valency.[4]

In New High German the meaning of the verb introduces a valency framework which, although it is slightly modifiable, as for instance in the case of optional complements, is quite stable for this particular meaning of polysemic lexemes.

A wider range of structures is often recognisable in historical periods of language, so that prototypes cannot easily be defined. Thus here, and this is the import of the following statement, historical valency is greatly influenced by co-textual and contextual factors.

f) The effect of the Indo-European meanings of the case. It seems that the meanings of the case in Old and Middle High German are still strongly influenced by their ancient Indo-European meanings, and more so in the cases of genitive and dative than for the accusative as the direct object case. In the Germanic dative, the Indo-European dative merges with the instrumental, locative and ablative. Until Old High German, there still are rare occurrences of instrumental and locative, whereas during the later language periods, the non-dative functions are generally expressed by prepositional phrases.[5]

Basically, the three morphological cases genitive, dative and accusative can appear as adverbial phrases. The disparity and diversity of meanings of genitive and dative render the assignment of semantic roles difficult.

3. Reasons for valency shifts

Before I look more closely at the idiosyncrasy of valency in historical language periods, I would like to put forward several arguments that help explain the phenomenon of valency shifts. The question is, which factors are responsible for prototypical clause patterns of the valency system in Modern German? Which factors condition these shifts? Valency shift is particularly affected:

a) by phonetic shifts, as a consequence of which a syncretism of form leads to re-analysis: the merging of different *s*-sounds in Late Middle High German influenced verb valency. Indeed, the fact that the differentiation between the inherited (MHG <s>) and the unvoiced *s* from the Germanic *t* (MHG <ʒ> or <ʒʒ>) in Late Middle High German was dropped (NHG <s> or <ss>) has made it impossible since Early Modern to distinguish between the neutral personal pronouns. In Middle High German, there were distinctive forms for the genitive on the one hand, that is to say *es* (today: *seiner* 'his') and the nominative and accusative on the other hand, that is to say *eʒ*. In Late Middle High German there is only one form, namely: *es*, for all three cases.[6]

(1)	a.	MHG	*es*	*verdriuzet*	*mich*
			compl (gen)	V	compl (acc)
			MHG *eȝ* (nominative and accusative singular)		
		NHG	*es*	*verdrießt*	*mich*[7]
			compl (nom)	V	compl (acc)
			'it	irritates	me'

The tendency to introduce a formal subject is illustrated in this example. In New High German impersonal structures without a subject, which are mostly ergative structures such as *mich friert* ['I am cold'] or *mich hungert* ['I am hungry'], are adapted to prototypical clause patterns with subject (experiencer) and object.[8]

The *s*-merging also affects the so-called strong declension of the adjective, which has a number of forms identical with the declension of the pronoun:

(1)	b.	LU Matt. 9,4			
		ENHG	*Warumb denckt jr*	*so arges*	*in ewren hertzen?*
				compl (gen) or compl (acc)[9]	
			'Why do you think such a bad thing in your hearts?'		

With the occurrence of the syncretism of form, a reinterpretation and thus re-analysis by the hearer/reader is possible, meaning that an earlier genitive as in the Lutheran example (*so arges*) can also be understood as an accusative form. The valency shift happens here through the re-organisation of the morphological case of a genitive into an accusative complement.

b) Another reason for valency shift is the decline of the morphological case for the benefit of analytically formed prepositional cases.

(2) *Sie rühmte sich ihrer Taten.* *Sie rühmte sich wegen ihrer Taten.*
'She prided herself on her actions.'
Sie würdigte ihn keines Blickes. *Sie würdigte ihn mit keinem Blick.*
'She did not deign to look at him.'

In sentences like these, the genitive phrase is becoming less common and is gradually being replaced by the prepositional phrase. It is common knowledge that verbs with a genitive complement have become rare. For Old High German, 198 verbs followed by the genitive were counted in Otfrid's

Evangelienbuch and at least 260 such verbs are recorded for Middle High German.[10] With around 40 verbs followed by the genitive, Modern German only retains 15% of the original number.[11]

c) Valency shift can be caused by a decrease in the variety of possible constructions linked with a gradual development of prototypical clause patterns:

There are many verbs with multiple valency patterns in Old and Middle High German which have simultaneously two possible valency patterns. In addition to the subject (or nominative complement) there is a genitive or accusative complement, occasionally a dative complement, apparently arbitrarily.

Subsequently, I would like to examine verbal patterns and thus show the idiosyncrasy of historical valency syntax in order to lay the basis for a diachronic valency. It is assumed that the distinction between genitive and accusative complements is not arbitrary but indeed deliberate and intentional.

4. Historical valency of German: Diachronic perspectives

As in Modern German, the meaning of the verb always has a great influence on valency. The distinction between genitive and accusative complements remains in Old High German particularly in verbs of certain groups, i.e.:[12]

action and effort	e.g. *biginnan* ['begin'], *geban* ['give']
striving and desire	e.g. *gerōn* ['desire'], *āhten* ['respect']
mental activity	e.g. *thenken* ['think'], *gilouben* ['believe']
speech and communication	e.g. *giwahan* ['mention'], *manōn* ['urge'], ['remind of']
question and request	e.g. *frāgēn* ['ask'], *bitten* ['ask for']
mental processes	e.g. *frewen* ['be glad'], *sorgēn* ['worry']
separation	e.g. *tharbēn* ['not participate'], *mīdan* ['avoid']

Alongside the meaning of the verb the Old Indo-European meaning of the case plays an essential part in the genitive. Genitive actually means "case of origin", which includes the functions of the ablative, such as separative. According to this definition, both the partitive meaning ('part of something') which was common in Old and Middle High German, and its relational meaning, which I could paraphrase as a relationship building function, are thus classified.

The next question is whether the difference in meaning for one and the same verb lies in alternating structural possibilities. I will thus now discuss the difference in meaning between the structure of the genitive complement on the one hand, and the accusative complement on the other.

Jacob Grimm (1837/1989: 646) had already noticed a difference and stated that genitive was the case of "geringere objectivisierung" ['case of the lesser objectification']. Its primary meaning is that of participation. The primary meaning of the accusative is that of involvement.[13]

Verbs of thought and perception such as *gedenken* ['think of'] offer the best opportunity to describe alternative structures.[14] Compare the example of *gedenken*, with a genitive complement:

(3) a. NL 1757,1 [1695,1]

Er	*gedâhte*	*langer mære, diu wâren ê geschehen*
compl (nom)	V	compl (gen)

'Er erinnert(e) sich an lange Geschichten, die einst geschehen waren'

'He remembered / he remembers long tales which once occurred'

The genitive complement has a looser relationship to the predication than the accusative. To some extent, the meaning expressed by the use of genitive externally influences that of the nominative (subject). It is not so much the agent as the experiencer, which is embodied in the subject.

In the example of the Nibelungenlied (3a), the existing meaning of the genitive appears independently of the range of influence of the verb. That is to say, the long tales already exist, before the action of *gedenken* is implemented. The meaning of the verb and the meaning of the case operate together. In this context *gedenken* ['think of'] includes the meaning 'think out', so that one knows or is reminded of.

The meaning 'remember' in *gedenken* is not coincidental. Indeed, the act of memorising uses a process of thought, that is, recalling. Therefore, the very frequent link between past tense and genitive complement is – probably – not a coincidence either. It is similarly the case with verbs such as *sich erschrecken* ['get a fright'], *vergessen* ['forget'] and *sich befreien* ['free so.'].

A very different meaning of the structure is introduced in the case of *gedenken* followed by an accusative complement, the case of the direct object:

(3) b. Herb. 13450

so	*gedenke*	*ich*	*wol*	*die list*
adjunct	V	compl	adjunct	compl
(caus)		(nom)	(mod)	(acc)

'Deshalb denke ich mir gutüberlegt die / meine Vorgehensweise aus'
'Therefore I think out well my action'

In this example, the meaning of the accusative complement is directly affected by the action of the verb. It is the result of the "thought process".

Here, the meaning of *über etwas nachdenken* ['think about something'] is linked with *etwas ausdenken* ['think something up']. The action of the verb governs the object, in a rather abstract way that emerges gradually or is created during the action. The meaning of the accusative is the content or the result of the action carried out. This is also the case with verbs such as *schreiben* ['write'] and *bauen* ['build'].

In these examples, the occurrence of valency arises through both the meaning of the verb and the meaning of the case. The genitive complement refers to an external, already present object (which is brought to light through the action of the verb), the accusative object refers to an internal emerging object, to an object of result.

A further distinction, connected with the dichotomy of external and internal object defines the choice of the case in Old and Middle High German. The semantic class of the object may also be influential. The accusative complement is used for an abstract noun, the genitive complement for a concrete noun. This is not so clear in the case of *gedenken,* but is easily recognisable in the case of the Old High German *niazan* ['enjoy, turn to profit']:[15]

(4) a. O 5,22,5

Thie selbun gotes liuti	*thār*	*niazent*	*liohto zīti*
compl (nom)	mod (loc)	V	compl (acc)

'Das Gottesvolk dort genießt die lichten Zeiten'
'God's people there are enjoying the bright times'

b. O 1,11,8

thaz	*se*	*erdrīches*	*niezēn*
conj	compl	compl	V
	(nom)	(gen)	

'... sofern sie das Erdreich (das Land) genießen'
'... while they enjoy the land'

There is undoubtedly a relic of the old partitive meaning in the genitive complement. Distinctions were later blurred, particularly in the eighteenth century, when abstract objects are expressed by the genitive complement.

This brings me to another essential point: when dealing with a verb that can take either a genitive or an accusative complement, textlinguistics play a central role alongside the external object and result object in choosing which case is appropriate. Especially Richard Schrodt (1992: 385; 2004: 82–83, § S 78) has referred to this point.

Depending on whether the object was previously mentioned or not, the genitive or the accusative, respectively, are used. The text-deictic and the text-phoric function are closely interrelated here: in the case of the genitive complement, the external object correlates with the factor of being previously mentioned or given, and in the case of the accusative complement the object of result correlates with the factor of being new. In the case of some verbs, verb valency depends essentially on the dichotomy of given and new, or on the structure of theme and rheme.

The verb *hōren* ['hear'] in Old High German (di- or trivalent pattern) might illustrate this: the person "who is being listened to or obeyed" is in the dative (beside the nominative), the command, which the person (subject) obeys, can be in accusative, dative or genitive or occur as a *thaz*-clause:

(5)	a.	with dative	G	'auf jmdn. hören, ihm gehorchen'
			E	'obey sb.'
		with accusative	G	'etw. hören, etw. erhören, auf etwas hören'
			E	'hear sth.; listen to sth.'
		with genitive	G	'auf etwas (schon Vorhandenes, schon Gesagtes) hören, es beachten'
			E	'listen to sth. (which has been said / mentioned before)'.[16]

b. T 52,7

sie	*hōrent*	*imo?*
compl (nom)	V	compl (dat)

'Gehorchen sie ihm?'
'Do they obey him?'

c. O 1,17,53

Thaz imbot	*sie*	*gihōrtun*
compl (acc)	compl (nom)	V

'Sie hörten den Befehl'
'They heard the order'

d. O 2,9,55–7
quad ... thaz er got forahta tho er sulīh werk worahta
'er sagte, ... dass er Gott fürchte, weil er eine solche Tat vollbrachte'
'he said ... that he feared God because he accomplished such an act'

Ioh	*sīnēro worto*	*er*	*hōrta*	*filu harto*
conj	compl (gen)	compl (nom)	V	adjunct (mod)

'Hinsichtlich seiner Worte (seinen Worten) gehorchte er nämlich sehr'
'As to his words he obeyed well'

In example (5d), the anaphoric reference is doubled, coded by the case and anaphors (personal and possessive pronouns *er*, *sīnēro*).

A further example: in the case of a question, the circumstances which are being questioned are previously mentioned or known.[17] Therefore, this verb is followed by the genitive. When the circumstances are unknown, it is followed by the accusative (or prepositional case):

(6) a. O 3,12,5

thes	*ich*	*nu*	*frāgēn*	*iuih*
compl (gen)	compl (nom)	adjunct (temp)	V	compl (dat)

'... wonach ich euch jetzt frage'
'... what I am going to ask you about'

b. T 170,30f.

[*tho quuat her imo*]			
uuaz	*mih*	*frāgēs*	*fon guote*
compl (acc)	compl (acc)	V	mod (prep) / compl (prep)

'[da sprach er zu ihm:]
Was fragst du mich nach den guten Dingen?'
'[Then he said to him:]
What are you asking me about the good thing?'

Very frequently, the use of the genitive complement in a textlinguistic function also involves the use of a pronoun as the part of speech which additionally intensifies the cataphoric function. This includes personal, possessive, demonstrative and relative pronouns.

The results presented here have so far been verified only with limited groups of verbs, namely the verbs of thought, perception and interrogation, of seeing and hearing, of eating and drinking and the like. Whether these characteristics are also found with other groups of verbs is at this time open to debate. As yet, we have no studies based on large corpora and they will not be undertaken until we have digital historical language corpora for the German language. The individual occurrences of verbs can then be analysed in context, including textlinguistic aspects, and statements on the frequency of certain types of occurrences can be made.

Another question is if polyvalency, especially the choice of genitive versus accusative complement for text linguistic reasons, is actually a phenomenon of verb valency or if it is merely a phenomenon of language use, such as omitting optional complements. If the latter were the case, it would not touch the level of the language system.

The distinction proves to be extremely difficult. In my opinion, there is only one, in practice vague criterion, which can hardly be employed for historical language periods: valency variation is rooted in the language system if the meaning of the verb changes depending on the choice of the case.

5. Conclusion

The verb valency of Old and Middle High German is determined by many different factors. Different possible structures are applied to increase the polysemy of verbs, much more so than in Modern German. The different partial significances are activated according to the structural framework which covers the range of meaning of *gedenken* from 'denken' ['think'] to 'erinnern' ['remember']; of *hōren* from 'etwas hören' ['hear something'] to 'etwas hören, gehorchen' ['obey'].

This diversity of meaning(s) is often still effective in New High German when connected to prepositional phrases. There are, however, particular lexemes which lexically codify the equivalent partial significance of Old High German polysemic verbs. This is essentially different from historical language periods.

The lexical meaning of Old and Middle High German is not clearly defined. It is formed within a context, and according to the combination of the meaning of the verb and the meaning of the case. Nevertheless, it remains variable and imprecise in lexicographical terms. It is difficult to compile polyvalency in verb valency dictionaries, and until Early New Modern German it is in my view almost impossible.

The differentiation of meanings according to context is conditioned by the scantiness of verbs. So far we have no verbs that take particles; at most they are polysemic simplex verbs. Until well into the eighteenth century, the vernacular language lacks something crucial: it lacks a *copia verborum*, an adequately varied vocabulary, which is an achievement of modern times. The specific meaning of the case plays a decisive role in activating the meaning of the verb. It is strongly determined by its Indo-European primary meaning, at least in the cases of genitive and dative.

Using this argument, I have tried to establish the differences in the use of polyvalent verbs, working from the primary meaning of the genitive as a linking case. One and the same verb (from a specific semantic group) is constructed with a genitive complement if the genitive meaning in the (extralinguistic) reality is already available – it carries the semantic mark of the concrete or has already been mentioned in the text.

However, the accusative complement is then used if the object is not yet available but appears through the use of the verb, which has a semantic mark of abstraction or has not previously been mentioned in the text.

The function of the case develops from this past relationship between meanings, i.e. the linguistic function of the text in the sentence, but also of the sense of coding of the given and new, of theme and rheme. This function is achieved through textual elements of New High German. Old and Middle High German valency is not only part of the grammar of the sentence, but also of the grammar of the text.

Notes

1. In the following English *complement* will correspond to German *Ergänzung* and *adjunct* to German *Angabe*.
2. Cf. in detail Greule (1982: 192–219, 1983: 85, 1995: 358–362).
3. On the declension of nouns cf. Paul (1881/1998: 184–207, § 174–195).
4. The variety of constructions found with Old High German verbs is documented impressively in Greule's valency dictionary (1999). The best-known phenomenon is that in the case of negation in a sentence an accusative complement can be replaced with a genitive phrase; cf. Ebert (1986: 38–39).
5. Cf. at length Delbrück (1893: 172–199, § 55–80) and Braune (1886/2004: 182–183, § 192e) with further reading.
6. On the declension of pronouns and on the merging of the *s*-sounds cf. Paul (1881/1998: 162–163, § 151–154 and 220–221, § 214) and Ebert et al. (1993: 110–113, § L 52, and 214–215, § M 63 Anm. 3).
7. Cf. Ebert (1986: 60).
8. Cf. Ágel (2000: 270–273); for the terminology cf. Fillmore (2003: 464).
9. It is also possible to interpret *arges* as a modifier (genitivus partitivus) to *so*.
10. Cf. Schrodt (1996: 78–82) and Rausch (1897: 54).
11. Cf. Kolvenbach (1973: 123). Lenz (1998: 3) still identifies 56 verbs followed by genitive, many of which however can be shown to be outdated or stylistically marked; cf. Dürscheid (1999: 34–37).
12. Cf. Schrodt (2004: 80, § S 75), Behaghel (1923/1989: 562–574, § 407–409), Ebert (1986: 40–43) and Paul (1881/1998: 341, § 361).
13. Cf. Delbrück (1893: 308, § 148, and 360–361, § 176).
14. This group of verbs has already been investigated by Milligan (1960). More attention has been directed to them through the works of Schrodt (1992: 372–377, 387–391, and 2004: 81–82, § S 76); cf. Donhauser (1998: 73–76).
15. Cf. Greule (1999: 184–185, cf. *niozan*) and Schrodt (2004: 83–84, § S 79).
16. Cf. Greule (1999: 130–133, cf. *hôren*).
17. Cf. Greule (1999: 82f., cf. *frâgên*) and Schrodt (2004: 83, § S 78).

References

1. Sources

Herb. = *Herbort's von Fritslâr liet von Troye*
1966 Reprint. Georg Karl Frommann (ed.), (Bibliothek der gesammten deutschen National-Literatur 5.), Amsterdam: Rodopi. Original edition, Quedlinburg/Leipzig, 1837.

LU = Martin Luther. *Biblia. Das ist die gantze Heilige Schrifft Deudsch auffs new zugericht*
1974 Reprint. Vol.3 Hans Volz (ed.), (dtv Text-Bibliothek 6033) München: Deutscher Taschenbuch Verlag. Original edition, Wittenberg, 1545.

NL = *Der Nibelunge Nôt. Mit den Abweichungen von der Nibelunge liet, den Lesarten sämtlicher Handschriften und einem Wörterbuche 1. Theil: Text; 2. Theil 1. Hälfte: Lesarten; 2. Theil 2. Hälfte: Wörterbuch*
1966 Reprint. Karl Bartsch (ed.), Hildesheim: Olms. Original edition: Leipzig, 1870; 1876; 1880.

O = *Otfrid's Evangelienbuch*
1982 Reprint. Paul Piper (ed.), Hildesheim: Olms. Original edition, Tübingen, 1882. 2d ed. Freiburg i. Br.

T = *Tatian.* Lateinisch und deutsch mit ausführlichem Glossar
1966 Reprint. Eduard Sievers (ed.), 293–515 (Bibliothek der ältesten deutschen Litteratur-Denkmäler 5.), Paderborn: Schöningh. 2d revised edition, Paderborn, 1892.

2. Secondary literature

Abraham, Werner
2005 *Deutsche Syntax im Sprachenvergleich: Grundlegung einer typologischen Syntax des Deutschen.* 2d improved and enlarged ed. (Studien zur deutschen Grammatik 41.) Tübingen: Stauffenburg.

Ágel, Vilmos
1988 Überlegungen zur Theorie und Methode der historisch-synchronen Valenzsyntax und Valenzlexikographie: Mit einem Verbvalenzlexikon zu den „Denkwürdigkeiten der Helene Kottannerin (1439–1440)". (Lexicographica Series Maior 25): Tübingen: Niemeyer.
2000 *Valenztheorie.* Tübingen: Narr.

Behaghel, Otto
1989 Reprint. *Deutsche Syntax. Eine geschichtliche Darstellung.* Vol. 1: *Die Wortklassen und Wortformen. A. Nomen. Pronomen.* Heidelberg: Winter. Original ed., Heidelberg, 1923.

Braune, Wilhelm
2004 Reprint. *Althochdeutsche Grammatik I. Laut- und Formenlehre.* 15th revised ed. Ingo Reiffenstein (ed.), (Sammlung kurzer Grammatiken germanischer Dialekte A, 5/1.) Tübingen: Niemeyer. Original edition, 1886.

Delbrück, Berthold
1893 *Vergleichende Syntax der indogermanischen Sprachen. Erster Theil.* (Grundriß der Vergleichenden Grammatik der Indogermanischen Sprachen 3). Straßburg: Trübner.

Donhauser, Karin
1998 Das Genitivproblem und (k)ein Ende? Anmerkungen zur aktuellen Diskussion um die Ursachen des Genitivschwundes im Deutschen. In *Historische germanische und deutsche Syntax. Akten des internationalen Symposiums anläßlich des 100. Geburtstages von Ingerid Dal, Oslo, 27.9.-1.10.1995*, John Ole Askedal (ed.), 69–86 (Osloer Beiträ-

ge zur Germanistik 21.) Frankfurt M./Berlin/Bern/New York/Paris/ Wien: Lang.

Dürscheid, Christa
1999 *Die verbalen Kasus im Deutschen. Untersuchungen zur Syntax, Semantik und Perspektive.* (Studia linguistica Germanica 53.) Berlin/New York: de Gruyter.

Ebert, Robert Peter
1986 *Historische Syntax des Deutschen II: 1300–1750.* (Germanistische Lehrbuchsammlung 6.) Bern/Frankfurt M./New York: Lang.

Ebert, Robert Peter, Oskar Reichmann, Hans Joachim Solms, and Klaus-Peter Wegera
1993 *Frühneuhochdeutsche Grammatik.* (Sammlung kurzer Grammatiken germanischer Dialekte A, 12.) Tübingen: Niemeyer.

Fillmore, Charles
2003 Valency and semantic roles: The concept of deep structure case. In *Dependenz und Valenz. Ein internationales Handbuch der zeitgenössischen Forschung,* Vilmos Ágel, Ludwig M. Eichinger, Hans-Werner Eroms, Peter Hellwig, Hans Jürgen Heringer, and Henning Lobin (eds.), 457–475. (Handbücher zur Sprach- und Kommunikationswissenschaft 25.1.) Berlin/New York: de Gruyter.

Greule, Albrecht
1973 Valenz und historische Grammatik. *Zeitschrift für Germanistische Linguistik* 1: 284–294.
1982 *Valenz, Satz und Text. Syntaktische Untersuchungen zum Evangelienbuch Otfrids von Weißenburg auf der Grundlage des Codex Vindobonensis.* München: Fink.
1983 Zum Aufbau einer dependenziellen althochdeutschen Syntax. *Sprachwissenschaft* 8: 81–92.
1995 Valenz im historischen Korpus. In *Dependenz und Valenz,* Ludwig M. Eichinger, and Hans-Werner Eroms (eds.), 357–363. (Beiträge zur germanistischen Sprachwissenschaft 10.) Hamburg: Buske.
1999 *Syntaktisches Verbwörterbuch zu den althochdeutschen Texten des 9. Jahrhunderts. Altalemannische Psalmenfragmente, Benediktinerregel, Hildebrandslied, Monseer Fragmente, Murbacher Hymnen, Otfrid, Tatian und kleinere Sprachdenkmäler.* (Regensburger Beiträge zur deutschen Sprach- und Literaturwissenschaft B 73.) Frankfurt M./Berlin/Bern/New York/Paris/Wien: Lang.

Grimm, Jacob
1989 2d reprint. *Deutsche Grammatik.* Vol. 4, 2. Gustav Roethe, and Edward Schröder (eds.). Hildesheim: Olms. Original edition, 1837.

Kolvenbach, Monika
1973 Das Genitivobjekt im Deutschen. Seine Interrelation zu den Präpositionalphrasen und dem Akkusativ. In *Linguistische Studien IV. Festgabe für P. Grebe zum 65. Geburtstag. Teil 2,* 123–134. (Sprache der Gegenwart 24.) Düsseldorf: Schwann.

Korhonen, Jarmo

1978 *Studien zu Dependenz, Valenz und Satzmodell.* Vol. 2: *Untersuchung anhand eines Luther-Textes.* (Europäische Hochschulschriften II; 271.) Bern/Frankfurt M./Las Vegas: Lang.

1995 Zum Wesen der Polyvalenz in der deutschen Sprachgeschichte. In *Dependenz und Valenz,* Ludwig M. Eichinger, and Hans-Werner Eroms (eds.), 365–382. (Beiträge zur germanistischen Sprachwissenschaft 10.) Hamburg: Buske.

Lenz, Barbara

1998 Objektvariation bei Genitiv-Verben. *Papiere zur Linguistik* 58: 3–34.

Maxwell, Hugh

1982 *Valenzgrammatik mittelhochdeutscher Verben.* (Europäische Hochschulschriften 1.504.) Frankfurt M./Bern: Lang.

Milligan, Thomas R.

1960 The German verb-genitive locution from Old High German to the present: A study in structure of content. Ph.D. diss., New York University.

Paul, Hermann

1998 Reprint. *Mittelhochdeutsche Grammatik.* 24th revised ed. Peter Wiehl, and Siegfried Grosse (eds.), (Sammlung kurzer Grammatiken germanischer Dialekte A, 2.) Tübingen: Niemeyer. Original edition, 1881.

Rausch, Georg

1897 Zur Geschichte des deutschen Genitivs seit der mittelhochdeutschen Zeit. Ph.D. diss., University of Gießen.

Schrodt, Richard

1992 Die Opposition von Objektsgenitiv und Objektsakkusativ in der deutschen Sprachgeschichte: Syntax oder Semantik oder beides? *Beiträge zur Geschichte der deutschen Sprache* 114: 361–394.

1996 Aspekt, Aktionsart und Objektsgenitiv im Deutschen: Wie weit kann eine systematische Erklärungsmöglichkeit für den Schwund des Genitivobjekts gehen? In *Language Change and Generative Grammar,* Ellen Brandner, and Gisella Ferraresi (eds.), 71–94. (Linguistische Berichte, Sonderheft 7/1995–96.) Opladen: Westdeutscher Verlag.

2004 *Althochdeutsche Grammatik II. Syntax.* (Sammlung kurzer Grammatiken germanischer Dialekte A, 5/2.) Tübingen: Niemeyer.

The valency of experiential and evaluative adjectives

Ilka Mindt

1. Introduction and aim

This paper focuses on adjectives which are followed by *that*-clauses. An example is

(1) *It is obvious that sovereignty does not mean dictatorship.* (AMK 481)

The valency pattern for the adjective *obvious* in this example is given in *A Valency Dictionary of English* (VDE) as "[it] + (that)-CL" (Herbst et al. 2004: 559). The square brackets around the pronoun *it* indicate that the adjective *obvious* has to be preceded by impersonal *it*. The adjective *obvious* is followed by a *that*-clause. The round brackets around the conjunction *that* specify the conjunction *that* as an optional element. The conjunction *that* can occur but it need not occur as can be seen in (2) where a zero realisation is found.

(2) *It was obvious a storm was coming in.* (H9C 338)

The research reported here is part of a research project (for more details see Mindt forthcoming) which focuses on the 51 most frequent adjectives in the pattern "adjective + conjunction *that*". These 51 adjectives account for 75% of all adjectives in the pattern "adjective + conjunction *that*". For the research reported here about 44,000 cases, all taken from the *British National Corpus* (BNC), have been considered.

The aim of this paper is to offer a new description of adjectives in the pattern "adjective + conjunction *that*", which will then be compared with the valency patterns given in the VDE. Section 2 focuses on the description of the pattern "adjective + conjunction *that*" in three reference grammars of English. In section 3 the empirical approach is presented, which leads to a new classification of adjectives followed by *that*-clauses. A comparison between the description found in the reference grammars with the new classification is attempted in section 4 before the adjective classification is compared with the valency patterns presented in the VDE in section 5.

2. Description of the pattern "adjective + conjunction *that*" in three reference grammars

I will use the description of adjective complementation by *that*-clauses of three present-day reference grammars of English as a basis for comparison. Other studies which group adjectives followed by *that*-clauses are Householder, Alexander, and Matthews (1964) and Francis, Hunston, and Manning (1996). Their grouping of adjectives is similar to the one given in the three reference grammars. There are some studies that concentrate on one particular group of adjectives followed by *that*-clauses: namely adjectives in the construction "*it* + verb + adjective + *that*-clause". Examples are Erdmann (1987), Hunston and Sinclair (2000) and Kaltenböck (2004). These studies are not considered here in greater detail. The three reference grammars are:

a) *A Comprehensive Grammar of the English Language* (Quirk et al. 1985),
b) *Longman Grammar of Spoken and Written English* (Biber et al. 1999), and
c) *The Cambridge Grammar of the English Language* (Huddleston and Pullum 2002).

A Comprehensive Grammar of the English Language distinguishes between two sets of adjectives: (i) "Adjectives with experiencer as subject" and (ii) "Adjectives with anticipatory *it* as subject" (Quirk et al. 1985: 1223–1225). A typical example of an adjective with an experiencer as subject from the BNC is *aware* in (3), whereas the adjective *apparent* in (4) occurs with anticipatory *it* as subject.

(3) *I am also very aware that all this is relative*. (A0F 2162)
(4) *It was apparent that a genius had been born*. (EX1 463)

The type of grammatical structure found in (4) is referred to as subject extraposition[1] in the CGEL (Quirk et al. 1985: 1224). Quirk et al. (1985: 1391–1392) describe extraposition in terms of a postponement of nominal clauses. "The subject is moved to the end of the sentence, and the normal subject position is filled by the anticipatory pronoun *it*." (Quirk et al. 1985: 1391). Quirk et al. state that postponement is "more usual" (1985: 1392) for clausal subjects – *that*-clauses in my research – "than the canonical position before the verb" (1985: 1392). An example taken from the BNC of a *that*-clause occurring before the verb in subject position is given in (5).

(5) *That this was clearly a tactical decision quickly became apparent.* (AHK 85)

Extraposition is a special device in order to structure the information. It is employed when end-weight or focus should be given to the postponed element.

The *Longman Grammar of Spoken and Written English* (Biber et al. 1999: 671–674) differentiates between (i) "Adjectival predicates taking post-predicate *that*-clauses" as in (3) and (ii) "Adjectival predicates taking extraposed *that*-clauses" as in (4) (1999: 672).

The Cambridge Grammar of the English Language (Huddleston and Pullum 2002: 957–964) distinguishes between (i) "Adjectives in predicative function" (2002: 964) which may take declarative content clauses as exemplified in (3) and (ii) adjectives with extraposed subjects as in (4) where the *that*-clause can also occur as the subject (see [5]).

All three grammars basically distinguish two groups of adjectives. One group comprises adjectives which are followed by a *that*-clause. These adjectives are described differently in the three reference grammars. Quirk et al. state that they occur with an experiencer in subject position. Biber et al. and Huddleston and Pullum do not comment on the subject in the matrix clause. They just describe this group of adjectives as being complemented by a *that*-clause as opposed to the second group of adjectives. The second group consists of adjectives which can occur with extraposed subjects. They are referred to as "Adjectives with anticipatory *it* as subject" by Quirk et al. (1985: 1224), as "Adjectival predicates taking extraposed *that*-clauses" by Biber et al. (1999: 672) and as "adjectives taking a clause as (extraposed) subject" (2002: 964) by Huddleston and Pullum.

Table 1 lists examples of the two groups of adjectives as given by Quirk et al. (1985: 1223–1225). Only those adjectives are listed in table 1 which are found in the CGEL and are also considered in the empirical research outlined in section 3.

Table 1. The grouping of adjectives by Quirk et al.

adjectives with experiencer as subject	adjectives with anticipatory *it* as subject
afraid, angry, anxious, aware, certain, confident, disappointed, glad, grateful, happy, hopeful, pleased, sad, sorry, sure, surprised	*apparent, appropriate, arguable, certain, clear, essential, evident, important, inconceivable, inevitable, likely, obvious, odd, possible, probable, sad, strange, surprising, true, unfortunate, unlikely, vital*

In the following, I will not use the term anticipatory *it* but instead refer to the pronoun *it* in so-called extraposition as impersonal *it*. This terminology is in accordance with the VDE (Herbst et al. 2004: xx). Impersonal *it* must be distinguished from another use of the pronoun *it* as in (6).

(6) *The commission says it's adamant that the public will have the final say.* (K1R 897)

The pronoun *it* in (6) will be termed referring *it*, because the pronoun *it* refers to the noun phrase *the commission.*

3. An empirical approach to adjectives followed by *that*-clauses

The aim of the empirical approach described here is to arrive at a systematic description of adjectives followed by *that*-clauses, which accounts for all cases without any exception. The approach is not based on any linguistic theory or framework. The findings rest exclusively on the language samples. The analysis of the language samples leads to a new classification of adjectives and is based on the subject types of the matrix clause. It will be explained in the following (for more details see Mindt forthcoming).

The adjectives are first distinguished according to whether they cooccur with a subject or without a subject.

(7) *Keith kept up a brisk pace, glad that it was a full moon.* (HUA 1319)

(8) *But he was glad that there was no mirror in this room.* (ADA 824)

In (7) no subject precedes the adjective *glad* whereas in (8) the subject *he* co-occurs with *glad*. Cases with a subject are then further distinguished according to the following subject types:

a) pronominal subject vs. non-pronominal subject and
b) intentional subject vs. non-intentional subject.

The subjects *we* and *it* in (9) and (11) are examples of pronominal subjects, *environmentalists* in (10) and *the Bible* in (12) are non-pronominal subjects. The subjects *we* (9) and *environmentalists* (10) are intentional subjects, *it* (11) and *the Bible* (12) are non-intentional subjects.

(9) *We are hopeful that it will be a true festival of football.* (A9N 135)
(10) *Environmentalists are worried that the fumes from the fire are hazardous.* (K23 1445)
(11) *It's likely that trade will rise, but it doesn't automatically follow.* (HYN 63)
(12) *The Bible is quite clear that these evil spirits (and the things that they do) are dangerous.* (C8N 916)

The four subject types can be cross-classified as shown in table 2.

Table 2. Cross-classification of subjects

	intentional subject	non-intentional subject
pronominal subject	*we*	*it*
non-pronominal subject	*environmentalists*	*the Bible*

The pronouns *I*, *you*[2], *he*, *she*, *it* (both impersonal *it* and referring *it*), *we* and *they* are pronominal subjects, all other subjects are non-pronominal. An intentional subject can act intentionally or may be able to act intentionally. This distinguishes it from a non-intentional subject. The subject *we* in (9) is an intentional subject which does not perform an intentional action because the adjective *hopeful* refers to a feeling. Non-intentional subjects as impersonal *it* in (11) or *the Bible* in (12) cannot act intentionally. Impersonal *it* as a non-intentional subject is used in (11) as an option in the English language to make a statement about the likelihood of something without explicitly naming the source who/that considered this as likely. The subject *the Bible* in (12) is also non-intentional because no intentional action can or may be performed by it. For more details on intentional and non-intentional subjects see Mindt (forthcoming).

The subject types of all 44,000 cases have been analysed. The analysis of the subject types into intentional and non-intentional subjects cannot be made on the basis of formal criteria but has to be carried out by the researcher for each individual case. The decision on whether the subject is intentional or non-intentional has to be made on the basis of the context.

The next step in the research was to discover if co-occurrences exist between the different subject types and the 51 adjectives. Because of the large number of cases it would have been prohibitive to analyse them manually. But statistical procedures provide powerful tools to explore relationships between the subject types and the adjectives. I have employed hierarchical cluster analysis. The purpose of cluster analysis "is to group objects on the basis of the characteristics they possess" (Hair et al. 1998: 473). This means that the adjectives are grouped together into clusters on the basis of their subject types.

Hierarchical cluster analysis yields two clusters of adjectives (see Mindt forthcoming for further details on the application of cluster analysis). The two classes of adjectives are presented in table 3.

Table 3. Classification of adjectives

Experiential adjectives	Evaluative adjectives
adamant, afraid, angry, anxious, aware, certain, concerned, confident, conscious, convinced, delighted, disappointed, glad, grateful, happy, hopeful, pleased, sad, satisfied, sorry, sure, surprised, unaware, worried	*apparent, appropriate, arguable, certain, clear, essential, evident, good, great, important, inconceivable, inevitable, interesting, ironic, likely, natural, obvious, odd, possible, probable, sad, significant, strange, strong, surprising, true, unfortunate, unlikely, vital*

The adjectives *aware, adamant, glad, hopeful,* and *worried* (examples [3], [6-10]) belong to the first class. The adjectives *obvious*, *apparent*, *likely*, and *clear* in examples (1), (2), (4), (11), and (12) are part of the second class. The adjectives of each class have one semantic characteristic in common. The adjectives of the first class are all experiential. Experiential adjectives either convey a feeling or express certainty and confidence. Those of the second class are evaluative because they convey a judgement or an assessment. The adjectives *certain* and *sad* can occur as members of both classes. Examples of the adjective *certain* are given in (13) and (14).

(13) *An informed insider told me last night: "It is absolutely certain that Nigel has done the deal."* (CH3 3179)

(14) *He is almost certain that they went up Charterhouse Street.* (ANL 1315)

In (13) the adjective *certain* co-occurs with the non-intentional subject impersonal *it*. The adjective *certain* conveys an evaluation. On the other hand, the subject *he* in (14) is intentional and co-occurs with the experiential adjective *certain* which expresses a meaning similar to that of *sure* (see Mindt forthcoming for more details).

The adjectives have been classified with regard to their subject types in the matrix clause and thus reveal typical co-occurrence patterns. Experiential adjectives co-occur with intentional subjects, evaluative adjectives with non-intentional subjects. But it is also an inherent semantic property of experiential adjectives to favour intentional subjects because an intentional subject is the carrier of the emotion or certainty/confidence expressed by the adjective. Evaluative adjectives – on the other hand – co-occur with non-intentional subjects. In contrast to an intentional subject, the non-intentional subject cannot act intentionally. The evaluative adjective expresses the judgement or assessment which is assigned to the non-intentional subject. By using impersonal *it* as a non-intentional subject, a speaker or writer has the possibility to express a judgement or an assessment without explicitly naming the source of the evaluation. Impersonal *it* as a non-intentional subject expresses the evaluation from a non-involved, neutral and indeterminate point of view. This view is also shared by Collins, who states that a speaker, when using impersonal *it* as the subject in the matrix clause, ascribes "to an unspecified source the responsibility for an assertion" (1994: 19). The empirical research outlined above shows that the non-intentional subject impersonal *it* refers to such an unspecified source.

The terms "experiential" and "evaluative" illustrate the semantic characteristics of the adjectives. They should be considered as umbrella terms that cover the specific meanings of these adjectives.

4. Differences in the adjective classifications

The grouping of the adjectives in the three reference grammars (Quirk et al. 1985; Biber et al. 1999; Huddleston and Pullum 2002) mainly rests on a syntactic criterion which has been described as extraposition. Adjectives occurring with extraposed *that*-clauses and thus with impersonal *it* in subject position are differentiated from adjectives which are not followed by an extraposed *that*-clause. Quirk et al. also introduce a semantic criterion for adjectives followed by a *that*-clause: they have an experiencer as subject. The adjectives comprising each group can then be further subdivided according to their semantics (see for example Quirk et al. 1985: 1223–1225 or Biber et al. 1999: 671–674).

The new classification of adjectives can be explained in terms of lexico-semantic features. One group of adjectives expresses either a feeling or certainty/confidence and thus has been described as experiential. The other group of adjectives conveys a judgement or an assessment and has been termed evaluative. The two classes of adjectives emerged on the basis of the co-occurrence patterns with their subject types. Experiential adjectives typically co-occur with intentional subjects. These intentional subjects are the carriers of the emotion or certainty conveyed by the adjective. Intentional subjects are expressed by different forms of subjects, the most frequent being a personal pronoun. The personal pronouns *I*, *you*, *he*, *she*, (referring) *it*, *we*, and *they* account for 78% of all intentional subjects. Evaluative adjectives co-occur with non-intentional subjects of which impersonal *it* is the most frequent, accounting for 96.9% of all evaluative adjectives with non-intentional subjects (for more information on frequency distributions see Mindt forthcoming). By using impersonal *it* as the subject, a speaker or writer can make a judgement or an assessment without the need to explicitly refer to the source of the evaluation. Another example of a non-intentional subject co-occuring with an evaluative adjective is *the Bible* in (12).

The empirical analysis of more than 44,000 cases of adjectives followed by *that*-clauses shows that there is no group of adjectives which exclusively occurs with impersonal *it* as their subject. The class of evaluative adjectives co-occurs with non-intentional subjects, of which impersonal *it* is one possible form. A subclassification of evaluative adjectives into those which co-occur with impersonal *it* only and those which do not occur with impersonal *it* results in two classes which list the same adjectives. Such a subclassification does not reveal any contrast and is therefore useless.

The grouping of adjectives given in the reference grammars as well as the classification of the adjectives based on an empirical analysis revealed two groups or classes of adjectives. The adjectives which comprise these two groups or classes are largely identical (compare tables 1 and 3). The group of adjectives which have been described in the reference grammars as complemented by a *that*-clause largely match those which have been termed experiential adjectives. The adjectives which are followed by an extraposed *that*-clause are mostly part of the class of evaluative adjectives. This means that the classification of adjectives into two classes as outlined by the empirical research resulted in the same division of the individual adjectives which has already been described by the reference grammars.

The main difference between the two accounts lies in the fact that the distinction in the reference grammars is based mainly on syntactic criteria whereas the new classification reflects systematic co-occurrences of the adjectives with their subject types and can additionally be explained in terms of lexico-semantic features inherent in the two adjective classes.

Cases such as (12) above or (15) below are not accounted for explicitly by the reference grammars. The adjective *clear* is listed in all three reference grammars as being followed by an extraposed *that*-clause. This is not the case in (12) and (15).

(15) *The Equal Opportunities Commission says the Sex Discrimination Act is clear that restricting taxi cab jobs to one sex is potentially unlawful*. (K26 1633)

Within the new adjective classification the adjective *clear* is considered as an evaluative adjective co-occurring with non-intentional subjects of which both *The Bible* and *the Sex Discrimination Act* are examples.

Huddleston and Pullum (2002: 964) mention cases similar to (16) ("*I'm quite clear that* …").

(16) *Our audiences are clear that we are the most trusted source of information and news in Britain*. (J1L 62)

The subject *our audiences* in (16) as well as *I* in the example given by Huddleston and Pullum is analysed in the empirical research as an intentional subject. The meaning of the adjective *clear* in both examples is similar to the meaning of *certain* or *sure* and conveys the semantic characteristics of an experiential adjective. In a small number of cases which account for less than 1% of all 44,000 cases an experiential adjective may acquire an evaluative meaning or an evaluative adjective (as *clear*) may be analysed as an experiential adjective. This shift in meaning is also reflected by the co-occurrence of experiential *clear* with an intentional subject, whereas the evaluative adjective *clear* co-occurs with a non-intentional subject.

Impersonal *it* is the most frequent form a non-intentional subject takes. It can only be assumed that the high frequency of impersonal *it* is the reason why cases with this subject have been considered separately in previous accounts of adjective classifications. The high frequency might also be the reason why cases with impersonal *it* have received so much attention and are the topic of many studies within different grammatical frameworks and theories.

5. Valency patterns

In section 5.1. I will briefly refer to two accounts that have analysed impersonal *it* in terms of its valency. Section 5.2. discusses the valency patterns of experiential and evaluative adjectives as given in the VDE.

5.1. Analysing impersonal *it*

Herbst (1983: 33–38) argues that adjectives should be described in terms of patterns. He states that impersonal *it* fulfils merely a syntactic function, but goes on that impersonal *it* is necessary in terms of the structural requirements of a sentence and thus should be regarded as a complement in a valency description. This implies that impersonal *it* is assigned a valency. Herbst analyses adjectives that occur with impersonal *it* in subject position as divalent (1983: 37): "Zwar läßt sich argumentieren, daß it, auch wenn es nicht gegen andere Elemente austauschbar ist, eine Valenzstelle besetzt, also die Funktion von E 1 wahrnimmt; dennoch erscheint es sinnvoll, bei einer Valenzbeschreibung anzuführen, ob E 1 nur von it oder auch von anderen Elementen besetzt werden kann" (1983: 33). In this quote he expresses his view on the pedagogic description of cases with impersonal *it* in subject position: when impersonal *it* occurs as a complement which cannot be substituted by other elements then the valency pattern should make it clear that impersonal *it* is the only subject of this particular adjective.

Seppänen (2002: 452–459) employs valency to analyse the status of impersonal *it* in constructions as *It is raining* or *It is cold.* He states that "[a]ll the verbs and multi-word predicates quoted above are – in the relevant weather sense – zero valent, rather than monovalent" (2002: 452). He does not give an analysis of the valency in constructions such as (1). Seppänen cites examples identical in structure to (17) where impersonal *it* is in direct object position and analysed as a placeholder for the *that*-clause following the adjective. This leads to the conclusion that the verb *make* is trivalent, taking a subject, a direct object and an object complement or PC, as Seppänen calls it. Herbst et al. (2004) also consider the verb *make* to be trivalent. Herbst et al. give the following valency pattern for *make* which describes (17) and (18): "+ N_P/V-ing$_P$ + ADJ / it + ADJ-pattern" (2004: 514).

(17) *In another extract Morton makes it clear that the Queen has supported Diana*. (CEK 2749)
(18) *Recent work makes us much less confident that any such clear correlation is possible*. (A6S 1278)

(17) consists of impersonal *it* followed by an adjective (*clear*) and a *that*-clause which is dependent on the valency pattern of the adjective. This is depicted in the valency pattern "+ it + ADJ-pattern". (18) consists of the object *us* and the adjective *confident* followed by a *that*-clause. The valency pattern "+ N_P + ADJ" describes this construction. It is clear from this outline that the *that*-clause is not part of the valency pattern of *make* but is a feature of the adjective.

5.2. Adjectives in the VDE

The distinction of adjectives into two classes (evaluative and experiential) is reflected in the valency patterns found in the VDE. Not all adjectives which have been considered in the empirical approach are listed in the VDE. Those that have been included in the VDE are presented with the following pattern description for each of the two classes of adjectives:

a) experiential adjectives: "+ (that)-CL" or "+ that-CL", and
b) evaluative adjectives: "[it] + (that)-CL" or "[it] + that-CL"

The valency pattern of experiential adjectives takes the form of a *that*-clause with or without the conjunction *that*. The adjective *surprised* is an experiential adjective and the valency pattern is reflected in the VDE in examples (19) without the conjunction *that* and in (20) with the conjunction *that*.

(19) "The family were *surprised* she'd found someone else so quickly." (Herbst et al. 2004: 834)
(20) "I was *surprised* that the police hadn't followed me to New York." (Herbst et al. 2004: 834)

Evaluative adjectives are also described in the VDE as being followed by *that*-clauses with or without the conjunction *that*. Additionally, all adjectives classified as evaluative in the empirical research are specified in the

VDE according to their subject: impersonal *it*. Examples for the evaluative adjective *possible* taken from the VDE are found in (21) and (22).

(21) "It was *possible* they had been at the gatehouse for only a few days." (Herbst et al. 2004: 600)
(22) "It is *possible* that he thought that by alliance with her his career would progress." (Herbst et al. 2004: 600)

The valency patterns in the VDE serve a descriptive and a pedagogic purpose. Its descriptive purpose is to provide the dictionary user with the most frequent valency patterns. This is reflected in the valency pattern for experiential and evaluative adjectives. Whereas experiential adjectives co-occur with a wide range of different intentional subjects, it has been outlined above that the most frequent form a non-intentional subject takes when co-occurring with an evaluative adjective is impersonal *it*. Almost 97% of all occurrences of evaluative adjectives are found with impersonal *it* in subject position. The pedagogic purpose of the valency patterns in the VDE is to give the dictionary user a clear outline of the valency for each adjective. The pedagogic purpose is fulfilled in that evaluative adjectives are all assigned the valency pattern "[it] + (that)-CL" or "[it] + that-CL" and experiential adjectives the valency pattern "+ (that)-CL" or "+ that-CL".

The adjectives *certain* and *sad* have been classified in the empirical research as belonging to both classes of adjectives. This is also reflected in the VDE. The adjective *certain* as an experiential adjective is assigned the valency pattern "+ (that)-CL" (Herbst et al. 2004: 120). An example from the VDE is (23). *Certain* co-occurs with an intentional subject and conveys an experiential meaning.

(23) "He was *certain* that no one he knew had seen him." (Herbst et al. 2004: 120)

As an evaluative adjective *certain* is assigned the valency pattern "[it] + (that)-CL" (Herbst et al. 2004: 120), an example from the VDE is shown in (24).

(24) "Now it seems *certain* that elections will go ahead." (Herbst et al. 2004: 120)

In (24) the evaluative adjective *certain* – similar in meaning to *true* – co-occurs with the non-intentional subject impersonal *it*.

The adjective *sad* has also been assigned two different valency patterns in the VDE: as an experiential adjective it is followed by a *that*-clause, reflected in the valency pattern "+ that-CL" (Herbst et al. 2004: 716), as an evaluative adjective it is described with the pattern "[it] + that-CL" (Herbst et al. 2004: 716). An example from the VDE for the experiential adjective *sad* is given in (25), for the evaluative adjective *sad* in (26).

(25) "I'm *sad* that we are leaving." (Herbst et al. 2004: 716)
(26) "He had a truly original talent, and it is *sad* that in the end there was so little to show for it." (Herbst et al. 2004: 716)

In (25) the experiential adjective *sad* co-occurs with the intentional subject *I*, the non-intentional subject impersonal *it* is found in (26) together with the evaluative adjective *sad*.

The adjective *clear* has been classified as an evaluative adjective. As has been outlined above it may also be found as an experiential adjective, co-occurring with an intentional subject. Of all cases of the pattern "*clear* + *that*-clause" in the empirical research only 2.9% occur with an intentional subject. In all of these cases, the adjective *clear* has an experiential meaning. This difference is also taken into account in the VDE. The adjective *clear* can be complemented by a *that*-clause, which is reflected in the valency pattern "+ that-CL" (Herbst et al. 2004: 137). *Clear* is also described as an evaluative adjective, corresponding to the valency pattern "[it] + (that)-CL" (Herbst et al. 2004: 137). Again, the examples given in the VDE clearly show that experiential *clear* co-occurs with intentional subjects ("I", "The security forces"; Herbst et al. 2004: 137), whereas evaluative *clear* co-occurs with impersonal *it*.[3] The frequency distribution based on the empirical research is also corroborated by the information found in the VDE. In the empirical research, the experiential adjective *clear* is only found in 2.9% of all cases, whereas the evaluative adjective *clear* accounts for 97.1% of all cases of the adjective *clear* in the pattern "adjective + *that*-clause". In contrast to the valency pattern "+ that-CL" the valency pattern "[it] + (that)-CL" is labelled "frequent" in the VDE (Herbst et al. 2004: 137).

6. Conclusion

The aim of the research reported here is twofold: first, a new classification of adjectives followed by *that*-clauses has been presented. Second, it has been demonstrated that this classification is also reflected in the valency patterns of adjectives given in the VDE.

The classification of adjectives into evaluative adjectives and experiential adjectives is based on more than 44,000 cases occurring in the pattern "adjective + conjunction *that*". By employing an empirical approach which neither rested on previous descriptions of adjectives nor attempted a preselection of cases it was possible to present a novel description of the pattern "adjective + conjunction *that*". This description not only leads to a new classification of adjectives, but also accounts for all cases in the pattern "adjective + conjunction *that*".

The results from the empirical approach are reflected in the valency patterns given in *A Valency Dictionary of English* (VDE). The VDE accounts for both classes of adjectives. Experiential adjectives co-occur with intentional subjects which take a wide range of forms and are therefore not accounted for in the VDE. Evaluative adjectives occur most frequently with only one subject: impersonal *it*. This is also reflected in the valency patterns of the VDE.

Notes

1. Cases of so-called object extraposition are not considered in this paper. They are discussed in Mindt forthcoming.
2. The pronoun *you* refers both to the singular and plural usage.
3. Two of the four examples in the VDE have the structure "make it clear that" as in "He has made it *clear* that he does not want the job." (Herbst et al., 2004: 137). These are considered as examples of object extraposition and are not part of the research reported in this paper. For more information on the structure *make it clear that* see Mindt forthcoming.

References

Biber, Douglas, Stig Johansson, Geoffrey Leech, Susan Conrad, and Edward Finegan
1999 *Longman Grammar of Spoken and Written English.* London: Longman.
Collins, Peter
1994 Extraposition in English. *Functions of Language* 1: 7–24.
Erdmann, Peter
1987 It-*Sätze im Englischen.* Heidelberg: Carl Winter.

Francis, Gill, Susan Hunston, and Elisabeth Manning
1996 *Collins COBUILD Grammar Patterns 2: Nouns and Adjectives.* London: HarperCollins.

Hair, Joseph F., Rolph E. Anderson, Ronald L. Tatham, and William C. Black
1998 *Multivariate Data Analysis.* New Jersey: Prentice Hall.

Herbst, Thomas
1983 *Untersuchungen zur Valenz englischer Adjektive und ihrer Nominalisierungen.* Tübingen: Narr.

Herbst, Thomas, David Heath, Ian F. Roe, and Dieter Götz
2004 *A Valency Dictionary of English. A Corpus-Based Analysis of the Complementation Patterns of English Verbs, Nouns and Adjectives.* Berlin: Mouton de Gruyter.

Householder, Fred. W. Jr., Dee Alexander, and Peter H. Matthews
1964 *Adjectives before That-Clauses in English.* Indiana University Linguistics Club, Indiana University. Indiana: Bloomington.

Huddleston, Rodney, and Geoffrey K. Pullum
2002 *The Cambridge Grammar of the English Language.* Cambridge: Cambridge University Press.

Hunston, Susan, and John Sinclair
2000 A local grammar of evaluation. In *Evaluation in text. Authorial Stance and the Construction of Discourse,* Susan Hunston, and Geoffrey Thompson (eds.), 74–101. Oxford: Oxford University Press.

Kaltenböck, Gunther
2004 *It-Extraposition and Non-Extraposition in English. A Study of Syntax in Spoken and Written Texts.* Wien: Braumüller.

Mindt, Ilka
forthc. Adjective complementation by *that*-clauses: An empirical study.

Quirk, Randolph, Sidney Greenbaum, Geoffrey Leech, and Jan Svartvik
1985 *A Comprehensive Grammar of the English Language.* London: Longman.

Seppänen, Aimo
2002 On analysing the pronoun *it*. *English Studies* 5: 442–462.

Valency rules? The case of verbs with propositional complements

Michael Klotz

1. Introduction

Almost 20 years ago Noam Chomsky (1986) suggested that syntactic valency properties of verbs (or c-selection in his terminology) may be seen as an automatic consequence of the semantic properties of the verb and its complements (or s-selection): "Let us assume that if a verb (or other head) s-selects a semantic category C, then it c-selects a syntactic category that is the 'canonical structural realisation of C' (CSR(C))" (Chomsky 1986: 87). Investigating the verb *persuade* he concludes that

> ... the lexical entry for *persuade* need only indicate that it s-selects two complements, one a goal, the other a proposition. All other features of the VP headed by *persuade* are determined by general properties of the UG. A child learning English must, of course, learn the meaning of the word *persuade* including its properties of s-selection ... . Nothing more must be learned ... . In particular, no properties of c-selection and no rules of phrase structure are required in this case. (Chomsky 1986: 88)

That these were more than just casual remarks can be seen from the fact that Chomsky reiterated that view nine years later in 1995, when he noted "... that subcategorization follows almost entirely from θ-role specification" (Chomsky 1995: 31).

Of course, most of the grammatical machinery that Chomsky proposed in the 1980s has been thrown overboard since, but the questions underlying his remarks remain: rephrased in valency terminology we might ask to which extent the syntactic valency of verbs can be reduced to semantic facts. Are there (semantically motivated) valency rules or must we consider valency as a purely lexical property of individual words? As Herbst suggests elsewhere in this volume, the two views at stake here are those of rule vs. storage.

If we accept the rule view for the moment, there seem to be at least three kinds of semantic basis from which the form type (cf. Huddleston and Pullum 2002: 1173) of complements could be deduced:

Firstly, the form type of the complement may depend on the meaning of the verb itself. In this vein, the *COBUILD Grammar Patterns 1: Verbs* (Francis, Hunston, and Manning 1996) correlates syntactic patterns with verb meanings. As John Sinclair puts it in the foreword (1996: iv): "… verbs can be subdivided according to pattern, and patterns can be seen to correlate with meaning – that is to say, verbs with similar patterns have similar meanings".

Secondly, the form may depend on the semantic (or theta) role relation between the valency carrier and its complement. This is what Chomsky seems to have in mind when he talks about subcategorisation following almost entirely from θ-role specification (see above).

Thirdly, the form type itself may be associated with meaning. Thus, in connection with non-finite clausal complements of verbs Quirk et al. (1985: 1191) suggest that "the infinitive gives a sense of mere 'potentiality' for action … while the participle gives a sense of the actual 'performance' of the action itself".

Other authors, however, doubt whether the syntactic valency behaviour of verbs can be predicted from such semantic facts. Thus Gazdar et al. (1985: 32) conclude "that there are restrictions on contexts of occurrence for lexical items which the grammar must specify, and which cannot be reduced to facts about meaning". Helbig (1992: 9) essentially takes the same line when he asserts, „[d]ass diese verschiedenen Valenzebenen nicht einfach isomorph aufeinander abbildbar sind“ [that these different levels of valency cannot be mapped isomorphically onto each other]. Noël (2003: 369) reviews several authors who believe that syntactic constructions are essentially semantically driven, but remains "convinced that in the absence of convincing evidence to the contrary the clausal complements of the kind considered here, do not have a different semantics". Huddleston and Pullum (2002: 1241) take an in-between position, asserting that "we cannot assign distinct meanings to the form-types and treat the selection as semantically determined. On the other hand, the selection is not random: verbs with similar meanings tend to select the same form-types …".

The present study is a contribution to this ongoing discussion. In particular, it will attempt to empirically test the assumption of a correlation between the lexical meaning of and syntactic patterning around a valency carrier by investigating the data contained in the *Valency Dictionary of English* (Herbst et al. 2004). Taking its lead from Chomsky's *persuade* example, the study focuses on verbs which take propositions as arguments. Although on the syntactic level these propositional arguments can be realised in a considerable variety of ways, we will limit ourselves to cases where the entire valency pattern to the right of the verb is made up alternatively by the following three basic form types:

VERB +	that-clause N to-INF N V-ing

The latter two non-finite constructions will be considered as the most important constructional equivalents to the *that-clause*, because like the *that-clause* they also overtly express subject and predicate.

The following discussion will provide statistical data which shed some light on the following two hypotheses:

- Hypothesis 1:
  That-clause, *N to-INF* and *N V-ing* are constructional synonyms of each other, i.e. they can replace each other in the same context (i.e. after a given verb).
- Hypothesis 2:
  Differences in complementation behaviour correspond to differences in verb meaning.

2. *That-clause*, *N to-INF* and *N V-ing* as constructional synonyms

In order to test hypothesis 1, all occurrences of the above mentioned three form types as complements to verbs were extracted from the electronic text of the *Valency Dictionary of English*. Here it has to be pointed out that both non-finite form types can be further subdivided so that we are actually not looking at three single form types but rather three families of form types. For example, with respect to the *N to-INF* as well as *N V-ing* type the *Valency Dictionary of English* differentiates between cases like *expect* and *leave* where the noun phrase can become subject of the passivised matrix clause and cases such as *demand* and *mind* where it cannot. Compare the following examples from the *Valency Dictionary of English* (VDE) and the *British National Corpus* (BNC):

(1)	a.	*This year I* ***expect*** *market conditions ... to improve somewhat ...* VDE	N_p to-INF
	b.	*The meeting is* ***expected*** *to last two days.* VDE	
(2)	a.	*I* ***left*** *the engine running and the lights on.* VDE	N_p V-ing

	b.	*Thomas Seton was **left** dangling in the air, swinging and twitching grotesquely* ... BNC	
(3)	a.	*They **demanded** more planes to be made available.* VDE	N to-INF
	b.	**More planes were demanded to be made available.*	
(4)	a.	*Where're you from, if you don't **mind** me asking?* VDE	N V-ing
	b.	* ... *if I am not **minded** asking.*	

Both types were included in the count. Also included was the *N INF* type as well as the *for N to-INF* type; the latter because the introductory *for* acts as a construction marker (Matthews 1981: 59–61; cf. also Allerton 1982: 16–17) rather than a lexical preposition.

(5)	*Instantly, unmistakably, he **felt** her recoil.* VDE	N INF
(6)	*Originally the scheme **allowed** for pensions to be calculated on the best twenty years of earnings.* VDE	for N to-INF

In contrast, constructions with prepositions followed by *N V-ing* as in *account for them being here* were excluded from the statistics, because here the prepositions are much more variable and lexical in character. They often form a semantic unit with the verb, i.e. a prepositional verb in the sense of Quirk et al. (1985: 1150–1167). In the following we will revert to simply talking about form types, but it should be born in mind that this includes their respective variants.

Combining the three form types in all logically possible ways results in seven complementation classes:

Table 1. Seven complementation classes

	that-CL	N to-INF	N V-ing
class 1	×	×	×
class 2	×	×	
class 3	×		×
class 4		×	×
class 5	×		
class 6		×	
class 7			×

The *Valency Dictionary of English* contains 511 verbs. Of these, 211 take one or several of the form types under study as their second complement. The following statistics show the number of verbs in each group.

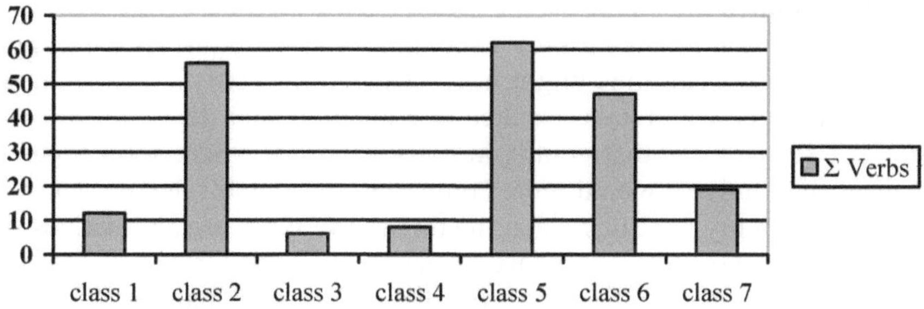

Figure 1. Number of verbs in each complement class

Several points are immediately apparent:

- Firstly, class 1 verbs which alternatively take all three form types as their second complement are relatively rare.
- Secondly, none of the seven groups is empty; this means that there is no form type which actually occurs with all verbs that take propositional complementation. Thus none of the three form types could be called a canonical realisation of propositional arguments in the sense that it could be applied invariably across the board whenever a propositional argument needs to be encoded in a grammatical form.
- Thirdly, the distribution of verbs across the classes is very uneven. Thus the *that-clause* and the *N to-INF* construction in class 2 are more likely alternants of each other than the *that-clause* and *N V-ing* in class 3.
- Fourthly, it is common for verbs to allow only one form type as realisation of the propositional argument. In fact, class 5 verbs which allow a *that-clause* but none of the non-finite constructions constitute the largest group.

The picture that emerges is complex but it clearly contradicts Chomsky's suggestion that the formal realisation is largely an automatic consequence of the propositional character of the argument. However, some important qualifications to the statistics presented above are in order.

Firstly, the statistics give the number of verbal lexemes in each class. However, it is generally accepted that valency is not a property of lexemes but rather of lexical units in Cruse's (1986: 80) sense, i.e. understood as "the union of a single sense with a lexical form". Thus, the co-occurrence of two form types in the valency of one verb in the statistics above does not mean that the two form types actually are constructional synonyms; they may just as well belong to different senses. However, using lexical units instead of lexemes in statistics of the above kind would have increased the complexity of the count considerably, all the more since the lexical unit is only well defined in theory.

For that reason it seemed safer to count lexemes and just speculate about how counting lexical units might have changed the statistics. Since counting lexical units would have resulted in a much greater degree of diversification, it seems clear that counts in classes 1 to 4, where form types co-occur as alternatives, would have come out considerably lower. The view emerging from my statistics – that the three form types are alternatives only to a very limited extent – would have been strengthened further.

The second qualification concerns those verbs which allow *N to-INF* or *N V-ing* but no *that-clause*. For a number of verbs there are good syntactic reasons which prevent the *that-clause*, as appears from the examples below, and these verbs should be counted separately.

(7)	*But in your particular case I* ***prefer*** *the precautions to be extreme.* VDE	N to-INF
(8)	*... their parents will have to attend a meeting of the school governors to try to* ***convince*** *them not to go ahead with the expulsion.* VDE	N + to-INF

The *N to-INF* type after *prefer* and *convince* as they can be seen in these example sentences are only superficially similar. Following Huddleston and Pullum (2002: 1201), we can draw a distinction between a raised object after verbs like *prefer* and an ordinary object after verbs like *convince*. Essentially, *prefer* must be seen as a verb taking two arguments whereas *convince* takes three. The *Valency Dictionary of English* makes the same distinction by distinguishing *N to-INF* from *N + to-INF* patterns.

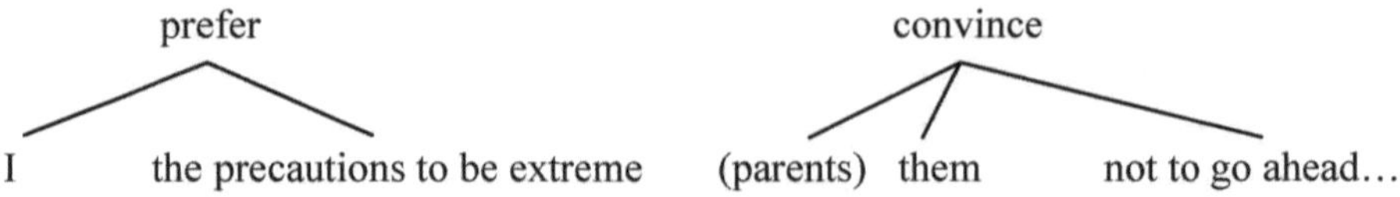

Since the *that-clause* always realises only one argument, it cannot replace *N + to-INF*, i.e. those cases, where *N* and *to-INF* have to be seen as realisations of separate arguments. The same is true for the *N V-ing* type respectively and the statistics have to take this distinction into account.

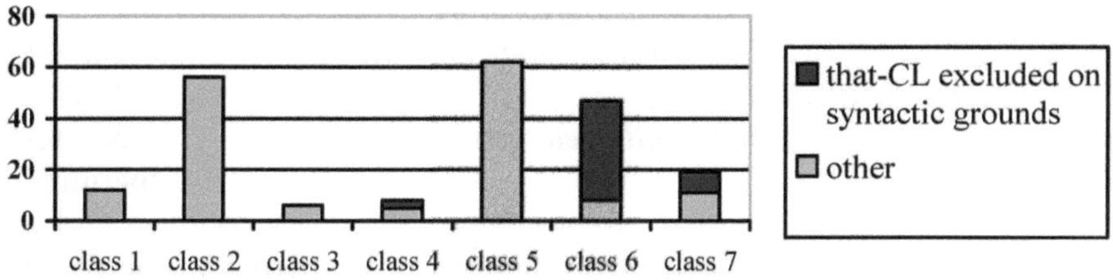

Figure 2. Number of verbs in each complement class – amended

The amended graph therefore shows those cases where the *that-clause* is excluded on syntactic grounds in dark grey. As can be seen, the number of cases where the *that-clause* does not function as an alternative to the *N to-INF* or *N V-ing* type as realisation of one argument is much more limited now. Thus, the *that-clause* is certainly the one form type which comes closest to being the canonical realisation of a propositional argument, however without being applicable in all cases either.

3. The correspondence of verb meaning and complement form type

We will now turn to hypothesis 2 and restate it here for matters of convenience:

– Hypothesis 2: differences in complementation behaviour correspond to differences in verb meaning.

To test the hypothesis, verbs were semantically classified for complementation classes 5 and 2, i.e. those verbs which only allow for a *that-clause* and those which alternatively admit the *N to-INF* type. With respect to the latter only those verbs were counted where the *that-clause* and *N to-INF* represented real alternatives. As has already been pointed out, two requirements have to be met for this:

Firstly, the *N to-INF* type has to represent a single argument. This excludes verbs like *promise*, where *N* and *to-INF* actually represent separate arguments.

(9) *She*$_{A1}$ *promised Beryl*$_{A2}$ *to keep an eye on him*$_{A3}$. VDE

Secondly, both form types have to be complements to the same lexical unit. This excludes verbs like *allow*, which has clearly different meanings in combination with the *that-clause* and *N to-INF*.

(10)	*I certainly would* ***allow*** *that things had taken an unfortunate turn.* VDE	+ that-CL 'admit'
(11)	*... my wife has never* ***allowed*** *me to see them.* VDE	+ N + to-INF 'permit'

In the analysis 112 verbal lexical units were classified into the following semantic groups:

- communication verbs: *add, admit, beg, claim, command, demand, deny, direct, explain, indicate, insist, joke, lie, maintain, object, pronounce, question, request, respond, rule, say, shout, signal, (let) slip, state, swear, threaten, whisper, write ...;*
- opinion verbs: *accept, agree, assume, believe, bet, conceive, consider, doubt, fear, gather, guess, know, question, suppose, suspect, think, trust*;
- fact finding verbs: *calculate, conclude, decide, establish, estimate, judge, learn, read, realize/realise, reason, recognise/recognize, reflect*;
- fact demonstrating verbs: *confirm, indicate, prove, reveal*;
- fact manipulating verbs: *conceal, hide, ignore*;
- fact establishing verbs: *arrange, check, ensure, guarantee, intend, plan, pretend, provide*;
- emotion verbs: *pray, desire, hate, hope*;
- imagination verbs: *dream, suppose;*
- unclassified: *respect, vote, wonder.*

The groups can be characterised in the following way: *communication verbs* constitute the largest class by far. As the name suggests, they all have in common that the proposition is communicated to somebody. Frequently, though not always, these verbs allow complementation by a direct quote. This latter fact distinguishes them from the *opinion verbs*; these verbs essentially express the AGENT's stance towards the truth value of the proposition on a scale from certainty (*know, believe*) to disbelief *(doubt*). *Fact finding verbs* are similar to opinion verbs, but in contrast to those they have an inchoative element to their meaning. Thus *realise* could be paraphrased as 'come to believe'. *Fact demonstrating verbs* also lead to opinions about the truth of a proposition, but their AGENTS are not those individuals who come to have these opinions; in fact, the AGENTS need not be animate at all. *Fact manipulating verbs* are those which signify some reaction by the AGENT to a true proposition. *Fact establishing verbs* like *check, guarantee* and *provide* put the onus on the AGENT to make the proposition a true one.

Emotion verbs signify the emotional stance of the AGENT towards the proposition. Nothing about the truth value of the proposition is implied. The group includes verbs like *pray, hope* and *wish*. Finally, there are the *imagination verbs dream* and *suppose*. Like emotion verbs they leave the truth value of the proposition entirely open, but they do not express an emotional stance either.

A few remarks about this semantic classification are in order: firstly, no claim is being made as to the completeness of these groups. There may be more semantic groups and the groups established may contain further verbs. Secondly, it is clear that polysemic verbs can occur in more than one semantic class. Thus *suppose* is an opinion verb in (12) and an imagination verb in (13).

(12)	*She **supposed** that there was a copy of the book in the library.* VDE	'believe'
(13)	***Suppose** somebody found an unlimited supply of energy ...*	'imagine'

Thirdly, there are a few verbs which could not be subsumed in any one of the semantic groups, but their number is surprisingly small. Most verbs could be included in one of the groups with some degree of confidence although it is clear that the groups should be seen as prototype categories which allow for some gradience. Such gradience is exemplified by the verb *fear* in

(14) *I **fear** that John will be late again.*

Like *hope* and *wish* it expresses an emotional stance towards the proposition. But in contrast to these emotional verbs it also expresses the AGENT'S stance towards the truth value of the proposition: a useful paraphrase might be 'I believe that John will be late again and I dislike this possibility'. For that reason, *fear* was classified as an opinion verb in the analysis.

The following graph shows the correlation between the semantic groups outlined above and complementation classes 2 and 5.

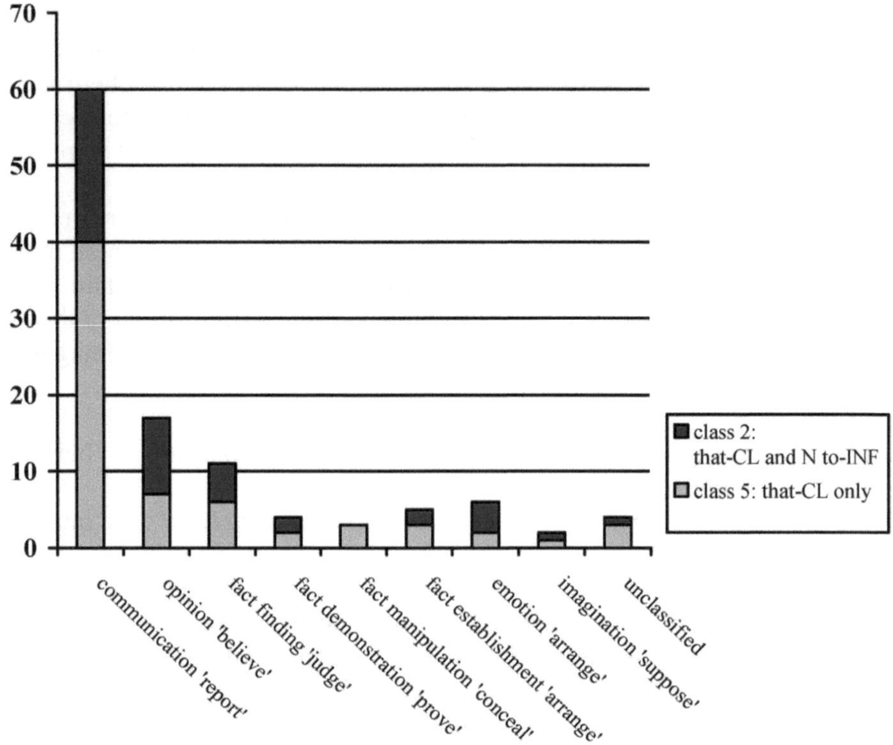

Figure 3. Correlation between semantic classes and complementation classes 2 and 5

It is immediately apparent that both complementation classes co-occur with all semantic groups. The only exception to this is the small group of the three fact manipulating verbs *hide, conceal* and *ignore*. However, given the small size of the group it is not clear whether this is actually a correlation between semantic and valency properties or simply a coincidence. Apart from this there is very little to suggest that the realisational possibilities of a propositional argument could be predicted from the meaning of the verb to which it belongs. The χ^2 test lends support to this conclusion: at df = 8 the resulting χ^2 value of 7.7 is only about half of what would be necessary for a significant result at the 95% level of confidence.

Slightly more significant results can be obtained, if we just compare the two largest groups, verbs of communication and opinion:

Table 2. Correlation between two semantic groups and complement classes 2 and 5

	communication verbs	opinion verbs
class 2	20	10
class 5	40	7

χ^2 (df = 1, N = 67) = 3,61
χ^2 (necessary for 95% confidence level with df = 1) = 3,84

Here we might tentatively conclude that communication verbs prefer the *that-clause* only, whereas opinion verbs show a slight preference for having *that-clause* and *N to-INF* as alternatives. However, even this distribution does not result in a χ^2-value which would be significant at the 95% level of confidence, although it is close to it.

Assuming that this distribution is not just coincidence, we are still nowhere near anything that might be called a regularity. If anything, it is rather a tendency, which begs the question whether such tendencies have a role to play from a psycholinguistic point of view. Although they obviously do not allow to make any predictions, one might suggest that the psycholinguistic correlate to such statistical tendencies may be certain expectations in the speaker which allow the speaker to retrieve the actual valency patterns more easily from memory.

In sum it seems fair to say that the statistical analysis of complementation data from the *Valency Dictionary of English* does not lend support to the view that the valency of a verb can be deduced from its meaning. The storage view of valency which sees it as an irregular lexical rather than semantically rule-based phenomenon is strengthened further.

References

Allerton David J.
1982 *Valency and the English Verb*. London/New York: Academic Press.
Chomsky, Noam
1986 *Knowledge of Language: Its Nature, Origin and Use*. New York: Praeger Publishers.
1995 *The Minimalist Program*. Cambridge, Mass.: Massachusetts Institute of Technology Press.
Cruse, David A.
1986 *Lexical Semantics*. Cambridge: Cambridge University Press.
Francis, Gill, Susan Hunston, and Elizabeth Manning
1996 *Collins Cobuild Grammar Patterns 1: Verbs*. London/Glasgow: HarperCollins.

Gazdar, Gerald, Ewan Klein, Geoffrey K. Pullum, and Ivan A. Sag
1985 *Generalized Phrase Structure Grammar*. Cambridge, Mass.: Harvard University Press.

Helbig, Gerhard
1992 *Probleme der Valenz- und Kasustheorie*. Tübingen: Max Niemeyer Verlag

Herbst, Thomas
2007 Valency complements or valency patterns? This volume.

Herbst, Thomas, David Heath, Ian Roe, and Dieter Götz (eds.)
2004 *A Valency Dictionary of English*. Berlin/New York: Mouton de-Gruyter.

Huddleston, Rodney, and Geoffrey K. Pullum
2002 *The Cambridge Grammar of the English Language*. Cambridge: Cambridge University Press.

Matthews, Peter H.
1981 *Syntax*. Cambridge: Cambridge University Press.

Noël, Dirk
2003 Is there semantics in all syntax? The case of accusative and infinitive constructions vs. that-clauses. In *Determinants of Grammatical Variation in English,* Günter Rohdenburg, and Britta Mondorf (eds.), 347–377. Berlin/New York: Mouton de Gruyter.

Quirk, Randolph, Sydney Greenbaum, Geoffrey Leech, and Jan Svartvik
1985 *A Comprehensive Grammar of the English Language*. London: Longman.

Valency issues in FrameNet[1]

Charles J. Fillmore

1. Introduction

This chapter describes the assumptions and practices of the Berkeley FrameNet project and shows how these have led to a particular treatment of the concept of *valency*.[2] The FrameNet project is dedicated to producing valency descriptions of frame-bearing *lexical units* (*LUs*)[3], in both semantic and syntactic terms, and it bases this work on attestations of word usage taken from a very large digital corpus. The semantic descriptors of each valency pattern are taken from frame-specific semantic role names (called *frame elements*), and the syntactic terms are taken from a restricted set of grammatical function names and a detailed set of phrase types. Sentences extracted from the British National Corpus provide both the empirical evidence for the analysis and an example database for both human and machine users. Sentences in the example database, chosen to illustrate each of the lexical units we analyze, are annotated according to the LU's semantic and syntactic combinatory properties, and the valency patterns are automatically derived from the annotations.

The treatment of valency in the FrameNet database differs from certain other electronic lexical resources in several ways, by: (1) relying on corpus evidence; (2) basing the semantic layer of valency on an understanding of the cognitive *frames* that motivate and underlie the meanings of each lexical unit; (3) recognizing various kinds of discrepancy between units on the semantic/functional level and patterns of syntactic form; and (4) providing the means of assigning partial interpretations to valents that are conceptually present, but syntactically unexpressed.

After a brief introduction to the work of the FrameNet project and a summary of the kinds of information it produces, the discussion will proceed to the special nature of building a frame-based dictionary and the ways in which such a commitment leads the analyst to a "splitting" rather than "lumping" approach to polysemy, ending with a survey of the discrepancies between the frame structures evoked by particular LUs and the syntactic structures which realize them.

2. The project

FrameNet is a lexicon-building project, one of whose missions is to construct valency descriptions for frame-bearing words in English – verbs, nouns, and adjectives, as well as some adverbs and prepositions. The meaning of *frame* and the scope of *valency* have determined the unique features of the descriptions produced by this research.

The project is administered at the International Computer Science Institute in Berkeley, California, and is in its eighth year. The original aim was purely lexicographic, but in recent years the project has taken on a number of frame-based *full-text semantic annotation* assignments.[4] The National Science Foundation provided two three-year grants for the lexicographic work[5] and two sub-contracts for text-analysis;[6] further support has been provided by the DARPA[7] and ARDA[8] agencies of the U. S. government.

Two important methodological and theoretical commitments assumed for FrameNet are the *corpus*[9] and the *frame* (Fillmore and Atkins 1992, 1994; Fontenelle 2003). We use corpus evidence to derive information about the combinatory possibilities of English lexical units, and to characterize the manner in which phrases that are grammatically dependent on the LU fill in details about the semantic frames which underlie each LU.

The process starts with extracting sample sentences from the corpus containing the words being examined, determining which of these contain instances of the LU under analysis, selecting sentences that show the varieties of that LU's combinatory properties in perspicuous ways, and annotating these with respect to their syntactic and frame-semantic properties.

The word *frame*[10] in this context is used to refer to a schematic representation of speakers' knowledge of the situations or states of affair that underlie the meanings of lexical items. The named components of a frame, called *frame elements* (*FEs*), stand for the participants, props, phases, and parts of the kinds of situations named by the frame.[11] For very schematic frames, such as those involving simple movement, the main FEs can be quite abstract: Theme (an object seen as moving), Source (the starting point of a movement), Goal (the endpoint or destination of a movement), and Path (information relevant to the itinerary of the movement). In sentence (1) below, the subject (*the horse*) expresses the Theme and the prepositional phrase (*out of the barn*) the Source. For narrowly defined frames involving complex scenarios, they can be quite specific. For example, in the Revenge frame, we recognize Avenger (the individual who carries out an act of revenge), Offender (the individual whose prior act is to be punished through an act on the part of the avenger's), Injured_party (the individual who is harmed or offended by the offender, who of course might be identical to the

Avenger), Injury (the act or insult perpetrated on the injured party), and Punishment (the act carried out on the offender by the avenger). In sentence (2) the subject (*I*) expresses the Avenger, the prepositional phrase (*at him*) is taken as indicating the Offender, and the prepositional gerund (*for insulting my sister*) stands for the Injury and indirectly indicates the Injured_party.

(1) [*The horse*] ***bolted*** [*out of the barn*].[12]
(2) [*I*] ***got back*** [*at him*] [*for insulting my sister*].

The segmentation seen in these examples show an important feature of FrameNet annotation. Since the purpose is to link the syntactic valents of the governing LU with its semantic valents, the syntactic and morphological *markers* of the relevant phrases are included in the sentence segmentations: thus, in the case of sentences (1–2), the words *out of*, *at*, and *for* are included within the marked-off phrases.

With respect to the naming of frame elements, we learned early that for many of the complex frames there is no non-arbitrary way of fitting them into the "standard" sets of *case roles* or *thematic roles* in recent literature,[13] except perhaps for the association of the familiar "Agent" with the primary active participant in a scene, e.g., the Avenger in the case of the Revenge frame.[14]

Using FrameNet terminology, a (frame-bearing[15]) lexical unit *evokes* a frame and a *valency description* of a given lexical unit presents the set of ways in which the syntactic accompaniments of the lexical unit introduce information about the meaning elements of the evoked frame – or, stated the other way around, the ways in which the semantic valents are expressed in the sentence or phrase built around the frame-bearing unit. Since words with different context requirements can evoke the same frame, the alignment of syntactic and semantic valents needs to be specified LU by LU.[16] For example, the grammatical markings of the Offender for various expressions in the Revenge vocabulary include simple direct object position in the case of *pay (someone) back*, and a variety of prepositional markings, as with *retaliation* ***against***, *get even* **with**, *wreak vengeance* ***on***, *get back* ***at***.

Since there are kinds of text annotation that seek to connect all of the information found in a sentence or text as tightly as possible, and since FrameNet examples are not limited to simple finite sentences, the limits of FrameNet annotation practice need to be made clear. In particular, for each targeted LU FrameNet annotates, just those realizations of the frame's FEs which are *in grammatical construction with* the LU itself. That is, for lexicographic purposes FrameNet records the amount of information about a frame that is provided in grammatically relevant positions within phrases headed by the LU that evokes the frame.[17]

Suppose we were to select sentence (3) as illustrative of the use of the verb *send out*:

(3) *My attorney requested the files early last week, and* [*they*] *were* ***sent out*** *the following morning.*

FrameNet annotation would record for the token of *send out* in this sentence that the pronoun *they* expresses one of its frame elements, as subject of the passive form of the verb, and that the other two FEs (the Sender and the Destination) are not locally identified *within the grammatical structure headed by that verb*.[18] This is distinct from the kind of annotation, built on principles of discourse coherence, that would probabilistically recognize that in the world of the text, *my attorney* stands for the intended recipient of this sending act and *the files* are the things that got sent. Since the phrases *my attorney* and *the files* hold no grammatical relation to the verb *sent* in this sentence, they are not part of the FrameNet annotation for this token of the verb in this sentence.[19] In other words, given FrameNet's lexicographic purposes, FrameNet sentence annotations alone cannot be interpreted as marking all of the participants in the situations evoked by the lexical units analyzed; sometimes frame-relevant information is outside of the valency range of the relevant lexical units.

3. The product

The database produced from FrameNet activities includes:[20]

1. a collection of informally characterized *frame descriptions*, including the assignment of names and definitions to the *frame elements*;
2. the set of *annotations* for each lexical unit, where each sentence is annotated with respect to one token of the LU whose function is illustrated in it;[21]
3. *lexical entries*, which identify, for each LU, the frame itself, and the variety of ways in which individual FEs are syntactically realized in the corpus (including zero realization), together with the full patterns of FE realizations found in individual sentences;[22] and
4. a network of *frame-to-frame relations*, showing how some frames are elaborations of others, how some frames are components of others, and so on.[23]

3.1. Frames

There are at present more than 700 frames recognized in the FN database. Frame descriptions are formulated informally, using the frame element names in definitional contexts as ways of indicating the frame elements. Among the collection of frames is one called Arranging, the description of which reads as follows: an Agent puts a complex Theme into a Configuration, which can be a proper order, a correct or suitable sequence, or spatial position.

The frame description mentions the *core* frame elements, Agent, Theme and Configuration. Non-core, or *peripheral* frame elements are separately described, and these include Manner, Location, Means, and several others. The core vs. periphery distinction is analogous to, but not identical with, the distinction in Tesnière (1959) between *actants* and *circonstants*. Core elements are those which are necessary to the central meaning of the frame, and peripheral elements provide aspects of the setting which can modify any frame of the relevant type, i.e., act, state, happening, or the like. The category *core* is not limited to obligatory elements, since we distinguish two main functions of missing FEs, and these apply only to core FEs. The distinction does not separate nuclear from "oblique" syntactic constituents, since many core FEs are expressed adverbially or in prepositional phrases. Core prepositional phrases can have their prepositions explicitly selected by the head LU; peripheral prepositional phrases have forms determined by their meaning, independently of the frame to which they are attached.

In order to have GF labels on all the phrases around a lexical governor, FrameNet annotations provide a third kind of FE, called *extrathematic*, a word or phrase which can be thought of as introducing a new frame, rather than filling out the details of the frame evoked by the head. Comparing sentences (4) and (5), we can see that each of them provides two layers of information about the same event. The Letter_writing frame gives the content of the event, and the Revenge frame gives an evaluation or interpretation of the event in respect to a larger scheme. The brackets decorating sentence (4) show core FEs in square brackets, peripheral in parentheses, and the extrathematic *in retaliation* in wavy brackets. A sentence bearing essentially the same information is sentence (5).

(4) [*She*] ***wrote*** [*the letter*] (*yesterday*) {*in retaliation*}.
(5) *Yesterday she retaliated by writing a letter to my boss.*

The fact that we cannot depend on a syntactic analysis that places such "adjuncts" outside the scope of the verbal predicator is suggested by the

VP-internal presence of a Beneficiary in certain sentences, e.g., in an apparent direct object position in a double-NP construction. Comparing sentences (6) and (7), note that the person indicated as *my sister* is a core participant in the activity designated by the verb *sell* in (6), but is understood as an intended participant in a secondary act in (7).

(6) [*I*] ***sold*** [*my sister*] [*a harmonica*].
(7) [*I*] ***bought*** {*my sister*} [*a harmonica*].

Recognizing *my sister* as the Beneficiary in (7) is acknowledging that this sentence evokes a complex scenario involving two phases or sub-events: the purchase of the harmonica and its subsequent presentation to the speaker's sister.

3.2. Annotations

As of this writing the FrameNet database has approximately 150,000 annotation sets,[24] each representing one valency possibility of a single target LU as exhibited in the sentence. Though there are large differences in the representativeness of attestations between highly frequent and infrequently occurring members of a given frame, the general goal is to include a small number of examples of each observed syntactic context. FrameNet does not present relative frequency information for frames, lexical units, or valency patterns, assuming that such information should be derived by procedures sensitive to genre, register, regional variation, and the like.

For the verb *arrange* in the Arranging frame we find such examples as those seen in figure 1.

[Agent *He*] [target *ARRANGED*] [Theme *the jharo*] [Configuration *in two pyramids*] [Location *at the edge of the roof, between the flowers*].

[target *ARRANGE*] [Theme *rice*] [Configuration *in a ring*] and place chicken in the centre. [Agent CNI]

[Theme *The waxworks*] *were* [target *ARRANGED*] [Configuration *in groups*] [Location *beyond a rope, which was supposed to separate them from their admirers*]. [Agent CNI]

Place a slice of avocado over each slice of grapefruit and [target *ARRANGE*] [Manner *attractively*] [Configuration *in lines down a serving plate*]. [Agent CNI] [Theme CNI]

Figure 1. Arranging.*arrange*.v: tagging of phrases by their frame element name

The annotations displayed in these samples identify only the constituent boundaries and the frame element name. In the corresponding XML representation the information characterizing the form of each syntactic valent is expressed, in two separate layers, in terms of *grammatical functions* and *phrase types*.

The principal GF names are External, Object, and Dependent: a distinction corresponding to that between arguments and adjuncts is not shown at the level of grammatical function, but in terms of the core vs. non-core distinction discussed above. Additional GFs are Appositive, Modifier, Head, Genitive, and Quantifier, important especially for nouns.

External and Dependent need special explanations. The External GF corresponds not only to the subject of a finite sentence, but also to the phrases that stand for the subject function of non-finite verbs, e.g., the controllers of subject roles in Raising and Equi constructions and subordinated participial constructions, and to the primary arguments of frame-bearing nouns and predicatively used adjectives. We do not use "Subject" because in many cases the relevant constituent is not, in its own location, a subject of anything, and because it does not seem natural to use the term as a GF of a noun. Thus, with annotations centered on the verb *release*, as in sentences (8) and (9), we categorize *the general's* (the Genitive modifier of *decision*) and *the general* (the Object of *persuade*) as the External argument of *release* in those contexts, and as being in grammatical construction with the target verb.

(8) *The [general's] decision to **release** the prisoners was surprising.*
(9) *We persuaded [the general] to **release** the prisoners.*

The decision to annotate these elements at all comes from the history of FrameNet annotation practice: we do not work with parsed sentences, within which controllers could in principle be recovered, and we have wanted the annotations to yield collocational information about "subjects" (here between *general* and the VP *release the prisoners*). Even a very large corpus cannot always be relied on to present examples for each verb in which a lexical subject (as opposed to a pronoun) is adjacent to a finite verb.

The function name Dependent is a cover term for all other dependents of an ordinary verbal predicate. Thus the "second object" in V+NP+NP patterns and their transformations is referred to as Dependent, i.e., as an "oblique nominal"[25], one of the areas in which the FrameNet annotation does not preserve theory-neutrality.

The phrase types recognized in FrameNet are those that we believe are relevant for the description of the lexically specified canonical syntactic contexts of English frame-bearing words, corresponding more or less to traditional *subcategorization features.* A near-exhaustive classification of such contexts can be found in Atkins, Fillmore, and Johnson (2003: 277–279).

3.3. Lexical entries

The lexical entry database includes for each LU a reference to its frame, a simple definition,[26] indications of how each FE is grammatically represented (the *complement inventories*, in Thomas Herbst's presentation), and patterns of FE realization (the *valency patterns*) found in corpus-attested sentences.[27]

Current valency pattern displays – automatically derived from the annotations – are organized in a brute force way, with the FEs in alphabetical order and the realizations given as pairs of grammatical function (GF) and phrase type. Figure 2 is a fragment of the valency description provided for the verb *accuse*, which is in the Judgment_communication frame, the frame for a situation in which a Communicator (the person uttering a judgment) speaks negatively of an Evaluee (the person whose behavior is being judged) and offers (or is understood to have) a Reason for this judgment. The active use is shown by the examples in which the Communicator has the GF "External" (Subject) and the Evaluee has the GF Object; in the passive use the Evaluee is the subject and the Communicator is realized either as CNI (unexpressed for constructional reasons) or as PP (by), i.e., with the preposition *by*. The Reason is given with the preposition *of* followed by either a NP or a gerund, or it is missing and given the DNI interpretation.

Total (54)	*Communicator*	*Evaluee*	*Reason*
(2)	CNI ---	NP Ext	PP(of) Dep
(9)	CNI ---	NP Ext	PPing(of) Dep
(4)	NP Ext	NP Obj	DNI ---
(8)	NP Ext	NP Obj	PP(of) Dep
(19)	NP Ext	NP Obj	PPing(of) Dep
(1)	PP(by) Dep	NP Ext	DNI ---

Figure 2. Fragment of the valency description for the verb *accuse*

The numbers in the left-most column indicate the number of sentences receiving the coding found on that line. The relevant part of a sentence for the first line is *Anyone could be arrested and accused of communist sympathies*. An example of the pattern shown in the fourth line is [*In your editorial*] *you accuse the Australian government of hypocrisy*. An example of the most common pattern, with *of*+gerund, is *The Defence Minister Moshe Arens accused the Fatah-affiliated Black Panther group of carrying out the attack*. The Reason is shown as DNI in the third and last lines, meaning that it is understood as contextually "given"; an example from the annotations is *Now she was accusing me in front of a stranger*.

In the case of *accuse* the alphabetical order of the FE names coincides accidentally with the familiar ranking of GFs, but in many cases this is not the case. Eventually the valencies will be shown in a normalized abstract form from which all of the actual realizations can be predicted, and this will require the identification of the nuclear GFs (subject in the case of verbs and adjectives, subject and object in the case of transitive verbs, parallels of these in the case of nouns derived from verbs or adjectives) together with information about lexically licensed valent omissibility.

With frame-evoking nouns of a particular type we occasionally find that a lexical unit that evokes a frame is itself (or is the lexical head of) the constituent in the sentence which represents one of the frame's FEs. This is true, for example, of the 'product' interpretation of the noun *replacement* in a sentence like *We need a replacement for this part*. Here the Replacement frame is evoked by the noun, and the NP *a replacement* counts as one of the FEs of that same frame (the other being *for this part*).

3.4. Frame-to-Frame relations

A system of frame-to-frame relations links semantically related frames to each other in any of several ways. One frame can be seen as a sub-type of another (*inheritance* relation), or as a component of another (*subframe* relation), or frames can be related as cause-effect (*causative* relation), or event-state (*inchoative* relation). There is also what we call a *perspectivizing* relation, by which one frame is seen as taking a point of view on a more abstract frame.

As an example (that isn't as perfect as it should be, but will do for illustrating the point), the verbs *buy*, *sell*, *pay* and *charge* have uses in which they give, or imply, information about the main individual transactions in a commercial event. They differ, however, in how they highlight the human participants' relation to the goods or the money. From one point of view, then, they all are capable of indexing all of the participants in a well-defined commercial event – and therefore can support inference operations about which party ended up owning the money and which ended up owning the goods – but *buy* and *charge* are instances of Taking, and *sell* and *pay* are instances of Giving, from the perspective of one human participant, and at the same time *buy* and *sell* are instances of Goods_transfer while *pay* and *charge* are instances of Money_transfer.

Certain kinds of semantic inferences can be read off of frame descriptions by way of frame-to-frame relations. For certain purposes, such informal descriptions appear to be satisfactory, since the descriptions can be the same – or can be paraphrases of each other – for a great many frames across languages. Sentences that report instances of the same frame, with FE instances being translations of each other, can at least partially be accepted as translation of each other. For more technical purposes, e.g., inferencing, the mapping of frame descriptions to semantic simulations or to logical expressions may be possible, but this is not included in the principal activity of the FrameNet researchers.[28]

A fragment of a display of such links, centered in Placing, is seen in figure 3.

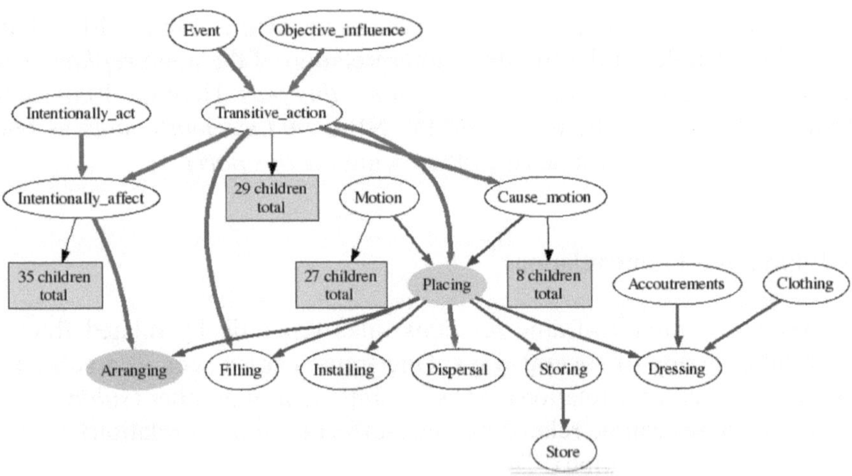

Figure 3. A fragment of a display showing frame-to-frame relations among a set of frames centered in Placing (i.e., putting something in a place). The various relations include inheritance and using.

The interpretation of the different relations indicated by the arrows (colored in various ways on the website) can be found on the FrameNet public website.

4. Frame-based vs. word-based progression

By working one frame at a time, rather than one word at a time from an alphabetical word list, frame-based lexicography necessarily pays attention to paraphrase relations and postpones thorough treatment of polysemy structures. That is, when we look for all the expressions that can be called on to talk about a particular well-defined situation type, we cannot simultaneously look into all of the *other* meanings of each of the words in our list.

Word-by-word lexicography, the traditional way to build dictionaries, tends to include all the senses[29] of each of the words *that have been included so far*. When an ordinary dictionary project is mid-way in its work there will be many words that have not yet been touched (possibly the project hasn't reached the letter "K" yet); a mid-stream frame-by-frame project is likely to have covered paraphrase-relations between expressions in each of the frames that have been included so far, but will not yet have all the meanings of each of the words in its current word list.

While working through an analysis of a single frame we try to accumulate all of the words that evoke that frame. For example, in the case of Revenge, mentioned earlier, the list will include nouns like *revenge*, *vengeance*, *retribution*, *reprisal* and *retaliation*; verbs like *avenge*, *revenge*, *retaliate* (*against*), *get back* (*at*), *get even* (*with*), and *pay back*; adjectives like *vengeful*, *retaliatory*, and *vindictive*, and a large number of support constructions – V+N examples like *take revenge*, *exact retribution*, *wreak vengeance*, and P+N examples like *in retaliation* and *in revenge*. To say that these LUs (these words in the intended meanings) are all members of the Revenge frame is to say that, in spite of their grammatical and organizational differences, they all evoke, and require an understanding of, the full Revenge scenario as described earlier. That is, independently of whether an instance of the frame evoked by a particular LU is asserted, presupposed, denied, or merely imagined, in that evoked scene an Avenger is meting out Punishment to an Offender in return for an Injury to an Injured_party.

There are at least two reasons for examining all of the words in a frame together, rather than describing one word at a time. First of all, frame-sharing words often need to be delimited from each other in ways we discover by doing corpus analyses of all of them, in parallel; sometimes we notice that what seemed like one frame at the beginning might in the end need to be separated into two or more. Secondly, since semantically related words, of the same part of speech, often have similar syntactic behavior – in spite of the variety just noticed for marking the Offender in the Revenge frame – the search parameters for finding example sentences in the corpus are largely reusable across a frame.

When the project is complete, the FrameNet lexicon will be of use to researchers working on broad-domain automatic sense selection, but at intermediate stages we are not in position to document all senses of each word. It is easy to see that having both goals simultaneously – exploring all the words in a frame and all the senses of each word – would have explosive ramifications. Starting with a word, you determine the different frames it belongs to – its different senses; taking each of these frames, you look for the different words that serve it; taking each of *these* words, you determine their frames; and so on.

To support this point with a concrete example, let's assume that our current target of analysis is the verb *depend* and that we have begun by describing its meaning in a sentence like (10). Calling this the Reliance sense, we examine samples of the word in context and notice that not all instances of the word in the corpus fit this frame. We then see the need to identify a Contingency sense as seen in example (11), where a connection is predicted between the weather and the success of a festival.

(10) *You can **depend** on me to get the job done.*
(11) *The success of the festival will **depend** on the weather.*

The Reliance frame involves humans trusting other humans to do what is expected of them. The Contingency frame poses a causing or enabling relation between occurrences. In order to pin down the details of the frame structures needed for each of these frames, we have to find out what *depend* has in common with the other words in each of these frames. We quickly realize that in the Reliance frame we also have the verbs *rely* and *count*, with essentially the same syntax and meaning, as seen in sentences (12) and (13).

(12) *You can **rely** on me to finish it in time.*
(13) *I hope we can **count** on the boys to get home before dark.*

Neither of these new additions to the Reliance frame is usable in the Contingency frame, as shown in the contrasts between acceptable and unacceptable versions of (14) and (15). (In [14] the thing depended on is unexpressed, i.e., is left implicit.)

(14) *That **depends**.* (**That counts.*[30] **That relies.*)
(15) *The salary level will **depend** partly on the age of the applicant.* (**count, *rely*)

We have made some progress towards including different senses of *depend*, but if we felt, in order to include *count*, we had to cover the rest of *its* meanings, we soon find what we might call a Validity or Importance sense[31] (*your vote doesn't count*), a Categorization sense (*I count you as a friend*), a Counting_out sense (*my grandson can already count to twenty*), and seven or eight others among the verbs, in addition to what we find with nouns sharing that form, including Nobility_rank (*the count and countess*), and a number of others in sports and weaving. In exploring each of these, we would need to deal with other words in *those* frames: the Validity frame will have the adjective *valid*; the Nobility_rank frame will have *duke*, *prince*, *earl*; and so on. The Categorization frame also contains *regard*, *consider*, *deem*, *categorize*, and many others, plus their nominal derivatives.

We at FrameNet want to explore all the words in a frame and to build up paraphrase relations. While this may be disappointing to those of our colleagues who expect to find all senses of each of the words that we touch, no rational plan of research is compatible with such conflicting goals, short of bringing the work to completion.

5. Polysemy and FrameNet

As noted, while traditional lexicographic practice leads immediately to an exploration of polysemy and provides data allowing the discovery of patterned polysemy structures, FrameNet's methods lead naturally to an exploration of paraphrase (and near-paraphrase) relations, showing how identical or similar semantic structures can be syntactically expressed in a variety of ways.

This does not mean that FrameNet researchers can ignore polysemy. There are both empirical and theoretical reasons for a concern with multiple meanings. The empirical issue is that we obviously have to choose the particular sense of a lemma that is going to define a particular LU, and this requires an initial survey of the most important of the word's *other* senses. Although it might not be possible to determine full descriptions of other meanings of a word from the start, we obviously need to delimit one particular LU from others that use the same form. The theoretical issue has to do with competing possible explanations of the same phenomena.

In the matter of deciding how many separate senses a word has, FrameNet is more closely aligned to the *splitters* than the *lumpers*. Monosemists[32] are semanticists who wish to cover word senses as generally or abstractly as possible. While a concern with maximal generalization may be attractive to the theoretician, it does not always satisfy the criteria according to which we need to decide which meanings belong to which frames. In FrameNet, we seek to maximize the regularity of LU-to-LU relations (antonymy, synonymy, etc.),[33] LU to valency patterns, LU to various grammatical patterns (tense, aspect, etc., in the case of verbs, determination and countability possibilities in the case of nouns, gradability in the case of adjectives and adverbs, etc.), inference possibilities associated with one sense rather than another, ambiguities not associated with complementation types, and morphological relations between words of different parts of speech. (To illustrate the last point, the nominalizations of two verbal LUs might have the same form: *deduce* > *deduction* vs. *deduct* > *deduction*; two verbal LUs with the same form might have different nominalizations: *observe* > *observance* vs. *observe* > *observation.* Arguments for the monosemy of *deduction* or *observe* will not be convincing.)

When asked for a synonym of *depend*, we need to know which frame it is in: *rely* fits in one frame but not in the other. When asked for a nominalization of *observe*, we need to ask which frame our inquirer has in mind: *observation* works in one frame, *observance* in the other. When asked about the valency of *remember*, it will depend on which sense of the verb is intended.

The case of *remember* is instructive. Monosemists are likely to find one meaning to this word, and to assign it a fairly large set of valency patterns. *Remember* has many different complement types, and it might be tempting to treat the differences in interpretation as explainable merely in terms of semantic accommodations to its various complement types. This verb can occur without an object, with a NP object, with a finite clause complement, with an infinitive complement, or with a verbal or clausal gerundial complement, and the verb can function as either a stative verb or an active verb.

In studying the language appropriate for describing episodic memory, we can create a frame called Remembering_experience. In this frame the verb *remember* has *recall* and *recollect* as its partners, as well as phrasal expressions like *have memories of.* Complements that participate in this meaning include VP gerunds or V-ing complements (16), sentential gerunds or NP V-ing complements (17), and simple NP (18).

(16) *I* ***remember*** *as a child* [*falling down the steps in my grandma's house*].
(17) *I* ***remember*** [*something touching me in the dark*].
(18) *I can still vividly* ***remember*** [*the accident*].

Another use of this verb has to do with Retaining_information, a sense in which it can be linked, through Frame-to-Frame relations, to *forget* (losing information) and *know* (having information). The complements of *remember* in this frame can be *that*-clauses (19) interrogative clauses (20), infinitival interrogatives (21), and NPs (22). As in the *remember* of Remember_experience, this LU can be used statively, representing an ability.

(19) *Everybody else* ***remembered*** [*that the meeting was scheduled for today*].
(20) *Do you* ***remember*** [*what she said*]?
(21) *They don't* ***remember*** [*what to do next*].
(22) *Do you* ***remember*** [*my phone number*]?

Yet another frame is needed for Remembering_to_do_something. This occurs with infinitive VPs (23) and simple NPs (24).

(23) *Did you* ***remember*** [*to feed the cat*]?
(24) *Did you* ***remember*** [*your umbrella*]?

This use of *remember* is paired with one sense of *forget* having the same presupposition about intending or resolving to do something, but has no semantic relation with *know*.

One syntactic complement type found in all three frames is the simple direct object. If all three putative senses can take NP objects, can we still find reasons for separating them in this context? The combination of differences in the kinds of NPs and aspect differences in the verb's main uses sorts these out. For episodic memory, a sentence like (25); for Remembering_to_do, something like (26); e.g., in the meaning 'did you remember to bring your umbrella'; and for retaining information a concealed question NP as in (27).

(25) *Do you* ***remember*** [*the umbrella*]? (*The one we gave you when you were seven, the one with the Mickey Mouse design*?)
(26) *Did you* ***remember*** [*the umbrella*]? (*Or did you leave it at home*?)
(27) *Do you* ***remember*** [*my name*]? (*Do you remember what my name is*?)

The separation of *remember* into different frames, then, permits association with synonyms: in one sense it goes with *recall* and *recollect*, with a variety of antonyms (senses 2 and 3 go with *forget*), associations with inferences, with *know*, with aspectual possibilities of the verb (senses 1 and 2 can be stative), etc., and with different ways of interpreting NPs. Importantly for present purposes, the three senses already identified – there are several more – have only partially overlapping valencies.

The theoretical issue of polysemy for FrameNet has to do with the extent to which frame-to-frame relations can make it possible to recognize both commonalities and differences between closely related frames. In the course of the project's treatment of what Fillmore and Atkins (1992) proposed as the Risk frame, what was regarded as a single frame at the beginning eventually split into three frames, all of them using a super-frame that recognized "risky" situations in the abstract. The polysemy issue here involves the verb *risk*. In one instance of *risk*, the verb has what can be called an Asset as its direct object: one *risks one's life*, *one's fortune*, *one's health*, and the like. Another has some unfortunate consequence (Mishap) as its complement: either a nominal object, as in *one risks failure*, *infection*, etc., or a verbal gerund as in *one risks losing one's job*, *falling off the cliff*, or a sentential gerund, as in *one risks everyone getting angry*. The third sense has an Action as its nominal or gerundial complement: *I wouldn't risk a trip into the jungle at this time*, *I wouldn't risk swimming in the dark*. The original analysis simply had Asset, Mishap and Action as different frame elements in the same frame, allowing any of them to be the primary verbal complement. The resulting three frames – called Jeopardizing, Incurring and Daring – allow a more systematic treatment of the data, a tighter recognition of synonymy relations and more consistent valency descriptions.

6. Discrepant links between semantic roles and syntactic constituents

In the simplest case, a linking of syntactic and semantic valents will have a *governor*, the valency-bearing word, and a set of *dependents*; each dependent in a given sentence will be assigned a syntactic status and a semantic role. A single lexical unit in the same frame might have more than one syntactic valency pattern, but for each one, in this starting idealization, a simple matching holds. Using everyone's first example of valency, we can assign Giver, Gift and Receiver to the three arguments of the verb *give*, mapping the Giver to the subject, the Gift to the direct object, and the Receiver to an oblique, marking it with the preposition *to*. Because of the so-called Dative Alternation and Passivization, of course, we can describe three other patterns involving different syntactic assignments to each of the semantic roles.

Limiting ourselves to the versions without passive ellipsis, a schema for the one-to-one linking of units of grammatical form (G) with the components of meaning (M) can look like this: {{Ga:Ma}, {Gb:Mb}, {Gc:Mc}}.[34] The combined syntactic/semantic valency is a set of linked relations pairing units of grammatical form with units of meaning (the frame elements), the linking suggested by the lowercase letters: the first valent of *give* in the primary valency mentioned above is Subject:Giver, where Subject is Ga and Giver is Ma.

There are numerous ways in which observed valency patterns differ from this simplest case:

1. There can be syntactic valents for which there is no corresponding semantic valent, schematically {{Ga:Mzero}, {Gb:Mb}, ...}.
2. There can be semantic valents for which there is no corresponding syntactic valent – i.e., there can be semantic roles that are understood but not expressed, schematically {{Gzero:Ma], {Gb:Mb}, ...}.
3. There can be single syntactic valents that incorporate more than one semantic valent {{Ga:Ma&Mb}, {Gc:Mc}, ...}.
4. There can be single semantic valents whose realizations are distributed over more than one syntactic constituents, schematically {{Ga&Gb:Mab}, {Gc:Mc}, ...}.
5. While the preceding examples show variations in the pairing of syntactic and semantic valents, other cases involve the frame-bearing words themselves. There can be simple-word valents of a verb (typically the particles of English *particle-verbs*, for which it makes most sense to claim that the verb and its particle jointly bear the verb's meaning).
6. And there are examples for which a frame-bearing noun participates as the syntactic dependent of a verb or preposition, where the verb contributes a subordinate semantic content, as with the *support constructions*.

The linkings examined in this section fall into a class of phenomena referred to by Francis and Michaelis (2003: 1–27) as *mismatches*. In our case the discrepancies are departures from the pattern that syntactic valents are expressors of semantic valents and that individual semantic valents are expressed by individual syntactic valents.

6.1. Syntactic valents with no assigned semantic role {{Ga:Mzero}, {Gb:Mb}, ...}

The semantically empty word *there* can occur in sentence formats expressing existence, and occurrence, as in sentences (28–30):

(28) ***There** suddenly appeared a great host of angels*. (Presentative)
(29) ***There** is some beer in the fridge*. (Locative/Existential)
(30) ***There** was a loud explosion*. (Support construction for event nouns)

The epenthetic pronoun *it* can serve as syntactic place-holder in the clause types known as *it*-extraposition, as seen in sentences (31–35):

(31) *I regard **it** as obvious that ...*
(32) ***It** is well-known that ...*
(33) ***It** is impossible to read this small print.*
(34) *See to **it** that the kids are home before dark.*[35]
(35) *You can depend on **it** that we'll be home before dark.*

In the extraposition case, the two constituents (*it* and the re-located clause) occupy well-defined syntactic positions relative to the governor.

6.2. Semantic valents with no syntactic expressors {{Gzero:Ma], {Gb:Mb}, ...}

Ignoring grammatical constructions of ellipsis, gapping and various kinds of coordination reduction, all of which do not target the dependents of *specific* governing words, we can describe two main kinds of lexically licensed ways of omitting valents in English. FrameNet annotations identify three kinds of valent omissions, but one of these is not treated as a part of specifically lexical descriptions. These are indicated with the symbols CNI, INI and DNI, paired with the name of the frame element that is not realized in the sentence.[36] The labels stand for: *constructional null instantiation*, *indefinite null instantiation*, and *definite null instantiation*.[37] Each of these will be treated in turn in the next three subsections.

6.2.1. CNI: Constructionally licensed valent omission

In the CNI cases the valent omissibility is not relevant to the description of individual lexical items, beyond whatever limits there may be in the conditions that limit lexical items to participating in the relevant constructions.[38] Examples are the missing subjects of imperative sentences (38), the missing "agents" of reduced-passive sentences (39), and the generic or "free" subject of locally interpreted infinitives or gerunds (40–41). CNI marking is included in the annotated sentences, if only to show how all valents are accounted for in the annotations. The omission of arguments in various sub-genres (recipes, instruction manuals, newspaper headlines, diaries, telegraphese, etc.) is also generally not determinative of lexically interesting principles (42).

(38) *Please leave the room.* (Imperative)
(39) *The work was finished years ago.* (Passive)
(40) *To expect more would have been foolish.* ("Free" a.k.a. PRO)
(41) *Sleeping in the park overnight is against the law.* ("Free" a.k.a. PRO)
(42) *Mix well and cook until done.* (Instructional imperative)[39]

All such absences are registered in FrameNet sentence annotations, to make it possible to see how all of the valents are accounted for, but are not included in information about the lexical units. In (38) the 'second person' indicator is missing; in (39) the passive's agent is unexpressed; in (40) and (41) a generically interpreted subject is unexpressed; and in (42) the implicit object of the verbs *mix* and *cook* is understood from a previous instruction.[40]

The other two Null Instantiation types are necessary components of the descriptions of individual lexical units.

6.2.2. INI: Indefinite null instantiation

Indefinite null instantiation has something in common with canonical Indefinite NPs, in that they both represent the introduction of something into the discourse and invite the understanding that the speaker is (or ought to be) prepared to say more about that. Thus, the speaker of (43) can be expected to say what his or her question is, perhaps in the next utterance. Similarly, with unspoken indefinite arguments, as with (44) or (45), the speaker can be expected to say something, on inquiry, about what has been being baked or what something depends *on*.

(43) *I have **a question**.* (indefinite NP)
(44) *I've been baking all day.* (missing object)
(45) *That depends.* (missing PP complement)[41]

FrameNet records only those missing elements that belong to the *core* type, since peripheral elements are always optional. One can assume that information about such *circumstantial* elements as Place, Time and Manner are open for inquiry at any time and so specific annotations indicating their availability for further elaboration in the ongoing discourse does not need to be included in sentence annotations.

6.2.3. DNI: Definite null instantiation, lexically licensed zero anaphora

Definite null instantiation has something in common with Definite NPs, in that it points back to something available in the interlocutors' context of discourse. Thus, in (46), the NP *the problem* refers to something already under discussion. DNI omissions, with similar contextual resolutions, can be found with adjectives (47), adverbs (48), nouns (49) and verbs (50).

(46) *I have a solution to* ***the problem***. (definite NP)
(47) *My answer was similar.* (similar to something given in the context)
(48) *That happened a year later.* (a year later than something just discussed)
(49) *Were there any witnesses?* (witnesses to an incident just identified)
(50) *When are they likely to arrive?* (arrive at the place we all have in mind)

Note that the link from DNI-marked valents to entities mentioned in previous discourse is similar to what is sometimes referred to as *indirect* or *bridging anaphora*. In the DNI case, it is *specific lexically-identified information* about unrealized arguments that invites the search for antecedents, and not real-world assumptions about what is likely to accompany particular referents in a text world.[42] Most discussions of bridging anaphora are concerned only with NPs, and in fact only with definite NPs. As the above examples show, the DNI phenomenon is not limited to such conditions; the unexpressed argument is what is construed as definite.

6.3. Syntactic valents incorporating more than one semantic valent {{Ga:Ma&Mb}, {Gc:Mc}, …}

We sometimes find situations in which a valency alternation allows reference to two entities to be expressed as a single syntactic valent in one case and as two syntactic valents in the other case.

With verbs of medical attention like *cure*, *heal* and *treat*, the situation calls for a Patient and a Disorder, and these can be represented jointly, as in (51), or disjointly, as in (52). The Disorder is implicit, as DNI, in (53). The generically interpreted sentences of (54) can be thought of as having the Patient as INI, the Disorder as incorporated, or the Disorder as Modifier.

(51) *The medicine* ***cured*** [*my asthma*]. (Patient as "possessor" of Disorder)
(52) *The medicine* ***cured*** [*me*] [*of asthma*].[43] (Patient and Disorder are separated)
(53) *The medicine* ***cured*** [*me*]. (Disorder is DNI-omitted.)
(54) *The medicine* ***cures*** [*asthma*].
(54') *The medicine* ***cures*** [*asthmatics*].
(54'') *The medicine* ***cures*** [*asthma patients*].

In the case of reciprocal or symmetric predicates, plural NPs can appear in subject (or object) position, representing the entities involved as a single syntactic constituent, or the two roles can be distributed over a subject (or object) and an oblique constituent. A number of examples are given below.

(55) [*John and his brother*] *are quite* ***different***.
(55') [*John*] *is quite* ***different*** [*from his brother*].
(56) [*Figures A and B*] *are* ***similar***.
(56') [*Figure A*] *is* ***similar*** [*to figure B*].
(57) *I find it difficult to* ***distinguish*** [*your sons*] [*from each other*].
(57') *I find it difficult to* ***distinguish*** [*John*] [*from his brother*].

Certain kinds of relational nouns, like *price*, *population*, etc., allow the relatum to be expressed in the NP headed by the relational noun, or allow the attribute to be identified in a separate oblique PP. This is clear in FrameNet's Change_position_on_a_scale frame, as seen in (58–59).

(58) [*The price of oil*] *is* ***rising***.
(58') [*Oil*] *is* ***rising*** [*in price*].
(59) [*The population of such communities*] *is* ***increasing***.
(59') [*Such communities*] *are* ***increasing*** [*in population*].

Frames dealing with body contacts allow such separate treatments between body-part names and their possessors, as in (60–61).

(60) *She* ***pinched*** [*my nose*].
(60') *She* ***pinched*** [*me*] [*in the nose*].
(61) *He* ***slapped*** [*my face*].
(61') *He* ***slapped*** [*me*] [*in the face*].

Another involves the relation between a role and the occupant of a role, as in (62).

(62) *We* ***elected*** [*Harry*] [*as president*]. (occupant and role as separate constituents)
(62') *We* ***elected*** [*a new president*]. (individual and role simultaneously represented)

6.4. Semantic valents distributed over more than one syntactic valent {Ga&Gb:Mab}, {Gc:Mc}, ...}

This description covers two situations, one of which does, and one of which does not, involve syntactically describable lexically headed constructions.

There are instances of discontinuities which could be thought of as interruptions of phrasal or clausal complements of verbs of speaking or thinking. FrameNet annotates these as discontinuous complements of the speech/thought verb, but there is nothing semantically or syntactically determinate about the pieces of the discontinuous structure. The point of separation is determined more by the structure of the complement clause than by any properties of the governing verb (see sentences [63–64]). FrameNet annotation uses the pseudo-phrase-type "Quotation" to represent the constituent as a whole, and assigns that label to each of piece of the discontinuity, whether or not the two parts can be given determinate phrase-type names.[44] The lexical heads tend to be – or to be construed as – verbs of speaking or thinking (*say*, *ask*, *think*, *suppose*, *sigh*, *huff*, etc.).

(63) *"But why," she* ***asked****, "did you do that?"*
(64) *The main issues are, I* ***think****, beyond resolution at this point.*

The phenomena of *preposition-stranding* and *prepositional passives* are further instances of contexts in which complements can be discontinuous. It is not an interesting property of either *put* or *shout*, beyond the reality that these verbs can take prepositional complements, that accounts for the discontinuities in (65) or (66).

(65) [*Which box*] *did you* ***put*** *it* [*in*]?
(66) [*I*] *don't like being* ***shouted*** [*at*]?

In other words, the ability to participate in such structures would not be separately described as significant parts of the valency of these verbs.

Secondary predication and raising are among the more lexically specific grammatical processes that create situations of distributed syntactic realization of single semantic role notions. Thus, all of the examples (67–70) have as their semantic complement Message, Proposition, or Content, depending on the frame, in which 'being my friend' is predicated of 'Harry', and the FE label is associated with both pieces.

(67) [*Harry*] ***appears*** [*to be my friend*].
(68) *I* ***consider*** [*Harry*] [*my friend*].
(69) *I* ***regard*** [*Harry*] [*as my friend*].
(70) *I* ***want*** [*Harry*] [*to be my friend*].

The complement of *appear*, *consider*, *regard* and *want* is expressed as the stretch 'Harry ... my friend' (give or take the "marking") in all four cases. The passivizability of the NP *Harry* in both cases suggests the correctness of assigning it a syntactic role on its own.[45]

6.5. Syntactic valents that are parts of multiwords

Syntactically viewed, the *particles* in English *particle verbs* are their dependents, but it is often useful to regard the combination of the verb and the particle as defining a single lexical unit. Alternatively it is possible to regard the verb itself as the frame-bearing element and specify that the particle is a semantically empty obligatory syntactic valent. These two views could be represented in the same way.

This will be the case for *put off* meaning 'postpone', *carry on* meaning 'continue', *check out* meaning 'examine', *call off* meaning 'cancel', and many hundreds of others. FrameNet does not give the same treatment to subcategorized prepositions, since these can be taken as markers of the relevant frame element. Thus for *put up* [*with*] meaning 'tolerate' the lexical unit itself is expressed as *put up*, and *with* is the selected marker of its complement.

6.6. Syntactic dependents that are semantic heads

While both nouns and verbs have valencies, in some cases, a noun that is a syntactic valent of a verb is itself the principal or only frame evoker, and the verb which syntactically governs it makes no (or little) contribution to the semantics of the clause, serving mainly to provide, within its own syntactic valence, frame elements in the noun's frame, while adding tense and aspect information: these are the *support verb constructions*. Many but by no means all of these are V+N paraphrases of morphologically related verbs, in the way that *have a fight* pairs with *fight*, *make a choice* with *choose*, *say a prayer* with *pray*, *give advice* with *advise*, and *take a bath* with *bathe*. The concept is not limited to deverbal nouns but also includes cases like *wreak havoc* and *wage war*.

Support verbs have many functions in addition to allowing a noun-evoked frame to be expressed in a verb-headed context. In some cases different support verbs for the same noun introduce different perspectives on a single event type: *perform* vs. *undergo an operation*, *inflict* vs. *sustain an injury*, *pay attention* vs. *draw attention*, etc. In some cases a manner or "setting" component varies with different support verbs for the same noun: *make* vs. *lodge*, *file* or *register a complaint*, for example.

There are more complex *lexical functions*, in the sense of Mel'cuk (1998), whose verbs share arguments with the noun's frame but identify subevents in a larger frame. *Giving* and *getting* ***advice*** express participating in an advising event; *taking someone's* ***advice*** presupposes participating in such an event but adds the concept of uptake; *making a* ***promise*** is a promising event, but *keeping* and *breaking a* ***promise*** are separate acts, on the part of the promiser, having to do with acting on the promise; *giving* and *taking a* ***test*** are perspectives on an examining event, but *passing* or *failing a* ***test*** are separate events, affecting the examinee, related to the "licensing" function of the test.

There are also prepositional supports, i.e., cases in which a preposition governing a frame-bearing noun creates a structure which functions as a predicate adjective (*in danger*, *at risk*, *on fire*, etc.) or as a verb-modifying adverb (*under pressure*, *in retaliation*). In such cases the primary valent of the frame is controlled by the surrounding syntax (subject of *be* as in *be under pressure*, object of *find* as *found him in trouble*, subject of an independent verb as in *acted under pressure*).

7. Summary and moving forward

In a frame-based lexicon words whose meaning descriptions require an appeal to a common underlying conceptual structure are described together. Somewhat analogous to word-grouping by frames is the practice in most dictionary projects of defining a standard way of describing words that differ from each other along clearly statable parameters. This includes color words, compass points, kinship terms, weekday names, weights and measurements, and perhaps a few dozen others. In the case of color words, for example, the style manual will likely dictate that the definitions are to be made with reference to (a) the color spectrum, in terms of neighbors within the spectrum, (b) the reader's knowledge of familiar colored objects, such as grass, blood, the cloudless daytime sky, etc., or (c) wavelength range, or some line-up of more than one of these kinds of information.

The difference is that for a frame-based lexicon, the grouping practice extends more or less to all words. Belonging to a semantic frame and having a valency are not identical. Color words have modifiers (tending, in English, to be adjectives – *light blue*, *dark green*, *pale yellow*, etc.) but they lack the kinds of FEs associated with relations, events, complex states of affairs, etc. Kinship terms have of course the terminals of the kinship relations (and in some cases an intermediary – *paternal uncle*), compass points used for indicating directions necessarily imply a starting point, and weights and measurements are the weights and measurements of something, and they are expressed in terms of types of units.

For words that don't really have valents in the usual sense, FrameNet chooses to treat categories of modification, including the *qualia* in the work of Pustejovsky (1995), whereby we can label the modifiers of simple nouns, for example, in terms of substance, dimensions, orientation, function, and a whole host of others. This has not been satisfying, in the way that modification in general provides some problems for semantic analysis. For a phrase like *angry child*, the adjective identifies a disposition of the child, but at the same time the noun stands as a semantic valent of the adjective.

It was pointed out above that semantic analysis in the FrameNet style begins by characterizing the kind of schema or event that motivates our understanding of the word's meaning. Once one has one such frame in mind, the question quickly turns around, and the analyst begins to ask what are the various means provided in this language for talking about the relations, processes and individuals within such a frame, and the kind of inquiry becomes *onomasiological*, or of the *encoding* type, rather than *semasiological*, or of the *decoding* type. This is part of what predisposes Frame-

Net researchers to assume a sense-splitting strategy, since a common word that has a special use within a particular frame is likely to seem like a separate sense of that word.

Much work in the semantic analysis of English modals has treated the monosemy/polysemy issue; there are persuasive arguments that the imagined differences of meaning of individual modals have more to do with the interaction of their uniform senses with differing contexts or domains of application (Sweetser 1990: 49–75). It's not likely that FrameNet researchers would even find a point in their research in which that question comes up. If the frame being worked on has to do with probability estimation, then the modal *may* of *He may retire early* is assigned to this frame (in a context where the intended meaning is clear); and if another frame is one of permission-granting, the *may* of *You may leave the room now* is assigned to this frame. Here the intellectual process by which a monosemist would seek to construct a single overarching sense to cover each of these uses has been foreshortened. The valence of the probability sense would undoubtedly be the (disjoint) predication that included both the subject and the VP complement of *may*; the valence of the permission sense would likely separate the subject (as the person receiving permission) from the VP complement (as the permitted action). I should point out that FrameNet has not yet tackled the modals.

One property of a valency description which FrameNet has not managed to provide directly is an account of the typical *semantic types* of the phrases that serve as frame elements. It is hoped that later research based on further corpus evidence can spot the semantic types found for particular FEs of particular LUs and incorporate such results in the valency descriptions – beyond such limited high-level indications as *animate*, *concrete*, and *abstract*. Various efforts to find nodes in WordNet to cover such categories as criminal acts (*murder*, *arson*, *treason*) for predicting the content of expressions occurring in contexts like *charged with* ___, *accused of* ___, *guilty of* ___, or *commit* ___, have been made, but they have not been impressively successful (Mohit and Narayanan 2003). Furthermore, there are many cases where particular FEs do not themselves have distinct semantic types, but pairs of FEs might be expected to have similar semantic types. Thus, for reciprocal structures, involving LUs like *similar*, *replace*, *combine*, etc., it is the pairing of similar semantic types that is typical. In "A can replace B", the A and B can both be holiday destinations, recipe ingredients, football players, words, etc., but there is simply no semantic type unique to either one of those positions.

Notes

1. The author is grateful to Miriam Petruck and Josef Ruppenhofer for their ears and their red pencils.
2. In all other writings on FrameNet or by FrameNet members, the word is given its American form *valence.* Since I want to use the noun *valent* to cover both semantic role notions (*semantic valent*) and syntactic dependents (*syntactic valent*), I resort to the form *valency* to avoid homophony between *valence* and *valents.*
3. Following Cruse (1986: 77) we use *lexical unit* to refer to a pairing of a word with a sense: in our case, it is the pairing of a word with the semantic frame to which it belongs. Thus, the *ties* in (a) *tie a knot*, (b) *research has tied cancer to smoking* and (c) *she tied the pony to a hitching post* are three different lexical units.
4. In standard FrameNet annotations, each sentence is annotated with respect to the single LU whose use is illustrated in it; in full-text annotation, the sentence is annotated – in multiple layers – with respect to each frame-bearing word found in it.
5. IRI-9618838, March 1997 - February 2000, "Tools for lexicon-building"; then under grant ITR/HCI-0086132, September 2000 - August 2003, entitled "FrameNet++: An On-Line Lexical Semantic Resource and its Application to Speech and Language Technology"; with a smaller but much appreciated supplement in 2004.
6. A subcontract from grant IIS-0325646 (Dan Jurafsky, PI) entitled "Domain-Independent Semantic Interpretation".
7. Defense Advanced Research Projects Agency, http://www.darpa.mil/. DARPA, FA8750-04-2-0026, "Steps Toward the Alignment of Complementary Lexical Resources and Knowledge Databases".
8. Advanced Research and Development Activity, http://www.ic-arda.org/. Since Sept, 2004, we have been a subcontractor on an ARDA contract for work on question answering through the University of Texas at Dallas, as part of the AQUAINT project; we are annotating AQUAINT texts, questions, and answers with frames and FEs, testing whether this will improve the QA results. Both the PropBank and the AQUAINT annotated texts are browsable on the FN public website.
9. The corpus used for most of the time of the project has been the British National Corpus (BNC). In recent years the BNC has been supplemented by samples of US newswire text provided through the Linguistic Data Consortium of the University of Pennsylvania (http://www.ldc.upenn.edu/), selected texts provided by funders, and some material from the WorldWideWeb.
10. In the author's personal history the concept "frame" evolved from an earlier use as "case frame", as readers who are over sixty may remember. The concept has obvious similarities to structures covered by terms like *frame, schema, scenario, script*, etc., common in educational, artificial intelligence and cognitive psychology research in past decades, but in our case it is limited

to such structures as they are keyed to – and "evoked by" – specific linguistic objects, i.e., words and grammatical patterns. See discussion in Fillmore (1985).

11. The FEs are to be taken as role names, not names of entities. As with the Revenge frame described below, the Avenger in a Revenge situation might be the same as or different from the victim of the original Injury, and may be a group of people rather than a single individual.
12. Although the FrameNet database is faithful to its corpus commitment, in that all annotated examples are attested in the corpus, the examples offered in this paper are simplified or invented.
13. Such lists are likely to contain agent, instrument, patient, theme, experiencer, source, goal and path among others. For examples see Fillmore (2003).
14. For various technical reasons we require that the FEs be seen as distinct for each frame, but rather than invent ever newer FE names for each new frame, we can satisfy this requirement by using dotted names that combine the frame name with the FE name: thus Placement.Theme is distinct from Arriving.Theme.
15. The qualifier "frame-bearing" is to distinguish the words that are directly targeted for FrameNet analysis from those that have mainly functions controlled by the grammatical system (tense, aspect, support verbs, etc.) or are determined by the subcategorization requirements of governing words, such as highly selected prepositions and particles in the case of phrasal verbs. Such words – together with vast numbers of names of artifacts, species, chemical compounds, as well as persons, places and institutions – do not receive treatment in the FrameNet database.
16. The groupings by which semantic and syntactic structures show parallel behavior, as in the important work of B. Levin (1985), do not always match frame-relationships of the kind developed in FrameNet.
17. This isn't quite true, but the places where we reach beyond the LU-headed phrase are precisely those places where familiar syntactic theories provide construals for "empty categories": the antecedents of gaps for WH-extracted elements, missing subjects in non-initial conjoined VPs, and the controllers of the subjects of non-finite VPs.
18. As will become clear below, the Sender is in fact recognized in the annotation, as unrealized in a way licensed by the passive construction, and the Recipient is indirectly expressed by the particle *out*.
19. It is for this reason, of course, that sentence (3) would not be valued as an illustration for the use of the verb *send*, and is not likely to be a valued entry in the FrameNet annotation collection. FrameNet does not seek to annotate the most frequent uses of a word. For a great many transitive verbs in English, the most frequent occurrences have pronouns in the nuclear syntactic positions; annotators are instructed to reject these in favor of examples whose components are semantically relevant to the nature of the frame, without needing to appeal to discourse context.
20. Details can be seen in the FrameNet public website:

http://framenet.icsi.berkeley.edu/.

21. In the full-text annotation work mentioned earlier, all words in a sentence are annotated. This would correspond to a full annotation set for each frame-relevant word in the sentence.
22. This distinction corresponds to the distinction brought up by Thomas Herbst during the conference as that between *complement inventory* and *valency pattern.*
23. The structure of the system of frame-to-frame relations is set up, but the details have not been completed as of this writing. Many FrameNet frames are elaborations of more abstract schemas of change, action, movement, experience, causation, etc., and the roles found in these are the ones that figure in linking generalizations; many of the more refined frames can be seen as perspectives on the more abstract frames, in the way that buying is a subtype of getting, selling and paying are kinds of giving, etc. Generalizations based on inferences about who possesses what before and after the transaction depend on the roles in the commercial transaction; generalizations about how syntactic roles are assigned to the arguments depend on the more abstract inherited schemas.
24. Annotation *sets* because the annotation for each targeted LU includes layered descriptions specifying (1) the target lexical unit (which might be a discontinuous character-string), (2) the syntactic labeling of the annotated phrases, (3) the frame element labeling of these phrases, and (4) various other kinds of information varying according the the target LU's part of speech.
25. In general the category of "oblique nominal" (an NP with GF Dependent rather than Object) is used as the second object of a ditransitive pattern, and as nominal non-objects in expressions like *ski Davos*, *shop Macys*, *walk the plank*, etc., where one can assume that a preposition has been omitted. By making the same decision with "second objects" we recognize the similarities between *give someone a medal*, *present someone a medal*, where *a medal* is regarded as an oblique NP, and *present someone with a medal*, where the same function is expressed with a PP: with *present* the preposition omission is optional, with *give* it is obligatory.
26. Where suitable the definitions are taken from the *Concise Oxford Dictionary*, for which we have permission from Oxford University Press.
27. A feature of the eventual lexical entries, not provided in the present state of the project, is an *abstract valency formula* upon which the observed realization patterns could be generated. Such formulas will be abstracted away from the realizations found in the annotated sentences, where displacements and ellipses are the product of syntactic processes independent of the purely lexical requirements of the lexical target. It has not been possible to devise an automatic way of deriving such valency formulas from the annotations, and the manual work of drawing up such descriptions on the basis of the annotations has not been done.
28. But see Narayanan et al. 2003.
29. At the level of granularity deemed relevant to the publisher's intended market.

30. Of course *That counts* is an acceptable sentence, but in the (still different) sense of Validity, seen in *Everybody's vote counts*.
31. A number of putative frame names introduced in this paragraph are tentative; not all these frames exist in the current database.
32. See Ruhl (1989) and the research he praises.
33. In principle this means that to say that a word like *remember* has n senses is to say that it belongs to n *synsets* in an idealized WordNet. Co-membership in a single frame in FrameNet, however, is not limited – as are synsets – to words in a single part of speech. Cf. Fellbaum (1988).
34. For each grammatical unit G*i* there is a single corresponding meaning unit M*i*.
35. In general *it seems that*-predicates requiring syntactic PP complements and semantic propositional complements require extraposition with *it* in order to satisfy both of these constraints.
36. A more complete inventory of missing valents and the conditions which call for them can be found in Ruppenhofer (2005).
37. The INI and DNI are equivalent to what Allerton (1982) refers to as *indefinite deletion* and *contextual deletion*, but without suggesting a layered grammatical representation that includes a deletion operation.
38. For example, only agentively construable verbs participate in the imperative construction, only passivizable verbs participate in the passive construction.
39. The point about (42) is the omission of the object; the subject omission as a feature of the imperative form has already been discussed.
40. In many cases of deleted objects with instructional imperatives the possibilities of valence alternation, which of course *is* lexically determined, does play a role. Thus in *stuff into a large pepper* and *stuff with ground pork* both have the direct object omitted, since the verb *stuff* allows both *stuff x into y* and *stuff y with x* as two variant valency patterns. Pragmatically the omissions in instructional imperatives are like those in DNI (see below), since the identity of the omitted entity has to be known in the context, but these are annotated as CNI since the behavior is more determined by grammatical constructions than related to lexically specific information.
41. The omission of the contingency is limited to the limited case where the subject is *that* or *it*. Notice the unacceptable: **Success depends*.
42. See the special issue on Associative Anaphora in *Journal of Pragmatics* (1991, 31 (3): 311–440), where the general assumption is that a definite NP that points to the existence in a text world of some specific kind of referent invites the assumption that other things that typically accompany such an object are likely to be present and permit referential pick-up.
43. It's clear that the role represented here by of asthma is a core frame element, since it gets the DNI interpretation in a sentence that mentions only the patient: *It cured me.*
44. The substructure of the interrupted phrase itself is determined by its own highest governor(s).
45. Grammatical tagging in FrameNet is intended to be theory-neutral, but where that is impossible (as in the case of the contested analysis of "raising to ob-

ject") we choose the version from which conversion to alternative analyses is most straightforward.

References

Allerton, David J.
1982 *Valency and the English Verb*. London: Academic Press.

Atkins, Beryl T. S., Charles J. Fillmore, and Christopher R. Johnson
2003 Lexicographic relevance: Selecting information from corpus evidence. *International Journal of Lexicography* 16 (3): 251–280.

Charolles, Michel, and Georges Kleiber (eds.)
1991 *Associative Anaphora*. Special Issue of *Journal of Pragmatics* 31 (3).

Cruse, D. Alan
1986 *Lexical Semantics*. Cambridge: Cambridge University Press.

Fellbaum, Christiane
1988 *WordNet: An Electronic Lexical Database*, Cambridge: MIT Press.

Fillmore, Charles J.
1968 The case for case. In *Universals in Linguistic Theory*, Emmon Bach, and Robert T. Harms (eds.), 1–88. New York: Holt, Rinehart, and Winston.
1977 The case for case reopened. In *Syntax and Semantics,* Vol. 8: *Grammatical Relations,* Peter Cole, and Jerrold M. Sadock (eds.), 59–81. New York: Academic Press.
1985 Frames and the semantics of understanding. *Quaderni di Semantica* 6 (2): 222–254.
1987 A private history of the concept of frame. In *Concepts of Case*, René Dirven, and Günter Radden (eds.), Tübingen: Gunter Narr Verlag.
2003 Valency and semantic roles: The concept of deep structure case. In *Dependenz und Valenz / Dependency and Valency: Ein Internationales Handbuch der Zeitgenössischen Forschung / An International Handbook of Contemporary Research,* Vol. 2, Vilmos Ágel, Ludwig W. Eichinger, Hans-Werner Eroms, Peter Hellwig, Hans-Jürgen Heringer, and Henning Lobin (eds.), 457–474. Berlin/New York: Mouton de Gruyter

Fillmore, Charles J., and Beryl T. Sue Atkins
1992 Towards a frame-based organization of the lexicon: The semantics of RISK and its neighbors. In *Frames, Fields, and Contrast: New Essays in Semantics and Lexical Organization*, Adrienne Lehrer, and Kittay Eva (eds.), 75–102. Hillsdale: Lawrence Erlbaum Associates.
1994 Starting where the dictionaries stop: The challenge for computational lexicography. In *Computational Approaches to the Lexicon,* Beryl T. Sue Atkins, and Antonio Zampolli (eds.), 349–393. Oxford: Oxford University Press.

Fontenelle, Thierry (ed.)
2003 *FrameNet*. Special issue of *International Journal of Lexicography* 16 (3).

Francis, Elaine J., and Laura A. Michaelis (eds.)
2003 *Mismatch: Form-function Incongruity and the Architecture of Grammar*. Stanford: CSLI Publications.

Levin, Beth
1985 *English Verb Classes and Alternations: A Preliminary Investigation.* Chicago: The University of Chicago Press.

Mel'cuk, Igor
1998 Collocations and lexical functions. In *Phraseology: Theory, Analysis and Aplications*, Anthony P. Cowie (ed.), 23–53. Oxford: The Clarendon Press.

Mohit, Behrang, and Srini Narayanan
2003 Semantic extraction with wide-coverage lexical resources. In *HLT-NAACL 2003: Companion Volume*, Marti Hearst, and Mari Ostendorf (eds.), 64–66. Alberta, Canada.

Narayanan, Srini, Collin Baker, Charles Fillmore, and Miriam Petruck
2003 FrameNet meets the semantic web: Lexical semantics for the web. In *The Semantic Web – International Semantic Web Conference 2003*, Dieter Fensel, Katia Sycara, and John Mylopoulos (eds.), 771–787. Berlin: Springer-Verlag.

Petruck, Miriam R. L.
1996 Frame semantics. In *Handbook of Pragmatics 1996*, Jef Verschueren, Jan-Ola Östman, Jan Blommaert, and Chris Bulcaen (eds.), Philadelphia: John Benjamins.

Pustejovsky, James
1995 *The Generative Lexicon*. Cambridge: MIT Press.

Ruhl, Charles
1989 *On Monosemy: A Study in Linguistic Semantics*. New York: State University of New York Press.

Ruppenhofer, Josef
2005 Regularities in null instantiation. Manuscript.

Sweetser, Eve
1990 *From Etymology to Pragmatics: Metaphorical and Cultural Aspects of Semantic Structure*. Cambridge: Cambridge University Press.

Tesnière, Lucien
1959 *Eléments de Syntaxe Structurale*. Paris: Klincksieck.

http://www.darpa.mil/
http://www.ic-arda.org/
http://www.ldc.upenn.edu/
http://framenet.icsi.berkeley.edu/

Section 2
Cognitive issues and valency phenomena

Valency and cognition – a notion in transition

Gert Rickheit and Lorenz Sichelschmidt

Valency, one of the key notions in linguistics, is particularly suited to demonstrate the development of this discipline during the past decades. The way linguistics views itself has changed from a placement among the arts or humanities towards cognitive or life sciences. Linguistic methods have changed from introspection to experimentation, using sophisticated techniques and the latest equipment. Even the subject of linguistics has changed: while, in its early years, the discipline has focused on the structure of verbal utterances, contemporary linguistics embraces language usage as well as language users (Rickheit, Sichelschmidt, and Strohner 2002). Presently, linguistics is further broadening its scope far beyond the cognitive processes in the production and comprehension of verbal utterances as it is venturing to embrace topics like the neurophysiological substrate of language use, or human conversation as the art of successful information interchange by verbal means. Along with the profile of linguistics as a science, the notion of valency as a classical concept in linguistics has undergone dramatic changes. By tracing those changes over the decades, we learn something about the development of linguistics, and hopefully, also about its prospects.

1. Valency – the classical approach

The introduction of the term *valency* into linguistics is frequently attributed to the French grammarian Lucien Tesnière (1959). Borrowing the term from chemistry, Tesnière, in comparing words to atoms that combine with a fixed number of other atoms of an opposite electrical charge, indeed laid the foundations of what is referred to today as dependency grammar. In his seminal book *Éléments de syntaxe structurale*, Tesnière (1959: 13–14) explained the idea of a structural dependency of the elements of an utterance as follows: “Les connexions structurales établissent entre les mots des rapports de dépendance. Chaque connexion unit en principe un terme supérieur à un terme inférieur. … L’ensemble des mots d’une phrase constitue … une véritable hiérarchie.” [The structural connections form dependencies between the words. Basically, every connection binds a superior to a subordinate element. … The words within a phrase … form a real hierarchy.]

In Tesnière's conviction, the verb plays the central role in the structure of an utterance. The verb requires particulars, which are to be specified verbally by means of appropriate phrases or clauses – the so-called arguments – or else have to be inferred from context. A verb like *talk*, for instance, requires at least the specification of some speaker as a subject, while a verb like *donate* requires specification of a donator, a donatee, and a donation. So it is the verb which basically controls how many dependent elements occur in a sentence. With this, valency, in its most basic quantitative sense, refers to the capacity of a verb to take a specific number of dependent units.

However, Tesnière was not the very first to think along these lines. The Indian grammarian Panini (ca. 480 B.C.) is widely credited as the scholar who first elaborated on structural dependencies between linguistic expressions. In his book *Astadhyayi*, Panini used formal production rules to describe the structure of sentences and compound nouns in Sanskrit in a manner quite similar to modern linguistic theories (Böhtlingk 1998).

Another precursor of the notion of valency can be found in early European psycholinguistics. The psychologist Karl Bühler, in his seminal book *Sprachtheorie* (1934: 249) has elaborated on the valency of verbs on the Latin example *Caius necat leonem* ['Caius killed the lion'] in the following way:

> Wo immer ein Verbum die Komplexion regiert, dort und nur dort sind Leerstellen, in welche primär Caius und der Löwe eingesetzt werden können. ... Warum provoziert das Verbum die Fragen wer und wen? Weil es der Ausdruck einer bestimmten Weltauffassung ... ist, einer Auffassung, die Sachverhalte unter dem Aspekt des (tierischen und menschlichen) Verhaltens begreift und zur Darstellung bringt.
> [Where a verb governs a complex structure, there – and only there – are slots which can be filled with *Caius* and *the lion*. … Why does the verb evoke questions like who and whom? Because it expresses a certain perspective of the world …, a perspective which analyzes and represents situations according to the behaviour (of humans and animals).]

Following Tesnière, the notion of valency became well established in European linguistics – mostly in foreign language teaching, but also, in a way, as a counterconcept to mainstream syntactic theory. Lyons (1981: 116), in distinguishing between two principles of grammatical relations, dependency and constituency, noted that "Chomskyan generative grammar has opted for constituency, in this respect following Bloomfield and his successors. Traditional grammar laid more emphasis on dependency". However, due to the fact that during the sixties, generative grammar was the dominant paradigm in linguistic theorizing, it was not until the seventies that theoretical linguistics rediscovered the notion of valency. Since then, the dependency framework has gained about as much recognition in theoretical linguistics as it has had in applied linguistics. To date, numerous theoretical and empirical papers have been published on diverse aspects of dependency, and their number is steadily growing (see Ágel et al. 2003).

Since, in the view of dependency grammar, the faculty of controlling the number of arguments in a sentence is an inherent property of the verb, valency provides a means to subclassify verbs in terms of their dependent units. These dependent units are basically equivalent, so that subject and object specifications have equal status. Also, "this notion of valency does not presuppose … that the dependents of a predicator are necessarily noun phrases. What are traditionally referred to as adverbial complements of time, place, etc., also fall within the scope of the definition of valency" (Lyons 1981: 116–117). A few examples of possible verb classes based on valency are listed below:

Table 1. Possible verb classes based on valency

verb class	arguments	English example
avalent	0	*It was raining.*
monovalent	1	*Holmes yawned.*
divalent	2	*Holmes spotted Moriarty.*
trivalent	3	*Holmes handed the letter to Watson.*

However, in attempts at subclassifying verbs according to their valency, a fundamental problem arises from Tesnière's division of arguments into complements and adjuncts, which was widely adopted (see Somers 1987). While complements (also termed *actants*) take the essential thematic roles and thus are necessary to render a sentence grammatical, adjuncts (also termed *circumstantials*) are of a more elaborative kind. Complements depend in form on the governing verb; adjuncts, in contrast, are freely appendable to the valency structure. To illustrate, in the sentence *Holmes travelled from London to Geneva via Dover,* only the arguments *Holmes* and *to Geneva* would typically qualify as indispensable complements; the others might (arguably) be regarded as adjuncts, so that, in effect, the verb *to travel* would be classified as divalent. The problem with the dichotomy is that the criteria for classifying an argument as a complement or an adjunct are anything but clear; after all, information which is essential to the interpretation of a sentence need not always be supplied explicitly. In consideration of this, some researchers have proposed a more subtle distinction as an alternative to the dichotomy (cf. Herbst and Roe 1996). Unfortunately, though, a finer-grained classification is not a solution to the problem of unclear criteria: a characterization of obligatory complements as "Glieder, die in der Regel nicht weglassbar sind" [elements that usually cannot be omitted] (Helbig 1992: 99) is far too vague to be of any help. What is required, then, is a clarification of criteria – which can be accomplished only by more thorough inquiry into the way language users actually utilize structural dependencies in producing or comprehending verbal utterances.

Another issue that deserves consideration is the extent to which arguments can be classified in terms of semantic qualities. Clearly, Tesnière's resort to syntactic case as an indicator of different semantic qualities of complements (notably, nominative, dative, and accusative case to indicate particulars about *who*, *whom*, and *what*, respectively) is inadequate when it comes to handling other types of assertions (as in *Holmes travelled from London to Geneva via Dover*), more complex dependencies, or implicit complements. However, the incorporation of semantic qualities leads to a different definition of valency. The valency of a verb, in this sense, is determined by the constellation of the complements (not just by their number). Such a qualitative approach to structural valency, however, necessitates the development of clear-cut criteria for a classification of arguments in terms of their semantic roles – a point which shall be taken up in due course. As an interim summary, valency, from a structural point of view, can be regarded as the capacity of language elements to combine with particular dependent units for the formation of larger units.

The structural approach to valency has proved to be empirically fruitful. Results from several studies suggest that the notion of valency has some cognitive relevance. In a vintage memory experiment, for instance, Wilczok (1973) read to her students a number of five-word sentences which varied with respect to the valency of the verb: she compared divalent verbs (as in *The lady swallowed the tablets*) to trivalent verbs (as in *The lady sold the tablets*) so that each participant heard only one (randomly assigned) version of each sentence, with versions balanced between two samples of participants. In a subsequent cued recall test, the participants remembered the divalent versions significantly better than the trivalent ones. In an extension of this study, Raue and Engelkamp (1977) also found that recall decreased with increasing valency; in addition, they found that recall increased along with the degree of semantic relatedness of the arguments.

The notion of valency has also proved useful in the investigations of language development. In a large-scale developmental study of child language, Rickheit (1975; 1978) pursued the idea that dependency might be a valid indicator of children's linguistic abilities at primary school level, with the valency hierarchy increasing in complexity in the course of language development. In the study, 600 primary school children (aged 6;0 to 12;0 years) gave oral or written personal recollections and object descriptions. These corpus materials were then transcribed and analyzed. For analysis, Rickheit categorized valency as to three hierarchy levels:

- Primary constitutive verbal complements depend on the specific valency of the verb (as in *Fritz gab Peter das Buch* [*Fritz gave Peter the book*]).
- Secondary constitutive verbal complements depend on the valency of primary complements (as in *Peter ist müde vom Reden* [*Peter is tired from talking*]).
- Tertiary constitutive verbal complements depend on the valency of secondary ones (as in *Er wollte sie ins Krankenhaus bringen lassen* [*He wanted to have her taken to hospital*]).

The results of the empirical investigations were as follows: children clearly preferred primary constitutive verbal complements over secondary or tertiary ones. In addition, children preferred uni- or divalent utterances over more complex ones. The three most popular patterns in primary school children's oral language were: univalent (e.g., *Wir haben viel gelacht* [*We laughed a lot*], 20%), divalent with an accusative-object complement (e.g., *Er trägt eine Brille* [*He wears glasses*], 12%), and divalent with an accusative-patient complement (e.g., *Sie hat mich gerufen* [*She called me*], 12%). The proportion of these patterns remained relatively stable over the years (45% for the 6-year-olds to 43% for the 9-year-olds), and so did their distribution. Altogether, the ten most frequent patterns accounted for 80% of the syntactic structures used. Children's oral and written language did not differ with respect to syntactic pattern preference: the "top ten" patterns were identical; there were, however, significant differences in the frequency distributions.

These studies clearly show that valency is indeed a concept of relevance to linguistic accounts of human language use. However, there are major problems with the structural approach to valency. To reiterate, argument classes are not unequivocally defined; neither purely syntactic criteria nor optionality considerations based on introspection – or would introspeculation be more apt? – are sufficient for an adequate account. For another, the proposed linguistic tests – above all, deletion or replacement tests – are not unambiguous: depending on the importance granted to individual knowledge and situational context, they may arrive at different answers.

For instance, the verb *to dwell* is usually but not necessarily divalent; counterexamples are occurrences of univalent usage like the catchphrase featured in some TV commercials of a European furniture dealer – "Wohnst du noch oder lebst du schon?" [Still dwelling, or already living?] (IKEA 2005). Finally, the dependency approach and hence, the notion of valency, merits some more thorough consideration of its extension beyond the verb. From a structural point of view, other word classes also govern dependent units. An adjective like *similar*, for example, can be considered divalent because it requires two structures to be compared, likewise, a noun such as *fear* requires some particulars about the experiencer and the cause.

2. A reappraisal of the structural approach

It was the linguist Charles Fillmore (1968) who opened a new vista for the structural approach to dependency. In his so-called case grammar, Fillmore foregrounded semantic aspects by focusing on the arguments, that is, on the determined units rather than on the elements that govern these. The idea was to define valency classes on the basis of the type of the arguments rather than on their number. Thus, the quantitative point of view on valency was supplemented by qualitative aspects, namely, the particular constellation of complements. To illustrate, the verbs *to dance* and *to die* are both univalent in that they demand one nominative phrase giving particulars on *who*; they differ, however, in that *to dance* requires particulars on an agentive entity while *to die* requires particulars on an experiencer. Thus, by capturing the thematic roles of the participants (also referred to as theta roles or case roles), the analysis was extended beyond syntactic case and surface function into the semantic domain.

Linguistic theories generally proceed from the assumption that, since people organize their knowledge in terms of relations between entities, states, and events, there is a finite number of thematic roles (Chafe 1970, Jackendoff 1987). The classic thematic roles are agent, patient (or experiencer), object, and instrument, plus a set of locational and temporal roles like time, place, source, and goal. In some languages, these roles may have distinctive morphosyntactic characteristics, such as unique case markings, or restrictions on aspect or modality. Turkish, for instance, has a rich system of syntactic cases which, in addition to the nominative, genitive, dative, and accusative case, comprises locative, ablative, and illative case to specify location, source, and goal, respectively. However, thematic roles are in principle conceived of as being universal and independent from surface syntax. In fact, arguments can surface in a number of ways (see Hörmann

1979: 230)): if, in a sentence, the role of the agent is occupied, the instrument may surface in a *with*-clause (e.g. *Adrian opened the door with a crowbar*). However, if the role of the agent is not occupied, it can be assumed by the instrument using a noun in the nominative case (e.g. *The crowbar opened the door*).

It goes without saying that thematic roles are dynamic structures; after all, an agent is only an agent at the bidding of and for a particular verb. This fact has been exploited in order to classify verbs according to their typical patterns of thematic roles – their valency structures, or case frames, to use Fillmore's (1968) terminology. For instance, the valency of the verb *to open* has been assumed to unfold in a case frame that has an object as an obligatory argument and an agent and an instrument as optional arguments. Various sentence structures are compatible with this case frame; among them *The door opened*, *Adrian opened the door*, and *Adrian opened the door with a crowbar.*

In dependency grammar, such valency structures are regarded as the syntactic-semantic basis of sentences (Welke 1995). Accordingly, valency dictionaries for languages such as German, French, and – recently – English have been compiled (e.g. Helbig and Schenkel 1968; Herbst et al. 2004; Schumacher 1986) which list the verbal entries by their case frames.

The semantic view of valency has also found its way into theoretical linguistics (e.g. Haegeman 1991; Jackendoff 1990). At that, the original conception of arguments in terms of thematic roles has been modified in diverse ways. Dixon (1991), for instance, has divided case frames into some 50 verb classes, each of which has one to five distinct thematic roles. On the other hand, Dowty (1991) has attempted to trace back the plethora of thematic roles to only two thematic proto-roles – a proto-agent (which involves characteristics like causation, perception, and volition) and a proto-patient (which involves characteristics like effectiveness, responsiveness, or change of state). However, the basic idea that valency, conceived of in terms of argument constellations, is a useful starting point for a comprehensive account of the semantics of sentences, has remained largely unchanged.

Taken together then, case grammar as a semantic variety of the structural approach to valency has opened new avenues for linguistic research. It has proved useful not only in describing the dependency relations that hold among the elements of a sentence; it is also suited to explain phenomena like the occurrence of an intransitive use of a transitive verbs (as in *Paddy doesn't drink*), so that certain arguments are left unspecified. Above all, the structural approach to valency indisputably has some potential to systematically relate what – in transformational grammar – has been termed the surface and the deep structure of an utterance, thus smoothing the way towards an in-depth study of linguistic semantics. On the other hand, the notion of valency, as developed so far, has a few shortcomings: it is restricted to structural aspects in that it attempts to provide a description of the meaning of words and sentences – regardless of the fact that any verbal utterance is awarded (at least part of) its meaning through its use in a particular situation. The notion of valency is restricted in that analyses of dependencies proceed in a post-hoc fashion and hardly ever transgress sentence boundaries – which fails to do justice to the fact that utterances are produced and perceived in context. And it is largely built on linguists' intuitions about the functions of valency rather than on factual evidence about its functionality in actual language use.

3. The functional approach

In the mid-seventies, linguistics – in its own view, the science of language structure and language use – received new impetus from the blossoming fields of psychology and cognitive science. As a consequence of the "cognitive turn", the structural orientation that had been prevalent in the domain was now supplemented (or, in psycholinguistics, almost replaced) by a functional orientation. In the course of this development, the subject matter of linguistics has broadened so as to additionally comprise the language user. Scientific interest gradually shifted away from verbal structures towards mental structures. Research now focused on questions like how language is represented in people's minds, or how people actually produce and comprehend verbal utterances. Along with this new approach, the canon of linguistic methodology widened. Experimentation on cause-effect relationships has played an increasingly important role in the discipline ever since (Sichelschmidt and Carbone 2003).

As one side effect of the "cognitive turn", the dependency idea was reinterpreted in functional terms. After all, semantics is not a matter of words depending on each other but ultimately, a matter of concepts. In line with this, valency, from a functional point of view, was reinterpreted as referring to the capacity of concepts to combine with particular dependent concepts for the formation of more complex ideas. In this sense, not only verbs, nouns, or adjectives may serve as predicators that have valency, but conjunctions or prepositions as well since these also govern the use of other concepts. Engelkamp (1976) proposed three major conceptual classes of predicators:

- Attributive predicators are those that specify a feature, a state or an affiliation of an entity (as in the phrase *an old book*).
- Processional predicators are those that specify a change of a feature, a state, or an affiliation of an entity (as in *an intermittent light*).
- Actional predicators are those that specify an action, a transaction or a transformation (as in *a heart-breaking song*).

"It is important to note that the predicators reflect the structure of our world knowledge," Engelkamp (1976: 25) remarked. "These are the structures that guide our thinking, calling forth expectations also about verbal information."

The metamorphosis of valency from a linguistic notion to a mental notion was finalized by the psychologist Walter Kintsch. In an immensely influential book on *The Representation of Meaning in Memory*, Kintsch (1974) gave a comprehensive account of a dependency-based metalanguage for the description of the meaning of verbal expressions in general. Meaning, Kintsch argued, can be represented by structured sets of propositions. Though no explicit reference is made to Tesnière, the metaphor at the bottom of Kintsch's propositional account closely corresponds to the classic: a proposition is a sort of "meaning molecule" which comprises exactly one predicator plus a number of arguments. A predicator can be expressed by a verb, an adjective, a conjunction, a preposition, or the like, but more abstract concepts like *implication* or *consequence* are also permitted. Thematic roles such as agent, experiencer, instrument, object, source, or goal are assigned as arguments; however, the propositional account also permits hierarchical embedding – which means that a proposition may function as an argument to a higher-level proposition. Kintsch advocated a functor-argument notation system for propositions which is illustrated in the following examples (after Kintsch 1974; modified):

Table 2. Notation of propositions

Wording	Propositions
The clown smiled.	SMILE (CLOWN)
Cliff sold Linda a book.	SELL (CLIFF, LINDA, BOOK)
Cliff sold Linda an interesting book.	SELL (CLIFF, LINDA, INTERESTING (BOOK))
The clown smiled and bowed.	AND (SMILE (CLOWN), BOW (CLOWN))
Jane slept on the sofa.	SLEEP (JANE, ON, SOFA)
The baby did not spill the milk.	NOT (SPILL (BABY, MILK))
Not the baby spilled the milk.	NOT (SPILL (BABY, MILK)) & SPILL ($, MILK)

It should be noted that Kintsch's propositional account is meant to be truly semantic: it is an abstraction from the actual wording (tense, for instance, is not represented locally, nor is definiteness or indefiniteness of reference), it includes resolution of ellipses or pronouns as a matter of course, and it comprises inferences (for instance, in the affirmative proposition that *someone other than the baby spilled the milk*). Another remarkable feature of the propositional account is that it is easily expandable to larger texts. Local coherence, the paramount characteristic that distinguishes text from non-text, can be accommodated in the propositional account by evaluating the recurrence of particular arguments, and thematic progression as well as long-range dependencies can be treated by assigning a relevance weight to each proposition, with the weight gradually decreasing along with progress in the analysis of the text.

Several experiments have supplied empirical evidence as to the cognitive status of propositions. In a timed reading study (Kintsch and Keenan 1973), participants had to read sentences which were displayed on a screen one after another. The sentences had 16 words each (including punctuation); they varied in the number of propositions (from 4 to 9) in the base structure.

- Sample sentence with 4 propositions: *Romulus, the legendary founder of Rome, took the women of the Sabine by force.*
- Sample sentence with 8 propositions: *Cleopatra's downfall lay in her foolish trust in the fickle political figures of the Roman world.*

Reading time for the sentences varied along with the number of propositions; on average, it took participants almost one extra second per proposition (the least square regression model was $t = 6.34 + 0.94\ n_{prop}$). Moreover, the likelihood of recall of a proposition varied with the number of its arguments and with its level in the recurrence hierarchy: propositions that appeared early in a text and had many recurring arguments were recalled better than those of a lower rank.

Also, the cognitive relevance of particular arguments has been put to test (see Shapiro, Nagel, and Levine 1993). A memory experiment conducted by Obliers (1985) has provided evidence against the assumption that arguments are independently governed by the predicator. In the experiment, participants were given trivalent sentences (e.g. *The maid put the vase on the desk*) and were asked to underscore arguments of a particular type. In a subsequent incidental recall test, neither the verb nor any of the thematic roles played a central role in reactivating the sentences. Rather, focus on agents led to an increased recall of agents, focus on patients increased recall of patients plus objects, focus on objects did not increase recall at all, and focus on locatives increased recall of locations as well as of patients. These observations point towards syntagmatic – and unidirectional – dependencies among the various thematic roles, suggesting that combinations of the predicator and one or more arguments form gestalt-like semantic units with higher order meaning.

The propositional approach to semantic structure has subsequently developed into a comprehensive theory of text processing (Kintsch and van Dijk 1978). According to this theory, text processing comprises the stepwise, iterative extraction of propositions; these are temporarily stored in the recipient's working memory, where they are assembled to form a coherent hierarchy, the so-called text base. This "bottom up" account of text processing reveals several advantages, but also a few shortcomings of the propositional approach. On the positive side, predicator-argument constellations are functionally useful as elements of a versatile metalanguage for the description of semantic structures; moreover, they appear to constitute cognitively adequate processing units that can be tied down to the original notion of valency. On the negative side, propositions require human expertise and interpretation in order to accomplish reference and coreference resolution, to handle indirect meaning in a plausible way, and to cope with non-contingent constituents (as in *Hank took his hat off – Hank took off his hat*). Most importantly, the cognitive mechanisms in the identification and extraction of predicator-argument constellations need to be explored in detail.

In order to study the role of the predicator in on-line sentence processing, Rickheit, Günther, and Sichelschmidt (1992) have taken advantage of the flexibility of German word order. The authors hypothesized that, in case of a verb-first expression, the verb – due to valency – will enable the reader to mentally establish a relational link between arguments yet to be specified. In case of a verb-last expression, though, any argument noun phrases will have to remain standing alone for some time since the information necessary to integrate the arguments into a coherent conceptual structure is supplied only when reading the verb. Hence, verb reading times should be shorter with verb-first expressions than with verb-end expressions, whereas noun reading times should be slightly prolonged. This hypothesis was tested by comparing verb-first versions of 16 German sentences to verb-last versions in a self-paced word-by-word reading experiment with 40 student participants. For example, the verb-first clause *...und so treiben die Bauern das Vieh auf die Weide und...* was compared to the verb-last clause *...so dass die Bauern das Vieh auf die Weide treiben und...* [*drive* with the arguments *the farmers*, *the cattle*, *to the pastures*].

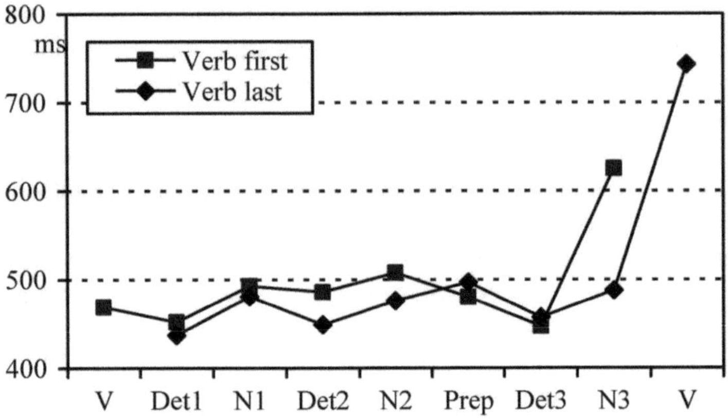

Figure 1. Word reading times (in ms) for trivalent verb-first and verb-last clauses

The analysis of word reading times (figure 1) showed that verb-first and verb-last versions differed significantly in reading times for the verb and for the last-mentioned noun: as predicted, the verb took longer to read when it occurred after the arguments than when it occurred prior to them. On the other hand, the last noun took longer to read in a verb-first expression than in a verb-last expression. The latency profiles indicate that supplying readers with the verb at an early point during reading indeed facilitates comprehension, whereas reading the arguments prior to the predicator is detrimental to processing because it increases working memory load. So far, the expectations have been substantiated empirically. Contrary to the predictions, however, verb fronting did not lead to a general increase in noun reading times. So there is no empirical support for the idea that tying an argument node to a relation link takes longer than merely installing it as a stand-alone. Hence, the decelerating effect of verb fronting observed at the last noun should perhaps be attributed to the fact that, in verb-first versions, the last noun occurred at the end of the clause. This suggests another mechanism to be operative in German sentence comprehension: readers may want to postpone the cognitive integration of predicator and arguments until attaining some degree of semantic saturation. In consequence, integrative processes in comprehension are contingent on reading the last element of a clause. This should become manifest in prolonged reading times for the final element of an expression – which was exactly the pattern of results found in the experiment.

4. The procedural approach

With considerations like these, the discussion of valency has taken still another turn. Dependency and valency have now become genuine mentalistic notions. The basic idea is that valency, being (proverbially) in the mind of the beholder, is assigned on-line and thus can be observed only by means of scrutinizing the cognitive processes in language comprehension and production. Pointedly, one might say that valency is not any longer a characteristic of verbal expressions that may take an effect on processing but rather, valency is an outcome of cognitive processes that may become manifest in typical constellations of verbal expressions.

The renewed metamorphosis of the approaches to the notion of valency – its transition from a functional to a procedural notion – coincided with the emergence of constructionist thinking in psycholinguistics (Rickheit, Sichelschmidt, and Strohner 2002). Emphasis was now on knowledge-based "top down" processes in text comprehension. The fundamental idea – reminiscent of Bühler's (1934) – was that readers or listeners take a text as a ground for activating knowledge which enables them to mentally construct a comprehensive model of the states of affairs described in that text. The cognitive scientist Philip N. Johnson-Laird (1983) has conceived of such "mental models" as holistic, dynamic knowledge structures which, unlike other forms of representation, have two important characteristics: mental models represent the situation in question in such a way that the structure of the representation depicts the structure of the represented, and they may, in their representational function, go far beyond what is explicitly stated in the text (see Rickheit and Sichelschmidt 1999; Zwaan 1999).

With respect to the procedural approach to valency, two concomitants of the rise of constructionist theories are of relevance – the re-emergence of the construct of cognitive schemata, and the placement of emphasis on inference as a fundamental mechanism in language processing.

Cognitive schemata (Bartlett 1932) are abstract, stereotypical macro-concepts of objects or situations which provide language users with a framework for the organization of knowledge. Schemata are often thought of as providing slots (variables) and default slot-fillers (values) which can be specified in actual use. To illustrate, a schema of a *car* may comprise general features of typical cars (such as 'has an engine', 'has four wheels', 'has left-side steering', 'seats five', and the like) which readers of the word *car* may use to develop an enhanced representation of the object referred to. Schemata serve important purposes in language processing; among them selection (the filtering of information according to relevance) and instantiation (the establishment of conceptual defaults). Experiments have demonstrated the importance of cognitive schemata as knowledge organization units at various levels of processing. For instance, a question like *How many animals of each kind did Moses take on the Ark?* will invoke some biblical schema which may prevent recipients from detecting the anomaly (it was not Moses who did). In contrast, a question like *How many animals of each kind did Mozart take on the Ark?* which does not invoke a unitary schema will make almost all recipients notice the anomaly (e.g. Sanford and Garrod 1994).

From a procedural point of view, the notion of valency lends itself to interpretation in terms of schematization: encountering a predicator will license the establishment of an appropriate argument frame, and accordingly, the thematic roles can be filled with default concepts. In fact, there is empirical evidence as to such a cognitive mechanism: using a single-word priming technique, Ferretti, MacRae, and Hatherell (2001) have demonstrated that verbs immediately activate knowledge of typical agents, patients, and instruments but not locations (e.g. arresting activates cop and criminal). At that, the activation of agent and patient thematic role concepts was modulated by syntactic cues. These findings have led the authors to conclude that schematic world knowledge is tied tightly to on-line thematic role assignment, and thus should be considered as part of thematic role knowledge.

Inference, the other phenomenon that is relevant to valency, relates to the fact that people often understand more than what is explicitly stated in a text (see Rickheit and Strohner 2003). Knowledge-based schemata provide a basis for the generation of inferences, that is, for the enrichment of meaning by default. The current state of psycholinguistic research on inference in text processing can briefly be summarized as follows: for one, inference is an everyday cognitive mechanism which can be observed in any kind of human information processing. For another, inference is not a uniform phenomenon; researchers widely agree on a distinction between two broad classes of inferences in text processing (cf. Rickheit, Sichelschmidt, and Strohner 2002):

- Obligatory inferences are those that are required for text coherence (e.g. suppositions about the referent of a pronoun). They occur frequently and do not take much cognitive effort.
- Optional inferences are those that elaborate on the text (e.g. schema-based speculations about the particulars of a situation). They occur less frequently, depend on circumstances and take comparatively much cognitive effort.

Since the latter inferences are at the core of constructionist theorizing (and at the same time, subject of dispute), contemporary psycholinguistic research primarily pursues the question under which conditions, how, and when in the course of processing people generate which optional inferences.

In this context, the notion of valency is brought into play when addressing the issue of whether or not thematic roles can be inferred, and if so, under which conditions, how, and when in the course of processing which thematic role information is activated. Evidence from priming studies and eye movement measurement has indicated that certain thematic roles such as instruments can indeed be activated by inference. Garrod et al. (1990), for example, have analyzed readers' eye movements in order to detect any differences in processing between four kinds of sentences:

- unspecific statements (e.g. *He assaulted her with his weapon*);
- specific statements (e.g. *He stabbed her with his knife*);
- statements with a specific predicator (e.g. *He stabbed her with his weapon*);
- statements with a specific argument (e.g. *He assaulted her with his knife*).

Eye movement patterns did not discriminate between the latter three conditions; they were, however, significantly different from those observed with unspecific statements. Apparently, thematic roles need not be made fully explicit; an appropriate thematic role frame can be established by specific predicators or arguments alike.

Other experiments have focused on inferences of other types of arguments. Mauner, Tanenhaus, and Carlson (1995) have employed a "stop making sense" reading task to investigate if people instantiate an agent when reading short passives like *The door was shut*, in which no agent is explicitly given. In the experiment, participants had to read sentences word by word, either pressing a "yes" key to make the next word appear or a "no" key to stop the procedure and indicate that they felt the sentence to be unacceptable. The authors compared short passives like *The door was shut to reduce the noise* to intransitives like *The door shut to reduce the noise*. Intransitives, naturally, would have to be considered unacceptable because a door, being an inanimate object, cannot act on purpose. Passives, on the other hand, would make sense provided that readers inferred the presence of an animate agent.

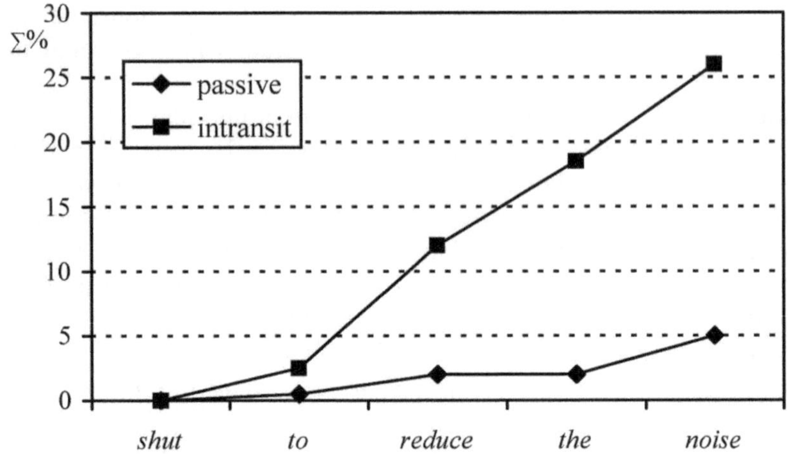

Figure 2. Cumulative % of "no" answers (after Mauner, Tanenhaus, and Carlson 1995)

The low percentage of "no" answers in the "passive" condition (figure 2) indicates that people did indeed infer an agent when reading short passives. In contrast, the sharp rise of "no" answers in the "intransitives" condition after encountering a clause that implies purposeful action of some agentive entity indicates that valency-related inferences are made on-line, that is, immediately during reading.

Finally, a recent series of studies conducted by Knöferle et al. (2005) shall be outlined which sheds still another light on the intricate relationship of valency and cognition. In these studies, the authors have addressed the question of whether the process of on-line thematic role assignment is influenced by nonverbal information. Participants in the experiments viewed pictures of complex scenes (e.g. a fencer drawing a picture of a princess who is taking a photograph of a pirate) while hearing German sentences like *Die Prinzessin malt offensichtlich den/der Fechter* [Obviously, the princess is painting / being painted by the fencer]. In these sentences, the thematic role of the princess is initially ambiguous. The ambiguity can be resolved only on hearing the second noun phrase: the accusative case determiner *den* renders the princess an agent while the nominative case determiner *der* renders the princess a patient. However, by relating the verb to the depicted events, thematic role assignment can be facilitated. Analysis of people's eye movements, in particular, anticipatory fixations of the appropriate agent or patient entity, showed that verb-mediated visual event information allowed early on-line disambiguation. This was corroborated in a further experiment which demonstrated that with verb-final expressions, intonation cues enabled role disambiguation even before people processed the verb. Taken together, these findings suggest that the verb is just one among several cues that contribute to the on-line establishment of an appropriate thematic role frame. The results support a notion of valency which includes nonverbal relationships as well as action and event schemata in addition to arguments; they suggest that people, in the comprehension of verbal utterances, exploit a rich inventory of semantic categories which go far beyond the linguistic domain.

With this, the notion of valency has eventually made its way from linguistics into cognition, a transition from a structural concept to a procedural one. Ultimately, valency has developed from a characteristic attributed to verbal entities unto a characteristic inherent to the way language users perceive situations. However, during these decades of transition, the notion of valency has lost nothing of its value for the organization of human information processing. Capturing the tendency of human beings to organize their environment in terms of "belonging together", in terms of partitioning wholes or grouping elements so as to arrive at meaningful, workable, and communicable units – this is perhaps the ulterior motive behind the linguistic and psychological attempts to draw on valency as an explanatory concept. And explanatory it is – provided that it has been given a comprehensive explanation.

References

Ágel, Vilmos, Ludwig M. Eichinger, Hans-Werner Eroms, Peter Hellwig, Hans-Jürgen Heringer, and Henning Lobin (eds.)
2003 *Dependenz und Valenz – ein internationales Handbuch der zeitgenössischen Forschung.* Berlin: de Gruyter.

Bartlett, Frederic C.
1932 *Remembering*. Cambridge: Cambridge University Press.

Böhtlingk, Otto
1998 *Panini's Grammatik.* Hamburg: Buske.

Bühler, Karl
1934 *Sprachtheorie. Die Darstellungsfunktion der Sprache.* Jena: Fischer.

Chafe, Wallace L.
1970 *Meaning and the Structure of Language.* Chicago: University of Chicago Press.

Dixon, Robert M. W.
1991 *A New Approach to English Grammar on Semantic Principles.* Oxford: Oxford University Press.

Dowty, David R.
1991 Thematic proto-roles and argument selection. *Language* 67: 547–619.

Engelkamp, Johannes
1976 *Satz und Bedeutung.* Stuttgart: Kohlhammer.

Ferretti, Todd R., Ken MacRae, and Andrea Hatherell
2001 Integrating verbs, situation schemas, and thematic role concepts. *Journal of Memory and Language* 44: 516–547.

Fillmore, Charles
1968 The case for case. In *Universals in Linguistic Theory*, Emmon Bach, and Robert T. Harms (eds.), 10–88. New York: Holt, Rinehart and Winston.

Garrod, Simon C., Edward J. O'Brien, Robin K. Morris, and Keith Rayner
1990 Elaborative inferences as an active or passive process. *Journal of Experimental Psychology: Learning, Memory, and Cognition* 16: 250–257.

Haegeman, Liliane
1991 *Introduction to Government and Binding Theory*. Oxford: Blackwell.

Helbig, Gerhard
1992 *Probleme der Valenz- und Kasustheorie*. Tübingen: Niemeyer.

Helbig, Gerhard, and Wolfgang Schenkel
1968 *Wörterbuch zur Valenz und Distribution deutscher Verben.* Leipzig: Verlag Enzyklopädie.

Herbst, Thomas, David Heath, Ian F. Roe, and Dieter Götz
2004 *A Valency Dictionary of English. A Corpus-Based Analysis of the Complementation Patterns of English Verbs, Nouns, and Adjectives.* Berlin: Mouton de Gruyter.

Herbst, Thomas, and Ian F. Roe
1996 How obligatory are obligatory complements? An alternative approach to the categorization of subjects and other complements in valency grammar. *English Studies* 2: 179–199.

Hörmann, Hans
1979 *Psycholinguistics. An Introduction to Research and Theory.* 2d ed. New York: Springer.

Jackendoff, Ray
1987 The status of thematic relations in linguistic theory. *Linguistic Inquiry* 28: 369–412.
1990 *Semantic Structures*. Cambridge, MA: MIT Press.

Johnson-Laird, Philip N.
1983 *Mental Models. Towards a Cognitive Science of Language, Inference, and Consciousness*. Cambridge: Cambridge University Press.

Kintsch, Walter
1974 *The Representation of Meaning in Memory*. Hillsdale: Erlbaum.

Kintsch, Walter, and Janice M. Keenan
1973 Reading rate and retention as a function of the number of the propositions in the base structure of sentences. *Cognitive Psychology* 5: 257–274.
Kintsch, Walter, and Teun A. van Dijk
1978 Toward a model of text comprehension and production. *Psychological Review* 85: 363–394.
Knöferle, Pia, Matthew W. Crocker, Christoph Scheepers, and Martin J. Pickering
2005 The influence of the immediate visual context on incremental thematic role assignment: Evidence from eye movements in depicted events. *Cognition* 95: 95–127.
Lyons, John
1981 *Language and Linguistics. An Introduction.* Cambridge: Cambridge University Press.
Mauner, Gail, Michael K. Tanenhaus, and Gregory N. Carlson
1995 Implicit arguments in sentence processing. *Journal of Memory and Language* 34: 357–382.
Obliers, Rainer
1985 Zur Revision prädikatzentrierter Satztheorien. *Archiv für Psychologie* 137: 175–200.
Raue, Burkhardt, and Johannes Engelkamp
1977 Gedächtnispsychologische Aspekte der Verbvalenz. *Archiv für Psychologie* 129: 157–174.
Rickheit, Gert
1975 *Zur Entwicklung der Syntax im Grundschulalter.* Düsseldorf: Schwann.
1978 Zur Syntax gesprochener und geschriebener Sprache acht- bis zehnjähriger Kinder. In *Die Lernfelder des Lernbereichs Sprache in der Primarstufe*, Walter Popp (ed.), 150–174. Heidelberg: Winter.
Rickheit, Gert, Udo Günther, and Lorenz Sichelschmidt
1992 Coherence and coordination in written text: Reading time studies. In *Cooperating with Written Texts. The Pragmatics and Comprehension of Written Texts*, Dieter Stein (ed.), 103–127. Berlin: Mouton de Gruyter.
Rickheit, Gert, and Lorenz Sichelschmidt
1999 Mental models: Some answers, some questions, some suggestions. In *Mental Models in Discourse Processing and Reasoning*, Gert Rickheit, and Christopher Habel (eds.), 3–49. Amsterdam: North-Holland.
Rickheit, Gert, Lorenz Sichelschmidt, and Hans Strohner
2002 *Psycholinguistik.* Tübingen: Stauffenburg.
Rickheit, Gert, and Hans Strohner
2003 Inferenzen. In *Psycholinguistk. Ein internationales Handbuch*, Gert Rickheit, Theo Herrmann, and Werner Deutsch (eds.). Berlin: Mouton de Gruyter.

Sanford, Anthony J., and Simon C. Garrod
1994 Selective processes in text understanding. In *Handbook of Psycholinguistics*, Morton A. Gernsbacher (ed.), 699–719. San Diego: Academic Press.

Schumacher, Helmut
1986 *Verben in Feldern. Valenzwörterbuch zur Syntax und Semantik deutscher Verben.* Berlin: de Gruyter.

Shapiro, Lewis P., H. Nicholas Nagel, and Beth A. Levin
1993 Preferences for a verb's complements and their use in sentence processing. *Journal of Memory and Language* 32: 96–114.

Sichelschmidt, Lorenz, and Elena Carbone
2003 Experimentelle Methoden. In *Psycholinguistik – ein internationales Handbuch*, Gert Rickheit, Theo Herrmann, and Werner Deutsch (eds.), 115–124. Berlin: Mouton de Gruyter.

Somers, Harold
1987 *Valency and Case in Computational Linguistics.* Edinburgh: Edinburgh University Press.

Tesnière, Lucien
1959 *Éléments de syntaxe structurale.* Paris: Klincksieck.

Welke, Klaus
1995 Dependenz, Valenz und Konstituenz. In *Dependenz und Valenz*, Ludwig M. Eichinger, and Hans-Werner Eroms (eds.), 163–175. Hamburg: Buske.

Wilczok, Karin
1973 Satzbildungs- und Satzverarbeitungsprozesse mit semantisch unterschiedlich spezifizierten Verben. Unpublished diploma thesis, Department of Psychology. Bochum: Ruhr University.

Zwaan, Rolf A.
1999 Situation models: The mental leap into imagined worlds. *Current Directions in Psychological Science* 8: 15–18.

Valency grammar in mind

Rudolf Emons

0. Introduction

Why has valency grammar been so successful? Or to put the question more modestly: why has valency grammar survived? My first rather general answer is: it has been so successful because it has been a valency grammar and not a valency theory.

The conference program mentions the concept of *valency theory* only once, in the title of the concluding discussion: "The future of valency / Die Zukunft der Valenztheorie", suggesting perhaps that what in Anglo-Saxon countries is just valency is valency theory in thorough and deep-thinking Germany. In the past a seeming or apparent lack of theory building was a decisive reason for many of our colleagues to hold valency grammar in not too high esteem.

My aim is not to present different theoretical valency concepts here nor to discuss anew if the concepts of Tesnière, Fillmore, Heringer and others merit the denomination of theory or not. I rather want to provide some prolegomena for a real theoretical foundation of valency grammar. The theoretical foundation of valency grammar which I have in mind is not rooted in linguistics as it is taught at the vast majority of our universities.

It is very welcome that some linguists in the field of cognitive linguistics have taken important steps towards linking language and mind. However, it seems to me that these efforts still lack real interdisciplinarity. By real interdisciplinarity I mean a program like the one that Nobel Prize winning biologist Gerald Edelman has described in his book *Bright air, brilliant fire – On the matter of the mind:*

> It is high time for another view of the mental, for a neuroscientific model of the mind. What makes the one proposed here new is that it is based remorselessly on physics and biology. It is also based on the ideas of evolutionary morphology and selection, and it rejects the notion that a syntactical description of mental operations and representations … suffices to explain the mind. Others have held similar positions but have not united them in a single evolutionarily based theory, one that connects embryology, morphology, physiology, and psychology. (Edelman 1992: 147)

1. Colours

Edelman's program is also a preamble to a new kind of linguistics.[1] A shift of focus takes place here. The focus is now on the construction of social reality and on institutional facts. John Searle regards language as "essentially constitutive of institutional reality" (1995: 59). Thus language is a very important and a very complex social construct. This construct has to be theoretically explained through the interplay of biological evolution and of cultural evolution. I would like to explain and refine this program now.

Let me start with a quote from a work by the neuroscientist and evolutionary anthropologist Terrence Deacon, whose theory on language development plays a central role in my considerations:

> Language is a social phenomenon. To consider it in purely formal, psychological, or neurobiological terms is to strip away its reason for being. Social phenomena like language cannot be adequately explained without appealing to a social evolutionary dynamic as well as a biological one. The source of information that is used to "grow" a language lies neither in the corpus of texts and corrections presented to the child, nor in the child's brain to begin with. It is highly distributed across myriad interactions between children's learning and the evolution of a language community. (Deacon 1997: 115)

This lesson about the reason for the existence of linguistic universals – and predicates and their valency are such a universal – is more difficult to learn than some linguists have thought so far. There are grammatical universals that are, however, not just stored as such in our brains. So how does this work?

Deacon cites as an example the development of colour terms in different languages and societies and sheds new light on them. He takes the following considerations as a starting point: the number of possible mappings of colours and their linguistic terms is nearly unconstrained,

> because: (a) the name of a color can be any combination of human vocal sounds; (b) the human eye can see every gradation of color between certain limits of wavelength; and (c) people can assign any term to any point on the visible light spectrum. So any association between utterable sound and perceivable light frequency is possible, in principle. (Deacon 1997: 116)

Reality, however, is quite different: "The mappings of colour terms to light frequencies are not only limited, they are essentially universal in many respects." (Deacon 1997: 116). Prototype semantics shows:

> The best physical exemplars of particular color terms, irrespective of how many are present in the language, are essentially the same when chosen from an arbitrary set of color samples. In other words, though the boundaries between one color and the next for which one has a term tend to be graded and fuzzy, ... color terms do apparently have something like a category center; a best red or best green. Surprisingly, the best red and the best green, whatever the terms used, are essentially agreed upon by people from around the world. Though the words themselves are arbitrary and the colors continually grade into one another, words are not arbitrarily mapped to points on the color spectrum. They are universally constrained. (Deacon 1997: 117)

The explanation for this astonishing phenomenon lies in our brain physiology and is – very briefly – as follows: different wavelengths of light activate different kinds of receptors in the human eye and cause different neuronal responses in the brain for different colours.

The basis for universality lies in the interplay of sensory input and the brainphysiological processing of this input. Sensory input as well as brainphysiological processing are species-specific and are therefore obligatorily the same for all members of this species. So all languages name colours in practically the same way and cannot use the theoretical naming potential mentioned above, because nobody can choose to perceive for example red as green or vice versa. Colour blindness or red/green weakness therefore are not problems of deficient language acquisition but are rooted in a biological defect.

2. Not seeing the trees for the wood

When we apply an evolutionary matrix to language acquisition and thereby compare our species to other primate species that do not have language, we will find that a major difference between us and them is that we are a symbolic species, as Deacon so aptly puts it in the title of his book. Human communication does not work along just indexical lines but symbolically. We do not only know that certain tokens refer to certain objects but we also establish logical relations between the linguistic signs. Language is a system. Symbols are difficult to acquire. Nevertheless each child learns a language. Universal grammar has every reason to ask here why this is so. With knowledge of our brain physiology and of neuronal processes in our brain the answer, however, will be quite different from the answer that universal grammar is prepared to give. Deacon provides a fascinating answer:

> Symbol learning in general has many features that are similar to the problem of learning the complex and indirect statistical architecture of syntax. This parallel is hardly a coincidence, because grammar and syntax inherit the constraints implicit in the logic of symbol-symbol relationships. These are not, in fact, separate learning problems, because systematic syntactic regularities are essential to ease the discovery of the combinatorial logic underlying symbols. (Deacon 1997: 136)

A quick learner who learns details very well has great difficulties with the concept of symbolicity. He matches things to many indexical signs but he does not need the qualitative leap that allows him to establish logical relations between the signs themselves. A less gifted learner, who does not perceive details so well, paradoxically seems to have a great advantage in this respect: he takes the bigger picture without bothering about details. Children are learners of this latter type. It is easier for an immature brain to acquire a symbol as such than it is for a more mature brain. Language structures themselves depend on biological evolution because they are adapted to children's learning structures. Valency structures are such adapted structures. Second language acquisition becomes more difficult than first language acquisition because our neural cognitive resources have already been used up for first language acquisition. We all know that language change can take place at a much greater evolutionary rate than biological, genetic change:

> The relative slowness of evolutionary genetic change compared to language change guarantees that only the most invariant and general features of language will persist long enough to contribute any significant consistent effect on long-term brain evolution. ... For these reasons there is little possibility for mental adaptations to specific syntactic structures. But there are many features of languages, from the presence of words and sentence units to the noun-part/verb-part distinction and many more subtle and idiosyncratic features that are common to essentially every natural language. (Deacon 1997: 329)

Valency is such a general feature. Constant und invariant neural processes must correspond to such constant and invariant language features. Now we have to take a very careful look at the biological logic: linguistic universals are "by their nature" (Deacon 1997: 333) very variable in their surface representations. Therefore, those varying surface features have tended not to develop specific neural supports in the brain. The separation of deep and surface structure – no matter what form it takes – together with the assumption of the universality of deep structures is virtually impossible from the perspective of brain physiology and evolutionary psychology (Deacon

1997: 333). In the light of symbolicity, the evolutionary development of valency would have been like this: "The earliest symbolic systems would necessarily have been combinatorial and would have exhibited something like this operator-operand structure (and probably subject-predicate structure) right from the start. This is the minimum requirement to make the transition from indexical to symbolic reference" (Deacon 1997: 334).

This is intimately related to the development of consciousness in general, not only in human beings: "The ability to construct a scene related to the value-category history of an individual marks the appearance of the self" (Edelman 2004: 132). So valency is plausibly a deep structure and a surface structure.

3. Human cognition

I would like to start this section by approaching the program of cognitive linguistics from a certain angle. Michael Tomasello (1999) draws on work in cognitive and functional linguistics like Langacker (1987) and at the same time transcends this work by also integrating biological research.

> The central theoretical point is that linguistic symbols embody the myriad ways of construing the world intersubjectively that have accumulated in a culture over historical time, and the process of acquiring the conventional use of these symbolic artefacts, and so internalizing these construals, fundamentally transforms the nature of children's cognitive representations. (Tomasello 1999: 95–96)

Tomasello's theoretical assumptions in this area are fundamentally different from those of the primatologist Frans de Waal (2001). De Waal emphasizes the cognitive similarities between apes and humans, whereas Tomasello emphasizes the cognitive differences between the species. I will not go into any detail here. But de Waal's study would also be part of the framework of a new linguistics.

The valency grammarian will read Tomasello's statements on verb island constructions with great satisfaction:

> As children begin to produce utterances that have more than one level of organization, that is, as they begin to produce utterances with multiple meaningful components, the most interesting question cognitively is how they use those component parts to linguistically partition the experiential scene as a whole into its constituent elements – including especially the event (or state of affairs) and participants involved. And ultimately children must also learn ways to symbolically indicate the different roles the partici-

> pants are playing in the event, such things as agent, patient, instrument, and the like. (Tomasello 1999: 138)

He goes on:

> The verb island hypothesis proposes that children's early linguistic competence is comprised totally of an inventory of linguistic constructions of this type: specific verbs with slots for participants whose roles are symbolically marked on an individual basis .... At this early stage children have made no generalizations about constructional patterns across verbs, and so they have no verb-general linguistic categories, schemas, or marking conventions ... . To repeat, the inventory of verb island constructions – in effect a simple list of constructions organized around individual verbs – makes up the totality of children's early linguistic competence; there are no other hidden principles, parameters, linguistic categories, or schemas that generate sentences.
>
> This item-specific way of using language is not something that goes away quickly. Indeed, in the view of many linguists, more of adult language is item-specific than is generally realized, including idioms, clichés, habitual collocations, and many other "non-core" linguistic constructions (e.g., *How ya doing, He put her up to it, She'll get over it*; Bolinger, 1977; Fillmore, Kay, and O'Connor, 1988). (Tomasello 1999: 139–140)

One very important point here is that according to Tomasello children start from very concrete structures and proceed to more and more abstract constructions:

> The mastery of verb island constructions is a major way station on the road to adult linguistic competence – a kind of base camp that is the goal of the early part of the journey but that, once reached, becomes only a means to the end of more abstract and productive linguistic constructions. (Tomasello 1999: 141)

4. From head to foot

In the light of Deacon's theory on language development this is a rather traditional view of the development of syntax or – more specifically – of the cognitive development of valency structures in children. I will therefore try to turn Tomasello's theory on its foot in this section. Tomasello seems to get into some trouble with his traditional concept. Take the following quotation: "Their [children's] sentence-level constructions are verb island constructions that are abstract with respect to the participants involved (they have open participant slots) but are totally concrete with respect to the relational structure as expressed by the verb and syntactic symbols (word order and grammatical case marking)" (Tomasello 1999: 140).

By any reasonable understanding of the meanings of *abstract* and *concrete* it is the relational structure that we would regard as abstract. Also the view that idioms and habitual collocations are item-specific or concrete would have to deal with the fact that patients with severe brain damage are still able to reproduce those "specific" items despite the fact that these patients have otherwise very limited cognitive abilities and are no longer able to perceive the specificity of certain situations.

So it seems to be necessary to turn Tomasello's theory upside down in this respect. I would like to suggest a new interpretation of the acquisition of verb island constructions:

The base camp children start from does not consist of specific and individual verb structures but rather of an abstract valency concept. Thus, the child does not proceed from trees to forest or from verbs to valency, but it is rather the other way round. This also seems to fit much better into Tomasello's general model of children's cognition (1999: 180).

first stage	young infants	understanding others as animate beings
second stage	nine months old	understanding others as intentional agents
third stage	four year olds	understanding others as mental agents

This model also proceeds from more general to more and more specific perceptions.

5. Valency grammar in mind?

I would like to begin this last section by putting a question mark behind the main title of my article: valency grammar in mind? In addition, I would like to raise two further questions in a similar form: valency theory in mind? and: valency in mind? The logical sequence of these questions would be theory, grammar, valency. What are the answers to these questions?

5.1. Valency theory in mind?

A really trivial answer is that someone who talks about a theory must have this theory in mind in one form or the other. So it is "yes".

A non-trivial answer can be given by making the following assumption: someone is unable to utter anything whatever about valency theory nor does she consciously know anything about it, yet she has valency theory in some innate or subconscious way in her mind: she cognizes valency theory. Modern research in the field of brain physiology and consciousness shows quite clearly that this assumption cannot be valid for a theory. So it is "no" for this case.

5.2. Valency grammar in mind?

The trivial answer is the same as for the theory question.

A non-trivial answer can be given against the background of Deacon's assumptions on the connection between neuronal brain structures and relatively variable language structures. The English and the German valency grammars exhibit quite different structures, and so the assumption that we have a valency grammar in mind seems rather improbable. So it seems to be "no" again.

5.3. Valency in mind?

The interesting, non-trivial answer is "yes". Valency is a universal concept and it is precisely because of this universality that it is present in the neuronal structures of our brains. This is of course restricted to our species, but we will find forerunners of valency in other species, too.[2]

So let me return to the beginning of this article. People working in the field of valency are invited to transcend the traditional linguistic limits. They will then come to an interdisciplinary view of the concept of valency and can happily combine their grammatical work with work in sociology and biology. In the light of Edelman's program the answer to the question if there is a *Valenztheorie* or theory of valency will get a very clear answer: "yes", there is a modern theory of valency and it is a model for a new kind of linguistics.

Notes

1. West has applied Edelman's Theory of Neuronal Group Selection very fruitfully to valency grammar and language and linguistics in general, relating it to knowledge and memory (2003: 272), and thus explaining the fuzziness of the distinction between complements and adjuncts with reference to neuronal processes within the brain. A different and more general focus on biological and brain processes is adopted in the following essay.

2. See Edelman (2004: ch. 9) for the causal interplay between brains, mental imagery, concepts and meaning.

References

Deacon, Terrence
1997 *The Symbolic Species: The Co-evolution of Language and the Brain.* New York: Norton.
De Waal, Frans
2001 *The Ape and the Sushi Master: Cultural Reflections by a Primatologist.* New York: Basic Books.
Edelman, Gerald
1992 *Bright Air, Brilliant Fire – On the Matter of the Mind.* New York: Basic Books.
2004 *Wider than the Sky: The Phenomenal Gift of Consciousness.* London: Penguin.
Langacker, Ronald
1987 *Foundations of Cognitive Grammar.* Stanford: Stanford University Press.
Searle, John
1995 *The Construction of Social Reality.* London: Penguin.
Tomasello, Michael
1999 *The Cultural Origins of Human Cognition.* Cambridge, Mass.: Harvard University Press.
West, Jonathan
2003 What can valency tell us about linguistic theory? In *Valency in Practice: Valenz in der Praxis*, Alan Cornell, Klaus Fischer, and Ian F. Roe (eds.), (German Linguistic and Cultural Studies 10.) Oxford: Lang.

The acquisition of argument structure[1]

Heike Behrens

1. Introduction

The concept of valency or argument structure is a powerful one in linguistics, although the current volume shows that there is still considerable debate as to how to characterise the valency of any given verb exactly. But if professional linguists and lexicographers encounter difficulties in defining the relationship between a verb's meaning(s) and its syntactic properties, how can a two-year-old manage?

Research on child language has focussed on argument structure or logical and syntactic valency rather than on semantic valency, that is the specification of the semantics of the arguments. This reflects the anglophone dominance in the field, but also emphasises the focus of interest, namely the role of the verb in the clause and the syntactic positions it opens. Consequently, I will follow this tradition and use the term *argument structure* rather than *valency* to refer to the acquisition research.

Argument structure acquisition has been a popular topic for the past 25 years, with shifting focus of attention. In the 1980s, a number of deductive accounts were proposed to explain which kind of knowledge helps children to identify the arguments a verb requires. These approaches relied on conceptual, semantic or syntactic cores, which could be universal and / or innate, and assume modular levels of representation. I will summarise these accounts under "bootstrapping" accounts, a metaphor used to explain how children could use information on one level of representation in order to get started (or to *bootstrap* in the technical sense) onto another level.

More recently, inductive learning accounts have gained popularity. In this view, children accumulate knowledge through usage events and derive generalizations about a given verb's syntactic and semantic properties only gradually. I will discuss such proposals under the heading "usage-based accounts" because they assume that children gain their knowledge about argument structure from observing the concrete usages of verbs in concrete discourse situations. Two types of approaches are of interest here. First, Construction Grammar accounts assume that the construction (a meaningful form-function unit) is the primary source of information, from which the properties of individual verbs can be derived. Second, there is research on the discourse and informativeness factors which determine argument realization in connected speech. These investigations use the concept of *Preferred Argument Structure*.

Since much research is ongoing, and since new results especially about crosslinguistic differences in argument structure are likely to lead to some modifications of earlier accounts, this paper provides pointers to previous and current research, rather than elaborating one of these aspects and theories in detail.

2. Deductive accounts of the acquisition of argument structure

The concept of argument structure assumes that verbs open up a number of semantically and syntactically specified positions. Typically, a verb like *put* opens positions for the putter, the thing being put and the location where the thing is put, as in *I put the book on the table*, whereas a verb like *see* opens two positions, namely the seer and the object being seen (*I see a boat*), but not a position of the location of the seeing or the object. This entails a relationship between events and the semantics of the verbs that encode these events, as well as a semantics-to-syntax mapping for these verbs.

Because argument structure seems such a logical and systematic concept, it is not surprising that researchers have made use of this concept for language acquisition. If argument structure is systematic, i.e., if there is a predictable relationship between a verb's semantics and the syntactic frames it occurs in, this relationship could provide a stepping stone for language learning because the verb "tells" the child about the linguistic items it goes with. But before observing the systematic syntax-semantics link, children could even make a connection between the event structure they observe in the preverbal phase, and possible argument structure patterns. Thus, if there is a systematic relationship between events, verb semantics and verb syntax, there are three possible entryways into the linguistic system. The assumption of such links leads to so-called bootstrapping accounts that predict that children use knowledge of one level of representation to bootstrap another level.

2.1. Conceptual starting points

Dan Slobin (1985) proposed a conceptual account for the acquisition of early syntactic relations. He argued that children all over the world will construe similar event representations and build up similar concepts, which will serve as the basis for linguistic encoding. That is, children learn to categorise events in the preverbal stage and try to find the linguistic entities that encode the participants in the event. For example, a common event is the so-called *Manipulative Activity Scene* where an agent does something to a patient. Children will form categories of such events and map them onto two-argument verbs.

> The central claim is that LMC [= language making capacity] constructs similar early grammars from all input languages. The surface forms will, of course, vary. What is constant are the basic notions that first receive grammatical expression, along with early constraints on the positioning of grammatical elements and the way in which they relate to syntactic expression. (Slobin 1985: 1161)

Transitive sentences will thus denote Manipulative Activity Scenes, before alternative, language-specific form-function mappings overrule this early alignment. That is, deviant language-specific patterns should be learned only in a second step.

Slobin's view was criticised by Melissa Bowerman, and later withdrawn by Slobin himself. Bowerman (1985) argues that children do not prefer Manipulative Activity Scene in their early transitive sentences. She concludes that there is no semantic basis for the acquisition of grammar. Based on a larger body of typological research and cross-linguistic acquisition studies, Slobin (1997, 2001) criticised his earlier views (Slobin 1985). He argues that there is no evidence for privileged grammatizable notions. Instead, children seem to be able to pick up any form-function relationship.

In a different vein, several authors suggested that children start out with conceptually simple, general-purpose verbs: Eve Clark (1993) formulated the "light verb hypothesis", and Anat Ninio (1999) the "pathbreaking verb hypothesis". These hypotheses claim that children start verb learning with semantically light verbs like *make, do,* and *put,* which can serve as pathbreaking verbs, and acquire semantically specific verbs only later. Thus, children initially only need fairly unspecific conceptual notions that serve a wide range of purposes, and differentiate their early unspecific concepts through extended exposure to a target language. However, this view was criticised from a crosslinguistic perspective because not all languages have a light verb vocabulary; e.g., Tzeltal (Mayan) has a vast array of semantically specific verbs, and it turns out that children from early on make a number of specific distinctions. Brown (1998) shows that children from early on have a rich and semantically rather specific inventory of eating verbs, for example, verbs to mean the equivalent of *eat soft things* versus *eat tortillas* or *eat crunchy things*. In a study of children's early usage of these verbs, Brown (2007) shows that children do not overgeneralise these semantically specific verbs to mean something more general, but use them adequately.

In sum, crosslinguistic analyses suggest that children make use of the affordances of the language they acquire. If a language has light verbs, they tend to be used frequently, although more specific verbs are used as well. But if a language does not provide such verbs, children quickly build up a rich repertoire of semantically specific verbs. To date, there is no evidence for a privileged conceptual starting point for the acquisition of verb syntax and semantics.

In the 1990s, two different approaches were much discussed. These approaches focus more narrowly on the mapping of syntax and semantics (cf. the review by Bowerman and Brown 2007). The so-called "semantic bootstrapping hypothesis" predicts that innate linking rules help the child to map the verb syntax onto already known verb semantics. The "syntactic bootstrapping hypothesis", in contrast, tries to explain how children can acquire and refine their knowledge of verb semantics by paying attention to the syntactic frames a verb is used in.

2.2. Semantic bootstrapping

Pinker (1994: 378) proposed that children use semantics to acquire syntax, because meaning is constrained by semantic factors:

> In the case of learning verb meanings, … not all logically possible construals of a situation can be psychologically plausible candidates for the meaning of a word. Instead, the hypotheses that a child's word learning mechanisms make available are constrained.

In his semantic bootstrapping hypothesis, Pinker (1989: 62) states that syntactic argument structure is predictable from semantic structure via the application of linking rules. The constraints on verb meaning interact with syntax in a systematic way: in the mental lexicon, verbs have rich semantic specifications. They project verb syntax by means of innate linking rules. The verb *hit*, for example, calls for an agent and a patient argument. Linking rules align the thematic roles to syntactically specified subjects and objects as in (1):

(1)	*Bert*	*hits*	*Ernie.*	
	AGENT		PATIENT	lexical representation
	↓		↓	linking-rules
	SUBJECT		OBJECT	syntactic structure

The hypothesis predicts that verbs with high semantic typicality should form the starting point for the acquisition of argument structure. For example, verbs with high semantic transitivity should be most easily aligned with transitive sentence structure.

Bowerman (1990) analysed English children's early transitive constructions and examined these predictions. She found that "best exemplars" are not acquired first. Instead, verbs like *have* and *see* are among children's early transitive verbs. They are high-frequency verbs, but have a non-prototypical linking between theta roles and syntactic structure, since the subjects are not typical agents and the patients are not typical patients. In a subsequent study, Bowerman (1996) examined the predictive power of Pinker's lexical rules for causative constructions. She analysed error patterns in children's encoding of causativity (as in *I disappeared the ball*) and found that the group of verbs that show errors differs from the group for which errors are predicted. In addition, Bowerman addresses the problem of cutting back on overgeneralizations. Some English verbs have alternative valency patterns and can be used intransitively or transitively (2a, b):

(2) a. *The stick breaks easily.*
b. *John breaks the stick.*

But alternating patterns can also be overgeneralised as in the following examples of non-alternating verbs (3a, b; Bowerman 1996: 454).

(3) a. *Button me the rest.*
b. *I said her no.*

Pinker (1989) proposed that broad-range linking rules, based on semantic categories, provide the *necessary* conditions for alternation. In order to account for the fact that some verbs do not alternate although they fit the semantic pattern, a set of more specific narrow-range linking rules is invoked which provides the *sufficient* conditions for distinguishing alternating and non-alternating verbs. Bowerman's (1996) summary of the data makes it seem unlikely that acquisition of argument structure patterns can be explained in terms of the interaction of broad- and narrow-range rules, especially since there is no evidence that children adhere to strict semantic groupings in the early stages of learning argument structure. Bowerman argues that instead children work with overly general assumptions about argument structure and have to learn to cut back on such errors.

One explanation for the low frequency of errors and their eventual disappearance is pre-emption. This means that errors are blocked because another verb or a related construction already occupies the semantic position of the possible alternate. When children know the construction *make disappear*, errors of the type *I disappeared the cake* will not occur because the semantic position is already filled. Pre-emption predicts that verbs for which the child knows the alternate construction should be less error-prone than verbs for which the child does not know the alternate construction. But a longitudinal study of two girls learning English showed that this is not the case (Bowerman 1996: 463-464).

Instead, usage-based factors could account for the relative infrequency of such errors, as well as for the disappearance of such errors, because repeated exposure to intransitive syntactic frames reduces the tendency to use verbs transitively (see also MacWhinney 1987).

The investigation of how the verb meaning can help to narrow down possible syntactic frames is just one side of the coin. If there is a predictable relationship between syntax and semantics, the process should work in the other direction as well such that knowledge of syntax should help to narrow down the possible meanings of a verb.

2.3. Syntactic bootstrapping

The syntactic bootstrapping hypothesis (Gleitman 1990) states that the syntactic frames a given verb occurs in are more informative about its semantics than a linking of the event itself to semantics, because any event is open to several ways of highlighting event participants. We can encode a "shopping" event from the perspective of the buyer (*Peter buys a book*), the seller (*Peter sells a book to Paula*), or the object (*The book cost Paula 10$*). Observation of an event alone does not help us to identify the linguistic perspective taken on an event. Moreover, Landau and Gleitman (1985) showed that blind children acquired the semantics of different verbs of vision, which demonstrates that the acquisition of verb semantics does not depend on the observation of events, but on the exploitation of linguistic structure. Gleitman (1990) predicts that the syntactic frames a given verb occurs in are systematically linked to verb semantics. For this hypothesis to work there needs to be a close alignment of argument structure and semantics:

> Verbs that describe externally caused transfer or change of possessor of an object from place to place (or from person to person) fit naturally into sentences with three noun phrases, for example, 'John put the ball on the table'. This is just the kind of transparent syntax/semantics relation that every known language seems to embody. It is therefore not too wild to conjecture that this relationship is part of the original presuppositional structure that children bring to the language learning task. (Gleitman 1990: 30)

Subsequent research by Naigles, Gleitman and Gleitman (1993) showed that children (mean age 2;9) can modify the verb meaning of familiar words when they hear it in a novel frame; e.g., they are likely to interpret the sentence *The zebra goes the lion* in a causative reading ('the zebra makes the lion go') in analogy to other cases where this structure encodes causativity. In a literature review on early verb knowledge, Naigles (2002) states that "form is easy, meaning is hard". Infants are good at processing form patterns (segmental, prosodic, structural), less good in handling semantic information. However, Naigles argues, later in development the occurrence of a verb in different formats or syntactic frames helps the child to narrow down the semantics (cf. also Naigles 1996).

Several authors found problems with the syntactic bootstrapping account. Pinker (1994: 382) criticised Gleitman's strong reliance on syntactic structure for the inference of verb meaning, because the other words in the sentence carry meaning as well. He argues that in sentences like *I filped the delicious sandwich and now I'm full*, the meaning of the pseudo-verb *filp* can be inferred from the lexical knowledge of the other words in the sentence without reliance on syntactic structure. This may explain why blind children learn verb semantics without having access to visual information. Furthermore, Pinker takes issue with Gleitman's claim that meaning cannot be learnt from observation of a word's usage in concrete contexts. Rather, for some semantically related verbs with the same argument structure, only the context can disambiguate subtle semantic differences; e.g., real world experience is needed to distinguish the manner of actions (e.g., *open* versus *close, tear* versus *break,* Pinker 1994: 394). Pinker's conclusion is that Gleitman's arguments are void if one assumes that children's word meanings are universally constrained such that they will not come up with nonsensical hypotheses about word meanings. Then, context information will provide sufficient information to derive the meaning distinctions between different verbs.

Wilkins (2007) points out another problem with the Gleitman's assumption that the syntax-semantics alignment of verbs is part of the "original presuppositional structure that children bring to the language learning task", because argument structure patterns are not the same crosslinguistically. Wilkins looked at the equivalents of the verbs *look* and *put* in Arrente, an Australian Aboriginal language. In English, the perception verb *look* is a classic example of a two-place predicate (agent and object), and the transfer verb *put* is a classic example for a three-place predicate (agent, object, location). In Arrente, however, by all linguistic tests, the verbs *arrerne* ['look'] and *are* ['put'] are three-place predicates that open positions for agent, object and location of the object put or seen. In the case of the verb *look*, the resultant meaning can, for example, come close to the English verb *find* (*to see something somewhere* denotes 'find it'). Thus, syntactic bootstrapping accounts would fail with Arrente, because there is no "natural" alignment between argument structure and verb semantics as proposed by Gleitman. Nonetheless, in a corpus analysis of spoken Arrente, Wilkins (2007) found that adults use these verbs in a different fashion: *look* is used as a two-place predicate more often than *put*. For *put*, the locative NP is realised more frequently than for *look*. Children follow this usage, and have particular problems with the third argument for *look*. These findings suggest that while there is no strict alignment between syntax and semantics that would allow children to bootstrap from syntax to semantics, in actual usage some argument structure realizations are more common than others. Children may use such distributional differences to induce verb meaning.

So far, we have seen that both syntactic and semantic bootstrapping do not work in a deductive way: the link between semantics and syntax regarding argument structure is not tight enough to allow full predictability. Consequently, inductive accounts of language acquisition gained ground in the past decade and can now be considered the dominant framework in acquisition.

3. Inductive accounts for language acquisition

The discussion so far has demonstrated that there seems to be little support for theories that assume a tight link between verb semantics and syntax that could be used to predict either syntax or semantics. But then how could children acquire argument structure? Alternative theories known under headings such as usage-based theories (Tomasello 2003) or emergentism (Elman et al. 1996; MacWhinney 1999) focus on the learning and categorization mechanisms itself. These theories assume that complex cognitive patterns can be induced from noticing distributional properties of the input language (Elman 2003). In addition to being able to use such probabilistic cues as early as in infancy (Saffran 2003; Gomez and Gerken 2000), humans also demonstrate the ability to perceive the intention of others in a concrete situation (Tomasello and Rakoczy 2003). If children are aware of other people's intention, however, this will help them to narrow down the possible meaning of what is being said. That is, the concept of the child as an intention reader replaces the Generative Grammar concept of the child as an hypothesis tester. Several studies have shown how intention reading contributes to early word learning; e.g., in an experiment a child and his/her mother played with three novel and unnamed objects. The mother went out and the child received another novel and unnamed object. When the mother came back in, she looked at the four objects and exclaimed "Oh look! A modi! A modi!". 24-month-old children significantly associated the word *modi* with the fourth object. They could not have done so by simple association but must have used social cognition, in this case their understanding that people get excited about new things (Akthar, Carpenter, and Tomasello 1996).

3.1. Usage-based models of syntax

Usage-based accounts of acquisition assume that learning takes place by generalising over concrete usage events (see Tomasello 2003 for a summary). They do not draw a distinction between universal and innate core grammar, which is acquired by deduction, and the periphery, which has to be learnt by induction. Instead, it is supposed that all properties of languages can be acquired from the input by powerful generalization abilities in connection with social cognition. The plausibility of usage-based learning is supported by a growing body of research which shows that even infants have a remarkable capacity for pattern recognition and statistical learning, regardless of whether the patterns are semantically motivated or not (see Saffran 2003 and Gomez and Gerken 2000 for a general introduction, and Newport and Aslin 2004 for more detail). Furthermore, research in computational linguistics shows that grammatical categories as well as information about constituency can be gained by data-driven parsing, without supplying "rules" to the computer (Redington, Chater, and Finch 1998; Keibel et al. 2006; Klein and Manning 2004). Finally, comparisons between child and input data show a close alignment between input patterns and the structures attested in children, which suggests that children pay close attention to the distributional properties of language use in the ambient language (Behrens 2006).

If acquisition is based on the evidence children get from the input, a number of predictions follow. First, acquisition should be item-specific because children have no access to a priori verb-general categories. Second, cross-linguistic differences are expected: if different languages show different alignments of syntax and semantics in language use, this should be reflected in acquisition.

3.1.1. Crosslinguistic variation

Recent investigations into "exotic", non Indo-European languages revealed that there is considerable variation both in terms of argument structure proper and in terms of argument realization. In general, high and/or substantial variation makes deductive account less plausible, because phenomena with large variability call for inductive learning processes.

Typological research has pointed out that semantic specificity has an impact on argument realization, because in lexically-specific verbs, the verb meaning may already incorporate some arguments. Compare, for example, the verb *kick* with the construction *push with foot*. In *kick*, the instrument *foot* is incorporated in the verb meaning and need not be specified as an extra argument. For *push*, in contrast, agent, object and instrument need to be specified. Consequently, languages with a richly specified verb lexicon tend to show more argument ellipsis than languages where the verb lexicon is rather small and semantically more general (cf. Bowerman and Brown 2007).

3.1.2. Item-specificity

In usage-based accounts for acquisition, the notion of verb-specificity has become very relevant. It is argued that the syntax of early child language is item-specific rather than abstract. This hypothesis has led researchers to reconsider the units children operate with: rather than to assume that verbs project syntactic structures based on their semantics, it is suggested that children work out form-function alignments based on individual verbs, and generalise over groups of verbs only later.

Tomasello (1992) analysed his daughter's development of verb syntax on a verb-by-verb basis. He did not find groups of transitive or intransitive verbs that show similar syntactic behaviour, but rather that each individual verb started out with its own, lexically-specific frame. At a given point in time, the child used the verb *cut* only in the frame *cut X*, while the syntactically similar verb *draw* was used in a wider range of frames (*draw X, draw X on Y, draw on X, draw X for Y*; Tomasello 2003: 117). These findings led Tomasello to propose the verb island hypothesis. It states that the best predictor for a given verb's use is not the use of other related verbs at the same time, but the child's previous use of that particular verb (Tomasello 1992: 256).

The item-specificity of early child language is related to the non-productivity of these utterances: if a child uses direct objects only with particular verbs, but not with all kinds of verbs that take direct objects, this may indicate that these early constructions are frozen or (semi-)formulaic concrete lexical units, rather than represented in an analytic or abstract fashion. Indeed, Pine, Lieven, and Rowland (1998) found that in the speech of twelve children learning English, the five most common slot-and-frame-patterns like *mommy X* or *want X* accounted for an average of 70% of all utterances containing verbs.

In the usage-based framework, the lexical robustness of early child utterances is considered as evidence that children operate with prefabricated "chunks" and do not generate utterances from scratch (Tomasello 2000). Similar conclusions can be drawn from the behaviour of individual verbs: Theakston et al. (2002) studied the used of word-forms of *go* (*go, goes, going, gone, went*) in eleven British children. They found little evidence for overlap of arguments across word forms. Instead, each word form seemed to have its own frames. In addition, children's use highly correlated with adult usage.

But what is the advantage of analysing child language in such a pattern-based approach? First, it directs the attention to the communicative function of the utterance, not to the syntactic or semantic representation of words in isolation. It is assumed that early formulae or patterns are linked by the same communicative function. Second, pattern-based approaches assign a different role to verbs. Rather than seeing verbs as the core elements that project syntax, verbs constitute just one, albeit important, aspect of communicative units. It is in this respect that recent acquisition theory draws a close connection to Cognitive Linguistics in general and Construction Grammar in particular (Tomasello 1998).

3.2. Constructions as predictor for language learning

In Construction Grammar, constructions are defined as entities of variable size, which are fixed pairings of form and meaning (see Fillmore and Kay 1993; Goldberg 1995 and 2006 for theory; Tomasello 1998 for acquisition). Tomasello (1998) claims that early acquisition is more adequately described in terms of constructions because the linguistic knowledge underlying early child language is tied to lexical items rather than being abstract or verb-general. Different structures need not be linked by rules, but could represent independent schemata, which may be analyzed only partially. There is no distinction between core and non-core-phenomena or between universal and language-specific factors because all of language is acquired bottom-up from language use (Tomasello 1992, 2003).

This approach differs crucially from the bootstrapping accounts described above, because the construction approach does not rely on syntactic or semantic primitives. It neither assumes the availability of abstract syntactic categories like word class or thematic roles, nor the availability of a detailed semantic analysis in terms of primitives that constitute the basis for syntactic acquisition. Instead, children use larger or smaller units to convey their communicative intention. In order to do so, it is not necessary that they have abstracted all the component parts of the construction, just like adults use idioms where the underlying structure remains opaque. What constructivist approaches then have to account for is how and when linguistic knowledge is abstracted. Linguistic creativity in both children and adults shows that at some point in development they are able to go beyond what they have heard and use their knowledge of the meaning of syntactic constructions to use lexemes in new and productive ways (cf. Fillmore and Kay 1993).

In fact, linguistic productivity would break down completely if children relied only on positive evidence and only used those constructions or arguments they had actually registered in the ambient language (Bowerman 1996: 464; Goldberg 1995). Recent experiments from a usage-based perspective therefore focus on generalization mechanisms. Goldberg and colleagues undertook a number of studies that tested how Construction Grammar can be used to predict the acquisition of argument structure (Goldberg and Casenhiser 2005a, b; Goldberg, Casenhiser, and Sethuranam, 2004; for summary and theoretical elaboration see Goldberg 2006). In a training study, 51 5–7 year-old-children were trained with a new argument structure pattern of the form "NP NP novel verb" (e.g., *the spot the king moopoed*) to encode appearance (the corresponding video showed a spot appearing on the king's nose). Within less than three minutes, the children saw 16 videos representing five new verbs. One group saw them in a skewed exposure (one video was shown eight times, the remaining four videos twice each). The second group had a more balanced exposure (three videos four times, two videos twice). It turned out that the group that was exposed to a skewed distribution generalised the new pattern best. This result confirms earlier findings from corpus studies that showed that within a particular syntactic construction, the distribution tends to be biased in that one verb represents a large number of tokens of that construction (Goldberg, Casenhiser, and Sethuranam 2004).

Based on these findings, Goldberg (2006) argues that the role of the construction has an important impact on acquisition. But what exactly determines the predictive power of verb-based constructions? At first glance, it seems that within a construction, verbs still have the highest predictive power because verbs are relational elements and therefore entail sentence meaning (i.e., who did what to whom, Goldberg 2006: 104). In a set of experiments, Goldberg and colleagues tried to test the relative contribution of verbs versus constructions in light of the fact that many verbs are polysemous such that their occurrence in different construction types is correlated with different meanings. Thus, under which circumstances are verbs better predictors, and under which circumstances are constructions the better predictor of sentence meaning? Goldberg argues that this is a matter of *cue validity*, a concept adapted from the competition model by Bates and MacWhinney (1987). This model hypothesises that all linguistic structures represent different formal and functional cues. Acquisition sequences are determined by the *cue cost*, the effort it takes to detect and process this cue (e.g., affixes are easier to detect and to segment than stem changes) and *cue validity*, the degree to which this cue is a reliable cue for this phenomenon (e.g., morphological paradigms with a 1:1 form-function correspondence have higher cue validity than paradigms with a high degree of syncretism and ambiguity). Regarding verb semantics, highly polysemous verbs like *get* have low cue validity regarding meaning. Here, the construction type can help to disambiguate possible readings and thus has a higher cue validity for meaning (see example 4; Goldberg 2006: 106).

(4) a. Pattern VOL: (Subj) V Obj $OBl_{path/loc}$ → caused motion
Pat got the ball over the fence.
b. Pattern VOO: (Subj) V Obj Obj → transfer
Pat got Bob a cake.

Based on corpus analyses and experiments, Goldberg and colleagues conclude that for early acquisition, verb-argument constructions (compatible to the verb-island constructions or slot-and-frame patterns discussed above) are better predictors of sentence meaning than the verb in isolation. This also holds for generalization in later stages of acquisition: the argument frame is at least as good a predictor of sentence meaning as the verb itself in isolation, because many high-frequency verbs are polysemous and have low cue validity for meaning (see Goldberg 2006: 105–126 for a summary of the results).

In sum, constructivist accounts point to the primary nature of the construction as the main conveyor of meaning since we talk in utterances, not in isolated words. These accounts also tend to be inductive, because they assume a usage-based vantage point where general learning mechanisms as well as social cognition regarding the intention of the other speaker allow children to induce linguistic knowledge on increasingly complex and abstract levels.

The impact of language use on argument structure is also studied in a different research tradition that investigates the influence of the discourse context on argument structure.

4. Preferred Argument Structure (PAS)

The studies reported so far focussed on a "context neutral" perspective of argument structure: which arguments does a given verb with a particular semantics call for? But in concrete connected speech or discourse, arguments can be dropped or provided for a number of reasons. First, there are language-specific structural reasons because some languages like Chinese show the phenomenon of topic drop: a topic once established needs not be encoded again, unless the topic changes. Second, there are various factors that influence context-dependent ellipsis. An argument can be assumed as "given", for example, because it is visible and can be pointed to or looked at. Furthermore, arguments need not be realised lexically, but can be encoded as pronouns or affixes on the verb. These factors determine argument realization. Discourse studies have shown that "givenness" in previous discourse is likely to lead to ellipsis or pronominal realisation, whereas "newness" is more likely to lead to encoding by a full NP. Several researchers are interested in "Preferred Argument Structure" and look at the structural (DuBois 1987) and discourse-pragmatic factors (Clancy 1997) that determine the number and nature of arguments that are realised in a particular language or a particular genre.

The concept of Preferred Argument Structure can be applied to child language. What is the effect of ellipsis, or pronominal versus lexical encoding in the adult language on acquisition? How does a child learn which arguments to provide and when? It is a common feature of early child language that arguments are omitted. For example, utterances often lack the subject as in *want milk*. Allen (2000: 484f.) identifies three explanations for this phenomenon. The first comes from a Generative Grammar perspective and hypothesises that children's grammar is consistent with adult grammar. In a parameter-setting version of Generative Grammar, children may assume that arguments are dropped unless positive evidence in the adult language tells them that they should be provided. Thus, the innate state would be that the child is equipped with knowledge about the circumstances under which arguments may be dropped (e.g., Hyams 1986). Second, performance factors are held responsible for argument omission. Researchers assume that children know the argument structure of a verb, but that their processing capacities are insufficient to handle all arguments. Thus, their representation of argument structure is adult-like, but provision of arguments is hindered by performance restrictions (e.g., Valian 1991). Thirdly, discourse-pragmatic accounts investigate which situational factors lead to the provision of arguments, without assuming that children's knowledge is adult-like (Clancy 1993).

Allen (2000) examined eight features of discourse-pragmatic prominence which contribute to the relative informativeness of arguments in the speech of four Inuktitut-speaking children aged 2;0 to 3;6. The "informativeness features" include knowledge features as well as confusion factors. For example, if one wants to talk about an object that is absent in the physical context, it must be realised as an argument unless it has already been established as the discourse topic. Likewise, one needs to realise arguments that one asks questions about. But "confusion features" also lead to the provision of arguments; e.g., if there are two or more possible referents in the discourse context, the intended referent has to be encoded overtly.

Inuktitut, a Inuit language spoken in Northern Canada, allows for massive argument ellipsis, and children between 2;0 and 3;6 years of age only provide about 18% of all arguments (Allen and Schröder 2000). When they do, their provision of arguments follows the predictions of DuBois' *Preferred Argument Structure* in that there is no more than one new argument per clause, and in that lexical arguments (as opposed to demonstratives or affixes) tend to encode new arguments (Allen and Schröder 2000). But the rampant omission of arguments in adult language raises the question why children provide arguments at all. Logistic regression analyses showed that argument provision by Inuktitut children is not random (Allen 2000). A model containing all eight features of pragmatic prominence is significantly more accurate at predicting which arguments will be overtly represented than a model containing none of these features. The presence of informativeness features also explains the overproductions of some types of arguments in early child language, as well as the omission of uninformative arguments by children where adults provide pronouns.

5. Summary and discussion

Generally speaking, inductive and deductive accounts can be distinguished by their vantage point: inductive accounts see linguistic categories as probabilistic concepts. For example, the "usual" case is for verbs with a transitive meaning to take two arguments, and for verbs of transfer to take three arguments. Deductive accounts assume that linguistic categories have a semantic or symbolic core, which is considered to be absolute such that children could make use of the link between the semantic and syntactic core in order to bootstrap another level of linguistic representation.

The semantic bootstrapping account comes closest to the traditional notion of *valency*. Valency in its core is a "projection" account: the verb exercises control over the arguments it occurs with. Consequently, there should be a systematic link between verb semantics and verb syntax that could be exploited in language learning since it would allow the child to predict the properties of semantically or syntactically similar verbs. The semantic bootstrapping account strives for full predictability of syntax on the basis of semantics (e.g., narrow and broad range linking rules) because it is assumed that learners are hypothesis-testing, thus grammar and semantics needed to be constrained in order to protect the learner from generalizing overly general grammars.

The syntactic bootstrapping account focuses on how children can use their syntactic knowledge for possible verb semantics. Syntactic bootstrapping cannot be the starting point for acquisition because it requires that children have built up some lexical as well as structural knowledge in order to deduce semantics based on structure.

More recently, the role of the construction has been emphasised in another framework, usage-based models of language. These inductive models are more lenient because they rely on probabilistic, not absolute cues. Since learners are assumed to be conservative, not hypothesis-testing, they will only generalise on the basis of positive evidence. They start out with lexically-based utterance schemas in order to encode their intentions and abstract semantic and syntactic components only gradually. It is important to note that constructions are defined as form-function units, thus form and function are equally important. The starting point need not be the semantic or syntactic "core" from which the periphery is acquired; instead, the core components would be the results of generalization over repeated experience. Research in this tradition focuses more narrowly on the exact learning processes that lead to more schematic and later fully abstract representations.

In usage-based models we observe a shift of attention from the role of the verb to the role of the syntactic frame or construction. This is psychologically plausible because humans communicate in order to convey intentions, and they do so using utterances, not words (Tomasello 2000). Thus, utterances are the primary source of information from which words and syntactic operations that combine them can be isolated or abstracted. For this to happen, there needs to be repetition *and* variation: repeated exposure leads to the entrenchment of that particular structure. However, without variation this structure would be unanalyzed and frozen, and productivity would break down. Variation in the structure is needed to acquire more general and abstract schemata; e.g., if a given verb is only used with prepositional phrases denoting location, the learner will probably not generalise this frame to manner information as well. Thus, a model that integrates both entrenchment and variation leads to more sophisticated mental models that allow for (frequency-based) generalisations and help to explain developmental as well as diachronic language change (cf. Bybee 2005).

One of the key problems is to determine in more detail how repetition and variation interact. Bybee (2005) alludes to exemplar-based models of language, which assume that each usage-event is an exemplar that acts on our representation because it leaves a memory trace. This theory thus relies on concrete (= substantial) usage that is stored. It is as yet not known whether we simply store more and more tokens upon repeated usage, or whether we store more repeated information on a more general and abstract level when available, or whether we do both. The latter is conceivable since first results suggest that we have access to multiple levels of specificity (Bybee and Scheibman 1999).

And finally, research on the exact nature of storage in the mental lexicon is required. Elman (2004) refutes the classic perspective of the mental lexicon as that of a "dictionary" in long-term memory with a passive storage for semantic and structural information. Alternatively, he proposes a dynamic model of the mental lexicon based on previous experience. With each new experience with words, the mental space of the lexicon is refined and redivided; e.g., each new exposure to the word *child* in context acts on our existing representation of the concept 'child'. We do not simply retrieve a fixed word meaning from memory in order to process the new sentence. Elman (2004: 305) proposes that there is a continuum from learning words to learning constructions: "Thus, knowledge of constructions is a straightforward extension, by generalization, of knowledge of groups of words that behave similarly". From a usage-based perspective, children's and adult's representations can be seen as a dynamic mental inventory of lexical items and constructions.

Notes

1. My interest in and knowledge about this topic goes back to the many intense and lively discussions in the *Argument Structure Project* at the Max-Planck-Institute for Psycholinguistics in Nijmegen in the mid 1990s. In particular, I would like to thank Shanley Allen, Melissa Bowerman, Penny Brown, Paulette Levy and David Wilkins for discussions on this topic. The inspiration for usage-based acquisition research came from many discussions at the Max-Planck-Institute for Evolutionary Anthropology in Leipzig, most notably with Mike Tomasello, Elena Lieven and Kirsten Abbot-Smith.

References

Akthar, Nameera, Malinda Carpenter, and Michael Tomasello
1996 The role of discourse novelty in early word learning. *Child Development* 67: 635–645.

Allen, Shanley E. M.
2000 A discourse-pragmatic explanation for argument representation in child Inuktitut. *Linguistics* 38: 483–521.

Allen, Shanley E. M., and Heike Schröder
2000 Preferred argument structure in early Inuktitut spontaneous speech data. In *Preferred Argument Structure: Grammar as Architecture for Function,* John W. DuBois, Lorraine E. Kumpf, and William J. Ashby (eds.), 301–338. Amsterdam: Benjamins.

Bates, Elizabeth, and Brian MacWhinney
1987 Competition, variation and language learning. In *Mechanisms of Language Acquisition,* Brian MacWhinney (ed.), 157–193. Hillsdale, NJ: Erlbaum.

Behrens, Heike
2006 The input-output relationship in first language acquisition. *Language and Cognitive Processes* 21: 2–24.

Bowerman, Melissa
1985 What shapes children's grammar? In *The Crosslinguistic Study of Language Acquisition.* Vol. 2: *Theoretical Issues,* Dan I. Slobin (ed.), 1257–1319. Hillsdale, NJ: Erlbaum.

1990 Mapping thematic roles onto syntactic functions: Are children helped by linking rules? *Linguistics* 28: 1253–1290.

1996 Argument structure and learnability: Is a solution in sight? In *Proceedings of the Twenty-Second Meeting of the Berkeley Linguistics Society (=BLS 22),* Jan Johnson, Matthew L. Juge, and Jeri L. Moxley (eds.), 454–468. Berkeley: Berkeley Linguistics Society.

Bowerman, Melissa, and Penelope Brown

2007 Introduction. In *Crosslinguistic Perspectives on Argument Structure: Implications for Language Acquisition,* Melissa Bowerman, and Penelope Brown (eds.). Mahwah, NJ: Erlbaum.

Brown, Penelope

1998 Children's first verbs in Tzeltal: Evidence from the early verb category. *Linguistics* 36: 713–753.

2007 Verb specificity and argument realization in Tzeltal child language: Implications for language acquisition. In *Crosslinguistic Perspectives on Argument Structure: Implications for Language Acquisition,* Melissa Bowerman, and Penelope Brown (eds.). Mahwah, NJ: Erlbaum.

Bybee, Joan L.

2005 From usage to grammar: The mind's response to repetition. Manuscript: University of New Mexico, Albuquerque.

Bybee, Joan L., and Joanne Scheibman

1999 The effects of usage of degrees of constituency: The reduction of "don't" in English. *Linguistics* 37: 575–596.

Clancy, Patricia

1993 Preferred argument structure in Korean acquisition. In *Proceedings of the 25th Annual Child Language Research Forum,* Eve V. Clark (ed.), 307–314. Stanford: CSLI.

1997 Discourse motivations of referential choice in Korean acquisition. In *Japanese / Korean Linguistics 6,* Ho-min Sohn, and John Haig (eds.), 639–659. Stanford, CA: CSLI.

Clark, Eve V.

1993 *The Lexicon in Acquisition.* Cambridge: Cambridge University Press.

DuBois, John W.

1987 The discourse basis of ergativity. *Language* 63: 805–855.

Elman, Jeffrey L.

2003 Generalization from sparse input. *Proceedings of the 38th Meeting of the Chicago Linguistics Society.* Chicago: Chicago University Press.

2004 A different view on the mental lexicon. *Trends in Cognitive Science* 8: 301–306.

Elman, Jeffrey L., Elizabeth A. Bates, Mark H. Johnson, Annette Karmiloff-Smith, Domenico Parisi, and Kim Plunkett

1996 *Rethinking Innateness: A Connectionist Perspective on Development.* Cambridge, Mass.: MIT Press.

Fillmore, Charles J., and Paul Kay
1993 *Construction Grammar Coursebook: Chapters 1 thru 11.* University of California at Berkeley: Department of Linguistics.
Gleitman, Lila R.
1990 The structural sources of verb meaning. *Language Acquisition* 1: 3–55.
Goldberg, Adele E.
1995 *Constructions.* Chicago: Chicago University Press.
2006 *Constructions at Work: The Nature of Generalization in Language.* Oxford: Oxford University Press.
Goldberg, Adele E., and Devin M. Casenhiser
2005a The role of prediction in construction learning. *Journal of Child Language* 32: 407–426.
2005b Fast mapping between a phrasal form and meaning. *Developmental Science* 8: 500–508.
Goldberg, Adele E., Devin M. Casenhiser, and Nitya Sethuranam
2004 Learning argument structure generalizations. *Cognitive Linguistics* 15: 289–316.
Gomez, Rebecca L., and Louann Gerken
2000 Infant artificial language learning and language acquisition. *Trends in Cognitive Science* 4: 178–186.
Hyams, Nina
1986 *Language Acquisition and the Role of Parameters.* Dordrecht: Reidel.
Keibel, Holger, Jeffrey L. Elman, Elena Lieven, and Michael Tomasello
2006 From words to categories. University of Freiburg: Unpublished Manuscript.
Klein, Dan, and Christopher Manning
2004 Corpus-based induction of syntactic structure: Models of dependency and constituency. *Proceedings of the 42nd Annual Meeting of the Association for Computational Linguistics (ACL 2004).*
Landau, Barbara, and Lila R. Gleitman
1985 *Language and Experience: Evidence from the Blind Child.* Cambridge, Mass.: Harvard University Press.
MacWhinney, Brian
1987 The competition model. In *Mechanisms of Language Acquisition,* Brian MacWhinney (ed.), 249–308. Hillsdale, NJ: Erlbaum.
MacWhinney, Brian (ed.)
1999 *The Emergence of Language.* Mahwah, NJ: Erlbaum.
Naigles, Letitia R.
1996 The use of multiple frames in verb learning via syntactic bootstrapping. *Cognition* 58: 221–251.
2002 Form is easy, meaning is hard: Resolving a paradox in early child language. *Cognition* 86: 157–199.

Naigles, Letitia, Lila R. Gleitman, and Henry Gleitman
1993 Children acquire word meaning components from syntactic evidence. In *Language and Cognition: A Developmental Perspective*, Esther Dromi (ed.), 104–140. Norwood, NJ: Ablex.

Newport, Elissa L., and Richard N. Aslin
2004 Learning at a distance: I. Statistical learning of non-adjacent dependencies. *Cognitive Psychology* 48: 127–162.

Ninio, Anat
1999 Pathbreaking verbs in syntactic development and the question of prototypical transitivity. *Journal of Child Language* 26: 619–653.

Pine, Julian M., Elena V. M. Lieven, and Caroline F. Rowland
1998 Comparing different models of the English verb category. *Linguistics* 36: 807–830.

Pinker, Steven
1989 *Learnability and Cognition: The Acquisition of Argument Structure.* Cambridge, Mass.: MIT Press.
1994 How could a child use verb syntax to learn verb semantics? *Lingua* 92: 377–410.

Redington, Martin, Nick Chater, and Steven Finch
1998 Distributional information: A powerful cue for acquiring syntactic categories. *Cognitive Science* 22: 425–469.

Saffran, Jenny R.
2003 Statistical language learning: Mechanisms and constraints. *Current Directions in Psychological Science* 12: 110–114.

Slobin, Dan I.
1985 Crosslinguistic evidence for the language-making capacity. In *The Crosslinguistic Study of Language Acquisition.* Vol. 2: *Theoretical Issues*, Dan I. Slobin (ed.), 1157–1249. Hillsdale, NJ: Erlbaum.
1997 The origins of grammaticizable notions: Beyond the individual mind. In *The Crosslinguistic Study of Language Acquisition.* Vol. 5: *Expanding the Contexts,* Dan I. Slobin (ed.), 265–323. Mahwah, NJ: Erlbaum.
2001 Form-function relations: How do children find out what they are? In *Language Acquisition and Conceptual Development*, Melissa Bowerman, and Steve Levinson (eds.), 406–449. Cambridge: Cambridge University Press.

Theakston, Anna L., Elena V. M. Lieven, Julian M. Pine, and Caroline F. Rowland
2002 Going, going, gone: The acquisition of the verb "go". *Journal of Child Language* 29: 783–811.

Tomasello, Michael
1992 *First Verbs: A Case Study of Early Grammatical Development.* Cambridge: Cambridge University Press.
1998 The return of constructions. Review essay on: Goldberg, A., 1995 'Constructions: A construction grammar approach to argument structure'. *Journal of Child Language* 25: 443–484.

2000 Do young children have adult syntactic competence? *Cognition* 74: 209–253.
2003 *Constructing a Language: A Usage-Based Account of Language Acquisition.* Cambridge, Mass.: Harvard University Press.

Tomasello, Michael, and Hannes Racoczy
2003 What makes human cognition unique? From individual to shared to collective intentionality. *Mind and Language* 18: 121–147.

Valian, Virginia
1991 Syntactic subjects in the early speech of American and Italian children. *Cognition* 40: 21–81.

Wilkins, David P.
2007 Same argument structure, different meanings: Learning 'put' and 'look' in Arrernte. In *Crosslinguistic Perspectives on Argument Structure: Implications for Language Acquisition,* Melissa Bowerman, and Penelope Brown (eds.). Mahwah, NJ: Erlbaum.

Section 3
Contrastive aspects of valency

Valency and the errors of learners of English and German

Ian Roe

1. Introduction

In contrast to the majority of contributions to the current volume, this essay is concerned primarily with valency not as a theoretical construct but as a learning (and teaching) tool. The first English valency dictionary (Herbst et al. 2004) has recently been published, the German tradition in this field is already well established both in terms of grammar and dictionaries, although only the recently published VALBU (Schumacher et al. 2004) comes close to meriting the term "user-friendly" and there is as yet no valency dictionary targeted at English-speaking learners.[1] The current essay seeks to investigate some of the areas that need to be addressed by a user-friendly valency dictionary for learners by drawing some comparisons, on the basis of a small analysis of errors, between the linguistic problems encountered by German and English advanced learners of the other language. Two questions need to be asked: what proportion (and what types) of errors might be seen as valency-specific? And what different conclusions might the compilers of English and German valency dictionaries need to draw?

2. Brief analysis of errors

2.1. German learners of English

A tempting short-cut to painstaking analysis in this field is, on the surface at least, Geoff Parkes's *Mistakes Clinic* (2001), which offers an analysis of over twenty years of work submitted by German learners of English, involving 4,000 errors of vocabulary and 5,500 errors of grammar and syntax. It is interesting to note that, in a list of the top twelve grammar mistakes, the most frequent is the use of prepositions, the fourth most frequent is confusion between *ing*- and infinitive-constructions. However, although Parkes's booklet provides useful examples and lists and is undoubtedly helpful for teachers of English, for our present purposes there is no attempt to distinguish complementation errors and other types of syntactical or grammatical error. As one example: where more detailed information is provided on prepositions by giving a top 20, the first four are all errors concerning adjuncts (e.g.**leave school with 16*, **in the last moment*), but the next five are valency-specific (which preposition is needed after *good, contact, pay, typical, depend*) and errors with *explain, connection, discuss, react, knowledge* are listed at 13 and 16-19 respectively (Parkes 2001: 125).

For a less extensive but, in the present context, more differentiated analysis I have used a small corpus of translations into English by German exchange students together with essays in English by German native-speakers.

Conflating the analysis of two sets of advanced translations, one finds that of 189 errors of syntax,

- 66 (one third of the total) were valency driven errors, of which 44 involved verbs, 13 nouns, and 9 adjectives;
- 123 were general errors (e.g. tense or aspect, misuse of articles, an adjective used instead of an adverb, word order, etc.).

The collection of essays produced a slightly different picture:[2] almost half (53) of the 114 errors were valency, and a rather higher percentage (21 of 53) were errors of noun valency, but that was perhaps inevitable in essays, as the errors occurred with nouns such as *argument, question, discussion, criticism*.

Taking the two sets together, 119 of 303 errors (39%) were valency-specific, and verbs accounted for 59% of the valency errors. Of the 119 valency-specific errors, 36 involved the wrong choice of clause, especially between infinitive and *ing*-constructions, 47 were wrong choice of preposition; there were also 13 examples of the wrong choice between noun phrase and prepositional complement (**She returned me my change*), although the majority of these latter errors involved problems with apposition (**the province Carinthia*, **the state Israel*). Of the 184 non-valency errors, 64 involved the wrong choice of tense or aspect (including wrong choice of simple or continuous [25], and incorrect use or omission of the auxiliary *do* [17]), 21 wrong prepositions, 25 wrong uses of the article, and 22 word-order errors (mainly the position of adverbials).

2.2. English learners of German

The parallel German corpus consists of two sets of translations into German by British final-year university students. The first set was written a number of years ago by 33 final-year students with, in most cases, nine years of German, including five or ten months in Germany or Austria. Dictionaries were not allowed in this earlier examination. Leaving aside errors of vocabulary, the 155 valency-specific errors can initially be analysed as follows:

- 126 errors of verb valency (plus a further 7 instances of the nominative used as an object);
- 14 problems of noun valency, although mainly the use of a plural subject with a singular verb;
- 1 adjective (*befürchtet*, which might therefore be seen as verbal);
- and 7 errors in the use of collocation (what Ágel [2003: 33] refers to as "syntaktische Ausdrucksvalenzträger"): *zu tun haben mit*, *Bescheid wissen*.

It is important, however, to note that there was a large variety of errors that were not valency-specific. Such general grammatical errors numbered 541 in total,[3] or 16.5 errors per student: arguably more, as multiple occurrence of identical or very similar errors was counted only once. The figure of 541 contrasts with 155 valency-specific errors (4.7 per candidate). Inevitably these figures are capable of variation, as analysis becomes difficult or almost impossible with a sentence such as the following: *Die neun Millionen Wörter, die über das Thema geschrieben worden, würden von ein Komputer gezahlt, hatten in Zeitungen erschienen während des letzten zwölf Monatens, in lautere Reden von Politiker und das Thema wurde von Fernseher behandelt, haben nicht gewirkt.*[4]

The second set is from a more recent examination (2003) taken by 24 students (again with a minimum of 8-9 years of German plus 5-10 months abroad). Dictionaries were allowed with this later examination. Again leaving aside errors of vocabulary, including wrong mode of address or confusion of *wann* and *als*, the 104 valency-specific errors can initially be analysed as follows:[5]

- 54 errors can be seen as verb valency; a further 6 might be seen in this category, but might be just confusion of cases (use of nominative, also one dative, as object; accusative used as subject of a passive sentence);
- 27 are noun valency: problems with *Gedanke*, *Idee*, *Art/Sorte*, *Ort/Stelle* (mainly arising from difficulty in producing a German equivalent of *the best place to go*);
- 1 possible example of adjective valency (the need for a complement with *für* with *verantwortlich*);
- 16 errors in the use of collocations such as *satt haben*, *leid sein*, *hungrig sein*.

Alongside these 104 errors in total (4 per candidate), which will be examined in more detail below, there were again a much larger number of non-valency-specific errors: the total of 339 general grammatical errors represents almost 14 per student.[6] This figure contrasts with 16.5 errors per student in the earlier set analysed, but the lower figure is explained to a considerable extent by the availability of dictionaries, which undoubtedly produced fewer errors in matters of gender and plural; if one discounts such errors, the error-count per candidate is approximately the same.[7] A small number of mistakes were difficult to categorise but were clearly not valency-specific (**keine Gedanke*, **sie haben ein deutschen Fest gefeiert*),[8] whilst as in the previous batch some sentences made an overall analysis difficult: **Man sollte zu dieser Zeit des jahres Deutschland als das zuletzten Land hinzufahren halt, oder?* or **Das Speise dorthin findest du nichts in einem erste-klasse Restaurants, jedoch wenn du kalt oder hungrish wärest denn dies wie das Beste überall schmecken würde.*[9]

Interesting by comparison was the very low occurrence of what one might rather unkindly categorise as "gibberish sentences" in the English written by German learners, an obvious consequence of the much longer and more constant exposure to the foreign language that marks out German learners of English from their British counterparts.[10]

3. Analysis of valency-specific errors in German

Valency-specific errors therefore accounted for 23% of grammatical and syntactical errors (compared to 39% with the German learners of English). If we collate the two analyses of the 252 valency-specific errors we find the following types of errors in particular:

Table 1. Types of valency-specific errors

number	type of error	example
8	omission of obligatory complements	with verbs such as *beantworten, beschuldigen, fühlen*
48	wrong case of noun complement	accusative used after *sein* or *werden*
21	noun phrase instead of prepositional complement	*antworten* + ACC
14	prepositional complement used instead of noun phrase	with *entstehen, geben*

1	adverbial complement used instead of noun phrase	*entstammen*
56	wrong choice of preposition, or preposition used instead of adverb phrase	*antworten zu/an*
10	correct preposition but wrong case	*geraten in, denken an*
19	wrong choice of clause complement	*sie erscheinen, dass ...*
10	wrong type of complement	*erweisen* and *beweisen* used with infinitive clause
5	wrong use of clause realisation of prepositional complement[11]	*es handelt sich um, dass ...*
7	wrong use of or omission of reflexive	*beweisen, erweisen*
43	wrong choice from semantically linked verbs[12]	*nennen* for *benennen*

4. Comparison of valency-specific errors in English and German

This analysis of the various sets of errors indicates some common ground between the errors made by learners of English and German but quite a number of key differences. The most obvious areas of common ground (speaking of types of problems rather than specific individual problems encountered) were:

- the choice of prepositional complement (almost 40% in English, 20+% for German);
- the choice of clause complement (30% for English, 12% in German);
- the choice between noun phrase and prepositional complement (including problems with apposition such as *the state Israel* or *die Art Gericht*) (11% for English, 14% for German).

It is especially worth noting that these three areas accounted for approximately 80% of the valency-specific errors of German learners of English.

A further area of common ground, but accounting for a relatively small number of problems, indeed far fewer than might have been expected, was the problem of the optionality of the complement (in constructions with *remind, allow, beantworten, fühlen, vorstellen*).[13]

Problems for German learners of English arose from:

- one specific aspect within the choice of structures already referred to, namely that between *+to-INF* and *+of V-ing*, especially with nouns such as *aim, intention, chance*;
- the need in English for use of a semantically empty noun as a correlate or stylistic filler, most particularly *the fact (that).* Empirical evidence suggests that this should be listed as common ground, but it was less of a problem in the German material analysed, either, as suggested above, because it was possible to avoid by the English-influenced use of nouns such as *Tatsache, Situation*, or because the relatively limited corpus resulted in only a few errors of the kind **es handelt sich um, dass ...* . A further use or non-use of correlates caused occasional problems for the learners of English, as revealed by errors sich as **Important was that / *I find interesting that / *Can I point it out to you that / *I cannot stand that you do that*;
- the choice of tense/aspect, which will be considered below.

Vilmos Ágel (2004: 27–28) has argued for an integration of word order into valency, but in the material analysed there was little evidence of valency-specific problems arising from restricted word order in English (i.e. errors of the type **I gave the book him* or **To Frankfurt he went*). Problems that might be seen as valency-driven were the result of incorrect use of the auxiliary *do*, but otherwise it was the position of English adverbials that most frequently resulted in word-order error.

Specific problems for English learners of German were:

- most obviously, and perhaps not surprisingly, the case system.[14] Some of these errors were valency-specific, not least the choice of case with prepositional complements, the incorrect use of the accusative after *sein*, and also the very English tendency to assume that any noun phrase after the verb should be an object, resulting in errors of the kind **Es besteht keinen Grund, daran zu zweifeln*;
- one particular aspect of that same overall problem is the relative inflexibility of the passive in German (a particular problem for English learners but less so for speakers of other Western European languages). By comparison, the passive was only occasionally a problem for German learners of English, with errors resulting from interference from German constructions involving the impersonal passive – **It has to be tried to ... / *There should not be made any attempt to ...*;[15]
- the choice between semantically related words requiring alternative structures (*antworten / beantworten*) also seemed much more of a problem for British learners of German, a further reflection perhaps of the

greater linguistic subtlety or awareness of German learners of English, as noted earlier in the context of "gibberish" sentences.

Alongside those valency-specific errors one must, however, also note the large number of problems arising from other aspects of the German morphological system, whether case-driven or convention-driven (e.g. strong and weak adjective endings).

5. Valency errors and the consequences for a valency dictionary

Despite the last comment in the previous section it is important to note that the number of valency-specific errors is still numerically high for English-learners of German; the complexity of German morphology, however, produces a much higher number of learner errors overall and in the process also a lower percentage of valency-specific errors. In respect of both languages it may be argued that valency-specific errors frequently relate to structure and are consequently more likely to detract from comprehensibility than (in German) incorrect plurals, gender or adjective endings, or (in English) incorrect word order or problems of tense and aspect.

The vital role of valency in learners' errors is not to be questioned, therefore, and it remains to ask, on the basis of the evidence analysed so far, what demands one should make of a good valency dictionary. That is of course to assume that our targeted learners do use dictionaries, although there is the frequent frustration for teachers that they do not, or that they rarely use the half of a bilingual dictionary in which the entries are in the target language. Petra Bräunling (1989) and more recently Monika Bielińska (2003) have underlined the even greater difficulty of getting FL learners or even FL teachers to use a valency dictionary. Leaving such caution aside, however, we may suggest that a valency dictionary should:

- concentrate on key difficult words, especially verbs.[16] This might be seen as stating the obvious, but some German valency dictionaries have taken a different line;[17]
- give cross references between semantically related words with different valency. English *comprise* or German *beantworten* do not themselves merit an individual entry, but users can be referred to the entries for *consist* and *antworten* respectively. A glossary or index of target-language words might be considered important here and even an index of cross references in the source language.[18]

Moving on to what are arguably the really crucial aims, a valency dictionary must provide:

- very detailed analysis of prepositional complements, especially where alternative realisations are possible: *agree* + *to/with*; *care* + *for/about*; *warten* + *auf/bis*; *bestehen* + *aus/in/auf*. The evidence analysed does not provide justification for detailed analysis of clause realisation of German prepositional complements, but it is possible that a more detailed analysis than was possible with the available corpus would suggest otherwise;
- detailed analysis of clause complementation, with specific reference to particular sources of error or confusion. In English this problem is further compounded by confusion between clause complements and preposition-plus-present participle structures. Recently Klaus Fischer has underlined the flexibility of complement clauses in English (2004: 223–224), the fact that a number of English clause-types are not found in German: to the list discussed by Fischer (including especially *+for N +to-INF*) one could add in particular the bolt-on infinitive such as *she had no one to turn to*. This flexibility is not often a source of syntactical error, and hence does not feature in the analysis of errors, but it can produce stilted English in sentences such as *She had no one to whom she could turn* or *It is rare that a house is built in two weeks* (instead of *for a house to be built* …). A German dictionary for English-speaking learners clearly needs to underline the lack of flexibility in this respect, and the incorrectness of a structure such as **Deutschland ist nicht der beste Ort hinzufahren*. A valency dictionary, which should be concentrating on key words, can play an important role in sensitising learners to wider stylistic possibilities rather than simply concentrating on grammatical and syntactic accuracy.[19]

Two areas that are more specific to only the one side of our present German-English comparison:

- especially in English one may ask to what extent tense or aspect are part of valency. Some areas might be expected to be covered in our ideal notion of a valency dictionary, such as the wrong choice of tense in indirect speech or *as if* clauses, for instance, but other aspects are not obviously valency-driven. Thomas Herbst and I have demonstrated (Herbst and Roe 1996) how the optionality of complements is affected by questions of tense and aspect and one might consider in more detail the extent to which other issues of tense are important: *She has written* sounds fine in context, whereas *She wrote* without an object seems less likely. There is however a very delicate question of balance involved here, as any move from lexeme-based valency to word-form valency can easily render a valency dictionary in any manageable volume impossible;[20]

- on the German side of the equation there is the question of the extent to which the seemingly endless problems caused by case and morphology can be integrated into a valency description. Clearly valency cannot be used to teach adjective endings or the plural of German nouns, or that *mit* is followed by a noun in the dative, and the current analysis suggests that even advanced learners of German make a large number of errors that require other teaching and learning approaches alongside that of valency grammar. Nevertheless the use of a valency approach can place great emphasis on case use in paradigmatic situations such as the function of the dative, the correct choice of case with prepositional complements, or the greater restrictions on the semantic role of cases (as in the relative inflexibility of passive transformations in German).

Some of these aspects could of course be more fully treated in a valency dictionary aimed at a particular linguistic group of learners: an English dictionary for German learners, for example, as opposed to one for all learners of the language. In such a targeted valency dictionary, problems of interference can be fully addressed, for example with warnings of the kind "note that you may NOT say …". Such an approach is envisaged in the proposed German dictionary for English learners referred to earlier (see note 1); to discuss it in the present context would, as Theodor Fontane or Günter Grass might have put it, be "ein zu weites Feld".[21]

Notes

1. A project for such a dictionary is underway, coedited by myself, Alan Cornell and Klaus Fischer; for an outline of the project, see Cornell and Roe 1999.
2. I am grateful to Alan Cornell for supplying this material.
3. These general grammatical errors include 139 wrong verb conjugations, 62 wrong plurals, 88 wrong genders, 36 incorrect choices of preposition in an adverbial phrase, 36 wrong cases after prepositions in adverbial phrases, 112 other wrong endings, 48 word order errors, and 2 misuse of articles.
4. Or, from a number of similar examples:
   Eine Frau aus Battersea glaubte, daß die Teilung der Konservativen aufgrund des Lusts Margaret Thatchers nochmal an die Stellung Premierministers sei ...
   jemand anderen dachte es hatte etwas mit die gleichen arbeit stunden für das gleicher geld für alle zu tun.
5. 4 per student, though some with an obvious native-speaker background had no valency-specific errors of any kind.
6. These non-valency-specific errors include 43 wrong verb conjugations, 43 wrong plurals, 22 wrong genders, 40 wrong cases after prepositions, 73 other wrong endings, 12 errors relating to relative pronouns, 29 incorrect uses of ar-

ticles, 27 incorrect choices of preposition in adverbial adjuncts, and 48 word-order errors.

7. 11.5 errors per candidate in the later (2003) examination compared to 11.8 in the earlier set, but the later translation was undoubtedly less difficult.
8. As Anke Lüdeling et al. (2005: 2–3) underline, categorisation of errors can indeed be problematic, although an experienced teacher accustomed to seeing mistakes by students with the same native language is usually able to make an accurate assessment of the type of mistake involved.
9. Or, again from many similar examples:
   Wenn du zum Weihnachten Kotzen finden und kann nicht es nochmal feiern dann fahrst du nicht nach Deutschland, oder?
   Ein Weihnachtsmarkt hat alles, dass Sie alle Hoffnung immer aufgeben, in Dezember in einer typischen britischen Hauptstraße zu finden.
10. Indeed the degree of opaqueness is arguably less even in those English sentences that do pose problems of comprehension:
    ... the respectable time historian Karl-Friedrich Bracher pointed at the power of seduction of how to handle certain terms linguistically.
    "Reading Haider and thinking of Hitler" was even said on banners.
11. The number of such errors is arguably much higher, as the problem was often partly avoided through stylistically unacceptable but grammatically just acceptable sentences of the type ?*es hat zu tun mit diesem Ding, wo wir alle die selben Stunden arbeiten für das gleich Lohn.*
12. Arguably some of these might be seen as errors of vocabulary rather than of valency. Furthermore, a small number of individual problems merit a brief mention. The German equivalent of *answer* was a particular problem, as despite the best efforts of lecturers and teachers *antworten* or *beantworten* was used wrongly by almost two-thirds of the candidates; especially *antworten* was used with either an accusative complement or with the wrong prepositional complement; frequent problems also occurred with passive constructions involving *stellen* or *fragen*; and many problems arose from the English sentences *Germany is not the best place to go at this time of year*, and also and perhaps more understandably, *The market place contains everything you always despaired of finding.*
13. Although it would not normally be considered an issue of valency, one may also note problems with the use or non-use of articles, despite the great similarities between English and German in this area of grammar.
14. See most recently Fischer (2004).
15. The theoretically interesting question of which elements in English can become the subject of a passive construction does not cause problems for foreign learners – presumably because they do not venture as far as complexities such as *Which film to see has not yet been talked about.*
16. The lack of problems encountered with the valency of adjectives was particularly noticeable in the material analysed, although this may be a result of the restricted corpus.
17. See especially Sommerfeldt and Schreiber (1996).

18. Bielińska (2003: 244–245) suggests that the use of valency dictionaries for learners may only become possible once the learner has come to the FL word via a bilingual dictionary.
19. The "sensitising" role of valency dictionaries is underlined by Alan Cornell (2003: 142).
20. This danger was underlined at one point of the conference in Erlangen when a participant was heard to comment that one might need one volume simply for the verb *put*. For an indication of the breadth of detail that is potentially possible, see Willems and Coene (2003) on *glauben*; also Kolde (2004).
21. See the example entry for *antworten* in Roe (2003: 196–197).

References

Ágel, Vilmos

2000 *Valenztheorie*. Tübingen: Narr.

2003 Wort- und Ausdrucksvalenz(träger). In *Valency in Practice: Valenz in der Praxis*, Alan Cornell, Klaus Fischer, and Ian F. Roe (eds.), 17–36. Oxford/Bern/Berlin/Bruxelles/Frankfurt M./New York/Wien: Lang.

2004 Prinzipien der Valenztheorie(n). In *Valenztheorie: Bestandsaufnahme und Perspektiven,* Speranţa Stănescu (ed.), 11–30. Frankfurt M.: Lang.

Bielińska, Monika

2003 Valenzwörterbücher – das Ideal und das Leben. In *Valency in Practice: Valenz in der Praxis*, Alan Cornell, Klaus Fischer, and Ian F. Roe (eds.), 241–258. Oxford/Bern/Berlin/Bruxelles/Frankfurt M./ New York/Wien: Lang.

Bräunling, Petra

1989 Umfrage zum Thema Valenzwörterbücher. *Lexicographica* 5: 168–177.

Cornell, Alan, and Ian F. Roe

1999 A valency dictionary for English-speaking learners of German. In *From Classical Shades to Vickers Victorious: Shifting Perspectives in British German Studies*, Steve Giles, and Peter Graves (eds.), 153–170. Bern: Lang.

Cornell, Alan, Klaus Fischer, and Ian F. Roe

2003 *Valency in Practice: Valenz in der Praxis*. Oxford/Bern/Berlin/ Bruxelles/Frankfurt M./New York/Wien: Lang.

Cornell, Alan

2003 Valency for learners of German: How do the customers feel? In *Valency in Practice: Valenz in der Praxis*, Alan Cornell, Klaus Fischer, and Ian F. Roe (eds.), 127–143. Oxford/Bern/Berlin/Bruxelles/Frankfurt M./New York/Wien: Lang.

Fischer, Klaus
1997 *German-English Verb Valency*. Tübingen: Narr.
2004 Deutsche und englische Ergänzungssätze: Zwei typologische Anomalien? In *Valenztheorie: Bestandsaufnahme und Perspektiven,* Speranţa Stănescu (ed.), 213–236. Frankfurt M.: Lang.

Herbst, Thomas, David Heath, Ian F. Roe, and Dieter Götz
2004 *A Valency Dictionary of English. A Corpus-Based Analysis of the Complementation Patterns of English Verbs, Nouns and Adjectives.* Berlin/New York: Mouton de Gruyter.

Herbst, Thomas, and Ian F. Roe
1996 How obligatory are obligatory complements? – An alternative approach to the categorization of subjects and other complements in valency grammar. *English Studies* 77: 179–199.

Kolde, Gottfried
2004 Gehört der Heckenausdruck *(so) (ei)ne Art (von) X* ins Valenzwörterbuch? In *Die Valenztheorie: Bestandsaufnahme und Perspektiven,* Speranta Stănescu (ed.), 133–146. Frankfurt M.: Lang.

Lüdeling, Anke, Maik Walter, Emil Kroymann, and Peter Adolphs
2005 Multi-level error annotation in learner corpora. http://www.linguistik.hu-berlin.designato.de/korpuslinguistik/projekte/falko/FALKO-CL2005.pdf (15 August 2005)

Parkes, Geoff
2001 *The Mistakes Clinic for German-speaking Learners of English.* Southampton: Englang Books.

Roe, Ian F.
2003 Layout of valency dictionary entries: Theory and practice. In *Valency in Practice: Valenz in der Praxis*, Alan Cornell, Klaus Fischer, and Ian F. Roe (eds.), 187–209. Oxford/Bern/Berlin/Bruxelles/Frankfurt M./New York/Wien: Lang.

Schumacher, Helmut, Jacqueline Kubczak, Renate Schmidt, and Vera de Ruiter (eds.)
2004 *VALBU – Valenzwörterbuch deutscher Verben*. Tübingen: Narr.

Sommerfeldt, Karl-Ernst, and Herbert Schreiber
1996 *Wörterbuch zur Valenz etymologisch verwandter Wörter*. Tübingen: Niemeyer.

Stănescu, Speranţa
2004 *Die Valenztheorie: Bestandsaufnahme und Perspektiven.* Frankfurt M.: Lang.

Willems, Klaas, and Ann Coene
2003 Argumentstruktur, verbale Polysemie und Koerzion. In *Valency in Practice: Valenz in der Praxis*, Alan Cornell, Klaus Fischer, and Ian F. Roe (eds.), 37–63. Oxford/Bern/Berlin/Bruxelles/Frankfurt M./New York/Wien: Lang.

Temporary ambiguity of German and English term complements[1]

Klaus Fischer

1. Introduction

In the assessment of the contrasts between English and German, there is a consensus that German is more semantically transparent or overspecified than English, has preserved more grammatical complexity and is thus a grammatically more mature language. One reason for the contrasts is seen in the contact-rich history of English which has lost much of its Germanic grammatical inheritance, possibly because of imperfect acquisition by Scandinavian settlers (McWhorter 2002: 253–265; Olga Fischer 1992: 207–208, but see Fennell 2001: 92; Thomason and Kaufman 1988: 275–306).

Comparisons of the two languages by John Hawkins (1986, 1992), John McWhorter (2002), Werner Abraham (2003) and Frans Plank (1984) have understandably concentrated on the extent and systematic nature of the contrasts. The perhaps unavoidable danger is that data that do not quite fit the broad picture but nevertheless inform the English-German contrasts, are ignored or not given the prominence they deserve.

In this article, I would like to adjust the picture that John Hawkins in particular has drawn but that is also more or less explicitly present in other accounts. I will address the claim that the English subject and direct object are syntactically and semantically more ambiguous than the German subject and direct object. I will also investigate German verb position that is linked to these claims.

2. Overspecification, complexity and maturity

Semantic transparency or overspecification refers to the degree of explicit expression that can be decoded contrary to implicit information that can be inferred (cf. Sperber and Wilson 1995: 1–117). For instance, German case-marked noun phrases contain information that English caseless noun phrases taken in isolation do not. The same applies to German directional adverbs (for instance *dorthin*) in comparison with their English counterparts (for instance *there*) that do not indicate direction explicitly.

Grammatical complexity is measured by the complexity of the grammatical description (Dahl 2004: 27; 49–50; McWhorter 2003: 219–220). For instance the grammatical description of German noun phrases is more complex than that of English noun phrases because of grammatical gender and case.

Grammatical maturity (Dahl 2004: 111–162) is complexity seen as an evolutionary product, as the result of grammaticalisation processes. Fusional morphology such as German case, gender and number morphology is the outcome of a staged development from ultimately free combinations of lexical items.

Semantic transparency or overspecification on the one hand and grammatical complexity or maturity on the other are not identical. Grammaticalisation often leads to forms with very abstract meaning:

(1) *Sie hat ihm die Hausaufgaben erklärt/gemacht.*
She explained the homework to him/did the homework for him.

The fusional dative form is more mature than its periphrastic prepositional counterparts but less semantically transparent: it only limits the semantic role to an abstract role that has been labelled *Betroffener* [‘concerned’] (Wegener 1985: 275) while the prepositional phrases differentiate between goal on the one hand and beneficiary/substitute on the other.[2]

John Hawkins generally discusses semantic transparency with a maturity bias: he stresses the information that mature German forms achieve but neglects to mention the semantic transparency of less mature English structures.

3. Corpus

The statistical data and most example sentences in this article refer to the following small corpus of communicative translations, using the abbreviations indicated in brackets:

- J.K. Rowling: *Harry Potter and the Philosopher's Stone* (1997), ch. 1 (= HP; 4581 words), and the German translation by Klaus Fritz (1998) (= HPD; 4825 words);
- Cornelia Funke: *Der Herr der Diebe* (2000), ch. 1 and 2 (= HD; 4162 words), and the English translation by Oliver Latsch (2002) (= HDE; 4390 words);

– Detlef Gürtler: Wohlstand für alle. Das Erfolgsgeheimnis der sozialen Marktwirtschaft. In *Deutschland. Forum für Politik, Kultur, Wirtschaft und Wissenschaft* 3, 2003, S. 8–11 (= D; 1798 words), and the English translation (= DE; 2179 words).

Thus my findings apply to written texts in the first instance.

4. Processing of argument-predicate structures

4.1. Hawkins's psycholinguistic processing model

The background for Hawkins's psycholinguistic processing model is his processing theory which concentrates on the rapid recognition of constituent structure. I will ignore *A Performance Theory of Order and Constituency* (Hawkins 1994) here as it concludes – albeit after some discussion – that English and German recognition of constituency structure works in parallel: English verbs construct the verb phrase, so does German case (1994: 397). In valency terms: case signals that a clause is to be constructed rather than something else. I suppose the idea, though debatable, is unproblematic from a valency point of view as whenever something is said the default assumption is that this is going to be a clause.

Assuming constituents have been established, they have to be matched with semantic predicate frames. The task takes on different facets depending on the verb position (see figure 1). As predicate frames are activated early in English, there is time to provisionally attach constituents to a predicate frame as they are encountered successively and later revise the decision. English therefore tolerates temporary ambiguity resulting from multiple predicate frames being associated with individual verbs and from lack of morphological argument differentiation. For instance, the initial string *My guitar broke* is compatible with three frames (see table 1) and might mislead or "garden-path" a listener. Because the German equivalents of *break* (*brechen/zerbrechen/zerreißen*) allow fewer predicate frames and/or have tighter semantic restrictions, no garden-pathing occurs.

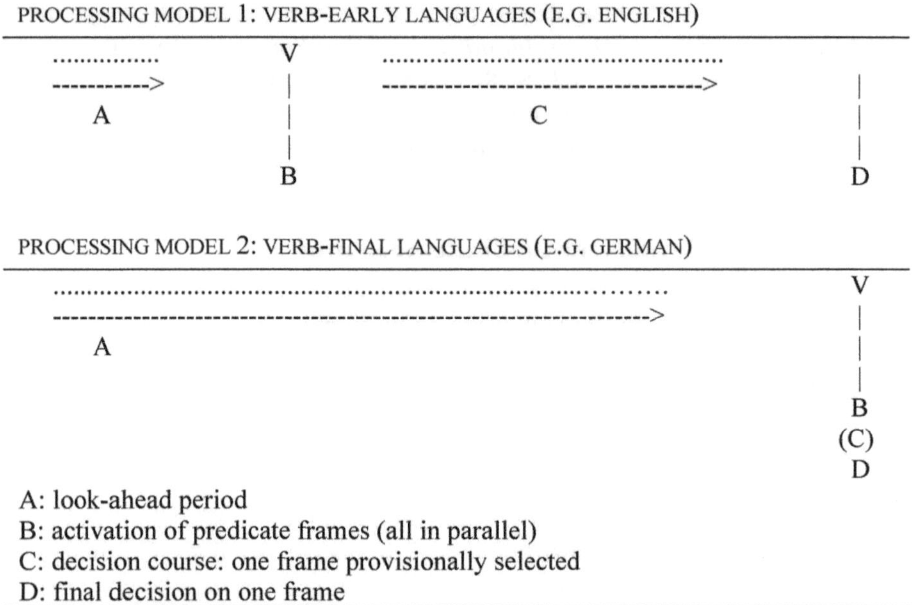

Figure 1. Processing in verb-early and verb-final languages according to Hawkins (1992: 122–124)

Table 1. Predicate frames of *break* according to Hawkins (1992: 121)[3]

Frame 1.	NP [Agent]	- V -	NP [Patient]	*John broke my guitar.* *John hat meine Gitarre zerbrochen.*
Frame 2.	NP [Patient]	- V		*My guitar broke.* *Meine Gitarre ist zerbrochen.*
Frame 3.	NP [Patient]	- V -	PP [Locative]	*A string broke on my guitar.* *An meiner Gitarre ist eine Saite zerrissen.*
Frame 4.	NP [Locative]	- V -	NP [Patient]	*My guitar broke a string.* **Meine Gitarre brach/zerriß eine Saite.*
Frame 5.	NP [Instrumental]	- V -	NP [Patient]	*My guitar broke a world record.* *Meine Gitarre hat einen Weltrekord gebrochen.*

John Hawkins sees German as having basic verb-final order. This puts interpreters of German sentences in quite a different position from interpreters of English sentences: the early English verb position allows time to decide between the different semantic frames while further phrases are encountered. For the same reason phrases do not have to carry information as to their thematic roles as there is time to address any temporary ambiguity.[4] Interpreters of German sentences only encounter the verb-induced list of semantic frames at the end of the sentence and have to take a quick decision before the next sentence starts. To ensure this rapid interpretation at the end, German case complements possess information that limits the possible scenario. Hawkins also maintains that German verbs are associated with a smaller set of sentence frames than English verbs. As a result, German clauses are claimed to possess less temporary ambiguity or garden path structures.

Hawkins (1992: 128) stipulates the following desiderata for verb-final languages:

- *argument differentiation*: phrases should indicate their thematic role so that they can be quickly mapped onto predicate frames;
- *predicate frame differentiation*: a low number of possible predicate frames helps quick recognition of the intended frame from surface structure;
- *clear argument-predicate attachment*: there should be no ambiguity as to which predicate a phrase is to be attached to by avoiding "argument trespassing" (raisings, *wh*-extractions).

Hawkins sees the three desiderata realised in German.

However, argument differentiation contains two steps: first, the identification and interpretation of lexical and formal syntactic means (position, morphology, prosody) which allows allocation of phrases to syntactic functions (see steps (a) to (c) in figure 2), and second, the allocation of a thematic role on this basis (see step (d) in figure 2).

(a) Recognition and interpretation of lexical (e.g. prepositions) and formal syntactic means (position, morphology, prosody)

|

(b) Recognition of constituent structure

|

(c) Recognition of syntactic functions

|

(d) Allocation of thematic roles

|

(e) Identification of scenario

Figure 2. Syntactic argument differentiation

Hawkins discusses (a) in relation to constituent structure but ignores it in relation to syntactic functions (cf. Fischer 2005a). In his discussion of temporary ambiguity he does not mention that the mapping of case forms onto syntactic functions is not always straightforward and therefore a source of temporary ambiguity: his comparison of German and English argument differentiation is only based on steps (d) to (e), which skews the result.

There are other problematic aspects of Hawkins's processing model that I can only briefly mention here: the failure to establish a link between verb meaning and complementation, that is to differentiate between inherent and combinatorial verb meaning (cf. Engel 1988: 358), and the consequent lack of differentiation between basic and extended or derived valency structures.[5] This cavalier treatment of valency leads to the doubtful idea of parallel activation of predicate frames (like a drop-down menu): hearers might realistically just construct one frame on the basis of all available information and, if problems are encountered, reconsider.

4.2. Ambiguity of English and German term complements

To what degree are German and English term complements ambiguous online? Hawkins's model suggests that English could afford a more ambiguous mapping of term complements onto syntactic functions and thematic roles than German.

English noun phrases in the narrow sense are not case-marked and therefore are ambiguous as to their syntactic function. However, a number of pronouns are case-marked as subjective or objective, third person personal pronouns to a higher degree than their German counterparts:

Table 2. Morphological marking of the differentiation between subject and direct object

	Personal pronoun								Noun			
	Singular					Plural			Singular			Plural
	1.	2.	3.M	3.F	3.N	1.	2.	3.	M	F	N	
German	×	×	×			×	×		×			
English	×		×	×		×		×				

The profile of English and German subject-direct object differentiation shows a graded difference that – with the exception of English second person pronouns – complies with typological hierarchies. Typologically unmarked forms are more likely to indicate subject-direct object differentiation than marked forms (Croft 2003: 130, 156, 161; < is less marked than):

personal pronoun < noun
singular < plural
1st/2nd person < 3rd person (in respect of number and animacy)
masculinum (M) < femininum (F) < neutrum (N)[6]
human < animate < inanimate

The lack of morphological subject-direct object differentiation in German noun phrases – it applies to feminine and neuter nouns in the singular and nouns of any gender in the plural (see table 2) – is no oddity or failure but typologically unremarkable. It has, however, severe consequences for on-line differentiation (see table 3).

Table 3. Morphological differentiation of subjects from direct objects

	German	English
NP (without proper nouns)	25.0%	0.0%
Pronoun	50.9%	64.0%
Total (including proper nouns and subject clauses)	34.9%	36.6%

Only 25% of all German noun-subjects were marked as non-accusatives in my corpus, for German pronoun-subjects the figure is 50.9%.[7] Overall, only 34.9% of German subjects were morphologically differentiated from accusative complements. This constitutes a considerable potential for temporary ambiguity.

As English pronouns mark the subject-direct object differentiation more strongly – 64.0% of pronoun subjects were marked as such –, a surprising 36.6% of English subjects were case-marked in my corpus. This means that English, which is not considered a case language, shows slightly higher morphological subject-direct object-differentiation than German.

The partial lack of subject-direct object-differentiation has very different consequences for on-line processing in both languages. Let us first turn to English: English subjects are easily identified in relation to verb position. The subject-verb axis is as fundamental to modern English sentence construction as verb-second is to German. Though inversion in English declarative main clauses, possibly a remnant of former English verb-second, has some text frequency – in my corpus, 5.04% (45/893) of declarative main clauses were inverted – it is limited to particular structures that exclude ambiguity: 4.37% (39/893) concerned preposed citations, of the remaining six cases five concerned the fronting of an adverb or a locative phrase headed by a preposition and one a qualitative *as*-phrase.[8] In three of these just the auxiliary was inverted, leaving three instances of main verb inversion. Below I give examples for the different types of inversion (subjects underlined):[9]

- preposed citation: 4.37% (39/893)

(2) *'It's – it's true?' faltered Professor McGonagall.* (HP: 15)

- other preposed phrases 0.67% (6/893)
  a. auxiliary inversion (3/893)

(3) *But only in very few of them* [*countries*] *do these organizations represent a dynamic element in the economy.* (DE: 10)

(4) ... *for neither as a cat nor as a woman had she fixed Dumbledore with such a piercing stare* ... (HP: 14)

b. main verb inversion (3/893)

(5) *Inside, just visible, was a baby boy, fast asleep.* (HP: 16)

(6) *In its window, between coffee machines and toasters, stood a few toys.* (HDE: 16)

An initial English noun phrase can thus be interpreted as subject or non-subject as soon as the next phrase is encountered:

Table 4. Disambiguation of English term complements

(7)

<table>
<tr><td>Peter</td><td>(,)</td><td>Claire</td><td>was</td><td>(desperately)</td><td>looking for</td><td>(not Paul).</td></tr>
<tr><td>NP_1</td><td></td><td>NP_2</td><td>V_{aux}</td><td>Adv</td><td>V</td><td></td></tr>
<tr><td rowspan="2"></td><td>pause,
new start</td><td></td><td colspan="3"></td><td rowspan="2"></td></tr>
<tr><td colspan="2">NP_1 shown as non-subject</td><td colspan="3">NP_2 shown as subject</td></tr>
</table>

The identification of English direct objects is similarly unproblematic. This is not what Hawkins's model suggests. Because of the early verb position, English clauses could tolerate a degree of complement permutation and ensuing ambiguity. However, they do not.

The topological grammaticalisation of English term complements makes case marking superfluous. It is tempting to see case marking in contemporary English as redundant overspecification. However, English case morphology has partially lost, or is about to lose, its relation to syntactic functions as insecurities in case assignment and the tendency to use objective case as default show (*Who has done this? Me.* Coll.: *Me and Peter had a good time.* [pseudocorrect usage: *between you and I*]).

The situation is quite different in German. While the preverbal position is a constructional sign for subjecthood in English, it is only a weak indicator of subjecthood in German: just 56.6% of German subjects occupied the first position in declarative main clauses as opposed to 37.9% in the third position. If a preverbal German noun phrase belongs to the 64.9% without definitive case marking, it can only be interpreted as a subject with a certain element of doubt and the interpretation might have to be revised. After all 10.4% of noun phrase-accusative complements occur *before* the subject where their identification is not topologically supported.[10] This means in effect that the majority of German sentences, quite unlike English sentences, feature an inbuilt ambiguity, forcing greater context reliance:

Table 5. Disambiguation of German term complements

(7')

<table>
<tr><td>Peter</td><td>hat</td><td>Claire</td><td>(verzweifelt)</td><td>gesucht</td><td>(nicht Paul).</td></tr>
<tr><td>NP_1</td><td>V_{aux}</td><td>NP_2</td><td>Adv</td><td>V</td><td></td></tr>
<tr><td colspan="6">no clear disambiguation
(not even with contrastive stress)</td></tr>
</table>

This creates obvious problems for English learners of German who might treat the preverbal position as a structural sign for subjecthood rather than a weak indicator for it and therefore ignore other clues (see table 6).

Table 6. Topological marking of the subject

<table>
<tr><th>English</th><th>German</th></tr>
<tr><td>NP (Adv) V
preverbal position: constructional sign for subjecthood
position decoded</td><td>NP V
preverbal position: weak indicator for subjecthood
position one of the clues that is involved in inference</td></tr>
<tr><td colspan="2">→
Language learning: interference</td></tr>
</table>

If an initial noun phrase is not morphologically marked as subject or accusative complement, agreement or the case marking of a later noun phrase can lead to formal disambiguation. But in many of these cases, i.e. if it is the second noun phrase in a main clause or verb agreement in a subordinate clause that resolves the temporary ambiguity, disambiguation is *later* than in English. Just considering the marked "accusative complement before subject" order, my corpus featured 29 cases – this represents 2.0% of all finite clauses – where temporary ambiguity was not resolved with the following constituent. In 10 cases – 0.7% of all finite clauses – there was no formal resolution of the ambiguity (SUB = subject, AKK = accusative complement):

(8) *Dass das Meer ... alles verschluckte: die Häuser und Brücken, Kirchen und Paläste,*
  a. *die* [AKK] *die Menschen* [SUB] *dem Wasser so frech aufs Gesicht gebaut hatten.* (HD: 7)
  b. *die* [SUB] *die Menschen* [AKK] *so lange erfreut hatten.*

Obviously, the ambiguities are resolved using non-formal means, namely verb meaning. Also, it is no accident that it is the contrast between subject and direct object that tends not to be marked cross-linguistically as the animate-inanimate opposition and others reduce ambiguity: the subject is more likely to be animate, definite or a pronoun than is the direct object. And permutations of German complements, while making on-line recognition of syntactic functions more difficult than in English, have well-known discourse advantages while the rapid recognition of English term complements has verbose[11] structures or, in Abraham's words, *sperrige Vertextungsmittel* ['unwieldy discourse organisers'] such as cleft sentences as a consequence (2003: 67).

But this does not detract from the fact that neither English nor German behave in the way that Hawkins's processing model suggests: in an important respect German clauses display regular temporary ambiguities which do not just irritate learners of German but catch out native readers as well.

5. Correspondence between syntactic functions and thematic roles

While Hawkins failed to discuss the mapping of phrases onto syntactic functions, presumably because he sees them as unproblematic, he discusses in depth syntactic restrictions and the mapping of syntactic functions onto thematic roles in his 1986 monograph. A number of German verbs are shown to have tighter semantic restrictions (1986: 28–35). Also, as a result of the collapse of the English case system, former English dative and genitive complements were turned into subjects and direct objects, mapping non-prototypical thematic roles onto these two syntactic relations and making them thereby less semantically transparent (1986: 53–73). The ensuing ambiguity of the English subject and direct object relation was compensated for by the early verb position, giving the hearer time to allocate thematic roles. Hawkins sees as another result of these changes that the English subject and direct object form supersets to the German subject and direct object. As a consequence, English subjects and direct objects should have higher text frequency than their German counterparts.

I established the text frequency of German and English term complements on the basis of the form-oriented classification widely used in German valency research. For English I used topology as the form equivalent of case (see endnote 1). Both the absolute number of each complement and the frequency per verb phrase or clause are indicated (see table 7). The statistics show that explicit English subjects have only a slightly higher text frequency while German accusative complements were more frequent than English direct objects. This surprising result even holds – at least proportionally – if markers of inherent reflexivity are discarded, of which the German texts had 77, the English one. This lowers the number of German accusative complements to 748 (= 0.460 per verb phrase) vs. 763 English direct objects (= 0.421 per verb phrase).

Table 7. Frequency of explicit term complements per verb phrase/clause (including dummy complements [*es, it, there*] and complement clauses; E = *Ergänzung* [complement])[12]

German			*English*
Case complements			Topological complements
Subjekt[13]	**0,889** 1296/1457	**0,927** 1356/1463	subject
Akkusativ-E	**0,508** 825/1625	**0,421** 764/1814	direct object
Dativ-E	**0,090** 146/1625	**0,025** 45/1814	indirect object (only noun phrases)
Genitiv-E	**0,0006** 1/1625		
Präpositiv-E	**0,120** 195/1625	**0,116** 210/1814	prepositional object

More interesting than the statistical data per se are the underlying reasons. The reason for the lower frequency of German subjects was a preference for co-ordinated clauses with subject deletion while English either used subordinated structures or, less often, was more reluctant to delete the subject in co-ordinated structures:
a) English subordinate clause vs. German co-ordinate clause with subject deletion (subjects underlined):

(9) *When Dudley had been put to bed, he went into the living-room …* (HP: 10)
Er brachte Dudley zu Bett und ging dann ins Wohnzimmer … (HPD: 10)

(10) *„Uns ist etwas verloren gegangen", sagte die Frau und schob ihm ein Foto über den Schreibtisch.* (HD: 9)
'This is what we've lost,' said the woman as she pushed the photograph across the desk. (HDE: 9)

b) English co-ordinate structure without vs. German co-ordinate structure with subject deletion:

(11) *Aber Prosper hatte ihm das Stehlen verboten und schimpfte ihn jedes Mal fürchterlich aus, wenn er ihn dabei erwischte.* (HD: 19)
Prosper had forbidden his brother to steal anything and he told him off very harshly every time he caught him. (HDE: 19)

(12) *„Du hast immer Hunger", stellte Prosper fest, öffnete die Tür …* (HD: 16)
'You're always hungry,' Prosper smiled. He opened the door … (HDE: 16)

c) In addition, subject ellipsis was more frequent in the German than in the English texts. German subject ellipsis vs. English lack of subject ellipsis:

(13) *„Tja, wäre schön gewesen."* (HD: 20)
'Well, it would have been nice.' (HDE: 19)

The higher text frequency of English subjects was not a result of more English verbs having a subject in their valency – all the verbs in the corpus required at least a dummy subject – but was brought about by a reluctance to delete subjects, incidentally leading to greater semantic transparency of the English texts.

A more faithful English form-argument correspondence is not limited to the subject. Rohdenburg (1990: 17; 1991: 18–25) has shown that a number of German indefinite deletions cannot be replicated in English (direct objects underlined):

(14) *Alkohol macht müde.*
  a. **Alcohol makes tired.*
  b. *Alcohol makes <u>you</u> tired.*

(15) *Sie befahl/forderte dazu auf, das Gelände zu verlassen.*
  a. **She ordered/requested to leave the premises.*
  b. *She ordered/requested <u>people</u> to leave the premises.*

Krone (2003: 104; 231–233) found in a study of German and English football match commentaries that German commentators are much more prone than English commentators to delete direct objects referring to the ball or to standard situations. Regularly German constructions with two complements corresponded to English constructions with three (*x flankt nach innen, lupft in den Strafraum, köpft zu Ziege* vs. *X plants <u>the ball</u> in towards the penalty area, heads <u>it</u> to the far side, nudges <u>it</u> out of play*).

What about the semantic flexibility of the English subject? There was some evidence that English verbs have indeed less tight semantic restrictions (subjects underlined):

(16) ... *the sign <u>that</u> said "Privet Drive"* ... (HP: 8)[14]
  a.? *das Zeichen, <u>das</u> „Ligusterweg" sagte*
  b. ... *das Schild mit dem Namen „Ligusterweg"* ... (HPD: 7)

Also some English verbs allow transitive and intransitive use while their German counterparts require a reflexive marker:

(17) ... *<u>Hagrid's shoulders</u> shook* ... (HP: 17)
  a. *<u>Hagrids Schultern</u> schüttelten sich*
  b. ... *<u>Hagrids Schultern</u> zuckten* ... (HPD: 21)

The texts in both languages featured a number of secondary subjectisations though it was difficult to delineate them from metaphorical usage. Counting generously, there were nine of them in the English and seven in the German texts, none as dramatic as the examples documented in Rohdenburg (1974) that Hawkins quotes (1986: 60–61). The semantic role allocations indicated below demonstrate the unusual status of the subjects. I have first listed thematic roles, which are largely situational, and second in italics construction-induced roles.[15] For instance, an agent or non-agent (thematic roles) might be construed as exercising control over the action or process, that is as an *Agentive* (construction-induced role) (cf. Fischer 1997: 55–65, Ickler in this volume):[16]

(18) [*ein Rollladen, breit und rostig*], *verschloss* [*die Eingangstür*]. (HD: 23)
[Instrument, *Agentive*] [Patient, *Objective*]

[*the entrance*] *was blocked off* [*with rusty shutters*]. (HDE: 22)
[Patient, *Objective*] [Instrument, *Co-presentive*]

(19) [*Auf seiner Nase*] *schälte* [*sich*] [*ein Sonnenbrand*]. (HD: 9)
[Locus, *Locative*] [*Objective*] [Cause/Patient, *Agentive*]

[*His nose*] *was peeling* [*from sunburn*]. (HDE: 9)
[Locus/Patient, *Agentive*] [Cause, *Originitive*]

But it was in the German texts that a number of marked subjects of verbs with active language constructions could be found (relevant subjects underlined, dative complements in bold):

(20) ***Uns*** *ist etwas verloren gegangen.* (HD: 9)
This is what we've lost.[17] (HDE: 9)

(21) ... *since Madam Pomfrey told me she liked my new ear muffs.* (HP: 14)
... *seit Madam Pomfrey mir gesagt hat,* ***ihr*** *gefielen meine neuen Ohrenschützer.* (HPD: 16)

These subjects are not first complements (or in other words: the last complements to be bound by the verb; cf. Zifonun et al. 1997: 1303) and feature non-prototypical thematic roles, making the German subject more abstract and ambiguous in Hawkins's sense.

Why are German accusative complements (direct objects) so numerous? One important reason is prefix verbs, especially verbs with the prefix *an-* (accusative complements and corresponding prepositional phrases underlined):

(22) ... *der sie von einem vorbeifahrenden Boot ankläffte* ... (HD: 13)
(22e) ... *barking at them from a passing barge* ... (HDE: 13)

(23) *Mr Dursley blinked and stared at the cat.* (HP: 8)
(23e) *Mr. Dursley blinzelte und starrte die Katze an.* (HPD: 7)

What Nichols (1986: 84) has called "headward migration" (of an adposition) has inflated the number of German accusative complements: the semantic transparency has, so to speak, moved from the complement to the verb. The thematic role of direction (for instance: *auf etwas/wohin starren*) is frequently mapped onto the accusative complement (*etwas anstarren*), turning it into the construction-induced objective role in the process. As a result German accusative complements quite regularly have English prepositional objects as their counterpart. While German prefix verbs are a mature phenomenon, they increase the ambiguity of accusative complements in Hawkins's sense (that is in relation to thematic roles, not in relation to construction-induced roles).

Some of Hawkins's semantic claims could be confirmed. But his subset relations, i.e. that the German subject and direct object are subsets of their English counterparts, had to be refuted. In addition, several of the phenomena that emerged as explanatory for relevant statistical data do not feature at all in Hawkins's typological account of the German-English contrasts. It seems that the typological profiling of languages should beware of possibly biased system accounts and supplement these with text-based analyses. My corpus-based argument thus has wider application: it makes a case for a "typology of *parole*".

6. Verb position

If the two central term complements of subject and direct object are, at least in a number of respects, more syntactically and semantically ambiguous in German than in English, but if German nevertheless allows discourse-induced permutations, then Hawkins's semantic processing model seems to have little relevance for modern German structures. Alternatively, one can question Hawkins's classification of German as a verb-final language.

Obviously, German has verb-object-verb order (V2 ...V) but can one of the two verb positions be established as basic or unmarked? The argument for verb-final is that the constituent order in German subordinate clauses mirrors the order by which complements are bound by the verb. But this grammaticographic perspective collides with the typological demand that basic orders be established in unmarked contexts. For clauses this is the declarative main clause in the indicative present active. German emerges as having "verb-object" as the unmarked order. This is borne out statistically:

Table 8. Verb positions in declarative main clauses (*Herr der Diebe* ch. 1+2)[18]

V2	V2 … V_{part}	v2 … V
281 (66,4%)	56 (13,2%)	86 (20,3%)

However, if all the different sentence types are considered, the picture is less clear. The main verb is in verb-second position in 45.8% of all clauses as opposed to 42% in verb-final position:

Table 9. Verb positions in *Herr der Diebe* ch. 1+2

V1	V1 … V_{part}	v1 … V	V2	V2 … V_{part}	v2 …V	… V
15 (2,4%)	4 (0,7%)	10 (1,6%)	281 (45,8%)	56 (9,1%)	86 (14,0%)	161 (26,3%)

It is also worth mentioning that verb-final features in all the sentence types while verb-first and verb-second define sentence types: the addition of all the clauses that use verb-final in some form adds up to a small majority of 51.7%.[19]

7. Conclusion

The German subject and accusative complement create considerable temporary ambiguity both because of ambiguous formal marking and the variety of thematic roles that can be associated with each of the two syntactic relations. The positional marking of the English subject and direct object is far less ambiguous than case marking in German. Somewhat surprisingly, the subject-direct object-opposition is less frequently morphologically marked in the case language German than in the non-case language English.

While there is evidence to support Hawkins's claim that the English subject and direct object have less tight semantic restrictions – at least with a number of frequently used verbs – and readily allow the mapping of a variety of thematic roles onto the two syntactic relations, the German subject and accusative complement have two quite frequently used sources of non-prototypical thematic role assignment: active language verb usages for the subject and prefixed verbs for the accusative complement (direct object). It is not a forgone conclusion whether the English or the German syntactic relations are more semantically transparent.

My findings are at odds with Hawkins's claim of greater argument differentiation in German because of its verb-final character. While the discussion about a basic verb position in German can probably be seen as futile as there is no speaker choice between the positions, typological markedness suggests that verb-second should be seen as the basic verb position. Statistically nearly 50% of German clauses in a narrative text showed the whole main verb in an early position. This somewhat relieves the need for German argument differentiation. Hawkins (1994) argued that German and English recognition of constituent structure runs in parallel left to right (rather than right to left in German as in true verb-final languages such as Japanese). More often than not, German and English scenario recognition works in parallel as well, starting with an early verb offering a basic scenario, which will be confirmed or changed by evidence from later complements.

If German case counts as more mature than the grammaticalised positions of the English subject and direct object, then the less mature English structures achieve greater syntactic-semantic transparency. Rohdenburg (1991, 1992) and Fischer (1997: 297–315) have shown that greater English semantic transparency applies to a number of constructions: for instance, the development of Old English deverbal nouns into gerunds (see Fanego 2004) ultimately led to a more complex and semantically more transparent system of English non-finite clauses than the German one.[20] Though the increase in English non-finite clauses – a change that very much informs the verbal character of Modern English[21] – was probably not driven by semantic transparency, it certainly has it as its side effect.

John McWhorter (2002: 250) might be right that the loss of complexity in the Middle English period has not been compensated by a concurrent or more recent increase in complexity. But the mature English structures that there are should be given due place in a typological assessment as should the semantic transparency of English and German structures, both mature and immature. A typological assessment of individual languages should take a comprehensive rather than selective approach. But not all structures are of equal importance in determining the character of a language: establishing the frequency of structures helped adjust typological claims about German and English. An encompassing typological assessment cannot afford to ignore texts.

While the lexically-centred valency approach with its bottom-up perspective naturally militates against taking typological shortcuts, it can also lead to typological abstinence ("lost in lexicography"). It is desirable that the recent re-discovery of a typological valency perspective (Ágel 2000; Fischer 2003), a perspective that was so important to Lucien Tesnière, the creator of valency as a linguistic framework, is taken forward.

Notes

1. Term complements are complements that refer to entities rather than localities or characterisations, so they are the subject and objects including prepositional objects (cf. Zifonun et al. 1997: 1065–1099). I will limit my discussion to the subject and direct object as the most central term complements. The use of the term *direct object* does not imply passivisability. The direct object is rather defined on the basis of proform replacement (both languages) and position (English): it is the *Akkusativergänzung* (accusative complement) of German valency work and the *direct complement* as defined in Fischer (1997: 99ff.): the only, or if there is more than one the second, postverbal NP in unmarked order that allows replacement by a personal pronoun in the objective case.

   I would like to express my gratitude to John Hawkins, from whose ideas and analyses, always lucidly expressed, I have benefited considerably. I would also like to thank John McWhorter and Ian Roe for having commented on a draft version of this article.

   I am indebted to London Metropolitan University and the British Arts and Humanities Research Board (now: Arts and Humanities Research Council) for supporting my research by granting me two sabbatical terms (Research Leave Scheme Award RL/AN6564/APN16978).
2. Olga Fischer implies that the replacement of the Old English object genitive by (ultimately) several prepositions led to "finer semantic role distinctions" (1992: 234).
3. One can add a further frame that has a similar relationship to Frame 5 as Frame 3 has to Frame 4:

Frame 6.	NP [Agent]	-	V	-	NP [Patient]	-	NP [Instrumental]	*I broke a world record with my guitar.* *Ich habe mit meiner Gitarre einen Weltrekord gebrochen.*

4. Hawkins (1986, 1992) uses the term *semantic role* which I reserve as a generic term for different concepts of roles.
5. See the lexically induced hierarchisation of predicate frames in Willems and Coene (2003) and the concept of a structured *Satzmusterparadigma* ['paradigm of sentence patterns'] derived from inherent verb meaning in Coene (2004: 562). For *Grundvalenz* ['basic valency'] see Welke (1988: 27) and Fischer (2003: 27).
6. The gender hierarchy is sometimes given as "M, F < N" (e.g. Hawkins 2004: 72) as there are languages where F is less typologically marked than M. How-

ever, morphological marking and distribution in German support the original hierarchy.

7. Ulrich Heid has kindly drawn my attention to Evert (2004) and Evert, Heid, and Spranger (2004) who present data on the ambiguity of German noun phrases (64605 tokens of common nouns) derived from an automated analysis using the Negra corpus of German newspaper texts. Only 22.03% of noun phrases were unambiguously marked for case, 21.40% did not contain any case information at all, the rest was ambiguous between two or three cases. Looking at candidates for nominative noun phrases, only 9.48% were marked as non-accusatives. Though the data are not entirely comparable with mine – neither syntactic function nor actual cases were ascertained – they point at even greater ambiguity in journalistic texts than in the mainly narrative texts which I have investigated and thus confirm my findings.
8. While many of my findings will be valid for spontaneous spoken text, this does not apply in this case as inversions in declarative main clauses are largely restricted to formal and/or narrative texts. Those that do occur in informal speech are formulaic (*Here comes the postman*). (Cf. Quirk et al. 1985: 1379–1383)
9. Note that preposing of the non-subject phrases in examples (3) and (4) forces inversion, which thus constitutes a separate construction here, not just a constructional variant of a corresponding XSV-clause. The reason for this is the restrictive or negative adverb in the preposed phrase which introduces a scope restriction and the way in which the scope restriction is used: the statement is by implication rather about the excluded cases than about those in the scope restriction. Compare with: *But in some of the countries these organizations represent a dynamic element in the economy*. Inversion is optional, at least in principle, in the other examples (*'It's – it's true?' Professor McGonagall faltered*), but cannot be realised in (5) to avoid ending a sentence with *was*.
10. In spontaneous spoken language this figure is likely to be lower.
11. The term – other than Abraham's assessment – does not imply a value judgement (see Dahl 2004: 60).
12. Complement labels for German are based in part on Engel and Schumacher (1978), Engel (1988), in part on Zifonun et al. (1997). For English complement labels see Fischer (1997: 94–151).
13. The frequencies for *Subjekt* and subject were calculated on the basis of finite clauses, for all other complements nonfinite clauses were considered as well.
14. Italics in the original text of examples (16) and (16b) were replaced by quotation marks.
15. The thematic roles are the Fillmore-type thematic roles used by Hawkins (see table 1), which capture a linguistic perspective only to a very limited degree. I have slightly changed some of the labels to emphasise this and to reserve labels ending in *-ive* for the construction-induced roles.
16. The dual role allocation demonstrates the problematic status of the various concepts of semantic roles. It is also meant as an implicit criticism of Haw-

kins's analysis of secondary subjectisations that solely relies on thematic roles and fails to address the semantic contribution of the construction.

17. The translation is rather free. (20) simply means: *We've lost something.*
18. V = main verb, v = auxiliary verb, V_{part} = separated prefix.
19. I have only presented statistics on verb positions for a narrative text with a fair amount of dialogue, but a separate count for a journalistic text confirmed the distribution (see Fischer 2005b: 246, footnote 37).
20. The increase in verbal complexity was matched by a decrease in nominal complexity as compact nominal structures were unravelled.
21. See the greater number of verbs in the English corpus texts (table 7).

References

Abraham, Werner
2003 Faszination der kontrastiven Linguistik ‚DaF': Der Parameter ‚schwere/leichte' Sprache unter typologischer Sicht. In *Deutsch von außen*, Gerhard Stickel (ed.), 34–73. (Jahrbuch 2002 des Instituts für Deutsche Sprache.) Berlin/New York: Walter de Gruyter.

Ágel, Vilmos
2000 *Valenztheorie*. Tübingen: Gunter Narr.

Coene, Ann
2004 Valenz und verbale Monosemie. Deutsche Kognitionsverben im Lichte der strukturell-funktionellen Semantik und Koerzionstheorie. Ph. D. diss., Faculteit der Letteren en Wijsbegeerte, Universiteit Gent.

Croft, William
2003 *Typology and Universals.* 2d ed. Cambridge: Cambridge University Press.

Dahl, Östen
2004 *The Growth and Maintenance of Linguistic Complexity.* Amsterdam: John Benjamins.

Engel, Ulrich
1988 *Deutsche Grammatik.* Heidelberg: Julius Groos.

Engel, Ulrich, and Helmut Schumacher
1978 *Kleines Valenzlexikon deutscher Verben.* 2d ed. Tübingen: Gunter Narr.

Evert, Stefan
2004 The statistical analysis of morphosyntactic distributions. In *Fourth International Conference on Language Resources and Evaluation*, Maria Teresa Lino, Maria Francisca Xavier, Fátima Ferreira, Rute Costa, and Raquel Silva (eds.), 1539–1542. (Proceedings 3.) Paris: ELRA.

Evert, Stefan, Ulrich Heid, and Kristina Spranger
2004 Identifying morphosyntactic preferences in collocations. In *Fourth*

International Conference on Language Resources and Evaluation, Maria Teresa Lino, Maria Francisca Xavier, Fátima Ferreira, Rute Costa, and Raquel Silva (eds.), 907–910. (Proceedings 3.) Paris: ELRA.

Fanego, Teresa
2004 The rise and development of English verbal gerunds. *Diachronica* 21 (1): 5–55.

Fennell, Barbara
2001 *A History of English: A Sociolinguistic Approach*. Oxford: Blackwell.

Fischer, Klaus
1997 *German-English Verb Valency. A Contrastive Analysis.* Tübingen: Gunter Narr.
2003 Verb, Aussage, Valenzdefinition und Valenzrealisierung: Auf dem Weg zu einer typologisch adäquaten Valenztheorie. In *Valenztheorie. Neuere Perspektiven*, Klaas Willems, Ann Coene, and Jeroen Van Pottelberge (eds.), 14–64. (Studia Germanica Gandensia 2003–2.) Akademia Press: Gent.
2005a Semantic transparency and 'parole': some statistical observations on German and English sentences. In *Getting into German. Multidisciplinary Linguistic Approaches*, John Partridge (ed.), 181–217. Bern: Peter Lang.
2005b Semantische Transparenz deutscher und englischer Satzstrukturen. In *Germanistentreffen Deutschland Großbritannien Irland. Dresden 2004*, 219–250. Bonn: DAAD.

Fischer, Olga
1992 Syntax. In *The Cambridge History of the English language*. Vol. 2: *1066–1476*, Norman Blake (ed.), 207–408. Cambridge: Cambridge University Press.

Hawkins, John A.
1986 *A Comparative Typology of English and German. Unifying the Contrasts.* London/Sydney: Croom Helm.
1992 A performance approach to English/German contrasts. In *New Departures in Contrastive Linguistics / Neue Ansätze in der Kontrastiven Linguistik*, Christian Mair, and Manfred Markus (eds.), 115–136. (Innsbrucker Beiträge zur Kulturwissenschaft. Anglistische Reihe 4.) Innsbruck: Universität Innsbruck.
1994 *A Performance Theory of Order and Constituency.* Cambridge: Cambridge University Press.
2004 *Efficiency and Complexity in Grammars*. Oxford: Oxford University Press.

Ickler, Irene
2007 Sentence patterns and perspective in English and German. This volume.

Krone, Maike
2003 The language of football. A contrastive study of syntactic and semantic specifics of verb usage in English and German match commentaries. Ph. D. diss., Department of Language Studies, London Guildhall University.

McWhorter, John
2002 What happened to English? *Diachronica* 19 (2): 217–272.

Nichols, Johanna
1986 Head-marking and dependent-marking grammar. *Language* 62: 56–119.

Plank, Frans
1984 Verbs and objects in semantic agreement: Minor differences between languages that might suggest a major one. *Journal of Semantics* 3: 305–60.

Quirk, Randolph, Sidney Greenbaum, Geoffrey Leech, and Jan Svartvik
1985 *A Comprehensive Grammar of the English Language.* London/New York: Longman.

Rohdenburg, Günter
1974 *Sekundäre Subjektivierungen im Englischen und Deutschen. Vergleichende Untersuchungen zur Verb- und Adjektivsyntax.* (PAKS Arbeitsbericht 8.) Bielefeld: Cornelsen-Velhagen & Klasing.
1990 Aspekte einer vergleichenden Typologie des Englischen und Deutschen. Kritische Anmerkungen zu einem Buch von John A. Hawkins. In *Kontrastive Linguistik,* Claus Gnutzmann (ed.), 133–152. (Forum angewandte Linguistik 19.) Frankfurt M.: Peter Lang.
1991 *Weitere Betrachtungen zu einer vergleichenden Typologie des Englischen und Deutschen.* (Series A Paper No. 302.) Duisburg: Linguistic Agency University of Duisburg.
1992 Bemerkungen zu infiniten Konstruktionen im Englischen und Deutschen. In *New Departures in Contrastive Linguistics/Neue Ansätze in der Kontrastiven Linguistik,* Christian Mair, and Manfred Markus (eds.), 187–207. (Innsbrucker Beiträge zur Kulturwissenschaft. Anglistische Reihe 4.) Innsbruck: Universität Innsbruck.

Sperber, Dan, and Deirdre Wilson
1995 *Relevance. Communication and Cognition.* 2d ed. Oxford: Blackwell.

Thomason, Sarah Grey, and Terence Kaufman
1988 *Language Contact, Creolization, and Genetic Linguistics.* Berkeley, CA: University of California Press.

Wegener, Heide
1985 *Der Dativ im heutigen Deutsch.* Tübingen: Gunter Narr.

Welke, Klaus M.
1988 *Einführung in die Valenz- und Kasustheorie.* Leipzig: VEB Bibliographisches Institut.

Willems, Klaas, and Ann Coene
2003 Argumentstruktur, verbale Polysemie und Koerzion. In *Valency in Practice / Valenz in der Praxis*, Alan Cornell, Klaus Fischer, and Ian Roe (eds.), 37–63. Genf: Peter Lang.

Zifonun, Gisela, Ludger Hoffmann, Bruno Strecker, Joachim Ballweg, Ursula Brauße, Eva Breindl, Ulrich Engel, Helmut Frosch, Ursula Hoberg, and Klaus Vorderwülbecke
1997 *Grammatik der deutschen Sprache.* Berlin/New York: Walter de Gruyter.

Sentence patterns and perspective in English and German

Irene Ickler

1. Sentence pattern and verb valency

It is my aim to show that sentence patterns can be related to specific functional meanings which can to a certain extent be described independently of the verbal lexeme. The functional meaning of the sentence pattern coordinates with verb valency in such a way that it either corresponds to part of the verbal meaning or adds to the (compatible) verbal meaning. Verbs can be compatible with different sentence patterns which is not surprising because sentence patterns are linked and related to one another. Verbal word formation may further reflect the functional meaning of a type of sentence pattern and so make the verb correspond to it.[1]

2. A systematic change of perspective

The meaning conveyed by the sentence pattern has to do with the perspective chosen by the speaker. Languages provide means to vary these perspectives in a systematic way.

I want to concentrate on one special systematic alternation of perspectives that is omnipresent and similar in English and German. It is the converse relation between two entities regularly referred to in verb complements: the Dynamic and the Static Entity. At any one time only one can be mentioned in a superior syntactic position. The relative position and status of these entities in a specific perspective is indicated by the grammar of the sentence pattern as a unit, especially by the combination of word order, cases, prepositions, prefixes and verb particles as well as the form of the perfect tense. It is important to stress that these formal features of a sentence pattern are more or less ambiguous if studied separately. Only in a combined construction are they able to convey functional meaning. In this approach the lexical meaning of the verbal stem or the complement nouns will only be drawn upon if the rest of the construction is ambiguous.

The criterion of passivizability will help to distinguish the two above-mentioned entities from the third main entity typically encoded as a verb complement: the Causative Entity.

2.1. Examples

Before I define these three basic semantic roles I would like to cite a set of examples that immediately demonstrates what I mean:

(1)	a.	*Sie*	*Desinfektionsmittel*	*auf die Wunde.*	*(sprühte)*
		She	*disinfectant*	*on the wound.*	*(sprayed)*
		X	Y	Z	

X is the Causative Entity that always fills the subject position if and only if the sentence is passivizable. Y is the Dynamic Entity which is found here in a position that is relatively central and superior to Z's position. Z is the Static Entity. Please note that there is no need to look at the verb in order to identify the Dynamic and the Static Entity. It is the divalent local preposition *auf/on* that clearly assigns a Static Entity to the NP following it and a Dynamic or potentially Dynamic Entity to the NP preceding it.

(1)	b.	*Sie*	*die Wunde*	*mit Desinfektionsmittel.*	*(besprühte)*
		She	*the wound*	*with disinfectant.*	*(sprayed)*
		X	Z	Y	

In sentence (1b) now Z, the Static Entity, is placed in the superior position. The non-local preposition *mit/with* introduces a prepositional object that carries the Dynamic Entity Y. So here the preposition *with* is converse to the local preposition in (1a).

(2)	a.	*Luft*	*in den / dem Ballon.*	*(strömt / ist)*
		Air	*into / in the balloon.*	*(streams / is)*
		Y	Z	

In (2a) the Dynamic Entity Y fills the subject position because there is no Causative Entity to claim its right to the highest position.

(2)	b.	*Der Ballon*	*Luft.*	*(verliert / enthält)*
		The balloon	*air.*	*(loses / contains)*
		Z	Y	

In (2b) we need the verb to tell us that the transitive-looking sentence is in fact non-passivizable, so that there is no Causative Entity to fill the subject position. But once that is found out, it is quite easy to conclude the functional meaning of this sentence pattern: it is the pattern of 'Having or Incorporating and opposite' (pattern 10) with the Static Entity Z superior to the Dynamic Entity Y.

The change of perspective in the sentences (a) vs. (b), where either Y or Z is central, is systematically indicated in speech. Below I list more sentence patterns that relate to one another in this respect.

2.2. The three basic perspective roles

Static Entity Z: the Static Entity Z has (= is represented as having) a stable local position relative to the other entities and to the speaker's standpoint: Z does not appear, does not disappear nor does it move from one place to another.

Dynamic Entity Y: the Dynamic Entity Y has no stable local position. In the representation of a process Y moves relatively to Z and to the speaker's standpoint: Y appears, disappears and moves from one place to another. In the representation of a state Y's position is seen as the more mobile or more uncertain in relation to Z's position.

Causative Entity X: the Causative Entity X acts either primarily on Z or primarily on Y. If X acts primarily on Z, it affects Z. If X acts primarily on Y, it effects Y, that is it either produces Y, extinguishes Y or it moves Y from one place to another.[2]

2.3. The specific perspective roles of the Static Entity Z and the Dynamic Entity Y

Y and Z are very basic semantic roles, but they are linguistic and perspective roles, as can be seen in *mother beside father,* where *mother* is set as the Dynamic Entity Y and *father* as the Static Entity Z, and the other way round in *father beside mother.* Y and Z each assume different specific perspective roles depending on the relative status they hold in a perspective:

- If Z has a more peripheral status in the perspective it is seen as a location (which may be split into source, path, goal and position). This location is not holistically affected by an action, process or state.

- If Z has a more central status it is seen as the entity that has, acquires or loses something or that changes a feature. This entity is seen as holistically affected by the action, process or state.
- If Y has a more peripheral status in the perspective it is seen as a feature added to or taken from Z.
- If Y has a more central status it is seen as an entity whose (change of) location or existence is of prime interest.

3. Hierarchy of grammatical functions

In a sentence pattern the specific perspective roles are assigned different grammatical functions according to their status (central or not) as well as their basic role (X, Y or Z).

Here I only want to refer to a section of the hierarchy of grammatical functions that shows the accessibility for grammatical regularities like pronominalization, passivization, congruence, case-marking, reflexivation and others:

(3) Subject > Direct Object > Indirect Object > Prepositional Objects/ Local Adverbials

As we shall see later, the indirect object can be seen as a threshold between the central functional complements that indicate different semantic roles in different patterns and the marginal (oblique) complements that indicate one specific semantic role.

The assignment of perspective roles and grammatical functions will be demonstrated in the following list of sentence patterns and stated again at the end of this paper.

4. List of sentence patterns and their functional meaning

In the following list twelve sentence patterns are marked by the grammatical functions of their complements, the assigned basic semantic roles, a convenient but not precise label for their functional meaning and the explicit functional meaning in brackets. They are exemplified by English and German model sentences and further verbs that fit the patterns. The patterns are not only listed but also linked to one another, i.e. I will mention connections to already introduced patterns.

I will start with the sentence pattern of "Transfer". This functional meaning is well-marked by the specific combination of complements. Three main types of verbal lexemes fit into this frame: 1, simplex verbs whose lexical meanings correspond totally or partly to the functional meaning of the pattern (e.g. *put, send*); 2, simplex verbs that do not carry this functional meaning intrinsically but that can be understood as compatible (e.g. *crash, rub*). The advantage here is that the verbal lexemes can add a great variety of modifying meaning to the functional meaning of the pattern; 3, particle or phrasal verbs that carry a part of the functional meaning in their particle. We will observe these complex verbs as we proceed.

I **SU + DO + L: 'transfer'**
X Y Z
(X causes Y to move/stay relatively to Z)

a. ***so. puts sth. somewhere:***
drive, roll, crash, pack off, bring away, send on, take down, carry off, drive back, drag out

b. ***so. removes sth. from somewhere:***
get, shake, throw off, exclude, extract, take out/off, sweep away, fish out, pull back, pick up

German:

a. ***jmd. tut etw. irgendwohin:***
bringen, kleben, einparken in, abschieben aus, umleiten nach, anbauen an, aufladen auf

b. ***jmd. nimmt etw. irgendwoher:***
zurückziehen, wegreißen, abwischen von, aufsammeln von, auspressen aus, entnehmen aus

The verbal particle specifies the directional movement of Y in relation to a Z which it implies. It also changes the status of the locational complement from obligatory to optional. The preposition of this complement is obligatorily di-valent and specifies a local relation between Y and Z. As peripheral Z splits up into source, goal, etc., the particle and the preposition can bind different aspects of Z. Interestingly, in English there seems to be a barrier to the particle and the preposition being congruent, whereas the opposite is the case in German.

The second sentence pattern is similar to the first, only the Static Entity Z is not merely marked as a location for Y but as a person who may receive Y. This special status makes Z the third entity in the speaker's focus of interest: it can be assigned a central position as an indirect object. Alternatively it can be assigned a more marginal position as a prepositional object:

II i) **SU + IO + DO**
X Z Y
ii) **SU + DO + PO** *to*: **'give'**
X Y Z
(X causes Y to be at Z's disposal and opposite)

a. ***so. gives so. sth. / so. gives sth. to so.:***
bring, offer, tell, show, hand on/over/up/down, send off, present (to), allow (to), supply (to)

b. ***so. charges so. sth. / so. takes sth. from so.:***
fine, deny, refuse, save, spare, envy, ask (of), demand of/from, steal from, take away from

German: i) **SU + IO + DO**
ii) **SU + DO + PO** *an/zu*

a. ***jmd. übergibt jmdm. etw./jmd. übergibt etw. an jmdn.:***
(weiter-)geben, anbieten, vorstellen, zuflüstern, aufbürden, liefern (an), bringen (zu)

b. ***jmd. nimmt jmdm. etw./jmd. nimmt etw. von jmdm.:***
abnehmen, wegnehmen, ausziehen, vorenthalten, entlocken, stehlen (von), kaufen von

Patterns i) and ii) differ slightly in perspective: in i) two personal individuals, the agent X and the receiver Z, are typically placed near each other in a central position. Where the agent acts, the receiver is expected to re-act in a mentally receptive way. This sentence pattern is twofold passivizable, which means that both objects can be made subject.[3] In ii) Z has more local features. The mentally re-acting feature is neutralized. Hence I would prefer to call Z 'addressee' in this construction.

Of course there are syntactic restrictions to the English intern IO, which is why nearly all verbs that fit into construction i) also fit into ii). But many verbs with a similar meaning are more or less restricted to construction ii); for example, verbs like *shout to* or *buy from* make do with the neutralized 'addressee'-construction. In German more fine-tuning is possible because of the dative case-marking combined with productive particle verbs like in *zurufen* or *abkaufen.* Here the particles are often used to make verbs correspond to this special pattern and therefore then the complements are obligatory (otherwise their function is similar to that in pattern I).

The third sentence pattern offers the possibility of expressing a perspective that is converse to both patterns I and II: here the Static Entity Z takes on the central position of the direct object.

III **SU + DO + PO** *with (of)*: **'provide with'**
X Z Y
(X causes Z to have Y and be holistically affected by this and opposite)

a. ***so. provides so./sth. with sth.:***
fill (up/in), deck (out), cover (up), surround, (over-/under-)stock, load (up/down), paste over
with PO *of*: *remind of, inform of, notify of, suspect of, accuse of*

b. ***so. rids so./sth. of sth.:***
deprive, rob, rid, relieve, clear of/from, discharge of/from, exonerate of/from, absolve from

German: **SU + DO + PO** *mit* **(GO)**

a. ***jmd. versieht jmdn./etw. mit etw.:***
(be-/ver-/ab-/an-/auf-/aus-)füllen, (be-/zu-)decken, einhüllen, überziehen, untermauern
with GO: *beschuldigen, bezichtigen, überführen*

b. ***jmd. befreit jmdn. von etw.:***
freisprechen, erlösen, entlasten, entbinden, reinigen, räumen, heilen
with GO: *berauben, entledigen, entwöhnen, entheben*

German pattern III entails quite regular and motivated verbal prefigation (*be-, ver-, über-, ent-*) that makes verbs correspond to the functional meaning of this pattern type. Strikingly, here the stressed local verb particles like *ein-, aus-, ab-, an-* in German or *in, out, up, down* in English have a somewhat different meaning as compared to patterns I and II. In pattern III they do not indicate a movement of the direct object entity, which is Z (e.g. *to fill up a bottle, to fill in a hole*). Instead, an aspectual meaning is added to them: the holistic and telic meaning of the sentence pattern is intensified or modified by them. In addition, they imply Y by stating its local relation to Z. So these particles in their converse variant can also be said to correspond to the sentence pattern. The third complement carrying Y is optional here, though the special form of GO/PO *of* is mostly only contextually optional.[4]

If we now reduce the trivalent sentence patterns I, II and III to just a divalent pattern of SU + DO, the structural meaning will be more ambiguous, because what we lose are the less central complements that disambiguate the meaning of the pattern. Still I find it justifiable to distinguish two patterns: pattern IV with a Dynamic Entity Y in the DO and pattern V with a Static Entity Z in the DO (e.g. *to wipe off crumbs* vs. *to wipe off the table;*

to supply food vs. *to supply shops*; similar in German with the verbs *abwischen; liefern* vs. *beliefern*).

IV **SU + DO: 'effect'**
X Y
(X causes Y to exist or to emerge somewhere and opposite)

a. ***so. produces sth. / so. takes sth. in / so. extinguishes sth.***
make, say, construct, set up, make up/out, bring up/about/along, erase, absorb, dispel

b. ***so. stores sth. up / so. removes sth.*** (can be extended to sentence pattern I):
write down, put away/across/out/off, box in/up, bottle, imbed, involve, exclude, give out

German:

a. ***jmd. bringt etw. hervor / jmd. nimmt etw. ein / jmd. löscht etw. aus:***
formen, erschaffen, aufbauen, aussagen, abgeben, aufnehmen, herstellen, (ver-)tilgen

b. ***jmd. speichert etw. / jmd. entfernt etw.*** (can be extended to sentence pattern I):
aufschreiben, einkellern, entsenden, auslagern, ab-/weg-/losschicken, hin-/herbringen

V **SU + DO: 'affect'**
X Z
(X affects Z holistically)

a. ***so. touches so. / so. treats sth.:***
caress, kiss, love, redden, clean, steam, damage, overbid, underestimate, wash (out)

b. ***so. (dis-)arms so.*** (can be extended to sentence pattern III):
crown, spice, colour, cork (up), roof in/over, plaster (up/over), depopulate, weed, heal

German:

a. ***jmd. berührt jmdn. / jmd. bearbeitet etw.:***
streicheln, küssen, röten, dämpfen, be-/anlächeln, verändern, überfahren, durchbohren

b. ***jmd. ent-/bewaffnet jmdn.*** (can be extended to sentence pattern III):
krönen, (be-)wässern, benachteiligen, verkorken, unterkellern, überdachen, einfetten

In spite of lexicalization there are typical prefixes and particles for each pattern. There tend to be more particle verbs in IV and more simplex and prefixed verbs in V (e.g. *Weizen anbauen / grow wheat* vs. *den Acker bebauen / till the soil*). In addition, denominal verbs in IV encapsulate Z (as in *einsargen / to coffin*) and denominal verbs in V encapsulate Y (as in *bewaffnen / to arm*).

If we reduce sentence pattern I by the Causative Entity X we get pattern VI (e.g *the boy rolls the ball across the road* vs. *the ball/boy rolls/goes across the road*). The Dynamic Entity Y advances into subject position and the Static Entity Z remains in its local adverbial. This pattern can offer a different perspective to sentence pattern V (e.g. *the boy crosses the road*), where the subject refers to a Causative Entity and the Static Entity has advanced from location to holistically affected entity.

VI **SU + L: 'move/stay'**
Y Z
(Y moves/stays relatively to Z)

a. ***so./sth. moves somewhere:***
go, come, crash, lie (down), sit (down), stream, drip, go off/out/back, run off/away from

b. ***so./sth. is somewhere:***
be (situated), stay, hang, remain, stick, live, lodge, occur, exist, sit, stand, lie

German:

a. ***jmd./etw. bewegt sich irgendwohin:***
gehen, kommen, tanzen, sich (hin-)setzen, einsteigen in, aussteigen aus, durchfahren durch

b. ***jmd./etw. befindet sich irgendwo:***
sein, sich befinden, sich aufhalten, bleiben, stecken, wohnen, vorkommen, stehen, sitzen

This pattern is not passivizable. The German verbs in (a) form their perfect tense with the auxiliary *sein*, even those that do not do so in other sentence patterns like *tanzen, krachen, schnaufen, tröpfeln,* or those that can also be used with transitive sentence pattern I, such as *fahren, fliegen, rollen, krachen.*

To indicate the distinction I would like to point out the similar sentence pattern VII, which is passivizable and in which the German verbs form their perfect tense with the auxiliary *haben.*[5] Here pattern I is not reduced by the Causative Entity X but by the Dynamic Entity Y.

VII **SU + PO: 'aim at'**
X Z
(X directs his action towards Z and may affect Z non-holistically because of that)
laugh at, look after, object to, rely on, comment on, believe in, break in on, dwell upon

German:
lachen über, aufpassen auf, anspielen auf, raten zu, glauben an, greifen nach, schwelgen in

The prepositions are similar to those in patterns I and VI, but instead of being divalent with the Dynamic Entity Y preceding them and the Static Entity Z following them, they are monovalent. We may think of Y as being the action itself, having melted into the verbal meaning, thereby attaching the preposition more closely to the verb and promoting Z from location to non-holistically, indirectly affected object.[6]

If we reduce sentence pattern II by the Causative Entity X we get sentence pattern VIII (e.g. *someone gave it to me* vs. *it belongs to me*). Again the Dynamic Entity Y advances to the subject position and the Static Entity Z remains in its position.

VIII **SU + IO (PO *to*): 'come to/ belong to'**
Y Z
(Y comes to / is with a mental Z and opposite)

a. ***sth. occurs to so. / sth. belongs to so.:***
happen to, appear to, go to, come (in handy) to, appeal to, be useful to, correspond to

b. ***sth./(so.) springs from so.:***
come from, escape from, slip (away) from, issue from, (fail so., escape so., slip so.)

German: **SU + IO** (NP dat)

a. ***etw./jmd. erscheint jmdm. / etw. gehört jmdm.:***
begegnen, widerfahren, unterlaufen, zustoßen, passen, einfallen, (aus-)reichen, auffallen

b. ***etw./jmd. entgeht jmdm. / etw. fehlt jmdm.:***
entfallen, entfahren, entgleiten, entweichen, entwischen, weglaufen, abgehen, ausweichen

This pattern is not passivizable and most German verbs form their perfect tense with the auxiliary *sein*.

To indicate the distinction I would like to point out a similar sentence pattern which is passivizable and in which the German verbs form their perfect tense with the auxiliary *haben*. Here pattern II is not reduced by the Causative Entity X but by the Dynamic Entity.

IX **SU + IO (PO *to*): 'pay attention to'**
X Z
(X directs his/her attention towards a mental Z and may initiate an interaction with Z because of this)
attend to, listen to, talk to, speak to, read to, write to, preach to, pray to, lie to, smile to

German: **SU + IO** (NP dat)
helfen, danken, gratulieren, zuhören, zustimmen, zulächeln, nachspionieren, vortanzen

If we reduce sentence pattern III by its Causative Entity X, we have pattern X with the Static Entity Z in subject position. Interestingly the Dynamic Entity Y can be stated in different syntactic positions, which means that there are subvariants:

X i) **SU + DO**
Z Y
ii) **SU + PO** *with/of:* **'incorporate/have'**
Z Y
(Z has/gets Y and opposite)

a. ***so. has sth. / so. gets sth.*** *(also intellectually):*
with DO: *possess, know, deserve (praise), contract (a bad habit), lack, need, want (care)*
with PO: *be full of, cope with, become possessed with, do with(out), be free of*

b. ***sth. contains sth. / sth. fills with sth.:***
with DO: *comprise, seat, house, fit, admit, emit, dispense, give, hold, shed, lose, leak, seep*
with PO: *fill with, charge up with, swarm with, buzz with, crawl with, be clear of*

German: i) **SU + DO**
ii) **SU + PO** *mit* / **GO**

a. ***jmd. hat etw. / jmd. bekommt etw.*** *(auch geistig):*
with DO: *besitzen, bekommen, erhalten, erfahren, ermessen, kennen, merken, verlieren*
with GO: *sich erfreuen, sich bewußt sein, bedürfen, entraten, ermangeln, voller Y sein*
with PO: *reichen mit, begabt sein mit, von sich geben, frei sein/werden von, voll sein von*

b. ***etw. enthält etw. / etw. füllt sich mit etw.:***
with DO: *beinhalten, (um-)fassen, einschließen, ergeben, betragen, wiegen, messen, kosten*
with GO: *ermangeln, voller (Y) sein/liegen/hängen,*
with PO: *sich füllen/anreichern/aufladen mit, vollhängen von, wimmeln von*

The transitive-looking pattern is in fact not passivizable. Pattern X offers a real converse to patterns VI (e.g. *water drips into/out of the basin* vs. *the basin fills with water / leaks water*) and VIII (e.g. *the ring belongs to Mary* vs. *Mary possesses a ring*).

If we now reduce the divalent patterns IV und V by the Causative Entity we get the two parallel monovalent patterns XI and XII. They are distinguished semantically by the fact that either the Dynamic or the Static Entity has advanced into subject position. Please compare the sentences in (4).

(4)	a.	*sth. has appeared*	b.	*so. has laughed*
		(ist erschienen)		*(hat gelacht)*
		so. has arrived		*sth. has reddened*
		(ist angekommen)		*(hat sich gerötet)*
		steam has developed		*the water has steamed*
		(ist entstanden)		*(hat gedampft)*
		water has leaked out		*the tank has leaked*
		(ist ausgelaufen)		*(hat geleckt)*
		SU		SU
		Y		Z

In (a) the subject entity has changed its local position or has come into existence. In (b) the subject entity has not changed its position; instead it is assigned a certain feature.

XI **SU: 'exist/appear/move'**
Y
(Y is or appears somewhere and opposite)

a. ***sth./so. appears/disappears:***
come (about/off/up), emerge, arise, break out, spring up, go (away/by/out), thaw (off)

b. ***sth./so. moves on/stays*** (can be extended to sentence pattern VI):
go (up/down/on/in), climb (up/down), drip (out), flow down/off, drain off, start off, be on

German:

a. ***etw./jmd. erscheint/verschwindet:***
entstehen, (an-)kommen, (er-)wachsen, aufkommen, austreten, (weg-)gehen, (ab-)schmelzen

b. ***etw./jmd. bewegt sich fort/bleibt*** (can be extended to sentence pattern VI):
(auf-/an-/ab-)steigen, auf-/ab-/fahren, (ab-)sinken, ausgehen, da/an/aus/weg/vorbei sein

XII **SU: 'characterization'**
Z
(Z has or changes a feature / gives off or takes on something)

a. ***so. laughs / sth. foams:***[7]
sleep, talk, read, sing, box, hunt, steam, sprout, hay, curse, dream, joke, drip, leak

b. ***so. blushes / sth. reddens / sth. is red:***
age, freeze, bleach, defrost, drain, mold, pale, open (up), close (down), shut (up), cool (down)

German:

a. ***jmd. lacht / etw. schäumt:***
schlafen, wursten, knallen, tropfen, abtauen (Kühlschrank), ausdunsten, aufheulen, abfärben

b. ***jmd. errötet / etw. rötet sich / etw. ist rot:***
altern, (ge-)frieren, trocknen, (er-)bleichen, veralten, aufbersten, (zer-)brechen, auslaufen

All German verbs in XI form their perfect tense with the auxiliary *sein,* but so do the transformative verbs in (XIIb). There tend to be more particle verbs in XI and more simplex but denominal and deadjectival verbs in XII. The particles in XI imply Z and those in XII have the converted, aspectual meaning. The denominal verbs in XII encapsulate Y (as in *smoke* > *emit smoke, haaren > Haare verlieren*) and those in XI encapsulate Z (as in *to emplane, sich einschiffen*).

5. Conclusion

5.1. Perspectives and their sentence patterns

In the following survey the perspectives I discussed are classified according to the presence of a Causative Entity (+X: "Causative Perspective" and –X: "Process/State Perspective") and according to the syntactic priority of Dynamic versus Static Entity (Y > Z: "Existence Perspective" and Z > Y: "Characterization Perspective"). These types are subclassified into their sentence patterns. Converse patterns are linked with a line.

I. CAUSATIVE PERSPECTIVE

A. EXISTENCE PERSPECTIVE	B. CHARACTERIZATION PERSPECTIVE
1 SU + DO + L 'transfer' X Y Z	3 SU + DO + PO (/GO) 'provide with' X Z Y
2 SU + DO + IO 'give' X Y Z	
4 SU + DO 'effect' X Y	5 SU + DO 'affect' X Z

II. PROCESS/STATE PERSPECTIVE

A. EXISTENCE PERSPECTIVE	B. CHARACTERIZATION PERSPECTIVE
6 SU + L 'move' Y Z	10 SU + DO (PO/GO) 'have' Z Y
8 SU + IO 'belong to' Y Z	
11 SU 'existence' Y	12 SU 'characterization' Z

The left side (which has to do with BEING somewhere) and the right side (which has to do with HAVING a feature), each combine with their typical variants of particles and prefixes in complex verbs. There is also a typical distribution of the auxiliaries *sein* and *haben* in German perfect tense.[8]

5.2. The naming of the specific perspective roles

Semantic roles have been identified and variously classified in many splendid studies, first and foremost by Charles Fillmore. The following open list of specific perspective roles is familiar but I would like to emphasize its anchorage in the syntactic construction of a sentence pattern through the three basic perspective roles:

SYNTACTIC FUNCTION	BASIC PERSPECTIVE ROLE	SPECIFIC PERSPECTIVE ROLE
SU	X 'Causative' Y 'Dynamic' Z 'Static'	Agent Existing Entity Characterized Entity
DO	Y 'Dynamic' Z 'Static'	Effected Entity Affected Entity
IO, PO *to/an*	Z 'Static'	Recipient, Addressee
L, PO *at/on/in*	Z 'Static'	Locative Entity, Indirectly Affected Entity
PO *with/mit/of/von*/GO	Y 'Dynamic'	Ornative Entity

Notes

1. This attempt is a development of Ickler (1985; 1990; 1993). My basic approach owes to or was encouraged by Hans Altmann as well as works by Fillmore (1988), Goldberg (1995), Langacker (1987; 1991), Wierzbicka (1988), Zaima (1987) and others.
2. Please note that "effect" is used in a broader sense than usual, also including the causation of an entitity's appearance or disappearance relative to a standpoint. By comparison, "affect" does not mean change of location or existence, but change of feature.
3. The dative-passive is much more restricted in German than in English and it requires its own auxiliary *kriegen/bekommen*. The use of dative in German may be extended to "mental" entities like in *dem Text etwas entnehmen, jemanden einer Richtung zuordnen,* but here no dative-passive is possible.

4. A verb having an optional complement just means that this verb is compatible with more than one sentence pattern. These patterns differ in length and functional meaning, but are, of course, related in form and meaning. Please see patterns IVb) and Vb) for examples.
5. In German the subjectless passive which basically can be applied to all actions can easily be applied here with all complements and their prepositions, compare: *Dazu wird (von dem Anwalt) geraten.* vs. **Dazu wird (von den Kindern) gegangen.* Similar in English: *It was objected to (by many members).* vs. **It was gone to (by the children).*
6. Compare *an etw. arbeiten* (non-holistically affected) and *etw. bearbeiten* (holistically affected), *an einem Roman schreiben* (non-holistically affected) and *einen Roman schreiben* (effected). Similar in English: *be at sth.* and *do sth.*
7. Many verbs in this pattern can be combined with an optional direct object, that is, they are also compatible with patterns 4, 5, or 10, e.g. *sing (a song), hunt (a deer), leak (oil).*
8. Typical complex verbs on the left side are combined with local adverbial particles like *in, out, off, up, down / ein, aus, ab, an* and prefixes like *con-, ex-, dis- / er-, ver-* and typical complex verbs on the right side are combined with aspectual particles (homophonous to the ones on the left side) or prefixes like *over-, under- / be-, ver-.*

References

Fillmore, Charles
1988 The mechanisms of "construction grammar". In *Proceedings of the Fourteenth Annual Meeting of the Berkeley Linguistic Society*, 35–55.

Goldberg, Adele
1995 *Constructions. A Constructional Approach to Argument Structure.* Chicago: University of Chicago Press.

Ickler, Irene
1985 Verb und Verbzusatz. Zur grammatischen Beschreibung von Partikelverben und partikelverbähnlichen Strukturen. M.A. thesis, Department of German Philology, University of Munich.
1990 Kasusrahmen und Perspektive. Zur Kodierung von semantischen Rollen. *Deutsche Sprache* 1: 1–37.
1993 Kasusrahmen und Perspektive im Deutschen und Englischen. *Germanistische Linguistik* 119–120: 151–200.

Langacker, Ronald
1987 *Foundations of Cognitive Grammar.* Vol. 1. Stanford: Stanford University Press.
1991 *Foundations of Cognitive Grammar.* Vol. 2. Stanford: Stanford University Press.

Wierzbicka, Anna
1988 *The Semantics of Grammar.* Amsterdam/Philadelphia: John Benjamins Publishing Company.
Zaima, Susumu
1987 "Verbbedeutung" und syntaktische Struktur. *Deutsche Sprache* 1: 35–45.

Contrasting valency in English and German

Brigitta Mittmann

In 2004, two large-scale monolingual valency dictionaries appeared – one for English (VDE) and one for German (VALBU). Now that most of the valency structures of these two languages have been recorded, the question of contrasting these structures in a bilingual reference work has become even more interesting. However, contrasting valency structures and patterns across languages is a complex task.

This contribution to the present volume explores different approaches to comparative valency research. It seems that for certain applied purposes – and not just for translating or lexicography – an approach which takes the text production situation into account and uses frames or constellations of semantic roles as *tertium comparationis* is the most useful one. More specifically, this paper looks at a set of verbs that are highly relevant for a particular text type. It uses them as a background for some observations on contrastive valency studies, on text types and text production, perspective, morphological forms, and dictionaries.

1. The "monosemy problem"

During the conference that this collection of articles is based upon, various speakers expressed the view that words are essentially monosemous. When comparing two languages, it is difficult to maintain this position, especially if one connects this notion with the idea – well-known from structuralist semantics – that the meanings of words are delimited by the meanings of other words. Imagine a two-dimensional model of the words of a language which is similar to a jigsaw puzzle with larger and smaller pieces. The larger pieces are those words which take on more metaphorical and metonymical *Lesarten*, and the smaller pieces are those words which have fewer of these metaphorical extensions. The problem is that once one starts comparing two languages, the situation becomes much more complex, for when the two jigsaw puzzles are put on top of each other, they do not match. There are plenty of intersections and large pieces from one language correspond to many parts of pieces from the other one. And of course the situation becomes yet more complex because word meaning is not just two-dimensional, but multi-dimensional.[1]

For this reason, it is not surprising that for practical purposes, compilers of bilingual valency dictionaries have treated words as polysemous and have also added further details about the selectional restrictions of the verbs in question (cf. e.g. Bianco 1996). Another way to come to terms with this complexity is to make bilingual valency dictionaries monodirectional, i.e. to use a selection of items from one language as a starting point, describe them in detail and give potential equivalents in the other language for these usages, rather than accounting for both languages at the same time (Schumacher 1995: 294).

2. Finding equivalents

Another problem is that of finding equivalents for the lexemes whose valency is to be compared. Fischer states that "[c]ontrastive valency dictionaries show syntactic and semantic parallels and contrasts in the environment of words that regularly occur as translations of each other" (1997: 217) and it seems that he used the same principle in a part of his own work. This is suitable for the aims that he pursues and it can show similarities and differences between the behaviour of words which are likely to be presented as potential equivalents in textbooks or language lessons. However, this does not necessarily mean that these are the equivalents that one should aim for in a given foreign language text production or L1–L2 translation situation, as most words can be translated in very different ways depending on the respective textual context and on factors such as register.

For example, Fischer (1999: 244–245) gives a long list of German and English verbs with prepositional complements together with equivalents from the other language which take a direct object or dative/accusative object respectively. This enables him to demonstrate potential differences between structures in the two languages. However, in several cases the proposed contrast is only true of the words chosen, but not of other potential equivalents. For example, Fischer contrasts German *an etw. zweifeln* with English *doubt sth.* Unlike *zweifeln,* the verb *doubt* does not take any prepositional complement. However, besides *an etw. zweifeln* German also has *etwas bezweifeln*, which – like *doubt* – can take an object without a preposition. It is not quite clear why Fischer discusses only *zweifeln* in this context. He is not alone in this preference for the non-prefixed form (i.e. *zweifeln* rather than *bezweifeln*). There seems to be a general tendency in German valency dictionaries and the core vocabulary lists that they are based upon to describe the prefixless verbs even though both are similar in meaning and there is hardly any significant difference in their frequency of occurrence. In fact, the lexeme *bezweifeln* occurs slightly more frequently in the large-scale written corpus (*Korpus W – Archiv der geschriebenen Sprache* of the *Cosmas II* project).

Similarly, Fischer contrasts *in etw. einsteigen* with *enter sth.* However, *in etwas einsteigen* might just as well be translated as *get into* (or even *onto*, if it is a translation of *in einen Bus einsteigen*), *go into*, *climb into*, etc., depending on the context and the register of the text. All of them are more similar to *in etw. einsteigen* as regards their valency.

One potential solution for this problem might be frequency: if there are verbs which can – broadly speaking – be considered synonymous, then the one that occurs more frequently should be chosen. However, frequency is also dependent on forms of the verb: while *zweifeln* and *zweifelst* are more frequent in the *Archiv der geschriebenen Sprache* in *Cosmas II* than *bezweifeln* and *bezweifelst*, the situation is reversed for *(be)zweifle*, *(be)zweifelt*, and *(be)zweifelte*. A second problem is that, ideally, what should be considered is not the frequency of the lexeme as a whole, but that of the lexical unit, i.e. the use of a particular meaning of a word. This, however, is a prohibitively time-consuming task.

Moreover, frequencies are also highly register-dependent. A few simple online researches in the *British National Corpus* support Fischer's choice in that they show that for the *BNC* as a whole, the forms of *enter* occur more frequently than those for *get into* and *go into* put together.[2] However, if one looks only at the frequencies for the conversations of the 'spoken demographic' part of the *BNC* only, one will find that the situation is reversed.[3] Here, the verbs with prepositional phrases as complements occur more frequently. And although the *BNC* as a whole contains mostly written English, most people arguably tend to use and be exposed to spoken English much more frequently than to the written registers.

Curcio's *Kontrastives Valenzwörterbuch der gesprochenen Sprache Italienisch-Deutsch* respects register specificities to a certain extent. She studies the 1000 most frequent verbs in spoken Italian (1999: 8) and arrives at potential German equivalents through translating relevant sentences taken from the corpus of the *Lessico di frequenza dell'italiano parlato* (LIP), which she uses as material for her research. While this is a suitable method for obtaining a variety of potential equivalents, one has to bear in mind that these counterparts from the other language may show signs of "translationese". In other words, they may not be the words that would be used in the same situations in natural spoken German. Moreover, if single sentences (rather than whole texts) are translated, this may influence the theme-rheme arrangement of the sentences and the selection of the verbs resulting from this.[4]

In Curcio's case, it was necessary to use a translation corpus, as no suitable parallel corpus of spoken German existed. If, however, such a parallel corpus is available, there is a more elegant solution to the problem. It will then be possible to identify what Jürgens (following Klix) has called *Geschehenstypen* (Krone 2003: 107), that is situations – reflected in sentences – which differ in many respects, but have identical constellations of semantic roles. This makes it possible to look for the *tertium comparationis* at the semantic role level. The following pages describe such an alternative approach. As it will become clear, this is very similar to the approach chosen in *FrameNet*, as it compares many different words which evoke the same frame.

3. Verbs in abstracts

When translating scholarly abstracts, translators may find that there is a certain group of verbs which have very similar meanings in this context, but for which bilingual dictionaries do not give enough reliable translations to keep the translators from repeating the same words all over. Amongst the verbs belonging to this group there are, for example, *sich befassen mit* and *sich einer Sache widmen*, as used in the following examples:

(1) *Nicola Würffel* ***beschäftigt sich*** *so mit der Methode des lauten Denkens als einem Mittel, um die Effizienz von Lernsoftware zu bestimmen.*
'In this context, Nicola Würffel discusses "think aloud protocols" as a means of determining the efficiency of pedagogical software.'

(2) *Die vorliegende Arbeit* ***befasst sich*** *mit den spezifischen Problemen der Behandlung von Kollokationen im zweisprachigen Wörterbuch.*
'The present study deals with the specific problems connected with the treatment of collocations in bilingual dictionaries.'

(3) *Die Arbeit* ***widmet sich*** *also einem der markantesten Problembereiche auf dem Gebiet von Theorie und Methodologie des zweisprachigen Wörterbuchs.*
'Thus, the book deals with one of the most prominent problem areas concerning the theory and methodology of bilingual dictionaries.'

(4) *Claus Gnutzmann* ***widmet sich*** *mit „Englisch als globale lingua franca" dem Problem der Herausbildung und Bedeutung des Englischen als Globalsprache und den sich daraus ergebenden didaktischen Konsequenzen.*
'In his contribution on "English as a global lingua franca", Claus Gnutzmann deals with the problems of the development of English into, and its significance as a global language, as well as with the consequences for teaching English which result from this.'

In abstracts, there can be very many verbs of this kind, like *sich beschäftigen mit, behandeln, sich widmen, eingehen auf, beschreiben, darstellen, erörtern, untersuchen*, and so on. These verbs can be grouped into various subcategories. *Verben in Feldern* (1986: 587–597, 709–718, 601–605), for example, mentions the following categories: (i) "Verben der geistigen Beschäftigung" [verbs of mental activity] like *es zu tun haben mit, sich zuwenden, ansprechen, sich beschäftigen mit, sich befassen mit, sich konzentrieren auf, sich auseinandersetzen mit, eingehen auf, behandeln*; (ii) "Verben des Diskutierens" [verbs of discussion] like *diskutieren, debattieren, erörtern, besprechen*; and (iii) "Verben des Untersuchens" [verbs of analysis] such as *untersuchen, analysieren, erforschen*. One could add a fourth group of verbs of description like *beschreiben* or *darstellen*.

Despite these subcategories, it is interesting to note that in abstracts they are all used to mean 'deal with', or perhaps even 'write about (in some detail)'. The text type determines a particular semantic interpretation.

4. General bilingual dictionaries

Traditional bilingual dictionaries do not offer much help when one is translating these words. For example, the fourth edition of the *Collins Großwörterbuch Englisch* (1999) offers the following translations for *sich mit etwas befassen*: first, the ubiquitous *to deal with something*, then *to look into something, to attend to something*, and *to work on something*. With all of the latter three, the reader may feel uncomfortable in this particular context.

befassen
1 *vr* **a** (= ***sich beschäftigen***) **sich mit etw** ~ to deal with sth; ***mit Problem, Frage auch*** to look into sth; ***mit Fall, Angelegenheit auch*** to attend to sth; ***mit Arbeit auch, Forschungsbereich etc*** to work on sth; (...)

In example (2) mentioned earlier, *den spezifischen Problemen der Behandlung von Kollokationen im zweisprachigen Wörterbuch* is the topic that the author writes about, so in a sense it can be interpreted as a *Problem*, a *Frage*, an *Angelegenheit* or even a *Forschungsbereich*, but neither of the verbs offered here seems quite appropriate. If one adopts the usual strategy of looking up another German word that can be used synonymously in the same context, this may be even less helpful. For *sich widmen*, for example, the reader is faced once again with *to attend to*, and also with *to devote oneself to* and *to apply oneself to*.[5]

> **widmen**
> **2** *vr +dat* to devote oneself to; (= *sich kümmern um*) *den Gästen etc* to attend to; *einem Problem, einer Aufgabe* to apply oneself to, to attend to; (...)

For a non-native user of English it will not become clear from this which of these suggestions can be used in translating *In Kapitel 6 beschäftigt sich der Autor mit Syntax*, *In Kapitel 6 widmet sich der Autor der Syntax* or even *Kapitel 6 beschäftigt sich mit der Syntax*.

The obvious solution for a dyed-in-the-wool corpus-linguist is to build her own corpus of abstracts. The corpus that was used here consists of eight reviews of linguistics books written by native speakers of English as contributions to the LinguistList. All of these reviews contain a section in which there is an abstract of the books' contents, and since many of the books are collections of articles, the abstract sections are often rather long and contain many of the verbs needed. For this reason, a very small corpus serves the current purpose.

Table 1. Verbs in the Reviews Corpus

31	*discuss*
19	*examine*
10	*explore, offer*
9	*demonstrate*
8	*describe*
7	*outline, present*
5	*cover, consider*
4	*provide, investigate*
3	*deal with*
2	*focus on, look at*
1	*analyse, chart, detail, pay attention to, pin-point, put forward, share, tackle, trace*

The most frequent verb in these abstracts was *discuss*, followed by *examine*, *explore*, *offer*, and many others. *Deal with* is also among them, but it is not one of the more frequent ones. These verbs were compared with those found in a small parallel corpus of German reviews.[6] The words which are used in the English abstracts seem to be more verbs of investigating and exploring than their German counterparts which in turn tend to be what are called "Verben der geistigen Beschäftigung" [verbs of mental activity (directed towards an object)] in Schumacher's *Verben in Feldern*. And while some of the verbs in the list, like *present* or *put forward*, can be said to describe quite literally what the author is doing in the text, this does not apply to others like *discuss*, *examine*, and *explore*. They only mean something like 'produce text about' in this context, though saying that they "mean something like 'produce text about'" is not very helpful. It is much more appropriate to describe their similarity with the help of semantic roles, or, for those who use a frame semantics approach, to say, that in scholarly abstracts, these verbs evoke the same frame, with the following frame elements, or roles: an [AUTHOR], a [TEXT], and a [TOPIC]. Not all of these have to be present in the sentences, as one can see in other sentences in the corpus where either the subject is not the [AUTHOR], but the [TEXT], as in examples (2) and (3) above, or where the verbs mentioned above are replaced by constructions like *consists of*, *is concerned with*, or *has to do with*. There are also other German constructions expressing the same frame: *es geht um, eine Rolle spielen, im Mittelpunkt stehen.*

5. Choosing a perspective – textual aspects

The choice of verb – and the choice of subject and voice – and thus also the choice of semantic roles and their order in the sentence – determine the perspective that is expressed in the sentence. It seems, however, that there is also a textual component in the selection. If one looks at the reviews in the corpus (and especially if one has previous experience of writing or translating abstracts) one gains the impression that there is something like a "sentence construction mechanism" underlying them. There are several reviews in it which consist in part of a long series of mini-abstracts, like the following:

(5) *[The first chapter (3–17), "American English: its origins and history,"]*$_{\text{text}}$ *[by Richard W. Bailey,]*$_{\text{author}}$ ***examines*** *[the genesis of American English varieties]*$_{\text{topic}}$ *through the lens of settlement history. [Bailey]*$_{\text{author}}$ ***demonstrates*** *[that the American English lexicon comes from a complex social situation, where Amerindian, European, and African languages and peoples coexisted]*$_{\text{topic}}$. *[He]*$_{\text{author}}$ *also* ***offers*** *[a brief account of early nineteenth century debates regarding the value of American English as a marker of national identity]*$_{\text{topic}}$.
[In Chapter 2 (18–38), "American English and its distinctiveness,"]$_{\text{text}}$ *[Edward Finegan]*$_{\text{author}}$ ***addresses*** *[the actual and perceived differences between American and British English varieties]*$_{\text{topic}}$. *[Finegan]*$_{\text{author}}$ ***examines*** *[variations in American and British pronunciations (represented with the International Phonetic Alphabet and pronunciation-based respellings), lexical items, grammar, semantics, discourse, and orthography]*$_{\text{topic}}$.
[Chapter 3 (39–57), "Regional Dialects,"]$_{\text{text}}$ *[by William A. Kretzschmar, Jr.,]*$_{\text{author}}$ ***points out*** *[the problems with broad generalizations regarding regional speech]*$_{\text{topic}}$, *yet acknowledges that Americans are justified in thinking that persons from distinct areas speak English differently. [Kretzschmar]*$_{\text{author}}$ ***presents*** *[historical origins of and linguistic examples from U.S. regional dialects]*$_{\text{topic}}$ *using maps and tables, including an explanation of the creation and use of these scholarly tools. ...*
(Shuttlesworth, <LINGUIST List 16.843>, 17-MAR-2005)

Even such a short stretch – and the review in question contains many more of these mini-abstracts – shows how many verbs there are in this text type which have the meaning 'to deal with' in this context. There is a limited number of sequences or role constellations which occur with the verbs in question.[7] Firstly, there is the sequence [AUTHOR]$_{\text{subj}}$ + VERB + [TOPIC], as exemplified in (6). This sequence can be expanded by an introductory adjunct ([*in* TEXT]$_{\text{adju}}$), as in (7).

(6) *Finegan* ***examines*** *variations in American and British pronunciations.*

(7) *In Chapter 2 (18–38), "American English and its distinctiveness," Edward Finegan* ***addresses*** *the actual and perceived differences between American and British English varieties.*

Alternatively, the [TEXT] can be the subject of the sentence, with an optional postmodification naming the [AUTHOR]. This results in the structure $[\text{TEXT}]_{subj}$ + ([*by* AUTHOR]$_{postm}$) + VERB + [TOPIC]:

(8) *Chapter 3 (39–57), "Regional Dialects," by William A. Kretzschmar, Jr.,* ***points out*** *the problems with broad generalizations regarding regional speech.*

Differences between the semantic roles become apparent in passivization: the [AUTHOR] appears as a *by*-phrase in a passive sentence, whereas the [TEXT] – if it does appear – is an adverbial of place. In many cases, however, neither are present:

(9) *The shift to English by immigrants* ***is*** *also* ***examined****, as are the classroom and untutored means immigrants use to learn English and the social, economic, and personal barriers to their success.*

(10) *In Chapter 2 sociological approaches to the relationship between language and society* ***are reviewed****.*

In German, the [TEXT] can also appear after the preposition *mit*, as in example (11).

(11) [*Claus Gnutzmann*]$_{subj}$ ***widmet sich*** [*mit „Englisch als globale lingua franca"*] [*dem Problem der Herausbildung und Bedeutung des Englischen als Globalsprache und den sich daraus ergebenden didaktischen Konsequenzen*].
'In his contribution on „English as a global lingua franca", Claus Gnutzmann deals with the problems of the development of English into, and its significance as a global language, as well as with the consequences for teaching English which result from this.'

According to the analysis of the *Valency Dictionary of English* – which will be followed here – these adverbials are of course not complements of the verb, but adjuncts. However, it is remarkable – and a computer which might one day translate or produce sentences like these would have to know this – that both the [TEXT] and the [AUTHOR] can be subject of the sentence, but only the [TEXT] can also be part of a prepositional phrase which in English usually functions as an adverbial of (more or less metaphorical) place, whereas the [AUTHOR] can appear in the *by*-phrase in passive sentences.

Psycholinguistically, it would be interesting to know if when writing texts like these abstracts, we first select the constellation of semantic roles for the sentence or the verb itself. The latter seems to be more in line with the ideas of most valency theorists, but some findings from analysing the spoken language – such as the verbless constructions in football commentaries mentioned by Krone (2003: 123) – would seem to contradict this. There is, of course, always the possibility of some kind of "co-selection" going on.

The selection of roles and the question of choosing a sequence seems to follow certain textual principles as well: firstly, as in example (5), there can be a tendency to impose a structure on the text and increase the cohesion of the text by starting paragraphs with the same semantic role sequence in the first sentence. Here, [TEXT] is always at the beginning of the sentence, twice as subject, once in the adverbial. On the other hand, with so many sentences in which the same role constellation is mentioned over and over again, there is of course also the principle of varying sentence structure and of avoiding too many similar and thus boring sentences. (This does not show up so much in this section, but it becomes quite clear in other reviews.)

6. Cross-linguistic differences in perspective

However, while these textual aspects are interesting from a text production point of view, they are not relevant for bilingual lexicography. What is more interesting in this context are the lexical aspects of sequencing roles and some other properties of the verbs studied here. There must be many cases like the following where the perspective (in active clauses at least) can be lexicalised in different ways in different languages:

[THEMA] ***steht im Mittelpunkt*** [eines TEXTES]
[AUTHOR] ***focuses on*** [TOPIC]

If we compare German *im Mittelpunkt stehen* with English *focus on*, we see that in German one makes a statement about something being located somewhere, whereas in English we talk about the activity of a person who is not normally mentioned in the equivalent German sentences. Cases like these can be very interesting, even though some researchers deliberately exclude them from their research because of their difference in structure. Here, once again, meaning-based approaches like *FrameNet* can be very useful, as they can compare many different words which evoke the same frame.

And indeed, if we look at the *FrameNet* homepage, we can find a frame which corresponds exactly to the set of verbs and other constructions which are at the heart of this paper:[8] if we look up the verb *discuss* in the lexical index (we will recall that it was the most frequent one of the set to be found in the corpus), we arrive at the frame labelled TOPIC which has the so-called "core frame elements" [COMMUNICATOR], [TEXT] and [TOPIC]. There are also some "marginal frame elements", namely [DEGREE], [MANNER], and [STATUS], which will not concern us here. And, as was pointed out earlier, although [COMMUNICATOR], [TEXT] and [TOPIC] are labelled as "core frame elements", they are not necessarily realised as complements of the verb in actual sentences, but may either be left out or be realised as adjuncts. The following examples are given for the frame TOPIC:

(12) *Chapter 5* ***discusses*** *the issue of transubstantiation.*
(13) *Smither's essay is* ***about*** *plane spotting.*
(14) *Ostrovsky* ***addresses*** *monetary policy in Chapter 5.*
(15) *This book is mostly* ***about*** *particle physics.*

The following lexical units are listed at the bottom of the page describing the frame: the prepositions *about*, *on*, *concerning* and *regarding*, the verbs *address*, *concern*, *cover*, *discuss*, *dwell_(on)*,[9] and *treat*, and the nouns *subject*, *theme*, and *topic*. As the research on the mini-corpus has shown, this list could be extended considerably. At present, of course, because the *FrameNet* project is still incomplete, there do not seem to be entries for many lexical units as yet. One that is missing, for example, is that for *explore*.

7. The new valency dictionaries

While the *FrameNet* database is, in theory, infinite and can accommodate many nuances of meaning, this is not the case with printed dictionaries. Nevertheless, both the VALBU and the VDE are much better at describing the 'deal with' set of verbs than the *Collins Großwörterbuch* – if, that is, they include these verbs in the macrostructure at all. Because of the fact that both dictionaries had to concentrate on a limited number of words, some had to be left out. Thus, for example, there is no entry for *explore* in the *Valency Dictionary of English*. However, for example, the VDE explicitly describes the 'write about' or 'deal with' use of a number of verbs and also mentions the fact that *cover*, *deal with*, *describe*, *discuss*, and *treat* can also be used with a [TEXT] functioning as grammatical subject. Nevertheless, there is also some, albeit limited, scope for improvement: for *examine* and *provide*, there is only an example in which the subject is a [TEXT] – and no mention in the note block – and for *look at* in the meaning 'deal with' there is not even an example. Even though the relationship between author and text is a well-known source of metonymies, it is not self-evident for non-native speakers that these verbs can be used with non-human subjects.

VALBU is very systematic in its treatment of these verbs. For instance, the "Belegungsregeln" [semantic scope] for the *Nominativergänzung* for *untersuchen* specify that it can be "derjenige, der etwas analysiert: Person/Institution/[auch geistiges Produkt]" [someone analysing something: person/institution/also "intellectual product"] and an example mentions an academic paper (2004: 761).

Both the VDE and the VALBU would treat cases like *In Kapitel 7 befasst sich der Autor mit Valenzgrammatik* and *Kapitel 7 befasst sich mit Valenzgrammatik* as the same meaning of the verb *sich befassen* (see example [2]). No new lexical unit is established. This is, of course, very sensible from a practical point of view – if one looks through just a few pages of either dictionary, one will come across a multitude of verbs with different lexical classes of subjects.

8. Large corpora reveal importance of morphological forms

This micro-study of the TOPIC frame shows how useful small specialised corpora can be. However, in order to find out about the distribution of these uses of the verbs in other text types, it is necessary to look at larger and more balanced corpora like the *British National Corpus*. In a random selection of 50 (out of a total of 1091) sentences for *looks at* (please note the inflectional form) almost half of the examples had the frame element constellation ([AUTHOR]) + ([TEXT/INTELLECTUAL PRODUCT]) + [TOPIC]. Two thirds of them had [TEXT] as subject. For *explores*, the figures are even higher: three quarters of the examples had the frame element constellation discussed here. Once again, two thirds of these had [TEXT/INTELLECTUAL PRODUCT] as subject.

This means that if one encounters the third person singular present tense of these verbs, it is very likely that one will also encounter this particular meaning and semantic role constellation, and also this particular choice of subject. Thus, this morphological form is linked closely to this frame and use of the verb, even though if one asked a native speaker to produce sentences with *looks at* and *explores*, these are likely to be more like the sentences in pre-corpus editions of learners' dictionaries. Native speakers of German who were asked to produce sentences with *behandeln, sich befassen, sich widmen* and *untersuchen* gave, amongst others, *Der Arzt behandelt die Magenverstimmung des Patienten, Die Rechtsanwältin befasst sich mit der Akte des Delinquenten, Der Großvater widmet sich seinem Enkel, Der Großvater widmet sich der Musik,* and *Der Geografieprofessor untersucht die vulkanischen Erscheinungen der Rhön.* The only one that came close and fitted the TOPIC frame was *Der Professor behandelt das Thema in der Vorlesung.*

9. Summary

Thus, to sum up, the perfect bilingual reference work on valency would be a comprehensive database in which the *tertium comparationis* lies at the frame or semantic role level and which includes all verbs, nouns and adjectives of the languages in question (or at least those that occur reasonably frequently in a large corpus). This database should also take into account certain other constructions like *im Mittelpunkt stehen* (or, in fact, *take into account*) and should give information about the frequencies of synonymous patterns, perhaps even in different text types. So one must hope that it will be possible to extend the project that Boas (2001; 2002) has described in his articles on creating a bilingual version of *FrameNet*. It would certainly be very useful for the material described here.

Notes

1. Other authors have also drawn attention to this, e.g. Schumacher (1995: 294).
2. At http://sara.natcorp.ox.ac.uk/lookup.html (August 5, 2005). These were simple formal queries disregarding the meanings that these lexemes can take on. This is crude but can still give an indication of general tendencies.
3. The spoken demographic part of the *BNC* contains around four million words of spontaneous conversation.
4. In another part of her book, Curcio (1999: 149) remarks that in 98,6% of sentences the Italian subject corresponded to the German subject in the translations. It is quite possible that this figure was influenced by the translation process.
5. The writers of this dictionary seem to assume that the user will understand that *vr+dat* refers to constructions like *sich einer Sache widmen.* In fact, it is likely that even well-trained dictionary users will overlook this code.
6. This corpus contains one abstract and seven reviews. For details see bibliography.

7. Note that with this group of verbs, the [TEXT] cannot be the object of the active clause (or the subject of the corresponding passive clause). Verbs like *write* belong to a different group of verbs, even though they may have the same role constellation in examples like *J.K. Rowling has written a new book about Harry Potter* (invented example) or *A new book has been written about Harry Potter* (invented example) where the role constellations are [AUTHOR]$_{subj}$ + VERB + [TEXT] + ([*on/about* TOPIC]) and [TEXT]$_{subj}$ VERB$_{PASS}$ ([*on/about* TOPIC]) respectively.
8. http://framenet.icsi.berkeley.edu/ (March 25, 2005).
9. In contrast to the other verbs mentioned so far, *dwell (on)* is of course used to indicate that the [AUTHOR] spends too much time dealing with the [TOPIC].

References

Bianco, Maria Teresa
1996 *Valenzlexikon Deutsch-Italienisch. Dizionario della valenza verbale.* (Deutsch im Kontrast 17.) Heidelberg: Julius Groos.

Boas, Hans C.
2001 Frame semantics as a framework for describing polysemy and syntactic structures of English and German motion verbs in contrastive computational lexicography. In *Proceedings of the Corpus Linguistics 2001 conference*, Paul Rayson, Andrew Wilson, Tony McEnery, Andrew Hardie, and Shereen Khoja (eds.), 64–73. (*Technical Papers*, 13.) Lancaster: University Centre for Computer Corpus Research on Language.
2002 Bilingual FrameNet dictionaries for machine translation. In *Proceedings of the Third International Conference on Language Resources and Evaluation.* Vol. 4. Manuel González Rodriguez, and Carmen Paz Suárez Araujo (eds.), 1364–1371. Las Palmas, Spain.

Curcio, Martina Lucia
1999 *Kontrastives Valenzwörterbuch der gesprochenen Sprache Italienisch-Deutsch. Grundlagen und Auswertung.* (amades 3.) Mannheim: IDS.

Fischer, Klaus
1997 *German-English Verb Valency: A Contrastive Analysis.* (Tübinger Beiträge zu Linguistik 422.) Tübingen: Narr.
1999 Englische und deutsche Satzstrukturen: Ein valenztheoretischer Vergleich mit statistischen Anmerkungen. *Sprachwissenschaft* 24 (2): 221–255.

Herbst, Thomas, David Heath, Ian F. Roe, and Dieter Götz
2004 *A Valency Dictionary of English. A Corpus-Based Analysis of the Complementation Patterns of English Verbs, Nouns and Adjectives.* Berlin/New York: Mouton de Gruyter. [= VDE]

Krone, Maike
2003 Valenzstrukturen in deutschen und englischen Fußballreportagen am Beispiel von Freistößen. In *Valency in Practice. Valenz in der Praxis*, Alan Cornell, Klaus Fischer, and Ian F. Roe (eds.), 105–126. Oxford/Bern/Berlin/Bruxelles/Frankfurt M./New York/Wien: Peter Lang.

Schumacher, Helmut
1986 *Verben in Feldern. Valenzwörterbuch zur Syntax und Semantik deutscher Verben.* Berlin/New York: Walter de Gruyter.
1995 Kontrastive Valenzlexikographie. In *Deutsch als Fremdsprache. An den Quellen eines Faches. Festschrift für Gerhard Helbig zum 65. Geburtstag*, Heidrun Popp (ed.), 287–315. München: Iudicium.

Schumacher, Helmut, Jacqueline Kubczak, Renate Schmidt, and Vera de Ruiter (eds.)
2004 *VALBU – Valenzwörterbuch deutscher Verben.* Tübingen: Narr. [= VALBU]

Terrell, Peter, Veronika Schnorr, Wendy V.A. Morris, and Roland Breitsprecher
1999 *Collins Großwörterbuch Deutsch-Englisch, Englisch-Deutsch.* 4th ed. Glasgow: Collins.

Corpora

The British National Corpus is a collaborative inititative carried out by Oxford University Press, Longman, Chambers Harrap, Oxford University Computing Services, Lancaster University's Unit for Computer Research in the English Language, and the British Library. The project received funding from the UK Department of Trade and Industry and the Science and Engineering Research Council and was supported by additional research grants from the British Academy and the British Library. For more details see http://info.ox.ac.uk/bnc/.

Cosmas-II-Projekt: *Korpus W – Archiv der geschriebenen Sprache.* For more details see http://www.ids-mannheim.de/cosmas2/ (August 2, 2005).

LINGUIST List issues 16.24 (Callahan), 16.163 (Willoughby), 16.314 (Unsworth), 16.467 (Hewitt), 16.577 (Maxwell), 16.601 (Wilcox), 16.757 (Henderson), 16.843 (Shuttlesworth).
See http://www.linguistlist.org/pubs/reviews/index.html (March 26, 2005).

Mini-Corpus of German Reviews and Abstracts. Contents: Jekaterina Boutina-Koller's abstract of her PhD thesis on *Kollokationen im zweisprachigen Wörterbuch* plus reviews by Claus Altmayer (jg-06-2), Dieter Kranz (jg-06-2), Haymo Mitschian (jg-09-1) and Guido Oebel (jg-09-3) from *Zeitschrift für Interkulturellen Fremdsprachenunterricht* (http://zif.spz.tu-darmstadt.de/earchiv.htm; downloaded on April 3, 2005) as well as reviews from *Philologie im Netz* (http://www.fu-berlin.de/phin/welcome.html, downloaded on April 3, 2005) by Christiane Maaß (PhiN 29/2004: 79), Susanne Mühleisen (PhiN 9/1999: 38) and Richard Waltereit (PhiN 4/1998: 53).

Valency in a contrastive perspective: Structure and use

Stig Johansson

1. Introduction

If we want to study verbs in a contrastive perspective, we can compare groups such as modal auxiliaries or mental process verbs. But how do we know what forms to contrast? We know that modality is expressed by other means than by modal auxiliaries, so a comparison of modal auxiliaries is clearly insufficient. Mental processes in English are often expressed by constructions containing the noun *mind*, and these go far beyond idiomatic forms like *keep in mind* and *make up one's mind* (cf. Johansson 1998: 16–18). Compare:

(1)	*in **my mind** it was as if*	*jeg **følte** det som* ['I felt as if']
	***my mind** fills with*	*jeg **tenker** på* ['I think of']

(2)	*sånn jeg **tenker*** ['the way I think']	*the way **my mind** works*
	*jeg **tenker** på alt annet* ['I think of everything else']	***my mind** fills with quite other things*

In (1) we find constructions with *mind* translated by Norwegian mental process verbs, in (2) Norwegian mental process verbs are rendered by constructions with *mind* in the English translation.

To identify what forms may be associated across languages, it is useful to turn to multilingual corpora. I will give some examples illustrating how such corpora can be used in a cross-linguistic study of verbs. My main claim is that this sort of comparison makes it possible to contrast both structure and use.

2. Material and method

The corpora I will refer to are the English-Norwegian Parallel Corpus (ENPC), the source of the examples above, and the Oslo Multilingual Corpus (OMC). The ENPC is a bidirectional translation corpus containing English and Norwegian original texts, both fiction and non-fiction, and their translations into the other language. The different parts are balanced to facilitate a comparison across languages. With this kind of model we can see both what forms are associated by translators, and we can control for translation effects (see Johansson 1998). The OMC is an umbrella term for a group of corpora developed at the University of Oslo, including a corpus of English, German, and Norwegian texts.[1]

When we compare verbs in a multilingual corpus, it is striking how great differences we may find even with cognates (or prototypical equivalents) in closely related languages. For example, Åke Viberg (1996; 2002) has shown that the cognate verb pairs *go/gå* and *give/ge* in English and Swedish correspond to each other only in about a third of the cases. I will now go on to examine correspondences for two verbs: English *spend* in expressions of time and a special construction containing the Norwegian verb *hende* ['happen']. By correspondences I mean the forms that are associated by translators.

3. The verb *spend* in expressions of time

The verb *spend* in expressions of time is an example of the "time is money" metaphor (cf. Lakoff and Johnson 1981: 7–9). Cross-linguistically, it has interesting correspondence patterns. Figure 1 summarizes the overall distribution in the fiction texts of the ENPC of *spend* and its most frequent correspondence in Norwegian, *tilbringe* ['pass time'; cf. German *verbringen/zubringen*]. We see that there is a wide difference in frequency in the original texts, suggesting that there are major differences in use between the English and the Norwegian verb, though the differences are evened out in translations. *Tilbringe* is much more common in texts translated from English than in Norwegian original texts; the same pattern has been found for Swedish *tillbringa* in a study by Gellerstam (1996: 59). For *spend* in expressions of time, we find the opposite effect. In other words, the ways of referring to passing/spending time appear to be influenced by the source language.

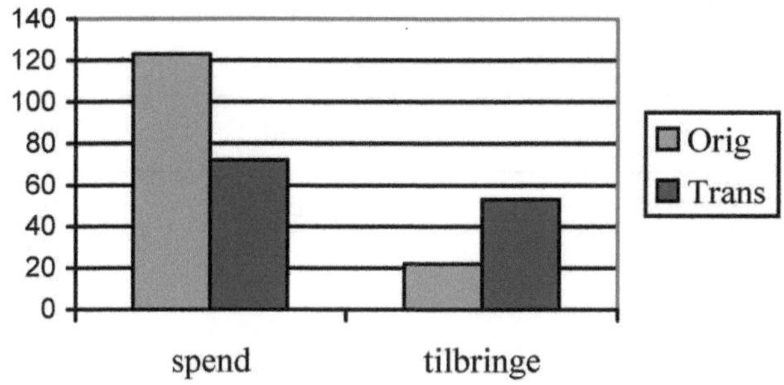

Figure 1. The overall distribution of English *spend* and Norwegian *tilbringe* in the fiction texts of the ENPC (30 texts of each type).

What correspondences do we find for English *spend*? At the time of the study I had 16 English original texts available with translations into Norwegian and German, and I decided to focus on this material. The material was not very large, but sufficient to show some very clear tendencies. There are congruent correspondences, which preserve the syntax of the English original, as well as cases of restructuring (see the overview of complementation patterns in table 1 and the summary of correspondences in table 2.) As shown in table 1, *spend* takes a temporal complement in the form of a noun phrase, typically followed by an adverbial and/or a verb in the *-ing* form.

Table 1. The distribution of complementation patterns of *spend* in 16 English fiction texts

spend + NP_{temp}			2
spend + NP_{temp}	+	ADV_{place}	21
		ADV_{accomp}	6
		ADV_{manner}	4
		$ADV_{place+accomp}$	2
		$ADV_{place+manner}$	1
		ADV_{place} + V-*ing*	2
spend + NP_{temp}	+	V-*ing*	28
Total			66

Table 2. Correspondence patterns for *spend* in German and Norwegian translations of 16 English fiction texts

			German	Norwegian
spend + NP_{temp}			*bleiben*	*bli over* ['stay over']
			sein	*gjennomgå* ['go through']
spend + NP_{temp}	+	ADV_{place}	*verbringen* (13)	*tilbringe* (11)
			intr/refl verb (7)	intr verb (7)
			other (1)	other (3)
		ADV_{accomp}	*verbringen* (4)	*tilbringe* (2)
			intr verb (1)	intr verb (2)
			other (1)	other (2)
		ADV_{manner}	*verbringen* (2)	*tilbringe* (1)
			zubringen (1)	
			nutzen (1)	*bruke* (3)
			verwenden (1)	
			intr verb (1)	intr verb (2)
		$ADV_{place+accomp}$	*verbringen* (1)	*tilbringe* (1)
			pass verb (1)	pass verb (1)
		$ADV_{place+manner}$	intr verb (1)	*tilbringe* (1)
		ADV_{place} + V-*ing*	*verbringen* (1)	
			intr verb (1)	intr verb (2)
spend + NP_{temp}	+	V-*ing*	*verbringen* (13)	*tilbringe* (9)
			zubringen (2)	
			verwenden (2)	*bruke* (9)
			V + ADV (10)	V + ADV (8)
				intr verb (1)
			other (1)	other (1)
Total			66	66

3.1. Congruent correspondences

Congruent correspondences with *tilbringe* or *verbringen/zubringen* are found with most of the patterns in table 2. These are the "standard" translations which are typically listed first in bilingual dictionaries for *spend* in expressions of time. Examples:[2]

(3) *He liked Sir Bernard Hemmings, but it was an open secret inside "Five" that the old man was ill and* ***spending less and less time in the office***. (FF1)
Er mochte Sir Bernard Hemmings, aber es war in "Fünf" ein offenes Geheimnis, daß der alte Mann krank war und ***immer weniger Zeit im Büro verbrachte.***
Han likte Sir Bernhard Hemmings, men det var en åpen hemmelighet i "Fem" at den gamle mann var syk og ***tilbrakte mindre og mindre tid på kontoret.***

(4) ***I spent most of the time sobbing in the protecting darkness of the great cathedral****, only half conscious of the endless stream of tourists shuffling past.* (ABR1)
Die meiste Zeit verbrachte ich damit, im schützenden Dunkel der großen Kathedrale zu schluchzen*, wobei ich mir des endlosen Stroms der vorbeischlürfenden* [sic] *Touristen nur halb bewusst war.*
Jeg tilbrakte det meste av tiden med å hulke i det beskyttende mørket i den store katedralen*, bare halvt oppmerksom på den endeløse strømmen av turister som subbet forbi.*

Other congruent correspondences have the verbs *nutzen* or *verwenden* in German and the verb *bruke* ['use'] in Norwegian, as in:

(5) *Look Brian, I've* ***spent two years on that investigation****.* (FF1)
Hören Sie, Brian, ich habe ***zwei Jahre auf diese Nachforschungen verwendet****.*
Hør nå, Brian. Jeg har ***brukt to år på denne etterforskingen****.*

(6) *I actually* ***spend time thinking about this.*** (MA1)
Ich ***verwende*** *tatsächlich* ***Zeit darauf, über diese Frage nachzudenken.***
Jeg ***bruker*** *faktisk* ***tid på å tenke ut dette.***

As shown in table 2, this type was only recorded with manner adverbials and *-ing* complements.

3.2. Restructuring

In spite of the translation effect established in the ENPC, there is a lot of restructuring. Most typically, we find intransitive or reflexive verbs: *sich aufhalten* [lit. 'keep oneself'], *bleiben* ['stay'], *verweilen* ['stay']; *bli* ['stay'], *bo* ['live, stay'], *oppholde seg* [lit. 'keep oneself'], *sitte* ['sit'], *være* ['be']. Some examples of restructuring are:

(7) *She informed us that she planned to* ***spend that night****, then go to church with us, and be back in Des Moines by suppertime.* (JSM1)
Sie teilte uns mit, daß sie vorhatte, ***die Nacht zu bleiben****, dann mit uns in die Kirche zu gehen und zum Abendessen wieder zurück in Des Moines zu sein.*
Hun kunngjorde at hun aktet å ***bli over*** ['stay'] *en natt, gå i kirken med oss neste morgen, og være tilbake i Des Moines til kvelds.*

(8) *I might even delve deeper into natural history and say, "The periodical cicada* ***spends six years as a grub underground****, and no more than six days as a free creature of sunlight and air."* (RD1)
Kann sein, daß ich mich sogar noch eingehender mit der Naturgeschichte befassen und sagen würde: "Die sich häutende Zikade ***bleibt im Puppenzustand sechs Jahre lang im Verborgenen*** *und verbringt nicht mehr als sechs Tage als freies Insekt in Licht und Luft."*
Jeg kunne trukket fram andre ting fra zoologien også: "Sikadens livssyklus er slik at den ***lever*** ['lives'] ***seks år som larve under jorda****, men bare seks dager som et fritt vesen i sola og lufta."*

(9) *"But I* ***spent the night at Rose's****."* (JSM1)
"Aber ich hab ***heut nacht bei Rose geschlafen****."*
"Men jeg har jo ***ligget over hos Rose****."* [lit. 'lie over']

(10) *Since the age of eighteen, he'd* ***spent an accumulated nine years in jail****.* (SG1)
Seit seinem achtzehnten Lebensjahr hatte er ***alles in allem neun Jahre im Gefängnis verbracht****.*
Siden attenårsalderen hadde han ***sittet inne i tilsammen ni år****.*
[lit. 'sit inside']

Example (7) is one of the rare cases where *spend* has no further complementation apart from the temporal NP. Both the Norwegian and the German translators have opted for intransitive verbs, and the same applies to (8), where the original has an adverbial of manner and a place adverbial (in addition to the temporal NP). In (9) the German translation has the intransitive verb for 'sleeping' (if you sleep in a place, you are there), while (10) has a congruent translation with *verbringen*. In both of these cases, the Norwegian translator has chosen a lexicalised expression for 'staying the night' and 'being in prison'.

The most interesting pattern is found where there is an *-ing* complement in the English original. In these cases there is often no verb at all corresponding to *spend*, and its place is taken by the complementing verb, which is so to speak "raised" to the superordinate clause, as in:

(11) *After leaving school at sixteen, Rawlings had* ***spent ten years working with and under his Uncle Albert in the latter's hardware shop****.* (FF1)
Nach seinem Schulabgang im Alter von sechzehn hatte Rawlings ***zehn Jahre in der Eisenwarenhandlung seines Onkels Albert gearbeitet****.*
Rawlings hadde sluttet på skolen da han var seksten år og siden ***arbeidet i ti år sammen med og under sin onkel Albert som drev jernvarehandel.***

(12) ***We spent a lot of the time driving****, in our low-slung, boat-sized* .... (MA1)
Die meiste Zeit fuhren wir *in unserem niedrigen, bootsförmigen Studebaker herum* ... .
Mye av tiden kjørte vi bil*, en lav Studebaker,* ... .

(13) ***Nights on end she spends flying****, beyond the reach of all that threatens her by day.* (ABR1)
Ganze Nächte hindurch fliegt sie *dahin, unerreichbar für alles, das sie tagsüber bedroht.*
Natt etter natt flyr hun*, utenfor rekkevidde av alt det som truer henne om dagen.*

(14) ***He spent pleasurable hours dithering*** *over questions of punctuation.* (AT1)
Er grübelte vergnügliche Stunden lang *über Interpunktionsprobleme* ***nach****.*
Han tilbrakte koselige timer med å gruble *over tegnsettingen.*

In (11) to (13) the German and Norwegian translators have opted for "raising". The same type of restructuring is found in the German translation of (14), while the Norwegian translator has relied on the "standard" translation, a form of *tilbringe*.

Apart from the correspondence types I have commented on above, there are other more sporadic renderings; for a more detailed account, see Johansson (2002).

3.3. Summing up: *Spend* in a contrastive perspective

We clearly have structures in German and Norwegian which correspond closely to the English original, but there are also many cases of restructuring. *Tilbringe* and *verbringen/zubringen* are possible choices in translating *spend*. To what extent, and in what contexts, are congruent structures overused as compared with their distribution in original texts in the target language? As the English-German-Norwegian subcorpus has not been developed sufficiently, I will restrict my remarks to the ENPC; see table 3.

Table 3. The distribution of complementation patterns of Norwegian *tilbringe* ['pass time'] in original and translated fiction texts of the ENPC (30 texts of each type)

		Original	Translation
tilbringe + NP_{temp} +	ADV_{place}	19	26
	ADV_{accomp}	2	6
	ADV_{manner}	0	9
	ADV_{place} + *med* ['with'] + V-inf	0	1
tilbringe + NP_{temp} +	*med/til* ['with, to'] + V-inf	1	11
Total		22	53

We see that *tilbringe* is more than twice as common overall in translated texts as in original Norwegian texts. Moreover, the overuse is found particularly with adverbials of manner and with infinitive complements (translating *spend* + V-*ing*). These types were found only once in original texts, as compared with twenty examples in texts translated from English. For translators, these results should be taken as an indication that they should look for more creative renderings than the "standard" translation with *tilbringe*. Such renderings are amply illustrated in the corpus material. I will come back later to what conclusions we can draw from this example as regards valency in a contrastive perspective.

4. The Norwegian *det* + *hende* construction

Formally, the *det* + *hende* construction consists of the dummy subject *det* [‘it’], a form of the verb *hende* [‘happen’], and a complement clause introduced by *at* [‘that’], though the conjunction is often omitted. This clause is placed at the end and cannot be fronted:

(15) ***Det hender at*** [‘it happens that’] *Elsa går på en utstilling, hvis Håkon kan være hjemme og se til barna.* (BV1)
Occasionally *Elsa goes to an art exhibition if Håkon can stay at home and look after the children.*
Cf. **At Elsa går på en utstilling hender* [‘That Elsa goes to an art exhibition happens’].

The construction can be expanded by modal auxiliaries and adverbials, as will be shown below, but generally it is unexpanded. The correspondences show very clearly that the bare *det* + *hende* construction is an expression of usuality, following the analysis of Halliday (2004), who regards usuality as a type of modality.

4.1. The bare *det* + *hende* construction

Most commonly, the English correspondence is a frequency adverbial, as in (15) above. The forms found most often in the material are *sometimes* and *occasionally*. Judging by these forms, the *det* + *hende* construction typically denotes a low degree of usuality. These are some more examples:

(16) ***Det har hendt at*** [‘it has happened that’] *du har sett på meg med akkurat det blikket.* (OEL1)
Sometimes *you’ve looked at me in exactly that way.*

(17) ***Det hendte*** [‘it happened that’] *han kom helt ut på kaia før han husket hodeplagget.* (HW1)
Sometimes *he got all the way out on the wharf before he remembered his headgear.*

(18) ***Det hender*** *vi slåss.* (MA1T)
Once in a while we fight.

In addition to frequency adverbials on their own, we find combinations of frequency adverbials and modal auxiliaries denoting habit or possibility (*would, used to, can, could, may, might*), as in:

(19) ***Det hendte at*** *gamle venner kom innom, tykke menn i flekkede tweeddresser, kvinner med usminkede ansikter.* (AB1T)
Occasionally *friends from the old days* **would** *drop in, fat men in stained tweed suits, women with unadorned faces.*

(20) ***Det hender*** *at man ser* [lit. 'it happens that one sees'] *dådyr mellom trærne.* (RR1T)
Sometimes *fallow deer* **can** *be seen among the trees.*

Sometimes the *det + hende* construction corresponds to a modal auxiliary on its own, as in:

(21) *Når Sofies mor var sur for et eller annet,* ***hendte det at*** *hun kalte huset de bodde i for et menasjeri.* (JG1)
Whenever Sophie's mother was in a bad mood, she ***would*** *call the house they lived in a menagerie.*

(22) *Når kvinner oppdrar gutter aleine,* ***hender det at*** *de kommer inn i den voksne verdenen ansiktsløse.* (ROB1T)
When women, even women with the best intentions, bring up a boy alone, he ***may*** *in some way have no male face, or he* ***may*** *have no face at all.*

The modals represented are *would*, *may*, and *could*, i.e. the same types of modals as were found in combinations with frequency adverbials.

4.2. Adverbial expansions

In all the cases we have seen so far, the *hende*-clause has disappeared in the translation. This correspondence type is also found where there is an adverbial expansion in the Norwegian material, as in:

(23) *Men* ***det hendte aldri at*** [lit. 'it happened never that'] *jeg hilste først.* (EHA1)
But I ***never*** *greeted them first.*

(24) ***Det hendte bare en eneste gang at*** [lit. 'it happened only a single time that'] *hun ikke kunne leksa det året.* (PEJ1)
Only once*, that whole year, did she not know her lesson.*

In (23) there is a frequency adverbial denoting that something does not occur, in (24) we find an adverbial referring to a single time in the past.

There are some examples where an expanded *det* + *hende* construction corresponds to a matrix clause with *happen*. Apart from a single example, these are found in translations from Norwegian. Examples:

(25) *"****Det har hendt før at*** *en kunstner forblir ukjent," sa han så, "men aldri for å dukke opp igjen som et geni på linje med de aller største."* (JW1)
*"****It has happened before that*** *an artist has remained unknown," he went on, "but never before to emerge again as a genius on a par with the very greatest."*

(26) ***Det hendte i Tuv som andre steder at*** *ungdommen fant seg kjærester når det var sommer og midnattssol og lyse netter.* (PEJ1)
It happened in Tuv, as it did in other places, that *young people fell in love in summer, when the days were longest and the nights were bright with the midnight sun.*

(27) ***Det hendte*** *han satte seg på kjøkkenet sammen med pikene, stjal seg til en kopp nypete og fortalte bløte vitser som alle hadde hørt før.* (BV1)
It sometimes happened that *he sat down in the kitchen with the girls, helped himself to a cup of rose-hip tea and told silly jokes which they had both heard before.*

(28) ***Det hendte*** *at Maria forsøkte seg på en sigarett, den gamle pianisten blunket til dem og spilte revyviser.* (BV1)
It might happen that *Maria* ***would*** *try a cigarette, and the old piano-player would wink at them and play tunes from the old musicals.*

Note that, in all these cases, the English *happen* clause has an expansion: in (25) a time adverbial, in (26) a place adverbial, in (27) a frequency adverbial, and in (28) a modal expansion.

4.3. Modal expansions

Det + *hende* constructions can also be expanded by modal auxiliaries, usually by the present-tense form *kan* ['can'], less often the past-tense form *kunne* ['could']. These constructions express possibility, as in:

(29) *Det er ikke noe farlig, men* ***det kan hende*** *du mister* [lit. 'it can happen you lose'] *litt av håret ditt, Herman.* (LSC1)
It isn't anything serious, but you ***might*** *lose a little of your hair, Herman.*

(30) *Etter et par timer* ***kunne det hende*** [lit. 'could it happen'] *at en og annen fant ut at han skulle handle litt.* (HW1)
After a few hours of that, one of them ***might*** *even remember that he was supposed to do some shopping.*

(31) *Nåja, hvis du må reise,* ***kan det hende*** *jeg blir.* (PDJ3T)
Well, if you have to go, ***maybe*** *I'll stay on.*

(32) ***Kanskje*** *var jeg* [lit. 'perhaps was I'] *ganske enkelt lei av å komme og gå. Det er forferdelig alltid å være i overgangen.* ***Det kan også hende at*** [lit. 'it can also happen that'] *jeg ville smake på denne verden … .* (BO1T)
It may simply have been that *I had grown tired of coming and going. It is terrible to forever remain in-between. It* ***may also have been that*** *I wanted to taste of this world … .*

(33) ***Det kan hende*** *at Robert M. Turner hadde gitt kelneren inntrykk av at … .* (FC1)
It could be that *Robert Turner had given the waiter the impression … .*

(34) ***Kan hende*** *det intime vennskapet mellom Scott og Wilson, blir den tilleggsbelastning på det psykiske plan som knekker Shackleton.* (KH1)
Perhaps *the intimate friendship between Scott and Wilson became the last mental straw which broke Shackleton's back.*

The English correspondences vary. Most often, there is no matrix clause in English, and the meaning is conveyed by a possibility modal (*may*, *might*, *could*), as in (29) and (30), less commonly by a modal adverb, as in (31). Where the English correspondence has a matrix clause in the material, the verb is *be* rather than *happen*, as in (32) and (33), testifying to the weakening of the meaning of the Norwegian verb. A further development is shown in (34) where the fixed sequence *kan hende* ['can happen'] is an adverbial corresponding to English *perhaps*. The same development is found with the more common *kanskje* [lit. 'can happen'], shown in the opening of (32).

Although *it* + *happen* constructions expanded by a possibility modal were not found as correspondences of similar Norwegian constructions, they are by no means excluded in English, as we shall see later (section 5). They seem, however, to be a less common option than in Norwegian.

4.4. Summing up: The *det* + *hende* construction

From the study we can draw the following conclusions (for a more detailed account, see Johansson 2005). There is generally no matrix clause in English. The correspondences clearly show that the bare *det* + *hende* construction denotes low usuality, most typically being rendered by an English frequency adverbial or by a combination of a frequency adverbial and a modal auxiliary denoting habit or possibility. Where the Norwegian construction is expanded, the meaning is guided by the expansion: with a frequency adverbial like *aldri* ['never'], as in (23), it means that something does not occur; with *en gang* ['once'], as in (24), that it occurs once; with a time adverbial like *før* ['before'], as in (25), the reference is to a particular time; and with modal expansions with *kan/kunne*, it denotes possibility. What is most striking cross-linguistically is that the *det* + *hende* construction only exceptionally corresponds to *happen* in English, chiefly in translations and when the construction is expanded by an adverbial.

5. A comparison with the English *it + happen* construction

English has a construction that is superficially similar to the *it + hende* construction, but the conditions of use appear to differ greatly. The bare *it + happen* construction is found only once in the English original texts of the ENPC. The Norwegian correspondence is *tilfeldigvis*, which means that something happens by accident and is quite different from the *det + hende* construction:

(35) *Intuition was telling me to turn this guy down, but* ***it happens that*** *the rent on my apartment was due the next day.* (SG1)
Min intuisjon fortalte meg at jeg burde avvise oppdraget, men husleien min forfalt ***tilfeldigvis*** *neste dag.*

In addition, there were a handful examples of expanded constructions, where the meaning is guided by the expansion; see the comments on (25–28) above.

The ENPC material is sufficient to show that the English and Norwegian constructions are quite different both in frequency and meaning. As the English construction was only rarely found in the parallel corpus, I have explored its use more fully with reference to the *Oxford English Dictionary* (OED) and the *British National Corpus* (BNC).

The OED has examples of *happen* used "impersonally, with or without *it*" from the end of the Middle English period. The earliest examples in the entry for *happen* contain a form of *happen + sa* (i.e. *so*) + a nominal clause. A text search in the OED quotations for the sequence *happens that* revealed that the great majority of the examples conform to these patterns:

- *it + so + happens + that*-clause
- *it* + frequency adverbial (*sometimes, rarely, often, frequently,* etc.) + *happens + that*-clause

Besides, there were some combinations with other adverbials (*easily, hardly, then, unfortunately*) and a few instances of the simple *it + happen* construction (chiefly found in *if*-clauses).

As the OED examples represent different time periods and can only be studied within the context of a single sentence, I turned to the BNC to examine the present-day English use of the *it + happen* construction more fully. The great majority of the present-tense examples are expanded and conform to the two most common patterns found in the OED, as in:

(36) ***It just so happens that*** *Berlin has expressed an interest in a loan show.* (A4A 28)

(37) ***It often happens that*** *young children find it enormously difficult to "surrender power".* (AM6 987)

The former refers to a particular situation, the latter to something occurring repeatedly. Where the bare *it* + *happen* construction occurs, it seems equivalent to *it so happens that*, as in:

(38) ***It happens that*** *my father is one of the top people in what is known as Work Study.* (FEU 45)

In the past tense the great majority of the instances are combinations with *so*, but there are also a good number of bare constructions, as in:

(39) ***It happened that*** *I called at Beatrice's house the last time Aunt Nessy visited there – the time before she was banished.* (AC7 940)

Sequences with the base form *happen* are of necessity expanded. The majority contain a possibility modal, usually *can* or *may*, as in:

(40) ***It can happen that*** *when an assistant is helping somebody to get dressed, the person suddenly gets violent.* (B32 604)

To sum up, the main uses of the *it* + *happen* construction in English are: (1) in combination with *so*, and less commonly in unexpanded constructions, it is used to refer to a particular situation; (2) in combination with a frequency adverbial, it refers to something occurring repeatedly; and (3) in combination with a modal auxiliary, sometimes expanded by a frequency adverbial, it refers to the likelihood of a situation. Unlike Norwegian, English does not have an unexpanded construction expressing usuality. Bare *it* + *happen* constructions refer to a single situation. Though the *det* + *hende* and the *it* + *happen* constructions are syntactically quite parallel, they have developed in different directions in Norwegian and English.

6. A note on similar constructions in other languages

Clauses of the *det* + *hende* type are found in other languages. Swedish *hända* is used in much the same way. An example from the OMC, with a sentence in Norwegian and translations into three other languages, may serve as a further illustration:

(41) ***Det hendte at*** *Dagnys bok eller sytøy ble søkk borte.* (HW2)
Es kam vor, dass *Dagnys Buch oder Nähzeug verschwunden war.*
Sometimes *Dagny's book or sewing disappeared.*
Il arrivait que *le livre de Dagny, ou son ouvrage de couture, disparaisse complètement.*

Judging by the material in the OMC, French generally uses an opening clause with *arriver* in such cases, although there are also many instances containing a frequency adverbial like *parfois* in the main proposition. The German translations are more evenly divided between constructions with a lexical verb, most typically *vorkommen*, and a frequency adverbial like *manchmal*. The English translations regularly contain a frequency adverbial. We may conclude that opening clauses of the *hende* type occur in a number of languages, although the extent to which they occur and the purposes for which they are used may vary.

Why does English stand out from the other languages I have referred to? The connection of the *it* + *happen* construction with a single situation may be a reflection of the historical origin of the verb. According to the OED, *happen* means "to come to pass (*orig*. by 'hap' or chance)", which suggests a reference to a single event. As already mentioned, the earliest examples of the *it* + *happen* construction are combinations with a form of *so*. The connection with a single event is quite clear with *happen to* + infinitive, as in *she happened to do it*, which typically corresponds to *tilfeldigvis* ['by chance']; cf. the rendering of the simple *it* + *happen* construction in (35) above.[3] To express usuality, *happen* must be combined with a frequency adverbial.

Another relevant question is why we find forms such as the *det* + *hende* and the *it* + *happen* constructions. Syntactically, it is natural to analyse them as matrix clauses. From the point of view of function, they can be viewed as clausal prefixes or utterance launchers. I will mention three possible motivations for these. In the first place, clausal prefixes allow expansions of different kinds. We can, for example, easily add a stance adverbial such as *of course*. Secondly, they seem to serve as thematisation devices. Note the initial position of the frequency adverbials in examples (15–20). Thirdly, it looks as if clausal prefixes of this kind could also have a function on the text level and introduce a longer stretch of text:

(42) ***Det hendte at*** *mamma dasket henne bak med håndflaten. Et lite klask. Men det var fordi hun ville at Tora skulle vite at hun var lei seg. De klaskene var aldri vonde.*
Det var ikke ofte mamma slo. Bare når hun måtte. Tora torde gråte når mamma slo. (HW1)
Sometimes *Mama swatted her on the bottom with the palm of her hand. A little swat.*
But that was because she wanted Tora to know she was aggravated. The swats never hurt. Mama didn't hit her often. Only when she had to. Tora wasn't afraid to cry when Mama hit her.

A clearer example of the text-structuring function, with a similar type of construction, is the opening of the Christmas gospel (*hende* and *happen* are not used in these translations, but they could easily be inserted):

(43) *Det skjedde i de dager at ...*
And it came to pass in those days that ...
Factum est autem in illis diebus ...
Ἐγένετο δε εν ταίς ήμέραις ...

All the versions have the same type of opening. Note, finally, that the structures I have dealt with have idiom-like features. In examining the material for this paper, I did not find any examples where the matrix clause was negated (i.e. not: *det hender ikke at …*; *it does not happen that …*). Some related expressions, such as Norwegian *kanskje* and English *maybe*, have gone all the way and become invariable single words (cf. section 4.3).

7. Conclusion

What do I mean by structure and use in the title of my paper? Both in the case of *spend* and *tilbringe* in expressions of time and the *det* + *hende* and the *it* + *happen* constructions, we clearly have equivalent structures in English and Norwegian, but there are differences in use. *Tilbringe* is a possible choice in Norwegian, but studies of Norwegian original texts show that some other form is often preferred. With *hende* and *happen*, we find exactly the same syntactic structures, but the meaning of the unexpanded constructions is totally different. When they are expanded, however, they can be used to express the same meaning: *it sometimes happens that ... / det hender iblant at ..., it can happen that ... / det kan hende at ..., it hap-*

pened once that ... / det hendte en gang at ... – here we have similar forms in both languages, though the conditions of use appear to differ. If by studying valency in a contrastive perspective we mean a structural comparison, it is clearly insufficient.

The conclusion I would like to draw is that cross-linguistic studies should not be limited to a comparison of structures. We have to consider conditions of use, including preferred ways of putting things (cf. Kennedy 1992). Such a study can best be done with reference to multilingual corpora.

Notes

1. For more information on the corpora, see our websites: http://www.hf.uio.no/ilos/forskning/forskningsprosjekter/enpc/ (ENPC) and http://www.hf.uio.no/forskningsprosjekter/sprik/korpus/index.html (OMC).
2. Corpus examples are accompanied by a text code. Text codes ending in T represent translations. For more information on the texts, see our websites.
3. *Happen to* + infinitive and the *it* + *happen* construction are, however, not equivalent, though space does not allow a discussion of this matter in the present paper. The bare *it* + *happen* construction frequently suggests that something is surprising or interesting and deserves special notice.

References

Gellerstam, Martin

1996 Translations as a source for cross-linguistic studies. In *Languages in Contrast. Papers from a Symposium on Text-based Cross-linguistic Studies, Lund 4-5 March 1994*, Karin Aijmer, Bengt Altenberg, and Mats Johansson (eds.), 53–62. (Lund Studies in English 88.) Lund: Lund University Press.

Halliday, M. A. K.

2004 *An Introduction to Functional Grammar*. 3d ed. Revised by Christian M. I. M. Matthiessen. London: Arnold.

Johansson, Stig

1998 On the role of corpora in cross-linguistic research. In *Corpora and Cross-linguistic Research: Theory, Method, and Case Studies*, Stig Johansson, and Signe Oksefjell (eds.), 3–24. Amsterdam/Atlanta, GA: Rodopi.

2002 Towards a multilingual corpus for contrastive analysis and translation studies. In *Parallel Corpora, Parallel Worlds. Selected Papers from a Symposium on Parallel and Comparable Corpora at Uppsala*

University, Sweden, 22-23 April, 1999, Lars Borin (ed.), 47–59. Amsterdam/New York: Rodopi.
2005 Some aspects of usuality in English and Norwegian. In *Semiotics from the North. Nordic Approaches to Systemic Functional Linguistics,* Kjell Lars Berge, and Eva Maagerø (eds.), 69–85. Oslo: Novus.

Kennedy, Graeme
1992 Preferred ways of putting things with implications for language teaching. In *Directions in Corpus Linguistics. Proceedings of Nobel Symposium 82, Stockholm, 4-8 August 1991*, Jan Svartvik (ed.), 335–373. Berlin/New York: Mouton de Gruyter.

Lakoff, George, and Mark Johnson
1981 *Metaphors We Live By*. Chicago: University of Chicago Press.

Viberg, Åke
1996 Cross-linguistic lexicology. The case of English *go* and Swedish *go.* In *Languages in Contrast. Papers from a Symposium on Text-based Cross-linguistic Studies, Lund 4-5 March 1994*, Karin Aijmer, Bengt Altenberg, and Mats Johansson (eds.), 151–182. (Lund Studies in English 88.) Lund: Lund University Press.
2002 The polysemy of Swedish *ge* 'give' from a crosslinguistic perspective. In *Proceedings of Euralex 2002*, Anna Braasch, and Claus Povlsen (eds.), 669–682. Copenhagen University.

The English-Norwegian Parallel Corpus (ENPC):
http://www.hf.uio.no/ilos/forskning/forskningsprosjekter/enpc/

The Oslo Multilingual Corpus (OMC):
http://www.hf.uio.no/forskningsprosjekter/sprik/korpus/index.html

Section 4
Computational aspects of valency analysis

Valency and automatic syntactic and semantic analysis

Dieter Götz

1. Putting valency information to use

In the *Valency Dictionary of English* (2004), the lexicographic treatment of verbs contains several sections of information – a complement inventory, a pattern and examples section and a note block. Basically, complements are described in formal terms: the dictionary lists patterns such as + N_P + *N* for *I'll call you a cab* or *He called me a nuisance*, where *N* stands for noun phrase and $_P$ indicates the ability of a complement to function as the subject of a passive clause. Thus, when looking up *call* in a string like *I'll call you a cab* you would have to consult the section *call* + N_P + *N* in the entry for *call* – as opposed to *call* + *N*, where you would find *I called my brother*.

If *I'll call you a cab* were your query, then the dictionary example *Olivia will be able to call you a cab*, within the section *call* + N_P + *N*, would suggest that you were about to hit your target, and this example would lead you to a note (> A, B, C etc.). For the meaning of *call* in *I'll call you a cab* the note reads as follows:[1]

(1) **A person[I] can call another person or a service such as the police, the fire brigade etc.[II] or call for them[II]**, i.e. attract their attention and ask them to come.

With this kind of information it should be possible to devise a program which could deal with e.g. *I'll call you a cab* as a dictionary query, and produce a syntactic analysis of the vicinity of the verb, plus the note, and plus an example. In other words, it would provide a syntactic-semantic analysis of the sentence or of parts of the sentence. The kind of note given to describe the semantic and lexical properties of valency complements in VDE thus seems to provide the ideal basis for computational processing.

Obviously, the notes in VDE were designed with the aim of providing information on possible complements in a way that can easily be understood by foreign speakers of English, i.e. human users. This means that in order to make them directly applicable to computational analysis, some of the VDE notes may have to be modified by applying a fixed number of categories more stringently. However, this could be done relatively easily, for instance the existing note covering cases such as *I call you Peter* could be rewritten in the following form:

(2) **If a person^{I} calls another person^{II} a word that is a name^{III}**, they will use that name for addressing and referring to the other person.

It should be understood that the considerations that follow are intended as a linguist's contribution towards a program, a program which might be used for automatic sentence analysis. These considerations are based on the general principles of VDE and take a slightly modified version of the valency dictionary as its basis (i.e. modified VDE-style entries). In particular, it should be noted that for reasons of simplicity some of the information actually provided by VDE – concerning passivizability, for instance – will be ignored.

2. Preliminaries

The query, still *I'll call you Peter*, needs tagging. The tagged version, e.g.

(3) I[N] 'll[mod] call[verb] you[N] Peter[N]

would enable the machine to stop at the asterisk below, in the entry for *call*, just before the example sentence and the letter for the respective meaning:

(4) call + N + N*
Give her another year and I reckon Olivia will be able to call you a cab as well as any doorman in Britain. >A
I'll call you Den. >B
I wasn't really what you'd call a public schoolboy – I wasn't from the same social strata as the other kids. >C

These three options are all of the type *call + N + N*. On a lower syntactic level they are, of course, not quite that ambiguous, the first is *IO + DO*, the second and third are *DO + OComp*.

Taking syntactic functions into account makes it necessary to rewrite the notes. Note (2) above would now be:

(5) >B: **If a SubjN1: person calls a DON2: person a OCompN3: name**, they will use that name for addressing and referring to the other person.

Given one pre-verbal N and two postverbal Ns, the machine can now decide whether *I* is a suitable candidate for the subject (matching 'person'), *you* a suitable candidate for a DO (matching 'person') and *Peter* a suitable candidate for 'name'. On the basis of note >B, as in (6) above, syntactic analysis and the semantic ranges of the Ns mutually confirm each other. The machine can now present a syntactic analysis, a simplified note giving the gist of note >B, as in above (6), and an example, in this case, *I'll call you Den*. It would, of course, exclude presenting *call you a cab* (because *a cab* is not a person) and *call you a public schoolboy* (because *a schoolboy* is not a name).

3. Range indicators

It is obvious that quite a number of range indicators are necessary or possible: relatively specific ones like *pilot*, fairly general ones like *business* (*He ran the business*) and general ones like *something/somebody* for *He looked at N*. In order to facilitate matching, the machine might be equipped with a smallish internal dictionary of the following type:

(6) nose: part of body
dexterity: quality
elephant: animal
anger: state of mind
officer: person, authority

It is known that defining vocabularies of about 3000 words can cope with up to two thirds of a text. This means that a lot of the material under analysis can be treated by internal resources of the program (but see below).

Range indicators are not confined to one word. Thus, a subset of the things that can be opened could be given by "*open* + DON2: structure, door, gate, barrier, window". If there is sufficient corpus evidence, even more details could be given: the use of *call* as in *I'll call you Peter* and *He called me a liar* very often shows a pronoun as DO, which would yield "DON2: person, me, you, him, her, us, them".

In case of e.g. *cut + N + with N* (*Someone cut the bread with a blunt knife*), we would have something like

(7) … cut a DON2: food, bread, meat, sausage, cheese, vegetable, wood, string, chord, paper, cloth withN3: instrument, knife, scissors.

What if the query were *Someone has cut the salami with a sharp dagger*? The machine might, since it cannot understand *dagger*, put *dagger* to WordNet or similar electronic lexicographic enterprises, and check paraphrase, synonyms, hyperonyms, meronyms etc. related to dagger. It will be able to understand *dagger* as soon as it meets *knife* or *instrument* as semantically related words. For some purposes, Windows Thesaurus might do. An assembly of WordNet, BNC, The Bank of English, FrameNet, wortschatz.uni-leipzig and the *Oxford English Dictionary* will certainly help in most cases.

The machine should perhaps have a command "search for collocates" outside the valency pattern, to the left and to the right (<COLL, COLL>, see below *open* in the meaning of 'rain').

4. Trials

The following is a trial run for the verbs *open* and *admit* with the respective VDE entries for *open* and *admit* rewritten in a short form (after the example, in bold, and abbreviated from a full meaning description as e.g. in [5] above).

(8) M

Suddenly the kitchen door opened and Alfred was standing there. **N1Subj: structure, door, gate, barrier, window**

A flash of thunder pierces the complacent, brown layer of smog. The Heavens open. A real rain falls.

<COLL; heavy, torrential, storm, rain, thunder; N1Subj: cloud, heavens, sky; COLL> heavy, torrential, storm, rain, thunder

D1

+ N

Fresh air is important throughout the day, and remember to open a window while you carry out any indoor exercises.

N1Subj: person, force, wind, gale; N2DO: structure, window, door, gate, barrier

He opened his eyes carefully. He was in different surroundings; he was sure of that, at least.

N1Subj: person, animal; N2DO: eyes

Wade heard the bottle being opened.
N1Subj: person, instrument; N2DO: container: bottle, can, box
My key opens both doors.
N1Subj: instrument, key, card; N2DO: structure, door, gate, lock
The Princess Royal has opened an exhibition of British life in the Ukrainian capital, Kiew.
N1Subj: person, authority, politician; N2DO: event, show, exhibition, presentation, display
The M1, Britain's first motorway, opened in the late 1950s to speed traffic between London and the Midlands.
N1Subj: person, authority, politician; N2DO: structure, building, road
Through the surgery, she heard that the Stroke Association was opening a local advice centre and applied for a job.
N1Subj: person, institution; N2DO: structure, institution
At least one person was killed when security forces opened fire to break up a disturbance in one village.
N1Subj: person, weapon; N2DO: fire
D2
+ by V-ing
President Mitterand opened by posing a number of questions.
N1Subj: person
D3
+ into N
The front door opens into a hall.
N1Subj: structure, window, door, gate; intoN2PC
D4
+ onto N/on to N
A wooden door in the stone wall opens onto a grassy terrace.
N1Subj: structure, window, door, gate; onto N2PC1
From here french windows open on to a small garden.
N1Subj: structure, window, door, gate; on to N2PC1
D5
+ to N
It may be that the gardens continue to open to the public.
D6
N1Subj: structure, building, event, institution; PC1: public, people, visitor
+ with N/N V-ing
This week's concert opened with the London premiere of John Casken's "Darting the Skiff".
N1Subj: event, performance, show, exhibition, presentation, display, event; PC1
The meeting opened with everyone giving their reasons for attendance.
N1Subj: event, performance, show, exhibition, presentation, display
D7
+ ADV
A year ago Friday, we opened. It's been hard.
N1Subj: person, institution, business; ADV: time, year, month, week, day, hour
There is simply no consistency about the museums of the world, or even of one given country. They all open at different times, on different days, during different seasons.

N1Subj: person, institution, business; ADV: time, year, month, week, day, hour
The film is due to open in London at the end of the year.
N1Subj: event; {ADV1: place; ADV2: time}
Some government offices open on alternate Saturdays.
N1Subj: person, institution, business; ADV: time, year, month, week, day, hour
The country's first National Bottle Museum has opened in Barnsley, Yorkshire.
N1Subj: event, show, presentation, exhibition; {ADV1: place; ADV2: time}
D8
+ ADV: QUAL
The door opened easily.
N1Subj: door, gate, window, container; ADV: quality
T1
+ N + by V-ing
He opened his speech by praising the Russian Federation President, Mr Boris Yeltsin.
N1Subj: person; N2DO: event, performance; ADV: by verb-ing
T2
+ N + to N
She refused to open her books to the auditors.
N1Subj: person, institution, organisation; N2DO: document, books; to N3: inquiry, examination, investigation, examiner, investigator
Mr Jackson appears to be ready to open his doors to business leaders.
N1Subj: person; N2DO: door; to N3: person
He decided to open his home to paying guests.
N1Subj: person, institution; N2DO: home, place, property, building; to N3: person
I know he had opened his heart to me and that I had found a place there.
N1Subj: person; N2DO: heart; to N3: person
T3
+ N + with N/N V-ing
You could open the door with a credit card.
N1Subj: person; N2: door, gate, lock; with N3: key, card

The vocabulary used for describing the ranges of N1Subj, N2DO etc. is, apart from necessarily specified ranges like *heart, fire*, fairly general. Writing an internal dictionary, as sketched above in (7) should therefore not prove too difficult, particularly if there is the WordNet option or another thesaurus option. Here is the trial run for *admit*:

(9) D1
+ N
Should she force him to admit the truth?
N1Subj: person, institution, organisation; N2DO: truth, crime, mistake, guilt, responsibility
Greycoat Commercial Estates and associated companies finally admitted defeat and sold their land interests to the GLC on 29 March 1984.
N1Subj: person, institution, organisation, military leader; N2DO: defeat, lose

Apparently, Barker admitted his mistake and apologised to Mujtaba afterwards.
N1Subj: person, institution, organisation; N2DO: truth, crime, mistake, guilt, responsibility
No-one has admitted responsibility for the murder.
N1Subj: person, institution, organisation; N2DO: truth, crime, mistake, guilt, responsibility
He admitted each of the delegates himself.
N1Subj: person, institution, organisation, rule, right; N2DO: person, things
Each ticket admits two people and is valid until the end of October. **N1Subj: person, institution, organisation, rule, right; N2DO: person, things**
I lay in my pallet waiting for sleep, with my window open to admit the bright autumn air.
N1Subj: structure; N2DO
D2
\+ V-ing
So far no group has admitted carrying out the murder.
N1Subj: person; N2DO: doing something, truth, crime, mistake, guilt, responsibility
But if he had something to do with it, why'd he admit being here?
N1Subj: person; N2DO: truth, crime, mistake, guilt, responsibility; N2DO: doing something wrong, truth, crime, mistake, guilt, responsibility
D3
\+ (that)-CL
I have to admit that I have bad handwriting, but that is not a moral fault of mine.
N1Subj: person; DO: *that-clause*
Philip admits he can't walk past a bookshop without going in.
N1Subj: person; DO: *clause*
I have to admit, sir, there's one thing that worries me.
N1Subj: person; DO: *clause*
D4
wh-CL
Perhaps, he muses, Milligan was terrified to admit how much pleasure he was missing out on.
N1Subj: person; DO: *wh-clause*
I am ashamed to admit what a relief this was.
N1Subj: person; DO: *wh-clause*
Some of the fur traders have been bold enough to admit why their industry has been hit.
N1Subj: person; DO: *wh-clause*
D5
QUOTE / SENTENCE
"I must admit, when we got to Sydney I really didn't feel very well at all," she said.
N1Subj: person; DO: *clause*
"I do not know yet," she admitted.
N1Subj: person; DO: *clause*
D6
\+ of N/V-ing
There will be slow growth and greater unemployment for years: our economic problems admit of no other solution.
N1Subj: person; of N2
If the link really were necessary, it would admit of no exceptions.

N1Subj: person; of N2
Not only do both works admit of being read either exoterically or esoterically: both works express precisely similar attitudes towards eternal life.
N1Subj: person; of V-ing
D7
+ to N/V-ing
Your father did not admit to his blindness and your mother, long after his death, continued to behave as if he had not died.
N1Subj: person; to N2
She described herself as an emotional person easily moved to laughter or tears and admitted to being rather shy.
N1Subj: person; to V-ing
T1
+ N + as N
The United Nations has voted to admit Namibia as its one-hundred and sixtieth member, one month after it gained independence from South Africa.
N1Subj: person, institution, organisation; as N2
T2
+ N + into N
Even Galiani admitted more of social forces into his utility theory than modern theorists would allow.
N1Subj: person, institution, organisation, structure; N2DO; into N3
The side arcades which with their tall arches above admit as much light into the nave as is possible.
N1Subj: person, institution, organisation, structure; N2DO; into N3
You will be admitted into the hospital either on the day of the procedure or possibly the night before.
N1Subj: person, institution, organisation, structure; N2DO; into N3
T3
+ N + to N
He is also in favour of women being admitted to his club, the United Oxford and Cambridge University Club.
N1Subj: person, institution, organisation; N2DO; to N3
Wu Man, a brilliant young virtuoso, was among the first group admitted to the Beijing Conservatory after the Cultural Revolution.
N1Subj: person, institution, organisation; N2DO; to N3
Six people are reported to have been admitted to hospital with bullet wounds or injuries from bomb explosions.
N1Subj: person, institution, organisation; N2DO: person; to N3
+ N + to N
He may never have admitted this even to himself.
N1Subj: person, institution, organisation; toN2: person, institution, organisation
T4
+ to N + (that)-CL
We don't admit to ourselves that we're playing games with our children.
N1Subj: person, institution, organisation; toN2: person, institution, organisation; DO: *that-clause*
I'm talking about the people who admitted to me they were guilty. **N1Subj: person, institution, organisation; toN2: person, institution, organisation; DO: *clause***

T5
+ to N QUOTE / SENTENCE
"I absolutely cannot compete with it all, or be natural or cheerful, when they won't treat me like a human being," he admitted to his mother.
N1Subj: person, institution, organisation; toN2: person, institution, organisation; DO: *clause*
Q
+ N + as N + to N
The Foreign Ministers of Lithuania, Latvia and Estonia say they have asked for the three Baltic states to be admitted as observers to the thirty-five nation human rights meeting taking place in Copenhagen.
N1Subj: person, institution, organisation; DON2: person, institution, organisation; as N3; to N4

5. Comment on the trial runs

100 occurrences of *admitted, admits* from the BNC, randomised, were checked against the above presentation. There were no occurrences of *admit** which were not captured by the re-written dictionary entry. Unfortunately, however, checking 200 randomised results for the queries *opens* and *opened* had proved less satisfactory. There is no denying it, some meanings are simply missing, or, at least, not sufficiently illustrated by examples, such as e.g. *open* plus *book, envelope, mail, open* plus *account, open* plus part of body (*abdomen*), *open* plus *something that is wrapped up or folded, open* plus *something in order to get to its interior parts*.

Some of these meanings can of course be added by expanding the ranges. Thus, in the appropriate line above there should also be *bag* and *case*, answering for *purse* and *wallet*, and adding *wings, hatchet* and *border* at the appropriate places would help as well. The next 50 randomised results yielded no new puzzles, except perhaps that the *pores opened.* Revision is necessary, but it should not prove too difficult.

Now suppose you had *He opened his fist*. The machine would, at the present stage of instructions, be baffled. In such a case it could look up *fist* in WordNet:

(10) **fist**, clenched fist (a hand with the fingers clenched in the palm (as for hitting))

and go from there to

(11) **clenched,** clinched (closed or squeezed together tightly) *"a clenched fist"; "his clenched (or clinched) teeth"*

which is where it would note one of the key concepts for *open*, namely *closed*. It could then copy the line and present it for inspection. To repeat the method: a word will be checked section by section of the WordNet entry until parts of the meaning description are found. For this, the machine would have to take words from the meaning block and check it against the outside dictionary or thesaurus information.

Unfortunately however, there are occurrences of *open*, particularly frequent metonymic and metaphoric usages, where this method fails. Decoding *I opened the whisky* requires finding *bottle of, cask of* in WordNet, but these collocations are not listed. It would require searching a corpus for collocations of the type *container* + *whiskey*.

We may encounter quite a number of similar verbs with a multitude of possible meanings. In these cases, the procedure might be to have two meaning blocks. One of them would be a "usage block", with notes as already presented. These notes would be presented in case of alleged certainty or high probability (as in *The gates opened and the chariot went through*). Incidentally, this kind of notes would be necessary anyhow if we wanted to add multilingual translation equivalents. From this usage block the machine would gather notes for presentation like:

(12) A door, window, etc. can open or be opened, i.e. … or
A container such as a tin can be opened, i.e. … or
A bag, a case, a chest can be opened, i.e. …

The other block would be a kind of "general meaning block", reverted to by default and presented as a whole to the human user:

(13) *Open* can mean 'become open, become no longer closed'. Most things that can be said to be closed can be opened.
(i) A door, window etc. can open or be opened, i.e. …
(ii) A container such as a tin can open or be opened, i.e. …
(iii) A bag, a case, a chest can open or be opened i.e. …
(iv) A lock can open or be opened i.e. …
(v) You can open something that is written: a book or a letter, i.e. …
(vi) You can open an account at a bank, i.e. …
(vii) Something that is folded or wrapped up can open or be opened, i.e. …
(viii) You can open something in order to access its interior parts, i.e. …
Open can mean 'start working, functioning, taking place'. etc…

With this general meaning information the human user could decode occurrences like *They opened his heart, The buzzard opened his wings, I opened the umbrella, I opened the sherry, I opened the watch.*

6. Other applications

Detailed notes might open up other applications. A machine might be able to answer *yes* to a question like *Did the show take place?* when given *The Princess Royal opened the exhibition.* And this could lead to more effective search machines. Else, you might put all notes together in a single file. There would be enough material to investigate issues like "other roles than agent in subject position" or "the semantics of direct objects with verbs of motion", or "nouns after verbs of saying".

Notes

1. The description uses Roman superscripts to indicate parts of the pattern in the order in which they normally appear, and specifies the semantic range to which these parts belong.

References

Herbst, Thomas, David Heath, Ian Roe, and Dieter Götz (eds.)
2004 *A Valency Dictionary of English. A Corpus-Based Analysis of the Complementation Patterns of English Verbs, Nouns and Adjectives.* Berlin/New York: Mouton de Gruyter.

Simpson, John, and Edmund Weiner (eds.)
1989 *The Oxford English Dictionary.* 2d ed. Oxford: Oxford University Press.

The Bank of English:	http://www.titania.bham.ac.uk/
British National Corpus:	http://info.ox.ac.uk/bnc/
Framenet:	http://framenet.icsi.berkeley.edu/
WordNet:	http://wordnet.princeton.edu/
Wortschatz Lexikon:	http://wortschatz.uni-leipzig.de

Handling valency and coordination in Database Semantics[1]

Roland Hausser

1. Sign-based vs. agent-based approaches to language

Most linguistic approaches are *sign-oriented* in that they analyze expressions of natural language as objects, fixed on paper, magnetic tape or by electronic means. They abstract away from the aspect of communication and analyze signs as hierarchical structures which are represented as trees and formally based on the principle of *possible substitutions*.

Database Semantics (DBS), in contrast, is *agent-oriented* in that it analyzes signs as the result of the speaker's language production and as the starting point of the hearer's language interpretation. Inclusion of the agents' production and interpretation procedures requires a time-linear analysis which is formally based on the principle of *possible continuations*.

The goal of Database Semantics is a theory of natural language communication which is complete with respect to function and data coverage, of low mathematical complexity, and suitable for an efficient implementation on the computer. The central question of Database Semantics is: how does communicating with natural language work?

In the most simple form, DBS answers this question as follows: natural language communication takes place between cognitive agents. These have interfaces for non-verbal recognition and action at the level of context, and verbal recognition and action at the level of language. Each agent contains a database in which contents are stored. These contents consist of the agent's knowledge, memories, current recognition, intentions, plans, etc. Contents are read into and out of the database by means of a time-linear algorithm. Cognitive agents can switch between the speaker- and the hearer-mode (turn-taking).

In a communication procedure, an agent in the speaker-mode codes content from its database into signs of language which are realized externally via the language output interface. These signs are recognized by another agent in the hearer-mode via the language input interface, their content is decoded, and stored in the second agent's database. This procedure is successful if the content coded by the speaker is decoded and stored equivalently by the hearer.

2. Complementation

In Valency Theory (cf. Ágel 2000) there is a basic distinction between valency carriers and valency fillers. Valency carriers have certain slots for which there must be suitable fillers in order for a sentence to be grammatical and complete. For example, the verb know is a valency carrier with valency positions for two nominal fillers, one serving as the subject, the other as the object.

In Dependency Grammar, the relations between a valency carrier and its fillers in a sentence are shown in the form of a tree, called dependency graph or stemma. Consider the following dependency graph of the sentence Julia knows John:

Example 1. Representing dependency relations as a tree

dependency graph (stemma)

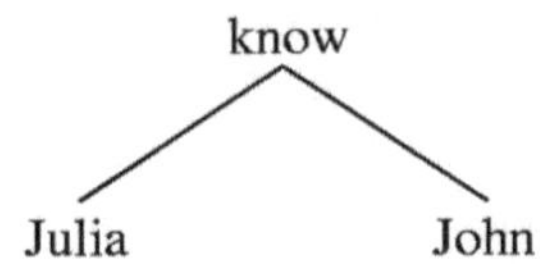

Supplying a valency carrier with suitable fillers is called complementation.

In Database Semantics, the grammatical structure of a sentence is represented as a set of proplets rather than a tree. Proplets are non-recursive (flat) feature structures in the sense that attributes may not take feature structures as values.

Example 2. Representing dependency relations as a set of proplets

sur:	sur:	sur:
noun: Julia	verb: know	noun: John
cat: nm	cat: decl	cat: nm
sem: sg	sem: pres	sem: sg
mdr:	arg: Julia John	mdr:
fnc: know	mdr:	fnc: know
idy: 14	prn: 6	idy: 15
prn: 6		prn: 6

The relations between the valency carrier *know* and its fillers *Julia* and *John* are coded by values for certain attributes. More specifically, the proplet *know* has the attribute arg with the values Julia John, and the proplets

Julia and *John* have the attribute fnc with the value know (bidirectional pointering).

Proplets belonging to the same proposition share a common proposition number (here prn: 6). Each proplet is an autonomous item which may be stored anywhere in memory without affecting the coding of grammatical relations. Thus, the grammatical relations characterized by sign-oriented approaches in the form of a tree are recoded equivalently in Database Semantics by means of values of certain attributes. They establish a bidirectional pointering between proplets of valency carriers and their filler proplets, regardless of where they are located in storage.

There is a total of eleven attributes in the proplets of example (2), the values of which have the following properties:

1. Surface attribute: sur
   Each proplet has a unique surface attribute. Its value is the language dependent surface of a proplet, needed for lexical lookup in the hearer-mode. After lexical lookup, the sur value is usually omitted.
2. Core attributes: noun, verb, adj
   Each proplet has a unique core attribute, which gets its value from the lexicon. From a sign-theoretic point of view,[2] the core values may consist of a *concept*, a *pointer*, or a *marker*, which corresponds to the sign kinds of *symbol, indexical* and *name*. While a verb-attribute can only take a concept as its value, an adj-attribute can take a concept or a pointer. The most general kind is the noun-attribute, which can take a concept, a pointer, or a marker as value.[3]
3. Continuation attributes: fnc, arg, mdd, mdr[4]
   Each proplet has several continuation attributes, which get their values by copying during the composition of proplets (cf. example [3]). The values consist of characters (char), which represent the names of other proplets. In complete propositions, the values of fnc, arg, and mdd must be non-NIL, while that of mdr may be NIL.

   Additional continuation attributes are pc (previous conjunct) and nc (next conjunct) in verbal proplets. They are used for connecting propositions in a time-linear sequence.
4. SynSem attributes: cat, sem
   Each proplet has the SynSem attributes cat and sem. They get their values in part from the lexicon, for example nm (for name), and in part by copying.
5. Book-keeping attributes: prn (proposition number)
   Each proplet has one or more book-keeping attributes, which get their values by the control structure of the parser and consist of numbers (integers). In connected proplets, these values must be non-NIL. Additional

book-keeping attributes are idy (identity), wrn (word number), and trc (transition counter).

Coding grammatical relations in terms of attributes and values is suitable not only for the treatment of complementation, i.e. obligatory and optional relations between a carrier and its fillers which are restricted in some grammatical way (for example agreement), but also for the treatment of adjuncts, which are usually excluded by lexical approaches to Valency Theory (cf. Herbst 1999; Herbst et al. 2004).

In other words, the handling of grammatical relations in Database Semantics applies not only to the traditional valency relations, but to functor-argument structures in general. Treating valency relations as an instance of functor-argument structure has several advantages, one of them being that valency relations are supplied with the standard semantic interpretation of functor-argument structure.

3. Basic model of communication in Database Semantics

Using the reconstruction of complementation in Database Semantics, we may illustrate the basic functioning of natural language communication. An agent in the hearer-mode receives a sequence of unanalyzed surfaces as input. During lexical lookup, these surfaces are matched with corresponding lexical proplets. Lexical proplets are *unconnected* in that the attributes' coding relations to other proplets have no values yet.

Example 3. Coding valency structure in the hearer-mode

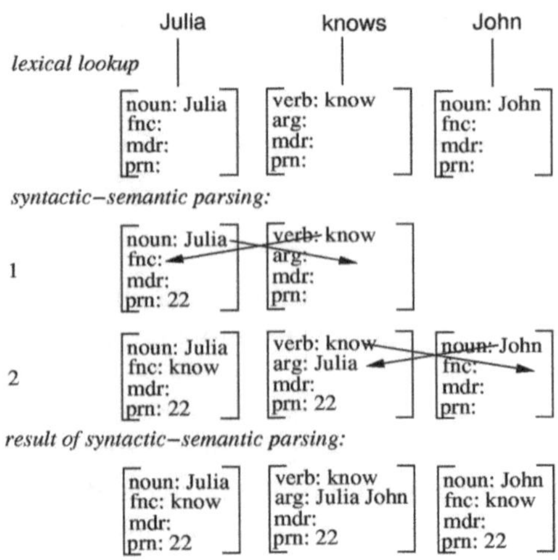

After lexical lookup, the proplets are connected by syntactic-semantic parsing. This strictly time-linear procedure is performed by an LA-grammar called *LA-hear*. It is based on copying values (here indicated by arrows) and by providing values to the book-keeping attributes (here the prn value 22).

The result of syntactic-semantic parsing in the hearer-mode is a(n unordered) set of proplets. For purposes of indexing and retrieval, these proplets are stored at the end of alphabetically ordered token lines. Each token line begins with the name of the core value and is followed by all proplets containing this core value. In this way, the content coded by the natural language expression Julia knows John is stored in the database of the hearer (see *hearer* on the left):

Example 4. Transfer of content from speaker to hearer

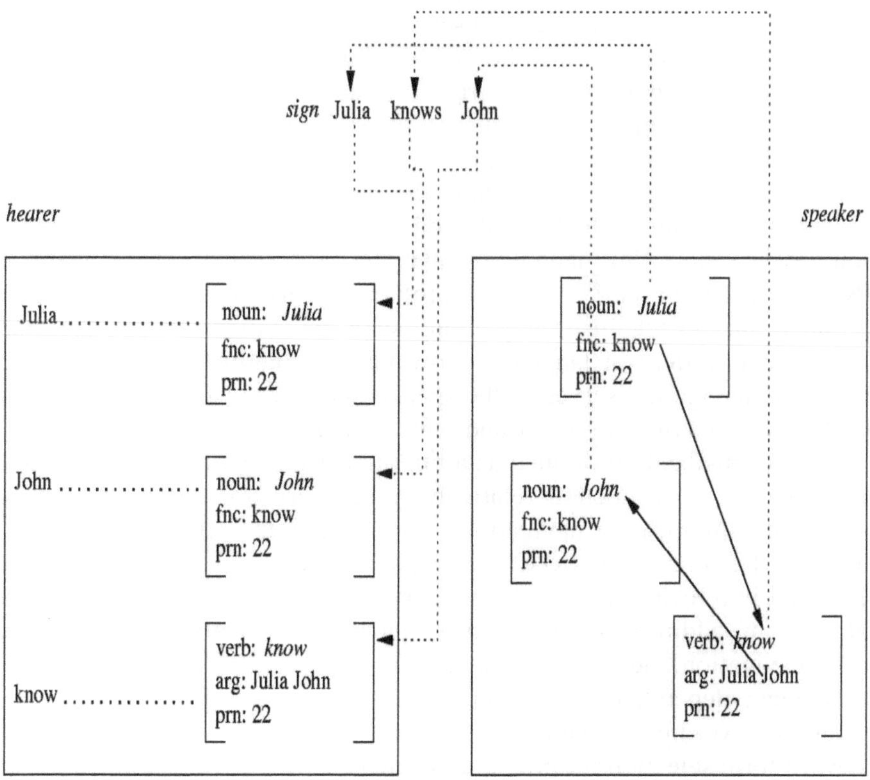

When the hearer turns into a speaker (see *speaker* on the right), stored content is activated by means of a time-linear navigation. Let us assume, for example, that *Julia* has been activated by the agent's control structure as the navigation-initial proplet. It has the attribute fnc with the value know and the attribute prn with the value 22. Based on these values, the continuation proplet *know* is being activated next (see arrow from *Julia* to *know*). The first value of its arg attribute, i.e. Julia, confirms the legality of the first navigation step. The second value, i.e. John, provides the information for continuing the navigation by activating a third proplet (see arrow from *know* to *John*).

Such a navigation through stored content serves as the basic model of *thought* in Database Semantics. Based on the grammatical relations between proplets (intrapropositional navigation) and between propositions (extrapropositional navigation), the navigation uses the standard retrieval mechanism of the database.

Because proplets normally provide more than one possible successor, the navigation algorithm, called *LA-think*, must make choices. The most basic solutions are either completely random choices or completely fixed choices, based on some predefined schema. For rational behavior, however, the *LA-think* grammar must be refined into a control structure which chooses between continuation alternatives based on the evaluation of external and internal stimuli, the frequency of previous traversals, learned procedures, theme/rheme structure, etc.

For present purposes, we assume the predefined schema of a standard navigation, starting with the verb and continuing with the arguments in their given order. This navigation may be represented schematically as VNN, with V representing the verb proplet, the first N the subject, and the second N the object. In principle, any such navigation through the word bank is independent of language. However, in cognitive agents with language, the navigation serves as the speaker's *conceptualization*, i.e., as the speaker's choice of *what to say* and *how to say it*.

A conceptualization defined as a time-linear navigation through content makes language production relatively straightforward: if the speaker decides to communicate a navigation to the hearer, the concept names (i.e., values of the core attributes) of the proplets traversed by the navigation are translated into their language-dependent counterparts and realized as external signs. In addition to this language-dependent lexicalization of the universal navigation, the system must provide

1. language-dependent word order,
2. function word precipitation, and
3. word form selection for proper agreement.

This process is handled by language-dependent *LA-speak* grammars in combination with language-dependent word form production. For example, the word form ate is produced from an *eat* proplet the sem attribute of which contains the value past.

Because word form selection for proper agreement involves a large amount of morphosyntactic detail, the language-specific production from the VNN navigation of our example is characterized by the following simplified format:

Example 5. Schematic production of Julia knows John. (speaker-mode)

	activated sequence	*realization*
i		
	V	
i.1	n	n
	V N	
i.2	fv n	n fv
	V N	
i.3	fv n n	n fv n
	V N N	
i.4	fv p n n	n fv n p
	V N N	

The letter 'i' stands for the number of the sentence produced. The letters n, fv and p are abstract surfaces for *name*, *finite verb*, and *punctuation* (here full stop), respectively.

The derivation begins with a navigation from V to N, based on *LA-think*. In line i.1, the N is realized as the n 'Julia', and in line i.2 the V is realized as the fv 'knows' by *LA-speak*. In line i.3, *LA-think* continues the navigation to the second N, which is realized as the n 'John' by *LA-speak*. Finally, *LA-speak* realizes the p '.' from the V proplet (line i.4).

The time-linear switching between *LA-think* and *LA-speak* is motivated not only by psychological considerations,[5] but also by computational efficiency. The reason is that realizing the surfaces of proplets as soon as possible (instead of navigating to the end of the proposition first) results in a more restricted set of candidates for matching by the LA-speak rules than having to consider the proposition's complete set of proplets.

The method of production shown in (5), based on an underlying VNN navigation, can be used to realize not only an SVO surface (subject-verb-object) as in the above example, but also an SOV and (trivially) a VSO surface (Greenberg 1963). The ordering and lexicalization are specified by the rules of an *LA-speak* grammar, whereby the design of these grammars is supported conceptually by abstract derivations like (5).

4. Treating adjuncts

Having outlined the basic mechanism of natural language communication in Database Semantics with a reanalysis of complementation, let us turn next to the treatment of adjuncts. Herbst (1999) presents the following example, shown here in simplified form:

Example 6. Dependency graph (stemma) with two-place verb and adjunct

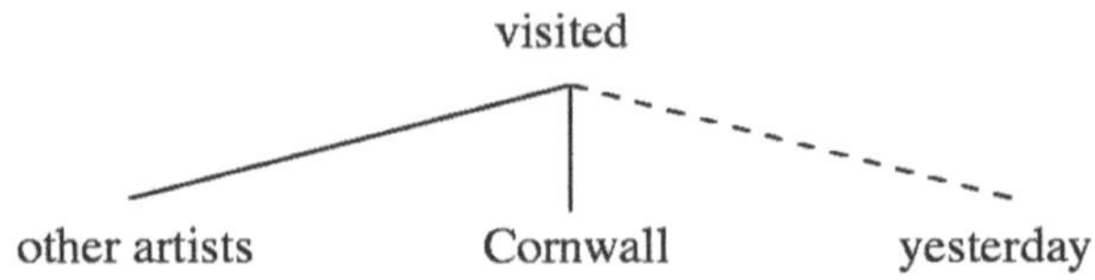

The optional character of the adjunct is indicated by the dotted line. In Database Semantics, the same example is represented as the following set of proplets:

Example 7. Corresponding representation in Database Semantics

sur: noun: artist cat: pnp sem: pl mdr: other fnc: visit idy: 16 prn: 7	sur: adj: other cat: adn sem: mdr: mdd: 16 artist prn: 7	sur: verb: visit cat: decl sem: past arg: artist Cornwall mdr: yesterday prn: 7	sur: noun: Cornwall cat: nm sem: sg mdr: fnc: visit idy: 17 prn: 7	sur: adj: yesterday cat: adv sem: mdr: mdd: visit prn: 7

There are two adjuncts, the adnominal modifier other and the adverbial modifier yesterday. The bidirectional pointering is between the modified (mdd), i.e. artist and visit, and the modifier (mdr), i.e. other and yesterday, respectively. The optional character of modifiers is treated as a property of the mdr attribute (typing), which may have the value NIL.

5. The treatment of certain function words (translatives)

One of the basic distinctions in Tesnière (1959) is between *mot plein* and *mot vide*, which may be translated as content word and function word, respectively. Examples of function words are determiners and auxiliaries, which are analyzed as "translatives".

In Database Semantics, function words are fused with associated content words during interpretation in the hearer-mode (absorption) and extracted during production in the speaker-mode (precipitation). Consider the following example illustrating absorption of a determiner and two auxiliaries in a hearer-mode derivation:

Example 8. Parsing The little dog has been barking in the hearer mode

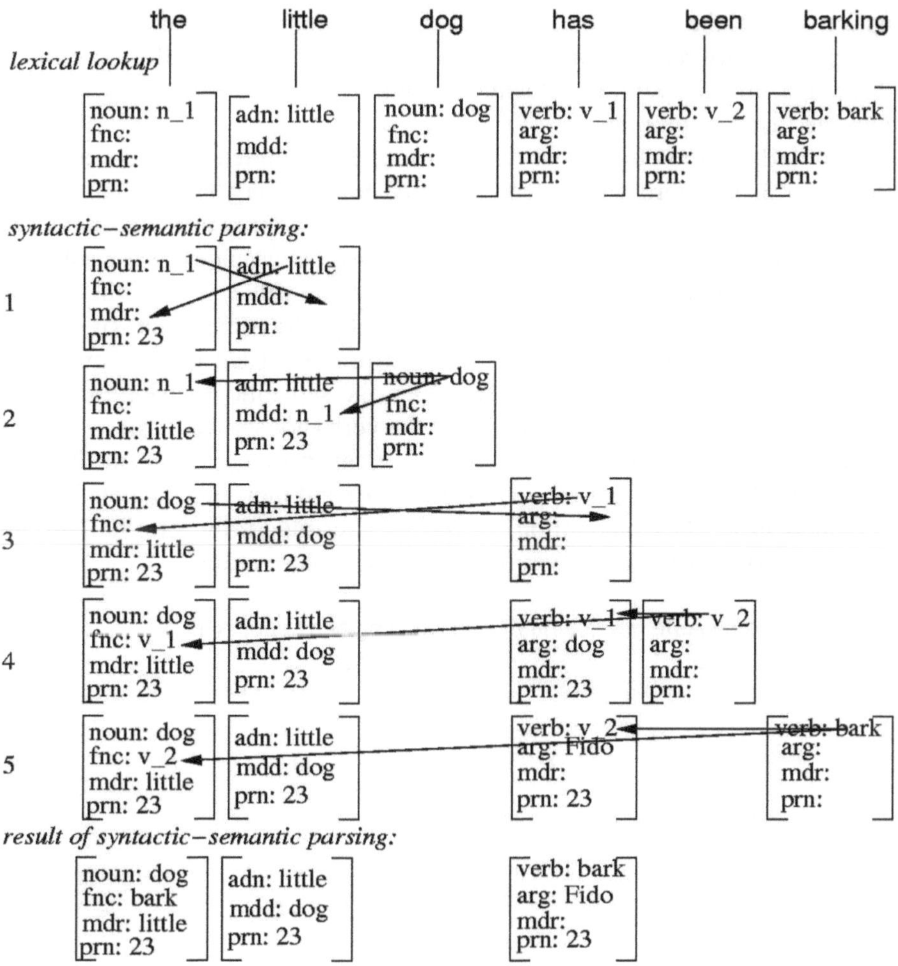

Because Database Semantics is strictly surface compositional, all word form surfaces in the input expression are lexically analyzed (see *lexical lookup*). The lexical analysis of function words is special, however, in that their core values are substitution values, e.g. n_1. During the *LA-hear* derivation, the substitution value of a function word is replaced by the associated content word.

Consider the time-linear derivation of the little dog in (8). In combination step 1, the adnominal little is copied into the mdr slot of *the*, and the substitution value n_1 of *the* is copied into the mdd slot of *little*. In combination step 2, the two occurrences of the substitution value n_1 in the first two proplets are replaced by the core value of *dog*. Then the third proplet is discarded. In this way, all relevant grammatical relations have been coded into the first two proplets.

Similarly in the time-linear derivation of the complex verb: in combination step 3, the core value dog is copied into the arg slot of the lexical analysis of has, and the substitution value v_1 is copied into the fnc slot of the *dog* proplet. In combination step 4, the two occurrences of the substitution value v_1 are replaced by the substitution value v_2 of the lexical analysis of been. In combination step 5, finally, the occurrences of v_2 are replaced by the core value bark of the last proplet. Then the last proplet is discarded. In the course of this derivation, the semantic contribution of the auxiliaries is coded into the sem slot of the verb (not shown here).[6]

The three proplets derived in this way can now be stored in the data base. Based on the values of the attributes arg and mdr, the proplets may be activated in a VNA navigation. In the speaker-mode, the original surface may be reconstructed as shown in the following derivation:

Example 9. Schematic production of The little dog has been barking.

```
     activated sequence                            realization
i
             V
i.1                        d                       d
             V             N
i.2                        d    an                 d an
             V             N    A
i.3                        d  n an                 d an n
             V             N    A
i.4          ax          d n    an                 d an n ax
             V             N    A
i.5       ax  ax          d n   an                 d an n ax ax
             V             N    A
i.6  ax  ax  nv           d n   an                 d an n ax ax nv
             V             N    A
i.7 ax  ax  nv p          d n   an                 d an n ax ax nv p
             V             N    A
```

Here, d, an, n, ax, nv, and p stand for determiner, adnominal, auxiliary, non-finite verb, and punctuation (full stop), respectively.

6. Coordination

The most important construction of natural language besides valency in particular and functor-argument structure in general is coordination. For Database Semantics, this presents the task of integrating the treatment of valency and coordination in a unified, functional system. The solution is illustrated below using a simple example of a nominal conjunction with the function word (junctive) and, serving as the subject:

Example 10. Lexicalization of The man, the woman, and the child sleep.

noun: n_1	noun: man	noun: n_2	noun: woman	cnj: &	noun: n_3	noun: child	verb: sleep
fnc:	fnc:	fnc:	fnc:		fnc:	fnc:	arg:
mdr:	mdr:	mdr:	mdr:		mdr:	mdr:	mdr:
nc:	nc:	nc:	nc:		nc:	nc:	nc:
pc:	pc:	pc:	pc:		pc:	pc:	pc:
prn:	prn:	prn:	prn:		prn:	prn:	prn:

The task of connecting these isolated proplets in a time-linear derivation (similar to example [8]) raises two basic questions. The first is how to build the grammatical relations between the conjuncts. In other words: what is the "connexion" between the elements of a conjunction in DBS? Consider the following solution:

Example 11. Relations within a nominal conjunction

noun: man &	noun: woman	noun: child	verb: sleep
fnc: sleep	fnc:	fnc:	arg: man &
mdr:	mdr:	mdr:	mdr:
nc: woman	nc: child	nc:	nc:
pc:	pc: man	pc: woman	pc:
prn: 26	prn: 26	prn: 26	prn: 26

Each conjunct specifies its predecessor in the pc (previous conjunct) and its successor in the nc (next conjunct) attribute. These attributes receive their values by downward copying in the hearer-mode, and are used for upward retrieval during conceptualization. The kind of conjunction, for example and versus or, is indicated after the concept value of the first conjunct (here man &). This treatment of coordination is strictly surface compositional and time-linear, in contrast to transformational systems such as Hellwig (2003).

The second question is how to integrate such a conjunction into the valency or functor-argument structure of a proposition. Consider the following solution:

Example 12. Relating a nominal conjunction to the valency structure

noun: man &	noun: woman	noun: child	verb: sleep
fnc: sleep	fnc:	fnc:	arg: man &
mdr:	mdr:	mdr:	mdr:
nc: woman	nc: child	nc:	nc:
pc:	pc: man	pc: woman	pc:
prn: 26	prn: 26	prn: 26	prn: 26

This analysis specifies the grammatical relations of a conjunction in a way which is as complete as necessary and as parsimonious as possible: only the first conjunct *man* specifies the verb in its fnc-slot, and the verb specifies only the first conjunct in its arg-slot. For retrieval, this has the following consequence.

When searching for sleeping child, for example, the *child* proplet in question merely indicates that it is part of a conjunction (pc: woman); in order to determine the associated verb, *LA-think* has to navigate to the first element of the conjunction, i.e. *man*, and check whether or not its fnc value is sleep. The verb proplet *sleep* also indicates that its argument is a conjunction (arg: man &). Therefore, the search for a non-initial conjunct is attempted only if the proplet belongs to a proposition which actually contains a conjunction.

The (re)production of the input sentence is based on a VNNN sequence.[7] The following derivation uses the new abstract surface cn, for conjunction:

Example 13. Production of The man the woman and the child slept.

	activated sequence				*realization*
i.					
	V				
i.1		d			d
	V	N			
i.2		d nn			d nn
	V	N			
i.3		d nn	d		d nn d
	V	N	N		
i.4		d nn	d nn		d nn d nn
	V	N	N		
i.5		d nn	d nn		d nn d nn
	V	N	N		
i.6		d nn cn	d nn	d	d nn d nn cn d
	V	N	N	N	
i.7		d nn cn	d nn	d nn	d nn d nn cn d nn
	V	N	N	N	
i.8	fv	d nn cn	d nn	d nn	d nn d nn cn d nn fv
	V	N	N	N	
i.8	fv p	d nn cn	d nn	d nn	d nn d nn cn d nn fv p
	V	N	N	N	

The conjunction is lexicalized from the first conjunct in line i.6. Due to this late realization, it appears between the penultimate and ultimate conjunct.

A second kind of intrapropositional conjunction are verbal conjunctions, as in John bought, cooked, and ate the pizza. The relations within a verbal conjunction are similar to those in a nominal conjunction. This approach works also for the combination of conjunctions as in the man, the woman, and the child bought, cooked, and ate the steaks, the potatoes, and the broccoli. The functor-argument structure of this example is that of the man& bought& the steaks&.

7. Conclusion

It has been shown in which way the notions of Dependency Grammar based on Valency Theory, such as valency carrier (functor) and valency filler (argument), adjunct (modifier), *mot plein* (content word), *mot vide* (function word, translative, junctive), connexion (grammatical relation), etc., have counterparts in Database Semantics. At the same time it became apparent that the realization of these notions and their location in the overall theories is different in the two approaches. This is mainly because Dependency Grammar and Valency Theory are sign-oriented while DBS is agent-oriented.

To further clarify the notions and distinctions in Database Semantics as compared to Dependency Grammar and Valency Theory, consider the following hierarchy:

Example 14. Hierarchy of notions and distinctions in Database Semantics

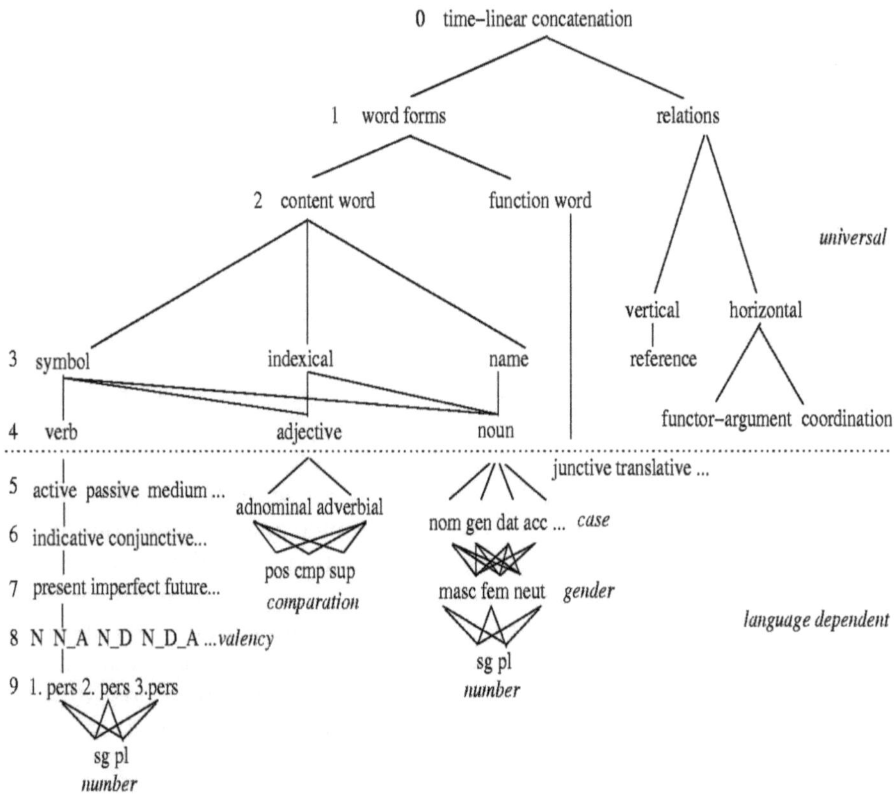

At the root of the tree there is the time-linear concatenation (level 0) of word forms which are in relations to each other (level 1). This most basic structural property of natural language is realized by the time-linear algorithm of LA-grammar (Hausser 1992) in its variants of *LA-hear*, *LA-think*, and *LA-speak* (Hausser 2001).

The word forms are divided into content words and function words (level 2). The content words are divided into the three basic kinds of signs, namely symbol, indexical, and name (level 3). In the branch of relations, the kinds of signs serve the "vertical" relation of reference, implemented as a matching between the levels of language and context.

The kinds of signs (level 3) are correlated with the parts of speech (level 4). Symbols can be verbs, adjectives, or nouns, indexicals can be adjectives or nouns, and names can be nouns only. This is shown graphically by the lines relating the kinds of signs and the parts of speech. In the branch of relations, the parts of speech serve the "horizontal" relations of functor-argument structure and coordination.[8]

The structures shown above the dotted line separating level 4 and 5 are universal: all natural languages are based on a time-linear concatenation of word forms, the distinction between content and function words, the three kinds of signs, the three parts of speech, the vertical relation of reference, and the horizontal relations of functor-argument structure and coordination. In Database Semantics, these structures are realized in the form of an artificial agent with interfaces for recognition and action at the context and the language level, the data structure of a word bank (database) containing proplets, and the algorithm of LA-grammar for reading content into and out of the database.

The structures shown below the dotted line are language-dependent. For the verb forms of the Indo-European languages, for example, this holds for the genus, modus, and tempus verbi (levels 5, 6, and 7), the valency structure of the verbs (level 8), as well as the person and number distinction (level 9). For the adjectives, it holds for the distinction between adnominal and adverbial use and for synthetic comparation. For the nouns, it holds for the different case systems, and the number and gender distinctions (which are missing, for example, in Korean). Language-dependent is also whether the coding of grammatical relations and distinctions is handled analytically by means of functions words (e.g. junctives, translatives) or synthetically in terms of morphology. In Database Semantics, these aspects are treated by language-dependent LA-grammars with a suitable lexicon, restrictions on variables for handling agreement, and a rule system for handling word order.

Notes

1. This paper benefited from comments by Jae Woong Choe (Korea University, Seoul), Besim Kabashi (Friedrich-Alexander-University, Erlangen), Haitao Liu (Communications University of China, Beijing), and Brian MacWhinney, (Carnegie Mellon University, Pittsburgh).
2. See Hausser (1999), chapter 6.
3. Seventh Principle of Pragmatics (PoP-7). See Hausser (1999: 107).
4. For functor, argument, modified, and modifier, respectively.

5. The *principle of incrementality* emphasizes the extent to which interpretation occurs in real time as new words are being heard (cf. MacWhinney 1987). The linkage of valency relations to incremental parsing found in the LA approach also provides a comprehensive approach to the aspects of the language learning problem known as the logical problem of language acquisition. In particular, MacWhinney (2004; 2005) has shown that children can induce the correct set of valency relations in their target language by focusing on meaningful relations in main clauses, along with their verbal complements.
6. For a more detailed analysis of the major constructions of English see Hausser (2006).
7. Note that VNNN can represent a three-place proposition like John gave Mary a flower or a one-place proposition with a nominal conjunction as in (12). The notation may be disambiguated by means of subscripts.
8. Treating coordination as a bona fide grammatical relation like functor-argument structure, handled in terms of the attributes and values of proplets, is in contrast to Lobin (1993a: 176): "the best way of dealing with coordination in syntax is not to deal with it at all, but 'process it away' immeadetly [sic]." See also Lobin (1993b).

References

Ágel, Vilmos
2000 *Valenztheorie*. Tübingen: Gunter Narr.

Greenberg, Joseph H.
1963 Some universals of grammar with particular reference to the order of meaningful elements. In *Universals of Language*, Joseph H. Greenberg (ed.), 73–113. Cambridge, Mass.: MIT Press.

Hausser, Roland
1992 Complexity in left-associative grammar. *Theoretical Computer Science*, 106 (2): 283–308.
1999 *Foundations of Computational Linguistics, Human-Computer Communication in Natural Language*. 2d ed. 2001. Berlin/New York: Springer-Verlag.
2001 Database semantics for natural language. *Artificial Intelligence* 130 (1): 27–74.
2006 *A Computational Model of Natural Language Communication: Interpretation, Inference, and Production in Database Semantics*, Berlin/New York: Springer-Verlag.

Hellwig, Peter
2003 Dependency unification grammar. In *Dependency and Valency. An International Handbook of Contemporary Research*, Vilmos Ágel, Ludwig M. Eichinger, Hans-Werner Eroms, Peter Hellwig, Hans-Jürgen Heringer, and Henning Lobin (eds.), 593–635, Berlin/New York: Mouton de Gruyter.

Herbst, Thomas
1999 English valency structures – A first sketch. *Erfurt Electronic Studies in English* (EESE) 6: http://webdoc.gwdg.de/edoc/ia/eese/artic99/herbst/6_99.html.

Herbst Thomas, David Heath, Ian F. Roe, and Dieter Götz (eds.)
2004 *A Valency Dictionary of English: A Corpus-Based Analysis of the Complementation Patterns of English Verbs, Nouns and Adjectives.* Berlin/New York: Mouton de Gruyter.

Lobin, Henning
1993a Linguistic perception and syntactic structure. In *Functional Description of Language*, Eva Hajicova (ed.), 163–178. Prague: Charles University.
1993b *Koordinations-Syntax als prozedurales Phänomen.* Tübingen: Gunter Narr.

MacWhinney, Brian
1987 The competition model. In *Mechanisms of Language Acquisition*, Brian MacWhinney (ed.), 249–308. Hillsdale, NJ: Lawrence Erlbaum.
2004 A multiple process solution to the logical problem of language acquisition. *Journal of Child Language* 31: 883–914.
2005 Item-based constructions and the logical problem. *ACL* 2005: 46–54.

Tesnière, Lucien
1959 *Éléments de Syntaxe Structurale*, Paris: Editions Klincksieck.

Pronominal clitics and valency in Albanian: A computational linguistics perspective and modelling within the LAG-Framework[1]

Besim Kabashi

1. Theoretical aspects: Pronominal clitics and valency

When reading Albanian texts, elements like *e*, *i*, *ia* cannot be overlooked. If they immediately precede the verb or if they are part of the verb form in non-negated imperative sentences, they are instances of *trajtat e shkurtra të përemrave vetorë* [short forms of personal pronouns; Domi 1995; 1997]. Buchholz and Fiedler (1987) call them *Objektszeichen* [object signs], Kalluli (1995) names them *clitics*. Like Newmark, Hubbard, and Prifti (1982), we will use the term *pronominal clitics* (*pCl*s).

1.1. Formal properties of pronominal clitics in Albanian

The following table gives an overview of the Albanian pCl forms:

Table 1. The personal pronouns in Albanian (left column) with their clitic forms (right column)

	1st Person				2nd Person			
	Singular		Plural		Singular		Plural	
Nom.	unë	-	ne	-	ti	-	ju	-
Dat.	mua	më	neve	na	ty	të	juve	ju
Acc.	mua	më	ne	na	ty	të	ju	ju

	3rd Person							
	Singular				Plural			
	Masculine		Feminine		Masculine		Feminine	
Nom.	ai	-	ajo	-	ata	-	ato	-
Dat.	atij	i	asaj	i	atyre	u	atyre	u
Acc.	atë	e	atë	e	ata	i	ato	i

PCls in Albanian indicate the person and number of the respective objects of the verb. They occur in dative and accusative case: dative pCls can be combined with accusative pCls. In most cases this results in *amalgamated forms* (*crasis*). For example *më* and *e* amalgamate to *ma.* The combination of *na* with *e, i,* or *u* does not involve amalgamation but *concatenation,* in which case the dative precedes the accusative: *na e, na i,* and *na u.*

There are two morphosyntactic types of pCls: bound and free. *Bound forms* occur within positive (non-negated) imperatives after the verb stem (*enclitic position*). In the plural they appear between the verb stem and the suffix *ni*, cf. the following example:

Example 1. Pronominal clitics as bound forms[2]

(1)		sill	V_{Stem}	No pCl; Sg;	'bring'
	a.	sille	$V_{Stem}+pCl_{A}$	pCl_{A}, Sg;	'bring it'
	b.	sillma	$V_{Stem}+pCl_{D+A}$	pCl_{D+A}, Sg;	'bring me it'
	c.	sillni	V_{Stem}+ni	No pCl; Pl;	'bring'
	d.	silleni	$V_{Stem}+pCl_{A}$+ni	pCl_{A}, Pl;	'bring it'
	e.	sillmani	$V_{Stem}+pCl_{D+A}$+ni	pCl_{D+A}, Pl;	'bring me it'

In cases with negation particles, pCls cannot occur as bound forms, e.g. *Mos **e** sill*! ['(You: Sg) do not **it** bring!', i.e. 'Do not bring it!'] and *Mos e sillni*! ['(You: Pl) do not **it** bring!', i.e. 'Do not bring it!']. As *free forms,* pCls always precede the finite verb (*proclitic position*).[3] Word order in Albanian is relatively free. Therefore, both subject and objects may appear in front of the verb complex, which allows for a large number of different sentence patterns for a given verb; the order of elements within the verb complex is fixed. If all of these elements occur, they are in the following sequence: negation, future marker/modal verb, subjunctive particle, pCls, finite and non-finite verb. The subject can be deduced from verb inflection and thus be left out.

PCls in Albanian appear either in addition to objects in the sentence (*object doubling*) or they replace objects in the sentence, so that the objects themselves can be left out (*object elimination*).

1.2. Object doubling

The following example (2b) shows the doubling of the accusative object:

Example 2. Accusative object doubling[4]

(2) S+V

Ne	*shohim.*	
Subject: N Pl1	Verb: Itr Pl1 Ind Prs Act Nad	
we	see	
'We (are able to) see.'		

S+V+O_A

a.	*Ne*		*shohim*	*studentët/ata.*
			Verb: Tr	O: A A Pl3 M
	we		see	the students/them

S+pCl_A+V+O_A

b.	*Ne*	*i*	*shohim*	*studentët/ata.*
		pCl: A Pl3		
	we	them	see	the students/them
	'We see the students/them.'			

The following example shows the doubling of dative (3, 3a, and 3b) and accusative objects (3a and 3c).

Example 3. Object doubling in dative and accusative[5]

(3) S+pCl_D+V+O_D+O_A

Ne	*u*	*dhamë*	*studentëve/atyre*	*librat/ato.*
Subject: N Pl1	pCl: u D Pl3	Verb: Tr Pl3 Ind Aor Act Nad	O: D D Pl3	O: A A Pl Det
we	them	gave	the students/ them	the books/ them
'We gave the students/them the books/them.'				

S+pCl_{D+A}+V+O_D+O_A

a.	*Ne*	*ua*	*dhamë*	*studentëve/atyre*	*librat/ato*
		pCl: *u+i* D Pl3 + A Pl3			
	we	them + them	gave	the students/ them	the books/ them
	'We gave the students/them the books/them.'				

$S+pCl_{D+A}+V+O_D$

b.	*Ne*	*ua*	*dhamë*	*studentëve/atyre*
	we	them + them	gave	the students/ them

'We gave the students/them them.'

$S+pCl_{D+A}+V+O_A$

c.	*Ne*	*ua*	*dhamë*		*librat/ato*
	we	them + them	gave		the books/them

'We gave them the books/them.'

Sentence (3) has two objects, one in dative and one in accusative case, and one pCl in dative case, which doubles the dative object. Whenever the verb has a dative valency, the dative pCl cannot be left out, regardless of the presence of a dative object in the sentence. In sentence (3a), both objects are doubled by means of the respective pCls. Only one object is doubled by the amalgamated pCl in sentences (3b) and (3c). Object doubling is also possible in imperatives, e.g. *Sill**ma** librin*! ['Bring+**me**+**it** the book!', 'Bring me the book!'], i.e. doubling of accusative object.

When the verb has a first or second person accusative or dative object, the pCls of the first and second person cannot be omitted, e.g. *Studentët **të** kuptojnë ty*. or *Studentët **të** kuptojnë*. ['The students understand you']. The form **Studentët kuptojnë ty*. is ungrammatical.

1.3. Object elimination

If a pCl occurs, the corresponding object can be left out.[6] This phenomenon has been called *Objektseliminierung* [object elimination] by Buchholz (1977), and Buchholz and Fiedler (1987). As there is no established English term, we will use the term *object elimination* as a translation of *Objektseliminierung*.[7] Example sentences where the objects are left out are (3b) and (3c). A sentence consisting only of pCl(s) and verb can be syntactically well-formed, cf. sentences (4a) and (4b) in the following example, where the subject is optional.

Example 4. Object elimination

(4) $*S+V+O_D+O_A$

**Ne*	_	*dhamë*	*studentëve/atyre*	*librat/ato.*
we		gave	the students/them	the books/ them

*'We gave _ the students/them the books/them.'

$S+pCl_{D+A}+V$

a.	*Ne*	*ua*	*dhamë.*
	we	them + them	gave
	'We gave them to them.'		

$S+pCl_{A}+V$

b.	*Ne*	*i*	*shohim*
		them	see
	'We see them.'		

The following patterns[8] are possible for doubling and elimination of accusative complements: $S+V+O_A$ (object without pCl), $S+pCl_A+V+O_A$ (object doubling) and $S+pCl_A+V$ (object elimination). For dative complements, the following patterns apply: $S+pCl_D+V+O_D$ (object doubling) and $S+pCl_D+V$ (object elimination). As shown in the examples above, these patterns can be combined with each other.

1.4. Pronominal clitics as valency fillers

Sentences (3b-c) and (4a-b) show the ability of pCls to function as *valency fillers*, as they can replace objects. The grammatical information of the pCl is sufficient to fill the valency of the verb; only the lexical content is missing, which has to be recoverable from the linguistic or extralinguistic context. Thus, if pCls occur, objects can be left out without making the sentence ungrammatical.

If objects are left out, the omission of pCls leads to the selection of a different valency pattern. This can (but does not have to) indicate the use of the verb in a different sense, cf. the difference of valency and meaning between sentences (2) and (2a), (2) and (2b), as well as in the following example adapted from Buchholz, Fiedler, and Uhlisch (1993):

Example 5. Different patterns/meanings of the verb *flas*[9]

(5) S+V

Ai	flet.
Subject: N Sg3 M	Verb: Itr Sg3 Ind Prs Act Nad
He	speak
'He speaks.'	

$S+pCl_D+V+O_D$

a.	Ai	i	flet	atij.
		pCl: D Sg3	Verb: Tr	O: D D Sg3 M
	He	him	scold	him

'He scolds him.'

$S+pCl_D+A+V+O_D+O_A$

b.	Ai	ia	flet	atij	një	libër.
		pCl: D Sg3 + A Sg3				A Sg1 M Undet
	He	him + it	promise	him	one	book

'He promises him a book.'

The role of pCls in the context of valency is different from the substitution of objects by pronouns, despite the fact that the pCls are short forms of personal pronouns. Personal pronouns, however, offer a more precise description of case and number (first and second person plural) and gender (third person singular) than pCls. First of all, the position of the pronoun is the same as the position of the object if a pronoun substitutes the object. A pCl has a fixed position in the verbal complex, regardless of the position of the object it replaces. While pronouns always replace objects, pCls are capable of either eliminating or doubling the objects they refer to. The appearance of the dative pCl is obligatory while the substitution of the dative object by pronouns is optional. The substitution of objects by pronouns does not change the structure of the sentence (which means the sentence matches to the same pattern), i.e. the O_A is only realized by a pronoun instead of a noun phrase, but the pattern $S+V+O_A$ remains the same. If a pCl appears, however, the pattern is changed, e.g. from $S+V+O_A$ to $S+pCl_A+V+O_A$ or to $S+pCl_A+V$. As shown above, pCls and pronouns can (and in some cases must, cf. section 1.2.) occur together in a sentence.

As the dative pCl cannot be left out without making the sentence ungrammatical, it always shares the dative valency slot with the dative object if the object is present. The pCl fills the valency slot itself, if the dative object is eliminated. In the case of the accusative, there is one more option: the object alone fills the valency slot of the verb, the object and pCl share the valency slot, or the pCl alone fills the valency slot. Thus in this analysis, there is a minimum number of required complements of 1 and a maximum number of required complements of 2 for the dative and the accusative valency slot (by analogy to Herbst et al. [2004], where the minimum and maximum valency of each verb is indicated); cf. the patterns $S+V+O_A$, $S+pCl_A+V$ and $S+pCl_D+V$ for minimum, and $S+pCl_A+V+O_A$ and

$S+pCl_D+V+O_D$ for maximum complements.

The fact that the dative pCl is obligatory even if the dative object is also present can be accounted for using the concept of structural necessity presented by Herbst (1999), which means that it is obligatory only on the syntactic level, not as a lexical property. As pCls can be correctly predicted by a set of rules, they are no idiosyncratic properties of lexical units and thus need not be specified in the valency frame of a lexical unit. It is enough to specify valency slots such as dative or accusative. Object doubling is always optional on the syntactic level; here semantic factors (needed for lexical content) as well as pragmatic factors (emphasis) decide whether doubling takes place or not. Additional functions and properties of pCls will not be discussed here.[10]

The properties of the pCl in the context of valency can be summarized as follows: in case of object elimination, the pCls indicate the verb valency and function as valency fillers, whereas in case of object doubling, both pCls and objects share the valency slot of the verb.

2. Practical aspects: The computational model

The formalism used in the following computational model is *Left Associative Grammar* (LAG).[11] LAG was developed as a formalism for the SLIM (*Surface compositional Linear Internal Matching*) language theory intended to model and reconstruct natural language communication on a computer.

2.1. The formalism

The formalism works according to the principle of possible continuations whereby every grammar rule concatenates the sentence start read so far with the next word. The result of this concatenation becomes the new sentence start to be concatenated with the next word again; this procedure is repeated until the end of the input is reached. For example the input *a b c d* is parsed in the steps $a+b \rightarrow ab$; $ab+c \rightarrow abc$; $abc+d \rightarrow abcd$, summarized as $(((a+b)+c)+d) \rightarrow abcd$. Ambiguities are handled by tracing several derivation paths in parallel. The most varied sentence types can be modeled with linear effort regarding complexity and parse time, because only the possible continuations matter in each LAG rule.

2.2. An example

Below, an algorithm for the treatment of dependencies between verb, pCls and objects is outlined using the sentence *Ai na i dha librat*. ['He gave us the books'].[12] It starts with the first word form and the matching rule *Subject* (start rule).

$Ai_{N\ Sg3\ M}$

❶ RULE: Subject
LVF = <Subject>;
Follow RULE pCl_D;

The subject is added to the list of valency fillers (LVF). In case of an omitted subject, the algorithm starts with the next rule, i.e. the parser searches for a rule with a matching start pattern. *Follow* means continuations, i.e. the next applicable rule, in this case *pCl_D*. When reading a word form, information required for recognition of the verb complex and for dealing with valency and congruency is provided by the lexicon or a morphological analysis component.

Ai	+	$na_{D\ Pl1}$

❷ RULE: pCl_D
LVF = <Subject, pCl_D_Object_elimination>;
Follow RULE pCl_A;

pCl_D is added to the LVF and labeled *Object_elimination* because the dative object can be left out. Since at this point it is not clear yet whether the actual pattern is *elimination* or *doubling*, the modification of the attribute to *pCl_D_Object_doubling* can be done when a matching object is encountered. If no matching object is found, the attribute is just left at the value set here. Here, two non-amalgamated (concatenated) pCls are used to demonstrate the *canceling* (filling) of valencies (valency slots). Amalgamated pCls have to be analyzed in the morphology component.

Ai na	+	$i_{A\ Pl3}$

❸ RULE: pCl_A
LVF = <Subject, pCl_D_Object_elimination, pCl_A_Object_elimination>;
Follow RULE finVerb;

pCl_A is added to the LFV just like *pCl_D* in the previous rule, also with the *Object_elimination* label.

Ai na i	+	dha $_{\text{Sg3 Aor Ind Act Nad <<D, A>, <A>>}}$

❹ RULE: finVerb
LVF = <pCl_D_Object_elimination, pCl_A_Object_elimination>;
Follow RULE Accusative_object;

The verb is read in and checked for agreement with the subject. The subject valency in LVF is canceled, the pCls, however, remain in the LVF because they can share their valency slot with an object and thus cannot be canceled before the respective object has been read or the sentence is finished. Because pCls always precede the verb, a (minimum) valency pattern that selects one or more of the possible lexical readings can be already constructed at this point.

Ai na i dha	+	librat $_{\text{A Pl3}}$

❺ RULE: Accusative_object
Replace pCl_A_Object_elimination by pCl_A_Object_doubling;
LVF = <pCl_D_Object_elimination, pCl_A_Object_doubling>;
Follow RULE Punctuation;

An accusative object is read in and modifies the *pCl_A_Object_elimination* entry in the LFV to *pCl_A_Object_doubling.*

Ai na i dha librat	+	.

❻ RULE: Punctuation
LVF = <pCl_D_Object_elimination, pCl_A_Object_doubling>;
RESULT = pCl_D_Object_elimination, pCl_A_Object_doubling;

The end of the sentence has been reached, the result is in LVF: object doubling for accusative and object elimination for dative.

Only the path that actually parses this sentence is shown above; other possible pathes were left out. After various rule applications, several continuations (parallel paths) would be possible and would have to be tried out by the algorithm. For example, after the rule *finVerb* the sentence may continue with punctuation, dative object, accusative object, a preposition, an adjunct etc.

As demonstrated in the example model, valencies can be canceled immediately when a potential valency filler has been read. Another possibility is end canceling, where the properties of all word forms read are collected in attribute-value matrices and are not canceled until a punctuation mark signals the end of the sentence. This has the advantage of transparency when handling constructions such as subclauses with the verb in final position, but one disadvantage is that ungrammatical constructions may not be rejected before they have been completely parsed.

When reading amalgamated pCl word forms such as *ma*, *ta*, *t'ia* etc., it is important to read and process the individual parts of the morphosyntactic information, e.g. *ma* ($më_{\mathrm{D\ Sg1}} + e_{\mathrm{A\ Sg3}}$). In this way, an amalgam can replace one object (object elimination) and double another at the same time, cf. sentences (3b) and (3c).

The following figure shows an example of a morphological analysis of the imperative one-word-sentence *sillmani*. As shown under the *Clitic* attribute, the enclitic form *ma* has been recognized as an amalgam of *më* and *e*.[13]

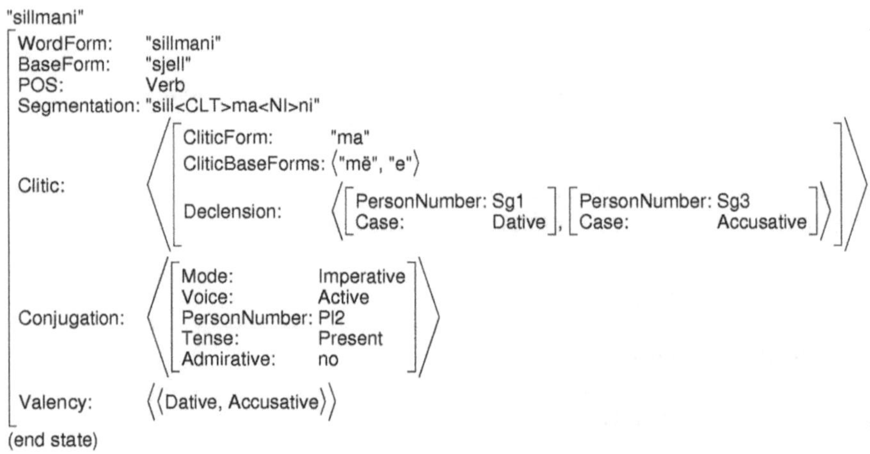

Figure 1. Morphological analysis of the word form *sillmani* from Kabashi (2003)

Here, valencies from the corresponding attribute are canceled with the matching cases from the clitic attribute *Declension.* It is necessary to check the information of lexical entries and morphological analysis to be able to select or construct the correct valency pattern, particularly with regard to the pCls that may be used with a verb. Information on possible valency patterns of a verb comes from its lemma in the base-form lexicon.

Figure 2 shows the result of syntax analysis and valency handling of the sentence *Ai na i dha librat.* treated above. The dative object is missing there, cf. the *FilledValencyFromObjects* attribute. A dative object was expected according to the verb's valency pattern but was not present. A dative pCl was found and thus the sentence can be analyzed as well-formed, cf. the *FilledValencyFromClitics* and the *DativeSlot* attributes. On the other hand the fact that both an accusative pCl and an accusative object are found, leads to object doubling, cf. the corresponding attributes, *FilledValencyFromObjects* and *AccusativeSlot*. The *Index* attribute indicates the position of a word form in the analyzed sentence. The actual pattern is derived from the attributes *Clitic_D*, *Clitic_A*, *Verb*, and *Object_A*. The *Meaning* attribute contains the meaning of the verb in the currently selected pattern.

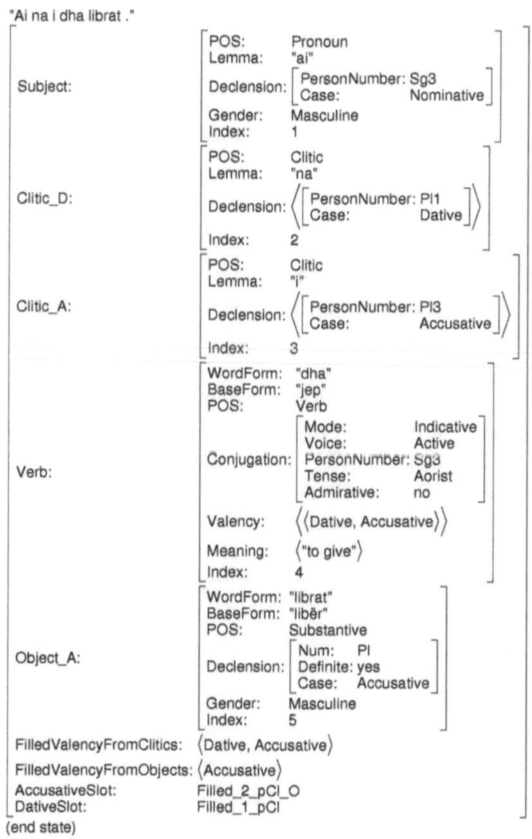

Figure 2. Syntactical analysis of the sentence *Ai na i dha librat.*

3. Conclusion

Acting as object substitutes (object elimination), pronominal clitics determine the verb's valency and assume the role of valency fillers. They play an important role in distinguishing between various possible valency frames of a verb and thus between different meanings. In the case of object doubling, they merely function as semantic and pragmatic markers for their respective object.

PCls supply grammatical information that can be very useful both in natural language communication as well as in natural language processing, e.g. for processing discontinued sentences during turn-taking in dialogue analysis.

In spite of the treated phenomenon's complexity, an efficient implementation of a parser is possible using the LAG formalism. As shown in the algorithm, canceling (filling) of verb valencies (valency slots) is easily solved despite the multitude of possible combinations and the consequently large number of sentence patterns.

Notes

1. For comments on the draft of this paper I would like to thank Jörg Kapfer, Matthias Bethke, and Peter Uhrig (all Friedrich-Alexander-Universität Erlangen-Nürnberg). Only the properties relevant to verb valency and computational modeling will be treated here. For further information on pronominal clitics left out here, see Buchholz (1977), Buchholz and Fiedler (1987), Domi (1995; 1997), Kallulli (1995), and Newmark, Hubbard, and Prifti (1982).
2. Here, the following abbreviations are used: A=Accusative, D=Dative, pCl_{D+A}= Amalgam of pCl_D and pCl_A, Pl=Plural, Sg=Singular, and V=Verb. Forms like *silleni* have alternatives in the form *sillnie*.
3. In subjunctive clauses, pCls are positioned after the subjunctive and future particles and precede the finite verb. In this case the pCl can be combined with these particles in one word, e.g. the amalgam *t'i* consisting of the subjunctive particle *të* and the pCl *i*.
4. Act=Active, Ind=Indicative, Itr=Intransitive, M=Masculine, Nad=Not admirative, N=Nominative, O=Object, Prs=Present, S=Subject, and Tr=Transitive.
5. Aor=Aorist (definite past), and Det=Determined.
6. An exception is the reflexive use of verbs, e.g. *Ai* ***e***$_{\text{(pCl: A)}}$ *lavdëron* ***vetën***$_{\text{(O: A, Reflexive)}}$ ['He (**him**) praised **himself**.', i.e. 'He praised himself.'], vs. *Ai e lavdëron.* ['He (**him**) praised.', i.e. 'He praised him.'].
7. This term is described in Buchholz and Fiedler (1987) as *Vertretung des Objekts* (which might be translated as *object replacement* or *object substitution*).

8. As we focus on the influence of pronominal clitics on verb valency, only direct and indirect objects (without prepositions) are treated here.
9. Undet=Undetermined. Other patterns of the verb *flas*, e.g. pCl(s) + *flas* + preposition, and other meanings not presented in Buchholz, Fiedler, and Uhlisch (1993) are not treated here. For more patterns/meanings cf. Kostallari (1980), where the pattern/meaning from sentence (5b) is marked as a dialect form. Cf. also Qesku (1999). Toçi (2002) does not list this pattern.
10. Buchholz and Fiedler (1987: 445–446) have described a group of verbs which cooccur with „,pleonastisch' verwendete Objektszeichen" ["pleonastically used" pronominal clitics]. These pCls are „nicht ... systematisch aus einem zur Grundstruktur gehörenden dir[ekten] Obj[ekt] ableitbar" [not derived in a systematic way from a direct object belonging to the base structure]. Thus sentences in which only one dative pCl would be expected can have two pCls or an amalgamated one consisting of a dative and an accusative pCl, like for example $Ia_{(\text{pCl: D+A})}$ $hipi_{(\text{V})}$ $kalit_{(\text{O: D})}$. ['He mounted the horse']; in this example the subject is left out. These verbs cooccur only with specific lexical entries (and so they must be marked in the lexicon to be considered during automatic syntactic and semantic analysis). According to Buchholz and Fiedler (1987: 445), this group contains, among others, the following verbs: *arrin, del, fillon, hipën, hyn, kërcen, mbath, merr, nis, pëlcet, shtron,* and *thotë.*

    PCls can also occur as ethical datives, cf. Buchholz and Fiedler (1987: 447–448). In this case, the verb valency must be treated differently as well.
11. For the formal definition of LAG see Hausser (1992; 2001a).
12. The version illustrated here is only a simple LAG. Information about valency in *Database Semantics* (*DBS*) can be found in the article *Handling valency and coordination in database semantics* by R. Hausser in this volume. For information on DBS see Hausser (2001b).
13. During the syntactic analysis both pCls would fill the corresponding attribute in the sentence structure while reading the verb.

References

Buchholz, Oda
1977 *Zur Verdoppelung der Objekte im Albanischen.* Linguistische Studien, Reihe A, Arbeitsberichte 34. Berlin: Akademie der Wissenschaften der DDR.

Buchholz, Oda, and Wilfried Fiedler
1987 *Albanische Grammatik.* Leipzig: VEB.

Buchholz, Oda, Wilfried Fiedler, and Gerda Uhlisch
1993 *Wörterbuch Albanisch–Deutsch.* München: Langenscheidt.

Domi, Mahir (ed.)
1995 *Gramatika e gjuhës shqipe.* Vëllimi I – *Morfologjia* [Grammar of the Albanian Language. Vol. 1: Morphology]. Tiranë: Akademia e Shkencave e Republikës së Shqipërisë.

1997 *Gramatika e gjuhës shqipe*. Vëllimi II – *Sintaksa* [Grammar of the Albanian Language. Vol. 2: Syntax]. Tiranë: Akademia e Shkencave e Republikës së Shqipërisë.

Hausser, Roland
1992 Complexity in left-associative grammar. In *Theoretical Computer Science*. 106 (2): 283–308.
2001a *Foundations of Computational Linguistics. Human-Computer Communication in Natural Language*. 2d ed. Berlin/New York: Springer.
2001b Database semantics for natural language. In *Artificial Intelligence* 130: 27–74.
2007 Handling valency and coordination in database semantics. This volume.

Herbst, Thomas
1999 English valency structures – A first sketch. *Erfurt Electronic Studies in English* (EESE). http://webdoc.gwdg.de/edoc/ia/eese/artic99/herbst/6_99.html.

Herbst, Thomas, David Heath, Ian F. Roe, and Dieter Götz (eds.)
2004 *A Valency Dictionary of English. A Corpus-Based Analysis of the Complementation Patterns of English Verbs, Nouns and Adjectives*. Berlin/New York: Mouton de Gruyter.

Kabashi, Besim
2003 Automatische Wortformerkennung für das Albanische. Master's thesis, Computational Linguistics. Universität Erlangen-Nürnberg.

Kallulli, Dalina
1995 *Clitics in Albanian*. (Working Papers in Linguistics 24.) Trondheim: University of Trondheim.

Kostallari, Androkli (ed.)
1980 *Fjalor i gjuhës së sotme shqipe* [Dictionary of Contemporary Albanian Language]. Tiranë: Akademia e Shkencave e RPS të Shqipërisë.

Newmark, Leonard, Philipp Hubbard, and Peter Prifti
1982 *Standard Albanian. A Reference Grammar for Students*. Stanford: Stanford University Press.

Qesku, Pavli
1999 *Fjalor Shqip–Anglisht. Albanian–English Dictionary*. Tiranë: EDFA.

Toçi, Fatmir (ed.)
2002 *Fjalor i shqipes së sotme* [Dictionary of Contemporary Albanian]. 2d ed. Tiranë: Toena.

The practical use of valencies in the Erlangen speech dialogue system CONALD

Günther Görz and Bernd Ludwig

1. Motivation

Within the broad spectrum of applications of computational linguistics the conversational computer is often regarded as the ultimate challenge: "The conversational computer paradigm provides a way to articulate the properties and challenges of natural language applications and the ways those challenges are being addressed within the field of computational linguistics (Cole et al. 1996)" (Resnik and Klavans 2003: 376).

2. Applications of language understanding

Linguistic computer applications do not just involve language per se, but also interactions between linguistic knowledge and other areas of knowledge. These interactions pose the main challenge for any more or less general approach to natural language understanding: constructing the meaning of a natural language phrase or sentence is guided by different principles than constructing sentences for a formal (artificial) language used for the representation of knowledge in a computing environment. There are two main differences:

2.1. Natural versus formal languages

Formal languages do not encode implicitly semantic relations between parts of a sentence. In contrast, in the natural language example

(1) *I want to watch a thriller tonight.*

grammatical markers (*subject*, *object*, and *attribute/adverbial*) are used to establish relations between the described intention *want to watch*, the agent *I* who has this intention, the TV programme *thriller*, and the indication of a time span (*tonight*) during which the programme should be on air.

In formal languages, such relations are non-ambiguous because each constituent of a sentence serves unambiguously as a functor or argument of another constituent:

```
want-to-see (I, thriller, tonight)
```

This functor-argument-structure defines precisely and unambiguously *tonight* as the time span when *want to see* should take place. This would probably be the standard interpretation for the natural language sentence as well.

However, depending on the content of the sentence, grammatical markers may be insufficient for avoiding ambiguities, as in the example:

(2) *I want to watch the thriller at 8 pm.*

In this sentence, there are no grammatical rules preventing the prepositional phrase *at 8 pm* from being attached to the noun phrase *the thriller*. As a consequence, it depends on the evaluation of both phrases which reading is the correct one. If there was a thriller recorded the day before it could be just the one the user wants to see, not necessarily a thriller broadcast when the utterance is made.

2.2. Context-dependent evaluation

The need to evaluate phrases in order to understand them suggests the execution of algorithms in order to make the evaluation effective. Such algorithms apply the information contained in phrases for input and compute output that is, in its turn, used to determine all the possible interpretations of an utterance and to react appropriately. A consequence of this approach is that the ability to understand an utterance are determined and limited by the ability to process given information with the help of problem-specific algorithms.

As an example, consider an intelligent interface to a TV set that tries to propose programmes to the user that match certain user-defined criteria. A programme is described formally by a filled data structure such as the following:

```
<programmes>
  <IsNowNext/>
  <TransportStreamId>1073</TransportStreamId>
  <OriginalNet-
    workId_ServiceId>93787</OriginalNetworkId_ServiceId>
  <EventId>43932</EventId>
  <StartTime>2005-07-28 12:00:00</StartTime>
  <Duration>00:30:00</Duration>
  <RunningStatus>1</RunningStatus>
  <Pil>238764127</Pil>
  <Title>Eisenbahnromantik</Title>
  <ShortInfo>Im Zug von Bratislava nach Ungarn</ShortInfo>
  <LanguageCode>7693668</LanguageCode>
  <ExtendedInfo>Der "Eisenbahnromantik"-Sonderzug fährt in
   die schöne Slowakei und nach Ungarn. Gefahren wird mit
   Diesel-, Dampf- und elektrischen Zügen. Der erste Teil der
   Reise führt uns über Bratislava, Zvolen, Poprad-Tatry an
   die ungarische Grenze.
  </ExtendedInfo>
  <ExtendedLanguageCode>7693668</ExtendedLanguageCode>
</programmes>
```


In order to evaluate the user query *Are there any documentaries about travelling now?*, three different types of pragmatic evaluation have to be distinguished:

- *documentaries*: look for programmes of this genre!
- *about travelling*: which programmes cover this topic?
- *now*: the programme should be being broadcast at the time of speaking.

Three different algorithms have to be employed for evaluating each of the above types:

- data base lookup to find the right genre,
- analysis of the ExtendedInfo field to find the right content,
- temporal reasoning to find the right time interval.

This is a typical situation complex software systems have to deal with. As a consequence, it is not practicable to rely on a single formal language to cover all types of evaluations. On the other hand, how can one nevertheless implement modules for natural language analysis that can be configured for different applications and therefore be used in contexts with totally different and often unpredictable types of evaluations?

Dialogue systems, e.g. for assisting human users in performing practical tasks, are a typical example of the variety of scenarios and applications just addressed: in cooperation with some technical application – e.g. a database system providing information of some kind – railway timetable, weather, stock market, theatre programmes, etc., a system to order merchandise, a system to control devices – a goal expressed by the user, usually in spoken language, has to be achieved, if possible. If not, the system should be able to explain why and provide further help.

Aside from dialogue systems, there are of course many other applications of computational linguistics such as

- information retrieval ("the Google challenge"),
- automatic machine translation,
- automatic text summarization,

but also

- evaluating linguistic hypotheses, as far as they are fully formalized,
- simulating human language processing,

and many more.

3. Grammar and valencies in natural language understanding

The solution we propose is that any formal representation of natural language within a natural language understanding system must resort to a formal language that is able to represent explicitly what is entailed explicitly and implicitly in a natural language utterance. This language must be sufficiently expressive to cover valencies, (generalized) quantifiers, modifiers, modalities, and coordination operators that are not available in almost every formal (logical) language due to limitations in computability and decidability.

In a second step towards understanding, a statement that represents the semantics of a natural language sentence or utterance has to be translated – by applying evaluation as in the example above, not just syntactical transformations – into an expression of the formal language(s) the underlying computational environment works with.

In this paper, we will focus the discussion on the use of valencies and address only marginally the broader problem of dialogue analysis and generation. For a better understanding of the role of valencies in our work, we first present the general framework and will then point out how valency plays an essential role in its linguistic analysis component.

3.1. The Erlangen dialogue system CONALD

Our research on language understanding is embedded in work on dialogue understanding. It aims at systems for rational dialogues based on a pragmatic approach. So, our overall perspective is that of language as action in which speech acts play a central role. As a consequence, the traditional "computational linguistics pipeline" – syntactic derivation, semantic resolution and inference, and, eventually pragmatic analysis – is turned upside down. Pragmatics gains control in that processing is controlled by a dialogue management module.

CONALD is a spoken language dialogue system which enables interaction between users and a technical system in dynamic environments.[1] The primary goal of its design is to achieve quick configurability for various applications. It combines deep syntactic and semantic analysis, discourse processing, and language generation and features a complex semantics-pragmatics interface in the sense of Brietzmann and Görz (1982). Semantics is defined in terms of an extended version of discourse representation theory (DRT). Discourse and application pragmatics are considered independent; user utterances affect application pragmatics when their speech acts are executed. They can be specified in a script language interpreted by the dialogue manager.

In dynamic environments, changes can be consequences of user requests as well as of external events in the application. The design of our system allows configuration for a wide range of applications (like household applications, the automotive environment, medical purposes, etc.). The user may give commands in natural language by speaking into a microphone.

The parser transforms the user's utterance into a semantic representation, from which the dialogue system derives a goal to change the environment. A plan to achieve this goal is computed and executed by a group of agents. Under the assumption of a closed world, the overall system features hierarchical planning, plan execution, and plan observation by several agents with different responsibilities and capabilities. In this way, system knowledge is distributed and organized hierarchically corresponding to the tasks each agent has to execute.

Agents are organized in a hierarchy of layers. On top there is the Assistance System (see figure 1) which plays the role of an interface between the application and the dialogue system. The main task of the Assistance System is to achieve the user's goals by computing and executing high-level plans.

Negotiation between system and users is handled by a dialogue manager. For user utterances, input from a speech recognizer is processed by a parser resulting in a representation of the meaning of the utterance.

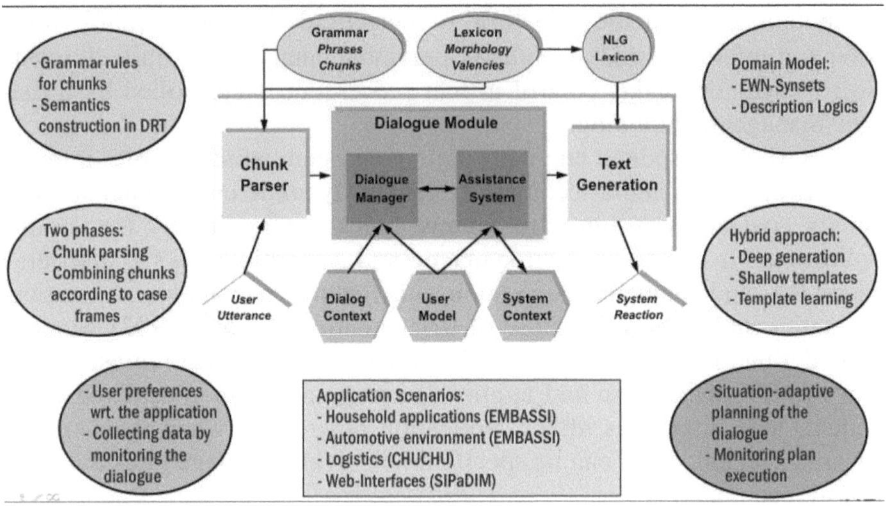

Figure 1. The CONALD system architecture

4. Incremental semantic composition

If we want human-computer dialogues to be natural, we must allow humans to talk to the computer as they do to humans. Spontaneous speech is often incomplete or incorrect, full of interruptions and self-corrections, leading to ungrammatical input to the parser. Additionally, given the error rates of speech recognizers, even with correct input the speech recognizer may produce an output which is not grammatical. Apart from that, parsing German input is difficult, as German is a language with fairly free word order, also allowing for discontinuous constituents. Therefore, the grammar cannot rely only on linear input sequences as its main concept. We try to overcome these problems by the design of a two-phase parsing process (as presented in Bücher, Knorr, and Ludwig 2002).

First, the speech recognizer's output is segmented into chunks (Abney 1991). These have to be translated into constraints for a (partial) description of a system state. For that purpose, an approach motivated by dependency theory is applied: valencies for the syntactic head of each chunk are analyzed if they can serve as the dependent for some other chunk (its regent). Dependent and regent have to meet three classes of criteria in parallel: syntactic constraints, semantic constraints (is the semantic part of the valency satisfied?), pragmatic constraints (can a constraint in the application domain be derived from the triple regent, thematic role, and dependent?). For the example utterance *I want to watch a thriller tonight!* the parser computes the following analysis:

Chunk	*Semantics (informal)*
I want to watch	assistance task
a thriller	object for task
tonight A	time span for task

4.1. Applying case frames to chunks

The three chunks shown above are connected by semantic relations which have to be identified during the second phase of the parsing process. It relies on a kind of dependency grammar which for each chunk of phase 1 gives a list of possible syntactic functions the chunk may have:

	C1 has *C2*	→	<synfunc>
	<constraint equation>		
example:	*VP* has *PP*	→	adverbial
	NP has *PP*	→	attribute
	VP has *NP*	→	subject
	NP agr case = nom,		
	NP agr num = *VP* agr num.		

The options are constrained by the morphological features of the chunk, e.g. an NP-chunk functions as subject only if it is in the nominative case.

For each chunk there is a case frame for its semantic head that stores information about the valencies.[2] The valencies of each chunk are filled by combining it with other chunks, e.g. building a VP from a verb and an NP that functions as its direct object, or expanding a VP by an adverb. The suitability of the combination of two chunks is determined by the semantic constraints of the application ontology. Take the case frame for *sehen*:

infinitive: *sehen*

syntactic function	thematic role	EWN concept
subject	involved-agent:	Person1
adverbial	involved-timespan:	TimeInterval1

From the case frame we derive hypotheses about possible fillers of a complement position of a chunk using the syntactic functions. Whether a hypothesis is satisfiable is determined by the concepts of the chunks. If they fit, the DRS can be computed.

In our example, the VP *want to see* can be combined with the NP *a thriller* and the adverbial *tonight* since in the case frame of *sehen* there are valencies allowing semantic relations to be established.

5. Building a case frame database

We use our approach to semantics construction in different applications. As a consequence, we have gathered a huge amount of semantic definitions (i.e. taxonomic chains) and case frames (i.e. thematic roles) defined by these applications. Some of these data are specific to a given application, whereas others are used by several applications. This created the need for a tool that enables efficient storage and easy and fast access and that prepares the data required by the parser.

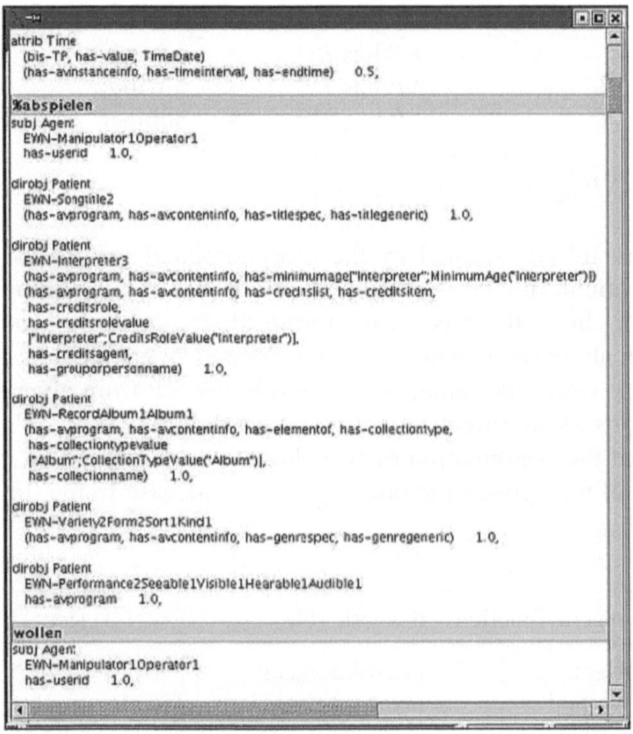

Figure 2. A screenshot of the valency editor

For this purpose, we have developed a lexicon tool that permits the editing of semantic data, checks their coherence according to the algorithm presented in section 4, and visualizes them as well (see figure 2). The tool depends on the following resources as a basis for its data:

- the EuroWordNet (EWN) ontology,
- the SUMO ontology (a generic reference ontology), and
- semantic lexica.

In this respect, it is worth highlighting the differences between our frame data base and FrameNet (Baker, Fillmore, and Lowe 1998). FrameNet is an online lexical resource for English based on the principles of frame semantics and supported by corpus evidence.[3] It can serve as a dictionary, for it includes definitions and grammatical functions of the entries. And hence entries are linked to the semantic frames in which they participate, FrameNet can serve as a thesaurus as well.

However, the information provided by FrameNet is not sufficiently formalized to be directly applicable within our system; in other words, it is not possible to use FrameNet to parse utterances directed to the system or to construct semantic representations for them. So, from a practical point of view, what we need is a formal specification for the information represented in FrameNet and which, on the one hand, can directly be encoded in Description Logic (which is the logical framework we use), and on the other hand, can be used with an efficient inference mechanism.

Another difference is that the current FrameNet is basically constructed for the English language and hence can be used only in systems based on English. Since our application is multilingual, our representation scheme is based on the ILI-representation of EWN, which makes our tool language independent.

6. Conclusions

To conclude, there are some points discussed in other contributions in this volume which are important to our work:

- first of all, *data-orientation* in general, which by the way is common in the speech recognition community, and in connection with that,
- the importance of *storage* of patterns in the lexicon, (which is, among other properties, a prerequisite for what in Artificial Intelligence is called *case-based reasoning*), and is perfectly compatible with the lexicalist character of our grammar,
- an emphasis on *pragmatics* and *context*, i.e., in our case, the conceptual domain model, the discourse context maintained in the dialogue man-

ager, and the situation context represented in the application system providing the key to disambiguation.

Furthermore, the success of any application system depends crucially on the availability of appropriate and comprehensive linguistic resources. Although this sounds trivial, the actual situation we face – at least for German – is not that easy.

It may improve within one or two years with the availability of a new generation of resources like GlobalWordNet and German FrameNet. In the long run, we would like to have access to a powerful valency lexicon database – in particular considering that multilinguality is of increasing importance – for the technical aspects of which we can give some advice from the viewpoint of computer science:

- As far as the formal representation of the lexicon is concerned, the expressivity of the language is of extreme importance. By that, we do not want to emphasize encoding in some XML language – which is state of the art – but rather its expressivity in logical terms, i.e. whether it can express conjunction, disjunction, negation, quantification, subsumption and inheritance, and whether it provides means to express non-monotonic notions like defaults, a notion which lies beyond standard first-order logic. And we must be aware that in a real, i.e. empirically based lexicon, we will be confronted with inconsistency, and we will have to deal with it.
- A minor, but nevertheless important issue is the interface, i.e., what is the expressitivity of the query language? And, furthermore: is access strictly sequential or is it possible to have parallel access?

Notes

1. Acknowledgment: Our work is supported by the Bavarian Research Association FORSIP. We would like to thank the current and former members of our research group for their contributions: Kerstin Bücher, Martin Klarner, Yuliya Lierler, Peter Reiss, Bernhard Schiemann, and Iman Thabet.
2. The term *case* is used as it is by Fillmore (1968) meaning thematic roles. The term *valency* is used here in a broader sense: it includes not only obligatory elements needed to make a phrase syntactically complete; more than that, the case frames list all semantically and pragmatically suitable modifications and their syntactic representations, e.g. attributes for nouns or adverbials for verbs.
3. http://www.icsi.berkeley.edu/framenet/.

References

Abney, Steven
1991 Parsing by chunks. In *Principle-based Parsing,* Robert Berwick, Steven Abney, and Carol Tenny (eds.), 257–278. Kluwer: Dordrecht.

Baker, Collin F., Charles J. Fillmore, and John B. Lowe
1998 The Berkeley FrameNet project. In *Proceedings of the COLING-ACL 1998*, 86–90. Montreal.

Brietzmann, Astrid, and Günther Görz
1982 Pragmatics in speech understanding – revisited. In *Proceedings of the Ninth International Conference on Computational Linguistics*, Ján Horecký (ed.), 49–54. Amsterdam: North-Holland.

Bücher, Kerstin, Michael Knorr, and Bernd Ludwig
2002 Anything to clarify? Report your parsing ambiguities! In *Proceedings of the 15th European Conference on Artificial Intelligence*, Frank van Harmelen (ed.), 465–469. Lyon.

Cole, Ronald A., Joseph Mariani, Hans Uszkoreit, Annie Zaenen, and Victor Zue (eds.)
1996 *Survey of the State of the Art in Human Language Technology*. New York: Cambridge University Press.

Fillmore, Charles J.
1968 The case for case. In *Universals in Linguistic Theory*, Emmon Bach, and Robert T. Harms (eds.), 1–88. New York: Holt, Rinehart, and Winston.

Resnik, Philip, and Judith L. Klavans
2003 Applications of language technology. In *International Encyclopedia of Linguistics*, 2d ed. Vol. 2. William J. Frawley (ed.), 376–377. Oxford: Oxford University Press.

Valency data for Natural Language Processing: What can the *Valency Dictionary of English* provide?

Ulrich Heid

1. Introduction

1.1. Objectives of this paper

This paper addresses two questions: a specific one and a more general one. The specific question could be phrased as follows: "*A Valency Dictionary of English* (VDE, Herbst et al. 2004) is available in a printed form and in the underlying electronic format. Could this dictionary be of use for Natural Language Processing (NLP)?" In trying to give an answer to this specific question, one is confronted with a second, more general issue: "What are requirements with respect to a valency dictionary for NLP and which data, which representation and which degree of detail are expected?"

We will try to briefly address both issues, starting with the more general one. Our views on NLP valency dictionaries will be influenced by the grammatical theory of Lexical Functional Grammar (LFG, Bresnan 1982a), as will be the answer to the specific question: we report in fact about an experiment in which an attempt was made to convert data from an early version of the VDE (July 2004) into the form and format of LFG and to use the result as a valency dictionary for an existing English LFG grammar. This experiment was assessed by means of an automatic analysis of the 25,000 example sentences contained in the VDE.[1]

1.2. Valency data in Natural Language Processing

All current symbolic approaches to syntactic analysis in Natural Language Processing (henceforth: NLP) rely on valency data; and in addition, many hybrid systems, which combine symbolic and statistical processing, do so in one way or another as well.

Valency (often called subcategorization in NLP work) is understood, here, as syntactic complementation, possibly related to predicate-argument structures. Thus, a predicate (a verb, adjective or noun) is described with respect to its capacity to have arguments, and in particular with respect to the syntactic form by which these are realized in sentences. To describe the behaviour of the verb [*to*] *substitute*, as used in *they substituted bricks for the expensive granite stone*, the fact will be mentioned that a subject and two complements show up in the syntactic environment of this verb.

NLP-oriented grammatical theories and the respective coding formalisms for lexical knowledge diverge considerably as to the details of valency description. However, they are unanimous in suggesting that the lexical description of predicates should go hand in hand with a grammatical rule that allows a system to derive a (syntactic and/or semantic) representation of a sentence which singles out the predicate and its arguments. These basic assumptions are true, irrespective of whether the representation follows rather a line of constituent structure[2] or of predicate-argument structure (such as LFG's F-structures), or whether it is inspired by dependency structures (cf. Tesnière 1959; Mel'čuk 1988).

A third component of valency-based implementations, besides lexical entries and grammatical rules, is a constraint system, which checks that only sentences are accepted (or generated) which contain all obligatory arguments of the predicate in question, and only these.[3] More details about approaches to valency in NLP can be found in the article by Roland Hausser in this volume.

2. Elements of an expectation horizon for a valency dictionary for NLP

In this section, a few NLP-related requirements for the lexicographic description of valency properties of words will be formulated. Starting from the current state of the art, we address needs with respect to the predicates and to a few specific valency phenomena to be covered; we also discuss the representation of valency data in the lexicon and preferences related to certain valency phenomena.

2.1. Types of predicates

In line with Tesnière's notion, the common understanding of linguists, lexicographers and NLP resource developers is that certain types of predicates are to be considered as valency-bearers. These include verbs, adjectives (as in [1]) and (mostly derived) nouns (cf. [2]).

(1) *He is proud of this exceptional success.*
(2) *John's proposal to postpone the meeting was accepted.*

For several languages, it has been observed that some (especially verbal) predicates can be "multiword expressions", i.e. composed of several lexemes. This is true of certain multiword idiomatic expressions such as German *in der Lage sein* ('be able to'), as in (3). Unless we consider *in der Lage sein* as a multiword predicate, it is hard to see how to assign it or its components a valency description. The expression requires a prepositional phrase with *zu* (or a pronominal adverb, *dazu*) or an infinitival with *zu*, cf. (4).

(3)	*Hans ist*	*in der Lage*	*die Aufgabe zu lösen.*
	Hans is	in the position	the task to do
	'Hans is able to do the task'		
(4)	*Hans ist zu allem in der Lage.*		
	Hans ist dazu in der Lage.		
	**Hans ist in der Lage.*		

Some multiwords which lexicography and linguistics would rather classify as collocations (and not as idiomatic expressions) seem equally to have subcategorized complements as a whole. German examples include *in Erfahrung bringen* ('understand'), *in Rechnung stellen* ('take into account') or *zu Papier bringen* ('write down'), which all can have an object clause (introduced by *daß* or by a *wh*-word), even though a sentential complement is restricted with the noun *Erfahrung* (no *wh*-clause) and impossible with *Rechnung* and *Papier*. If one counts the potential to take a subject clause (again with *daß* or *wh-*) among the valency properties of a predicate, German collocations like *zum Ausdruck kommen* ('be expressed'), *in Vergessenheit geraten* ('fall into oblivion'), *zum Vorschein kommen* ('appear') may be added to the inventory of multiword expressions with predicate character. It seems that little is known, at least for German, but also to some extent for English, about such phenomena; but we suggest for them an NLP treatment as valency-bearing predicates, simply because they would otherwise block automatic analysis.

2.2. Levels of linguistic description in a valency dictionary

Valency phenomena are often seen as concerning the interface between semantics and syntax. They involve argument structure (and thus the semantic description of the predicates) and at the same time the syntactic insertion of predicates into sentences. There is no agreement, however, as to whether this implies that lexical description and representation have to make explicit reference to both levels of description, syntax and semantics. Some approaches would tend to predict syntactic properties from a semantic description, others restrict themselves to a syntactic description, yet others cover both levels explicitly.

Many NLP grammars and lexicons mainly use descriptive devices pertaining to constituent structure. This is true of HPSG and of Tree-Adjoining Grammar. Another example is work on French in the framework of lexicon grammar (cf. Gross 1975), which uses abbreviations for noun phrases (N) and indexes as well as positional coding to indicate grammatical functions, as illustrated in (5):

(5) a. N_0 donner N_1 à N_2
b. *Jean donne la clef à son amie.*
'Jean gives the key to his girlfriend.'

Lexical Functional Grammar (LFG, Bresnan 1982a) is characterized by the use of two interrelated representations of sentences, one at the level of constituency (C-structure) and one at the level of predicate-argument structures (F-structures). LFG's lexical description makes reference to F-Structures: valency descriptions in lexical entries involve grammatical functions (subject, object, indirect object, etc.) and a notation which ensures a mapping to logic-like predicate-argument structures (cf. Zaenen 1988). In the grammar, a mapping between grammatical functions and grammatical categories is defined. An LFG entry for *donner* equivalent to (5) above, is given in (6) below:[4]

(6) donner, V:
(↑ PRED) = "donner<(↑ SUBJ)(↑ OBJ)(↑ INDIRECT-OBJ)>"

One of the most detailed and most explicit recent approaches to the lexical description of argument structure and valency is that of Frame Semantics (Baker, Fillmore, and Cronin 2003; Petruck 1996). It involves descriptive devices from three layers, namely constituents (NP, PP, etc.), grammatical functions (Ext[ernal argument], Obj[ect], Dep[endent]) and semantic roles ('frame elements' in Frame Semantics). In (7), we show an extract from FrameNet's valency tables[5], for a reading of the English verb [*to*] *substitute*, as exemplified in (8).

(7)

Agent	***New***	***Old***
CNI	NP	PP[for]
--	Ext	Dep
NP	NP	PP[for]
Ext	Obj	Dep

(8) a. *A young lady now substitutes for our former head of department.*
b. *They substituted bricks for the expensive granite stone.*

FrameNet's valency representation is attractive for NLP dictionaries, because it is rather explicit, remains close to observable phenomena and does not assume knowledge about correspondences between the three layers, which would otherwise need to be coded outside the dictionary.[6]

Because of these properties, FrameNet valency tables can also be used for the encoding of exceptions, of valency variation (e.g. *that*-clause vs. infinitive vs. noun phrase), for the comparison of near synonyms and morphologically related items (which would share frame elements, cf. *substitute* vs. *replace*, *read* vs. *readable*), or for relating single verb entries and entries for multiword predicates which are semantically close to each other. (9) is an example of the latter (cf. also Ruppenhofer, Baker, and Fillmore 2004). In our view, the three-layered representation is particularly flexible and particularly interesting for NLP.

(9) a. *John proposed to postpone the meeting.*
b. *John made the proposal to postpone the meeting.*
c.

predicates↓ / roles→	SPEAKER	MESSAGE
propose	SUBJ / NP	COMP / *to*-inf
make + proposal	SUBJ / NP	COMP / *to*-inf

2.3. Phenomena to be captured in an electronic valency dictionary

Above, in section 2.1, the needs of NLP in terms of predicate types were addressed; we now turn to complementation types and to the coocurrence of complementation types with other lexical properties.

2.3.1. Complementation phenomena

There is a huge literature on complementation facts to be covered by valency dictionaries, and we do not aim, in this section, to repeat the elements of the "standard" inventory. We only wish to point to a small number of facts which sometimes are not covered by dictionaries, and which merit treatment. We understand the following list as a proposal for additions to the usual typologies.

LFG's complementation theory includes a theory of control (cf. Bresnan 1982b) which predicts the subject of dependent infinitives. Some predicates seem not to fall under any predictable generalizations, and thus LFG dictionary entries typically include statements about the subject of the infinitive (cf. *promise* vs. *command* vs. *propose*). This proves vital for syntactic and semantic analysis.

Other phenomena which are sometimes not treated in sufficient detail are subcategorized adverbials (VDE has *she acted strangely*), subject and object predicatives and details on NP complements which are not objects. The latter include for example measure phrases (*the sessions lasted six hours*), complements of verbs like German *enthalten*, *erhalten*, *verlieren* ('contain', 'get', 'lose') and idiosyncratic cases like that of the German verb *halten* (*von jmdm/etwas* 'to have an opinion about sb/sth'), which requires a quantifying noun phrase as a complement, but a lexically very restricted one (*er hält viel/wenig/nichts/eine Menge von ihr*, 'he thinks a lot of her / does not think much of her').

From an NLP perspective, it would be useful if valency dictionaries could address such phenomena.

2.3.2. Contextual preferences related to valency

We know rather little, so far, about contextual preferences related to valency properties of predicates, i.e. about conditions under which certain, possibly exchangeable, valency patterns are particulary likely. These include the interaction with collocations, i.e. the fact that alternative valency constructions of a given verb are unevenly distributed across certain nouns which appear frequently as complements of this verb. Klotz (2000) has numerous examples of this phenomenon, and in table 1 we summarize a few of his findings (Klotz 2000: 178–179) for the verb [*to*] *ask*:

Table 1. Distribution of alternative valency structures of *ask* across certain nouns

Pattern			***favour***	***permission***	***asylum***
ask	sbdy	sth	+	??	??
ask	sbdy	for sth	+	+	+
ask	sth	from sbdy	??	+	??
ask	sth	of sbdy	+	??	??

On the basis of work towards VDE, Klotz has shown the use of corpus data for the identification of such preferences. According to this data,[7] many examples show up for the combinations marked with "+", and very few or none for those marked with "??". This knowledge is central for language generation and equally useful to guide expectations in the analysis of textual data.

Other preferences concern the cooccurrence of certain subcategorization patterns with certain tense and/or modalization forms (e.g. the possibility or not of dependent *wh*-interrogatives) or the position of German subject clauses with adjectives (cf. Heid and Kermes 2002). In fact, a subject clause of a German adjective may either be topicalized, as in (10a) or extraposed (10b):

(10) a. *Daß er kommt ist klar* ('that he is coming is clear')
b. *Es ist klar, daß er kommt* ('it is clear that he is coming)

(11) *Ob er kommt, ist unsicher/unklar/zweifelhaft*
('whether he is coming is unclear ...')

Across large amounts of German newspaper text, extraposed cases come out as more frequent than topicalized ones, if counted over all adjectives. However, certain classes of adjectives (e.g. *unklar, unsicher, zweifelhaft,* etc., 'unclear', 'unsure', 'doubtful') show clear preferences for topicalization of their subject indirect question clauses (cf. 11). This seems to have to do with their semantics, or it is explainable through the relationship between their semantics and information structure under topicalization; but for language learners (and obviously for NLP programs such as text generation), an explicit indication in the dictionary would be preferable.

2.4. Regularity and idiomaticity in valency descriptions

Some of the phenomena discussed in this section could be classified as subregularities, or as effects of idiomatization. Some of them are preferential in nature, rather than absolute. And they constitute contextual parameters of the valency description, which may be identified in large text corpora, at least as tendencies.

To our knowledge, these phenomena have not yet been studied in much detail, nor in large quantities, which is why dictionaries only sporadically mention them.

For NLP applications, and specifically for the analysis of large amounts of text and for natural language generation, it would however be desirable if valency dictionaries covered the phenomena we touched upon in this section. More generally, it seems that a large part of the regularity in valency behaviour of lexical items has been analyzed and described, at least for the major languages. But the domain of idiomaticity, or of local subregularities, needs to be explored in more depth and breadth, because it closely interacts with valency. In this sense, part of the present expectation horizon may seem ambitious, or it may be rather a work programme for the future.[8]

3. Comparing VDE and an English LFG grammar and lexicon

In this section, we will address the question whether the new *Valency Dictionary of English* (Herbst et al. 2004, VDE) could be used in Natural Language Processing. We use the expectation horizon discussed in section 2 in order to assess this, first in a broad quantitative form, then in qualitative terms. This assessment is the result of work by Spohr (2004), to which we add a few comments motivated by later work on an internal version of the VDE. The VDE itself is presented and discussed in articles by Herbst, Götz, Götz-Votteler and Klotz in this volume.

3.1. An experiment into dictionary reuse

The authors of the VDE kindly provided us, in spring 2004, with a prefinal marked-up WORD version of the full text of the VDE, along with explanations of its macro- and microstructure, its abbreviatory conventions etc.[9] Dennis Spohr then embarked on an experiment the objective of which was to feed an NLP grammar of English with data from the VDE. We used an

LFG grammar of English from PARC (Palo Alto Research Centre, version of 21.07.2004), designed using the Xerox Linguistic Environment, XLE, a platform and tool for parsing and generation developed from the *LFG Grammar Writer's Workbench* (cf. Maxwell and Kaplan 1996).[10]

The grammar and its lexicon are part of the multilingual Pargram project, the aim of which is to provide broad coverage NLP grammars and lexicons for several languages.[11] The PARC grammar of English comes with its own lexicon of verbal subcategorization. We wanted to check how the grammar performed, if we substituted the VDE for the existing PARC lexicon. To assess the results, automatic syntactic analyses of the example sentences of the VDE were produced. VDE contains over 25,000 example sentences, and we tested the performance of the grammar on this corpus if using the VDE lexicon, compared to the grammar with its existing lexicon. This test would allow us to use a substantial amount of VDE data in syntactic analysis, and to thoroughly assess the VDE against an NLP-oriented expectation horizon. A similar experiment has been reported on, for Danish, by Asmussen and Ørsnes (2005).

In order to be combinable with the NLP grammar, the marked-up WORD file of VDE was first metalexicographically analyzed and transformed into an XML representation. From there, a semi-automatic mapping into LFG-style lexical entries (cf. example [6] above) was performed (in fact into instances of templates which encode subcategorization patterns). The mapping from the printed-style dictionary to an XML version was not a trivial one, as the VDE makes use, among other things, of lexicographic text condensation devices: for example, in the notation of alternative valency patterns, the scope of the alternation symbol is not always automatically derivable; the string "*about wh-CL/wh to-INF*" needs to be translated into "*about wh-CL* OR *about wh to-INF*": in this example the "OR"-symbol groups a single-string expression (*wh-CL*) and a two-string expression (*wh to-INF*), which makes an automatic expansion less easy. Similarly, open lists of lexical constraints (e.g. a complement lexicalizable as *something/little/what* etc.) or approximative preference statements (*usually, normally, often*) cause difficulties in the mapping.

A by-product of this two-step procedure is a version of the (prefinal) VDE represented in XML, according to the CONCEDE DTD[12] (cf. Spohr 2004: 53–55). A major innovation of this XML version of the VDE over the original is the fact that it contains explicit links between VDE's descriptive indications (valency indications, verb senses, etc.) and its example sentences. Being able to relate example sentences with readings, and specific lexicographic indications with examples that illustrate them, contributes to a clearer addressing structure and to a richer microstructure. In an electronic dictionary, ideally all indications should be illustrated with example sentences. VDE has gone a long way along these lines, and the XML version completes VDE's intentions also on formal grounds, linking explicitly most of the 25.000 examples.[13]

More generally, for computational linguistics and knowledge representation (or knowledge processing), one would dream of many more links between the descriptive elements of the VDE entries. Patterns, subcategorization types, senses, semantic roles: all of these could ideally be part of a two-layered network-like structure. One layer would serve to describe and to (formally) constrain the descriptive vocabulary (the "attributes" and "value names" used by the lexicographers, and their interrelationships). The other layer would contain the actual entries, their links and relations among each other, and their links with the definitional layer.

We have worked out a prototype of such a structure for a collocations dictionary (cf. Heid and Gouws 2006; Spohr and Heid 2006) and it allows for interesting new kinds of queries, including ad-hoc queries not based on a particular entry (e.g. "give me all entries having a combination of properties x and y"). We think that a major task for both NLP and human-use lexicography of the coming years is to turn list-like dictionaries into network-like ones, by adding explicit relational data. VDE seems to have the ingredients to undergo such a transformation, even though this would still require some additional work.

3.2. Experimental results: Using the VDE for parsing

As mentioned above, the 25,000 example sentences of VDE were used as a test corpus, parsed with the existing PARC lexicon and grammar of English, and then with the VDE and an appropriately adapted grammar. The overall quantitative result shows a positive effect of VDE, but it does not look extraordinary at first sight. If the old PARC grammar produced at least one analysis for 78.5% of the sentences, the new grammar-cum-VDE goes up to 83.5% (Spohr 2004: 42): an increase in coverage by 5%. What is counted here is the number of sentences which receive at least one analysis (likely several analyses). This figure is indeed correlated with the quality of the subcategorization dictionary, because sentences for which there is no subcategorization entry available do not get any complete analysis, but at most a partial one.

A second, perhaps even more relevant figure concerns those sentences which got no analysis with the PARC grammar (over 4,500 sentences). An improvement through the use of VDE is visible here, since 27.59% of these do in fact receive an analysis if the VDE dictionary data are used.

Reasons why still a substantial portion of VDE's example sentences do not receive an analysis include, among others, the properties of these example sentences themselves: in fact, many of them are quite long (40 words not being exceptional) and rather complex; most of them have been taken from the *Bank of English* corpus, and they display the typical complexity of published written English. Other sentences are in fact dialogues: the grammar does not assign one common analysis to a sequence of turns but one per turn, while still counting, for the purpose of the quality assessment, the dialogue as one (failed) analysis task. In this sense, the above figures can be seen as the lower bound of the outcome of our experiment.

In conclusion, we have shown that VDE could indeed serve as a valency dictionary for a formal grammar, as its use leads to an acceptable syntactic analysis coverage of its own example sentences.[14] VDE is rich enough to provide good quality analyses, and it is richer than one of the most detailed NLP grammars and lexicons of English available, PARC's English LFG grammar and lexicon.

3.3. Learning from the experiment: A phenomenological comparison between VDE and Lexical Functional Grammar

Coming back to the expectation horizon discussed in section 2, we will now comment on parallelisms and differences between VDE and LFG. We do so by addressing in turn the treatment units covered, the levels of description available and the valency phenomena and preferences addressed in both resources.

Treatment units. The VDE covers nouns, verbs and adjectives; NLP systems need valency information for all three of these word classes, and only the most recent printed valency dictionaries, such as VDE or VALBU (Schumacher et al. 2004), go beyond verbs. VDE is much more detailed and complete than the version of LFG we used, as far as idioms and collocations and their valency properties are concerned. It provides a substantial number of entries for such items; the current LFG grammar, on the other hand, does not contain rules to analyze all of them. This problem is both a theoretical and a practical one, as the grammatical analysis of idioms is still a difficult task for NLP systems (cf. Sag et al. 2002). Thus, not all of VDE's entries for multiwords could be transformed into LFG.

Levels of description. VDE and LFG diverge as far as the level of linguistic description is concerned at which valency patterns or subcategorization frames are formulated: VDE uses grammatical categories (NP, AP, PP, etc.) and LFG uses grammatical functions. Consequently, the mapping from VDE to LFG was not an automatic one, as it required linguistic knowledge not explicit in VDE. More precisely, VDE is in some places underspecified with respect to the requirements of LFG, while at the same time being more specific on a few particular phenomena.

A lack of specificity is encountered, for example, with respect to LFG's treatment of complements of three-place verbs. While LFG distinguishes the grammatical functions "Object" and "Object2" (or: direct vs. indirect object), our (preliminary) version of VDE had a distinction between passivizable and non-passivizable NP complements, which is good for distinguishing "Objects" from other NP complements, but does not help, for example, to distinguish the two complements of *give* which are both passivizable. Similarly, non-passivizable NPs needed to be further split into predicative ones (*he died a rich man*) as opposed to nominal obliques (*to ski Tahoe; the balloon lost air*, etc.).

On the other hand, distinctions from VDE in the domain of sentential complements would merit being expressed in LFG grammars, too: for example, VDE distinguishes between *that*-complements, *wh*-complements and direct speech. English verbs seem (as German ones) to have specific requirements as to which of these they allow. This distinction is relevant in sentence generation and in (machine) translation; current LFG grammars tend to map all these complements to a grammatical function "COMP(lement)" (or to a sentential "OBJect"), which is underspecified with respect to constituency. The same holds for finite vs. infinite indirect questions (*they discussed who should do it* vs. *they discussed about how to do it*). Finally, the PARC grammar did not capture, before our experiments, passivizable prepositional objects (*freedom was marched for*).

In general, taking into account both grammatical functions and grammatical categories seems to be an ideal way of modeling valency patterns for NLP, in terms of detail and precision. However, such an approach would lead also to redundancy wherever it explicitly states twice what could be predicted from one level of description and from general principles.

VDE includes a semantic description in terms of semantic roles, at least for a considerable number of items. A general use of this device in all entries, in addition to grammatical categories and grammatical functions, would bring the valency description close to that of *FrameNet* (Baker, Fillmore, and Cronin 2003). The advantages of such a three-way description have been discussed above in section 2.2.

Valency phenomena covered. Above, in section 2.3, we mentioned a few facts of complementation which need to be described in an NLP dictionary. VDE has an excellent treatment of subcategorized adverbials (*she acted strangely* etc.) and of passivizability (cf. *freedom was marched for*). In both cases, VDE descriptions are much more fine-grained than the analyses available in the original LFG grammar and lexicon. Consequently, the grammar was enhanced to capture these phenomena.

A similar case was observed with verbs taking complex (i.e. multiword) prepositions; the authors of VDE consider, for example, the preposititional phrase *in favour of X* as subcategorized by the verb [*to*] *argue*, whereas the assumption in the original LFG grammar was that multiword prepositions would never be subcategorized. Here, clearly VDE throws up phenomena which have been overlooked in the PARC resources.

In the domain of control, VDE is less fine-grained than expected by LFG. In fact, the distinction between subject control and non-subject control in three-place verbs (*persuade* vs. *promise*) is not present in the version of VDE we analyzed.

Lexical and contextual constraints on valency. Being based on corpus evidence, VDE contains a substantial amount of data showing preferences or constraints attached to valency properties of predicates. In our experiments, quantification phrases (with predicates of duration, weight, length etc.) provided an example of the richness of such constraints, but also of the difficulty of capturing them in a formal way. VDE uses a subclassification of these measure phrases which is far more fine-grained than that of LFG, distinguishing, for example, quantifying NPs (of the kind [*to*] *weigh 50 lbs*, [*to*] *last 30 years*) from NPs without explicit quantification ([*to*] *last a lifetime*). For many predicates, the full range of possibilities is not fully explored. We think that further semi-automatic data extraction work, on the basis of very large corpora, is needed here to complete the picture.

4. Making a good thing even better

The experiment described in the previous section clearly shows that the VDE could indeed serve as a starting point for a detailed large-scale NLP dictionary of English valency.

Even if we could not document, in this paper, a comparison with COMLEX,[15] it seems that the entries of VDE contain more detail than those of COMLEX: multiword predicates, subcategorized adverbials, subcategorized quantifying phrases, to name but a few. VDE shares some properties with FrameNet (e.g. the use of semantic roles in some entries), but it differs from FrameNet in that it does not address the semantic aspects of valency in the same detail and coverage, and – obviously – in terms of the coverage of the vocabulary: as FrameNet is being created according to a framewise procedure, some high frequency items may be absent from FrameNet which are dealt with in the VDE.

In addition, we see VDE as a source of lexical information which lends itself easily to a systematic exploration of valency-related phenomena, such as variation in valency patterns, interrelationships between collocations and valency, etc. A fully formalized representation of VDE, perhaps one which would take Spohr's (2004) DTD or a similar modeling as a starting point, would allow to turn VDE into a network-like data source which could be explored in many and quite flexible ways.

Finally, to further improve on the side of contextual preferences, one could imagine using the VDE as a starting point for specialized corpus exploration. To this end, substantial amounts of illustrative examples for a given valency pattern would need to be collected and grouped. For example, the actual form and distribution of quantifying complements (cf. [*to*] *last 50 years*, [*to*] *last a lifetime*) could in this way be approximated, or subcategorized adverbials could be listed. Obviously, this would not alleviate the problem of how to generalize from the observed corpus data, but the mere fact of having quantifiable data on such phenomena available would already be an advantage. In a similar way, one could envisage providing corpus frequency data for the different valency patterns a predicate can have. Approximative data of this kind (in fact probabilities) have been provided, for example, by Schulte im Walde (2002), and a more fine-grained version could be the result of VDE-based corpus analysis.

Procedures to extract examples of valency patterns from text have been discussed in the NLP community for almost 20 years (see the overview by Schulte im Walde forthcoming), mostly with the objective to automatically learn verb subcategorization. Having VDE as a starting point, details about preferences, about frequency distributions etc. seem to be within reach. Instead of having to identify both at a time, valency patterns and the lexical and contextual properties associated with them, one could concentrate on the latter and include such contextual data, for example, in an electronic version of VDE.

In conclusion, VDE shows considerable affinity with NLP, even though it was not conceived with the use by automatic systems in mind. But the presence of a clear descriptive programme, its richness in details and its reproducible internal structure contribute to its multifunctionality.

Notes

1. The experiments were carried out by Dennis Spohr (cf. Spohr 2004), and the author should like to thank him in particular for making the results of his work available. All errors and inconsistencies in the present article are of the responsibility of the author.
2. As for example in Head-driven Phrase Structure Grammar (HPSG, cf. Pollard and Sag 1994), Tree-Adjoining Grammar (cf. Joshi 1985) or in C-structures of Lexical Functional Grammar (LFG).
3. Obviously, this leaves space for adjuncts (or: modifiers), but it raises the issue of handling optional arguments; typically, optionality gives rise to the disjunctive formulation of two or more (sub-)entries.
4. Uparrows are variables for the insertion of the entry into a grammar.
5. The top line of the table contains names of frame elements; each valency indication occupies two lines, one where phrase types are indicated and a functional one. The abbreviation CNI stands for 'contextual null instantiation'.
6. On the contrary, Spohr et al. (2007) have shown that valency descriptions can be derived from corpus data annotated with Frame Semantics roles, grammatical functions and phrase types: the interrelationships between the three layers then come out as preferred cooccurrences between facts from these layers, and variation can be captured without any extra effort.
7. Material from the Bank of English, cf. (as of 22.02.2007): http://www.cobuild.collins.co.uk
8. Part of the author's own ongoing work is devoted, among others, to the development of methods for identifying contextual parameters along with the extraction of data from corpus text; cf. the project B3 in the framework of the DFG-funded Special Research Centre SFB-732, URL (02.03.2007): http://www.uni-stuttgart.de/linguistik/sfb732/
9. We should like to thank Thomas Herbst and Dieter Götz, as well as all of their team for making the VDE available to us in a prefinal WORD version. Only this cooperation allowed us to assess the data in detail.
10. XLE and the grammar are property of Xerox and PARC; IMS Stuttgart has used both under academic usage licenses.
11. The languages include English, German, French, Norwegian, Korean, Japanese, Urdu, which all use parallel LFG-based methodology (cf. the URL (as of 22.02.2007): http://www2.parc.com/istl/groups/nltt/pargram/).
12. The CONCEDE project (Erjavec et al. 2003) provides a DTD into which the project transformed monolingual definition dictionaries. Spohr's version of the VDE DTD is extended with respect to the standard CONCEDE DTD.
13. An implicit link is obviously provided in the text version of VDE anyway, the XML version just makes it explicit.
14. One could have made more tests, e.g. with parts of the BNC. As this would have required filtering BNC data (to select relevant sentences), such a test would have gone beyond the experimental setup used here.
15. http://nlp.cs.nyu.edu/comlex/index.html

References

Asmussen, Jørg, and Bjarne Ørsnes
2005 Valency information for dictionaries and NLP lexicons: "Adapting valency frames from The Danish Dictionary to an LFG lexicon". In *Papers in Computational Lexicography COMPLEX 2005*, Ferenc Kiefer, Gábor Kiss, and Júlia Pajzs (eds.), 28–39. Budapest: Linguistic Institute, Hungarian Academy of Sciences.

Baker, Collin F., Charles J. Fillmore, and Beau Cronin
2003 The structure of the FrameNet Database. *International Journal of Lexicography* 16: 281–296.

Bresnan, Joan (ed.)
1982a *The Mental Representation of Grammatical Relations.* Cambridge, MA.: The MIT Press.

Bresnan, Joan
1982b Control and complementation. In *The Mental Representation of Grammatical Relation,* Joan Bresnan (ed.), 282–390. Cambridge, MA.: The MIT Press.

Erjavec, Tomaz, Roger Evans, Nancy Ide, and Adam Kilgarriff
2000 The CONCEDE model for lexical databases. *ITRI Technical Report Series*, ITRI-00-22. Brighton: University of Brighton.

Götz, Dieter
2007 Valency and automatic syntactic and semantic analysis. This volume.

Götz-Votteler, Katrin
2007 Describing semantic valency. This volume.

Gross, Maurice
1975 *Méthodes en Syntaxe.* Paris: Hermann.

Hausser, Roland
2007 Handling valency and coordination in database semantics. This volume.

Heid, Ulrich, and Rufus H. Gouws
2006 A model for a multifunctional electronic dictionary of collocations. In *Proceedings of the 12th Euralex International Congress*, Elisa Corino, Carla Marello, and Cristina Onesti (eds.), 979–988. Alessandria: Edizioni dell'Orso.

Heid, Ulrich, and Hannah Kermes
2002 Providing lexicographers with corpus evidence for fine-grained syntactic description: Adjectives taking subject and complement clauses. In *Proceedings of the 10th EURALEX International Congress*, Anna Braasch, and Claus Povlsen (eds.), 119–128. København: CST/KU.

Herbst, Thomas
2007 Valency complements or valency patterns? This volume.

Herbst, Thomas, David Heath, Ian Roe, and Dieter Götz
2004 *A Valency Dictionary of English.* Berlin/New York: Mouton de Gruyter.

Joshi, Aravind
1985 Tree adjoining grammars. How much context-sensitivity is required to provide reasonable structural descriptions? In *Natural Language Parsing: Psychological, Computational and Theoretical Perspectives*, David Dowty, Lauri Karttunen, and Arnold Zwicky (eds.), 206–250. Cambridge: Cambridge University Press.

Klotz, Michael
2000 *Grammatik und Lexik. Studien zur Syntagmatik englischer Verben.* Tübingen: Stauffenburg.
2007 Valency rules? The case of verbs with propositional complements. This volume.

Maxwell, John T., and Ronald Kaplan
1993 The interface between phrasal and functional constraints. *Computational Linguistics,* 19 (4): 571–590.

Mel'čuk, Igor A.
1988 *Dependency Syntax: Theory and Practice.* Albany, N.Y.: SUNY Press.

Petruck, Miriam R. L.
1996 Frame semantics. In *Handbook of Pragmatics*, Jef Verschueren, Jan-Ola Östman, Jan Blommaert, and Chris Bulcaen (eds.), 1–13. Amsterdam: Benjamins.

Pollard, Carl, and Ivan A. Sag
1994 *Head-Driven Phrase Structure Grammar.* Chicago: University of Chicago Press.

Ruppenhofer, Josef, Collin F. Baker, and Charles J. Fillmore
2002 Collocational information in the FrameNet Database. In *Proceedings of the 10th EURALEX International Congress*, Anna Braasch, and Claus Povlsen (eds.), 359–370. København: CST/KU.

Sag, Ivan A., Timothy Baldwin, Francis Bond, Ann Copestake, and Dan Flickinger
2002 Multiword expressions: A pain in the neck for NLP. In *Computational Linguistics and Intelligent Text Processing: Third International Conference: CICLing-2002*, Alexander Gelbukh (ed.), 1–15. Heidelberg/Berlin: Springer.

Schulte im Walde, Sabine
2002 Evaluating verb subcategorization frames learned by a German statistical grammar against manual definitions in the *Duden* dictionary. In *Proceedings of the 10th EURALEX International Congress*, Anna Braasch, and Claus Povlsen (eds.), 187–198. København: CST/KU.
forthc. The induction of verb frames and verb classes from corpora. In *Corpus Linguistics. An International Handbook*, Anke Lüdeling, and Merja Kytö (eds.). Berlin: Mouton de Gruyter.

Schumacher, Helmut, Jacqueline Kubczak, Renate Schmidt, and Vera de Ruiter (eds.)
2004 *VALBU – Valenzwörterbuch deutscher Verben.* Tübingen: Narr.

Spohr, Dennis
2004 Using *A Valency Dictionary of English* to enhance the lexicon of an English LFG grammar. M.A. study, Institut für maschinelle Sprachverarbeitung, Universität Stuttgart.
Spohr, Dennis, and Ulrich Heid
2006 Modeling monolingual and bilingual collocation dictionaries in Description Logic. In *Proceedings of the EACL Workshop on Multiwords and Multilinguality – ACL 2006*, Paul Rayson, Serge Sharoff, and Svenja Adolphs (eds.), 65–72. Trento: IRST/ACL
Spohr, Dennis, Aljoscha Burchardt, Sebastian Padó, Anette Frank, and Ulrich Heid
2007 Inducing a computational lexicon from a corpus with syntactic and semantic annotation. In *Proceedings of the Seventh International Workshop on Computational Semantics (IWCS-7)*, Jeroen Geertzen, Elias Thijsse, Harry Bunt, Amanda Schiffrin (eds.), 210–222. Tilburg: University of Tilburg.
Tesnière, Lucien
1959 *Eléments de Syntaxe Structurale.* Paris: Klincksieck.
Zaenen, Annie
1988 Lexical information in LFG. An overview. Ms. University of Essex.

Subject index

Author index

Bei Fragen zur Produktsicherheit wenden Sie sich bitte an:
If you have any questions regarding product safety,
please contact:

Walter de Gruyter GmbH
Genthiner Straße 13
10785 Berlin
productsafety@degruyterbrill.com